D1064373

WILSON:

Confusions and Crises
1915-1916

WILSON

CONFUSIONS AND CRISES

1915-1916

By ARTHUR S. LINK

PRINCETON, NEW JERSEY

PRINCETON UNIVERSITY PRESS

1964

Publication of this book has been aided
by the Ford Foundation program
to support publication through university presses
of works in the humanities and social sciences

Printed in the United States of America
by Princeton University Press
Princeton, New Jersey

5324

FOR

JOSEPH R. STRAYER

THIS fourth volume in my life and times of Woodrow Wilson, unlike its predecessors, has no central unifying theme. The period that it covers—from the early autumn of 1915 to the late spring of 1916—was a time of political controversy and confusion at home and of unending crisis in the foreign relations of the United States. Wilson's political leadership was taxed as never before when he tried to lead Congress to adoption of a preparedness program that satisfied neither champions of large defenses nor those who wanted no expansion of the armed forces at all. In foreign affairs he seemed momentarily to lose the control that he had achieved by so much effort in 1914 and 1915. Events in Mexico and the American Southwest set Mexico and the United States on a collision course, in spite of Wilson's efforts to avoid war. Events in Germany seemed to make war inevitable between that country and the United States. And one aspect of the German-American troubles, a potential controversy over armed merchant ships, had violent repercussions in Congress and stimulated a major challenge to Wilson's leadership. This volume relates these and other crises. It also tells how Wilson worked through controversy to a compromise solution on preparedness, laid the groundwork for a new political orientation, and re-established his mastery of Democratic forces in Congress in preparation for the campaign of 1916. It tells how Wilson, almost single-handed, averted war with Mexico. Finally, it relates how Wilson found new bearings for a policy toward the European belligerents and laid the foundation for a subsequent bold effort at mediation.

There is no need to repeat what I have recently said in *Woodrow Wilson and the Progressive Era* (Harper Torchbooks, 1963) and *American Epoch* (A. A. Knopf, Inc., 1963 edn.) about the sources for this period. But I should like to add a few supplementary comments about certain European sources. German materials for study of the era of the First World War are almost as abundant as American, and I have tried to work through the essential documents, memoirs, and published series. In this effort I have been greatly helped by Karl E. Birnbaum's monograph, *Peace Moves and U-Boat Warfare*. It is an important source book as well as one of the best studies in modern diplomatic history. I have also greatly benefited by way of background understanding of German policies from Fritz Fischer's *Griff nach der Weltmacht* and Ernest R. May's *The World War and American Isolation, 1914-1917*, even though I have not always agreed with Professor Fischer's and Professor May's conclusions.

British sources for most of the period covered by this volume are now very rich and revealing. In particular, the Asquith Papers at the Bodleian Library constitute one of the great manuscript collections of the twentieth century. The archives of the British Foreign Office are still closed to scholars, but it is now possible to see the essential Foreign Office materials bearing on Anglo-American and Anglo-French relations in other collections, and I doubt that access to the Foreign Office archives in London would have added much even by way of detail.

Thanks to the kindness of certain individuals who must remain anonymous, I was given access to an important French diplomatic archive that contains voluminous materials relating to Anglo-French, Franco-American, and Anglo-American relations during the period of American neutrality. The sole condition imposed was that I should neither quote directly from the documents nor cite them. This accounts for the absence of footnotes in many instances. I must ask my readers to believe that I have taken extraordinary care in copying, translating, and using documents in this collection.

It is now my pleasant duty to acknowledge my deep indebtedness to institutions, scholars, and other friends who have helped in various ways since I began research on this book in about 1948. I was able to do my first long stint of work in 1950-1951 thanks to a fellowship from the John Simon Guggenheim Foundation, supplemented by a grant from the College of Liberal Arts of Northwestern University. The Rockefeller Foundation underwrote work in British archives in 1958-1959. The University Research Committee of Princeton University provided funds for research in Paris and additional work in Great Britain in the summer of 1962. Finally, the Rockefeller Foundation and Princeton University cooperated to make it possible for me to have the academic year 1962-1963 free to write this volume. I thank these institutions from the bottom of my heart. I thank particularly Dean Simeon E. Leland of Northwestern University, Dr. Henry Allen Moe, former Secretary of the Guggenheim Foundation, President Robert F. Goheen and Dean J. Douglas Brown of Princeton University, and Dr. Kenneth Thompson, Dr. John P. Harrison, and Dr. Gerald Freund of the Rockefeller Foundation. They all gave generously in support and encouragement.

Librarians, both in the United States and abroad, have been, as always, unstinting in assistance, and it would be invidious to mention some and not all. But I cannot fail to acknowledge the help of the former Curator of the Wilson Papers in the Library of Congress, Miss Katharine E. Brand. I thank Professors Pierre Renouvin and J. B. Duroselle of the Sorbonne and Professor Max Beloff of Oxford University for their kindness and hospitality. Mrs. Maria P. Alter, Dr. Kenneth Negus, and Messrs. Nicholas Niles, Konrad Mueller, and Bert Thurber worked patiently with me through German newspapers, memoirs, and documents. Mrs. Donna Gunderson typed various drafts of this manuscript, and Mrs. Helen Spiro helped to check footnotes, quotations, and bibliography. Mr. Herbert S. Bailey, Miss R. Miriam Brokaw, and Mrs. Marjorie Putney, my copy editor, of Princeton University Press have guided this book to publication. The late President-emeritus Charles Seymour of Yale University gave permission to use the House Papers and Diary.

Finally, I take this occasion to acknowledge the extraordinary help, which went far beyond the call of friendship and duty, of persons who read this manuscript with the same care that they would have read their own: my wife and best editor, Mrs. Margaret Douglas Link; my former colleague at Northwestern University, Professor Richard W. Leopold; my present colleague at Princeton, Professor Arno Mayer; my former student, Professor William H. Harbaugh of Bucknell University; my colleague in the Papers of Woodrow Wilson, Dr. David W. Hirst; Professor Ernest R. May of Harvard University; Dr. T. H. Vail Motter; and Professor Gerhard Ritter and Dr. Klaus Schwabe, both of the University of Freiburg im Breisgau. I alone am responsible for whatever errors remain in this book.

The dedication is an inadequate expression of my admiration and affection for a great scholar and friend.

A.S.L.

Princeton, New Jersey
March 6, 1964

CONTENTS

W ILLUSTRATIONS W

Following page 178

Courtship and Marriage

LIFE began anew for Woodrow Wilson almost from the moment that he met Edith Bolling Galt on a bright afternoon in March 1915. She was born in 1872 and grew up in Wytheville, Virginia, the seventh of eleven children. Her family was poor but genteel. After scant formal education she moved to Washington and married Norman Galt, a jeweler, in 1896. He died in 1908, and Mrs. Galt set about, as she later put it, rebuilding the shattered timbers of her life. She first came into the White House circle through Helen Woodrow Bones, Wilson's cousin and hostess after Ellen Axson Wilson's death in August 1914. Miss Bones and Mrs. Galt had met in October 1914 through Doctor Cary T. Grayson, the White House physician. They soon became good friends, and they went on long walks through Rock Creek Park that were always followed by tea at Mrs. Galt's small house on Twentieth Street, Northwest.

One afternoon in March 1915 (it was probably March 20) Miss Bones announced that they would have tea *that* afternoon at the White House. Mrs. Galt said that her shoes were muddy and she was not properly dressed for a visit to the Executive Mansion. "There is not a soul there," Miss Bones replied. "Cousin Woodrow is playing golf with Dr. Grayson and we will go right upstairs in the elevator and you shall see no one." As fate would have it, they met the President and Grayson in the hall of the second floor as they came out of the elevator, and they all went to the Oval Room for tea before a blazing fire.[1] Wilson was most engaging during the hour's conversation. He was also much intrigued by the beautiful and gay Mrs. Galt. Miss Bones invited her to dinner on March 23, no doubt at Wilson's request. "I am just home from the White House," Mrs. Galt wrote that same evening, "where I spent the evening and dined informally with the President. He is *perfectly* charming and one of the easiest and most delightful hosts I have ever known. . . . They sent the big car for me & I picked up Dr. Grayson and there were no other guests but Col. [E. T.] Brown from

[1] Edith Bolling Wilson, *My Memoir*, pp. 53-56; Cary T. Grayson, *Woodrow Wilson, An Intimate Memoir*, pp. 50-51.

Atlanta, who was staying there. I sat by the Pres.['s] right & Dr. Grayson next to me and we had the most delightful dinner right after which we went up in the Oval Room where, before a big wood fire[,] we had coffee and all sorts of interesting conversation. . . . [Wilson] was full of interesting stories and a fund of information, and finally, at Miss B[one]'s request, read us three English poems—and as a reader he is unequalled."[2]

The President and Mrs. Galt had a long drive and dinner with Miss Bones two weeks later, and Wilson reminisced about his boyhood and described his father's influence on his life. Frequent meetings followed. Then, on May 4, less than two months after they had first had tea together, Wilson told Mrs. Galt, while they were sitting on the south portico of the White House, what he had known for some time—that he loved her. She later recalled her shocked answer: "Oh, you can't love me, for you don't really know me; and it is less than a year since your wife died." Wilson replied, describing his loneliness and heartache since Ellen Wilson's death and confessing his need for Mrs. Galt's love and companionship. He wanted her to marry him, he said, adding that he had already told his daughters and Helen Bones. Mrs. Galt later wrote that she had not thought of marriage and was not ready to give an answer. She would marry Wilson only if she knew that she loved him; she would not marry him out of pity, and certainly not because he was President of the United States. They agreed to continue seeing each other, and Wilson said that he would wait for her answer.[3]

The President did not wait patiently. He wrote daily, often twice a day, pouring out his love and pleading his need. His letters, sometimes twenty pages in length, were always written in prose of striking beauty and with the ardor of a young man in love for the first time. Some of them he drafted in his Graham shorthand before transcribing them in longhand. He also saw her as often as events of the hectic months of May and June 1915 would permit. Mrs. Galt was a member of the party that accompanied the President on the *Mayflower* to review the Atlantic Fleet in New York Harbor on May 17. "I feel like I was living in a story—and fear to move, lest I wake up and find it a dream," she wrote while they were at sea.[4] She also went with Helen Bones on June 21 to "Harlakenden," the summer house at Cornish, New Hamp-

[2] Edith B. Galt to Mrs. R. E. Bolling, March 23, 1915, the Papers of Edith Bolling Wilson, Library of Congress; hereinafter cited as the Edith Bolling Wilson Papers.
[3] Edith B. Wilson, *My Memoir*, pp. 60-62.
[4] Edith B. Galt to Mrs. R. E. Bolling, May 16, 1915, Edith Bolling Wilson Papers.

shire, that Wilson had rented for the third year. Wilson and other members of his party followed on June 23, and he and Mrs. Galt had a few weeks together. "Whenever my thoughts turn back to that wonderful summer," she recalled, "there seems about it all a halo of gorgeous colour from the flowers, and music made by the river where nearly every day we walked when the President was there." During the evening they would work together over correspondence and dispatches from Europe and Mexico. "Or if, happily, nothing was pressing, we sometimes read aloud, and discussed the things we both loved."[5]

All the while Wilson pressed his suit ardently. He was hard to resist, and Mrs. Galt lost her heart. She confessed as much to Wilson in early July but said only that she would marry him if he was defeated for re-election in 1916. Wilson returned to Washington alone on July 18 to discuss his third *Lusitania* note with Secretary of State Robert Lansing before dispatching it to Berlin. He came back to "Harlakenden" on July 24 for three weeks, returning to Washington on August 12. Mrs. Galt left on August 2 to visit friends in New York and New Jersey. Separation from her now seemed utterly unbearable to Wilson, and his letters grew desperately intense.

Wilson saw Mrs. Galt again on September 1, the day of her return to Washington. They had dinner together and then drove through Rock Creek Park. Wilson showed clear signs of the strain of the *Arabic* crisis, which seemed to threaten a break with Germany, and of the troubles in Mexico.[6] He had no right, he said, to ask her to help share the load that was almost breaking his back. "I know your nature," he went on, "and you might do it out of sheer pity." She turned impulsively, put her arms around his neck, and said, "Well, if you won't ask me, I will volunteer, and be ready to be mustered in as soon as can be." They did not agree on a date to announce the engagement. Mrs. Galt still wanted to wait until the election a year hence. Obviously, however, her resistance to an early marriage was weakening.[7]

Helen Bones was delighted, for she had encouraged the match all along. So, too, was Wilson's unmarried daughter, Margaret. "Isn't it wonderful to see Father so happy," she wrote to her uncle a short time later. "It makes me glad through and [through] to look at him, and

[5] Edith B. Wilson, *My Memoir*, p. 71.

[6] For events of the summer of 1915, see A. S. Link, *Wilson: The Struggle for Neutrality, 1914-1915*, especially pp. 551-628; hereinafter cited as *Wilson*, III.

[7] Edith B. Wilson, *My Memoir*, pp. 74-75.

to think of the sweet companionship that is to be his."⁸ Others were not so pleased. "Dr. Grayson . . . came to tell of the President's infatuation for Mrs. Norman Galt," Colonel Edward M. House recorded in his diary at the end of July. "It seems the President is wholly absorbed in this love affair and is neglecting practically everything else. Grayson says the President is using my approval as an excuse."⁹ Wilson had told House about his love for Mrs. Galt and asked his advice on June 24. House had discreetly suggested that Wilson's health demanded his remarriage and urged postponement until the following spring.¹⁰

None of Wilson's friends begrudged this lonely man his happiness, but some of them were terrified by the political consequences of marriage so soon after Ellen Wilson's death. They were too obvious and frightening to be ignored. As House put it, "I am sorry the President has fallen in love at this time, for he will be criticized for not waiting longer after Mrs. Wilson's death."¹¹ Joseph P. Tumulty, the President's secretary, feared that the step would be politically fatal.¹² News of the courtship of course reached members of the Cabinet and other Democratic leaders in Washington. They met in secret conference at some time in early September to discuss the matter and agreed unanimously that someone had to tell Wilson that his remarriage before the election in November 1916 would alienate women voters and cause Democratic defeat.

But who would carry the dangerous message? The conferees nominated Josephus Daniels, Secretary of the Navy, and asked Postmaster General Albert S. Burleson to tell the genial North Carolinian that he had been chosen for the mission. Daniels declined as soon as he could catch his breath. "Before giving a reply to the tender of the place of honor," he wrote in his memoirs, "I firmly applied my hands to be certain I was safe in the chair set apart for the Secretary of the Navy. That job was secure. . . . Having been called to that by President Wilson I did not feel inclined to exchange it for the difficult and, perhaps, dangerous high and exalted position of Minister Plenipotentiary and Envoy Extraordinary to the Court of Cupid on a mission in which

⁸ Margaret A. Wilson to Stockton Axson, c. November 1, 1915, the Papers of Stockton Axson, Library of William Marsh Rice University.

⁹ The Diary of Edward M. House, Yale University Library, July 31, 1915; hereinafter cited as the House Diary.

¹⁰ *ibid.*, June 24, 1915.

¹¹ *ibid.*, July 31, 1915.

¹² C. T. Grayson to E. M. House, September 10, 1915, the Papers of Edward M. House, Yale University Library; hereinafter cited as the House Papers.

neither my heart nor my head was enlisted and in the performance of which my official head might suffer decapitation. . . . Wilson was not warned."[13]

William G. McAdoo, Wilson's son-in-law and Secretary of the Treasury, now blundered into the delicate situation in a bit of meddling, the motives of which are still obscure. Grayson told him,[14] perhaps on September 17 or 18, that Wilson had sent $15,000 to Mrs. Mary Allen Hulbert, formerly Mrs. Peck, an old friend living in southern California with whom he had corresponded for many years. McAdoo, knowing of the scandalous rumors about Wilson's relationship with Mrs. Hulbert, "was very much disturbed, and in trying to find some way by which he could get the President to discuss it with him, told the President [almost certainly on Saturday, September 18] he had received an anonymous letter from Los Angeles saying Mrs. Hurlburt [*sic*] was showing his letters and was doing him much harm."[15]

Wilson did not take McAdoo's bait. This was not the first time that revelation of his letters to Mrs. Hulbert had threatened to destroy him, and he could think only of how to avoid embarrassing Mrs. Galt. He went to see her that evening, Saturday, September 18, and told her everything about his relationship with Mrs. Hulbert. Mrs. Galt said that she understood, but she was obviously hurt and confused. She sat through the night hours thinking. Then she wrote:

Dearest—

The dawn has come—and the hideous dark of the hour before the dawn has been lost in the gracious gift of light.

I have been in the big chair by the window, where I have fought out so many problems, and all the hurt, selfish feeling has gone with the darkness—and I now see straight—straight into the heart of things and am ready to follow the road "where love leads."

How many times I have told you I wanted to help—and now when the first test has come I faltered—But the faltering was *for* love—not lack of

---

[13] Josephus Daniels, *The Wilson Era, Years of Peace—1910-1917*, pp. 452-454.

[14] At least, according to Colonel House. House Diary, September 25, 1915.

[15] *ibid.*, September 22, 1915. Mrs. Wilson later wrote (*My Memoir*, p. 78) that Colonel House informed her afterward that *he* and McAdoo had told Wilson that Mrs. Hulbert was showing his letters because they feared that his marriage to Mrs. Galt would prevent his re-election, and they wanted to prevent it. Perhaps this was McAdoo's motive, but Mrs. Wilson was surely mistaken about Colonel House's part in the affair. House was not in Washington between September 3 (the day that Mrs. Wilson agreed to marry Wilson) and September 21, and it seems unlikely that House saw McAdoo during this interval. Moreover, House, if we may believe his diary, first learned about the matter on September 22, 1915.

love. I am not afraid of any gossip or threat, with your love as my shield—and even now this room echoes with your voice—as you plead, "Stand by me—don't desert me!"

This is my pledge, Dearest One, I will stand by you—not for duty, not for pity, not for honour—but for love—trusting, protecting, comprehending love. And no matter whether the wine be bitter or sweet we will share it together and find happiness in the comradeship.

Forgive my unreasonableness tonight (I mean last night, for it is already Sunday morning), and be willing to trust me.

I have not thought out what course we will follow for the immediate present for I promised we would do that together.

I am so tired I could put my head down on the desk and go to sleep—but nothing could bring me real rest until I had pledged you my love and allegiance.

Your own
Edith.[16]

Mrs. Galt sent this letter early in the morning of September 19. Wilson's burden lifted, and ecstasy returned as he read it.[17] He saw Colonel House at the White House on the next day and talked about the affair. "The President," House recorded, "at once took up his most intimate personal affairs. I could see he did it with reluctance, but with a determination to have it over. It showed remarkable courage, in which he is not lacking. He said many years ago the family had met at Bermuda a lady who was then Mrs. Peck. He had gotten to know her quite well. That there had never been anything between them excepting a platonic friendship, though afterward he had been indiscreet in writing her letters rather more warmly than was prudent. He understood there was much talk about his friendship with her and he wanted me to know the whole story.

"He said quite recently her son had gone into business in Southern California raising fruit, and that Mrs. Peck, who is now Mrs. Hurlburt [*sic*], wrote him, the President, saying as they were in need of money she had been trying to sell some mortgages which they owned but had been unsuccessful.[18] The President of his own volition and without being asked, offered to take up these mortgages. They amounted to $15,000.00."[19] Wilson then related his conversation with McAdoo on September 18. "He does not know now," House went on, "that the

---

[16] Edith B. Wilson, *My Memoir*, pp. 76-77.

[17] Mrs. Wilson's account of this episode (*My Memoir*, pp. 75-78) is entirely inaccurate.

[18] This was in mid-June 1915.

[19] Wilson had evidently forgotten the amount involved! He sent Mrs. Hulbert on September 14 a draft on a New York bank for $7,500 to purchase the mortgages.

anonymous letter was not genuine. However, he spoke to me about it with the greatest concern, telling me it was contrary to his idea of Mrs. Hurlburt and that he thought she must have fallen under some evil influence. He did not know that I knew the entire story both of the money having been sent and of the anonymous letter, and in order to protect McAdoo I could not explain.

"I advised him not to worry about it, for I was sure she was not showing his letters or attempting in any way to blackmail him. He showed me some of her letters so as to give me an idea of their tone. I was more convinced than ever that McAdoo was entirely wrong and that no trouble was brewing.

"I have never seen a man more relieved when I gave him this assurance. To illustrate how honest he is, he has told Mrs. Galt every detail concerning the matter. He expressed the desire, if any trouble were to come to him because of this indiscretion, he would like it to come now, and he would not, in any circumstances, allow anyone to blackmail him. They might publish if they pleased every letter he had ever written, and that while he might be humiliated in spirit, yet that would be preferable to having a sword continually hanging over his neck."

Wilson and House went on, discussing the impending marriage. It was obvious to House that Wilson's affection for Ellen Axson Wilson had never lessened. "I have never seen a man more dependent upon a woman's companionship," House wrote. "He was perfectly happy and contented with his wife. They had an ideal married life, as all her relatives will readily testify and have, indeed, to me. But his loneliness since her death has oppressed him, and if he does not marry, and marry quickly, I believe he will go into a decline. Dr. Grayson shares this belief. None of his family are with him, and his loneliness is pathetic. With the weight of the burdens upon him, it seems but a small concession which public opinion might make in behalf of this man not to criticize him too much for doing what one in a humbler station of life would be able to do without comment."[20]

Wilson's joy was now unbounded. He had to tell his friends even before the engagement was announced. He wrote somewhat briefly to Mrs. Hulbert on October 4 (he still signed himself "Your devoted

---

W. W. to Mary Allen Hulbert, September 14, 1915, the Wilson-Hulbert Correspondence (typed copies of Wilson's letters), Princeton University Library.

[20] House Diary, September 22, 1915.

friend") but he was more fulsome in letters to other friends. To Mary W. Hoyt, Ellen Wilson's cousin and dear friend of his own, he wrote first, on September 26:

"Something very delightful has happened to me which I am not yet at liberty to tell others but which I want you to know among the first. A great happiness and blessing has come to me in the midst of my loneliness. Mrs. Norman Galt, a lovely Washington woman (born in Virginia) whom I first met in April last through Helen [Bones], who had become her fast friend, has promised to marry me. When you know her you will know why it was inevitable that I should fall in love with her, for she is wholly delightful and lovable. She is known here for everything that is fine and for nothing that is touched with the small spirit of the society folk of the place. You would think that it was only love that was speaking if I were to tell you what she is like, how endowed and made distinguished in her loveliness, but you will, I am sure, find out for yourself how truly wonderful she is in gifts both of heart and of mind.

"Please for the present keep this as an absolute secret. We are not yet ready to let others know of it, though we shall, of course, make public announcement of the engagement in due time."[21]

He wrote again on October 5 to another friend:

"Before others know it, I want you to know what has happened to me. I am engaged to be married to a lovely lady here whom I met last April and who compels everybody who knows her to love her by the sheer charm of her character and whole personality,—Mrs. Norman Galt. I will not tell you about her: I want you to find her out for yourself.

"The last fourteen months have seemed for me, in a world upset, like fourteen years. It is not the same world in which my dear Ellen lived; and one of the very last things she said to me was that she hoped that what has happened now would happen. It seemed to me incredible then, and would, I think, have continued to seem so if I had not been brought into contact with Mrs. Galt. She seemed to come into our life here like a special gift from Heaven, and I have won a sweet companion who will soon make me forget the intolerable loneliness and isolation of the weary months since this terrible war began."[22]

[21] W. W. to Mary W. Hoyt, September 26, 1915, the Ray Stannard Baker Collection of Wilsonia, Library of Congress; hereinafter cited as the Baker Collection.

[22] W. W. to Edith Gittings Reid, October 5, 1915, the Papers of Woodrow Wilson, Library of Congress; hereinafter cited as the Wilson Papers.

Wilson was now determined to announce the engagement, and Mrs. Galt gave in on about October 4. They went into the President's study after dinner on October 6, and Wilson typed out an announcement to be given to reporters that same night. It read:

> The engagement was announced to-day of Mrs. Norman Galt and President Woodrow Wilson.
>
> Mrs. Norman Galt is the widow of a well known business man of Washington who died some eight years ago. She has lived in Washington since her marriage in 1896. She was Miss Edith Bolling and was born in Wytheville, Virginia, where her girlhood was spent and where her father, the Hon. William H. Bolling, a man of remarkable character and charm, won distinction as one of the ablest, most interesting and most individual lawyers of a State famous for its lawyers. In the circle of cultivated and interesting people who have had the privilege of knowing her Mrs. Galt has enjoyed an enviable distinction, not only because of her unusual beauty and natural charm, but also because of her very unusual character and gifts. She has always been sought out as a delightful friend, and her thoughtfulness and quick capacity for anything she chose to undertake have made her friendship invaluable to those who were fortunate enough to win it.
>
> It was Miss Margaret Wilson and her cousin Miss Bones who drew Mrs. Galt into the White House circle. They met her first in the early part of the present year, and were so much attracted by her that they sought her out more and more frequently and the friendship among them quickly ripened into an affectionate intimacy. It was through this association with his daughter and cousin that the President had the opportunity to meet Mrs. Galt, who spent a month at Cornish this summer as Miss Wilson's guest. It is, indeed, the most interesting circumstance connected with the engagement just announced that the President's daughters should have picked Mrs. Galt out for their special admiration and friendship before their father did.[23]

The White House correspondents tactfully quoted only the first paragraph and paraphrased the rest of the announcement in their reports.[24]

Letters and telegrams of congratulation poured into the White House on October 7, and callers at the mansion were struck by Wilson's broad smile and obvious happiness. He called on Mrs. Galt's mother, Mrs. William H. Bolling, at her home in Washington in the afternoon; that

---

[23] From the original copy in *ibid.* Ray Stannard Baker, *Woodrow Wilson: Life and Letters* (8 vols.), VI, ff. p. 50, prints a photographic reproduction; hereinafter cited as *Woodrow Wilson.*

[24] e. g., *New York Times*, October 7, 1915.

evening he entertained Mrs. Galt, Mrs. Bolling, Miss Bertha Bolling, John Randolph Bolling, and the McAdoos at dinner.[25]

The nation was buzzing with excitement, and people were eager to see the President's fiancée. Wilson and Mrs. Galt, accompanied by Mrs. Bolling, Miss Bones, Grayson, and Tumulty, went to New York on October 8. They received a warm demonstration at Pennsylvania Station and made their way through the crowds only with the help of Secret Service men. The Houses gave a dinner in their honor, and then the party, joined by Mr. and Mrs. Dudley Field Malone, went to the Empire Theater to see Cyril Maude in "Grumpy." The audience rose and cheered as the blushing President led Mrs. Galt to their box.[26] On the following morning the presidential party went by special car "Superb" to Philadelphia to see the Boston Red Sox and Philadelphia Phillies play the second game of the World Series. They returned to Washington in the late afternoon.[27] The next morning, a Sunday, Wilson, Mrs. Galt, and Wilson's cousins, Lucy and Mary Smith of New Orleans, drove to Baltimore so that Mrs. Galt could meet the President's brother, Joseph R. Wilson, Jr., and his family. They all attended service at Franklin Street Presbyterian Church.[28]

Life soon settled into a quieter routine. "The days were too full for us to see each other with regularity," Mrs. Wilson wrote later, "so we had a direct telephone line installed from the White House to my house. It did not go through the exchange, but connected one instrument with the other. By this means we could talk over things that needed immediate conference. On the days when we had no time for a visit the President would send me by messenger foreign and domestic information so I could keep in touch with his work. These always bore a pencilled line of comment or explanation. . . . In this way I followed day by day every phase of the mosaic which he was shaping into a pattern of statecraft, and we continued this partnership of thought and comradeship unbroken to the last day of his life."[29]

There were few opportunities for entertainment and public social events. On November 4 they went to New York, where Wilson delivered an address in the evening, and spent the following day seeing friends.[30] Three weeks later they returned to New York, accompanied

[25] Edith B. Wilson, *My Memoir*, pp. 80-81. The *New York Times*, October 8, 1915, printed a slightly different guest list.

[26] *New York Times*, October 9, 1915. [27] New York *Sun*, October 10, 1915.

[28] *New York Times*, October 11, 1915.

[29] Edith B. Wilson, *My Memoir*, pp. 81-82.

[30] *New York Times*, November 6, 1915.

by Wilson's sister, Mrs. Annie W. Howe, Miss Bones, Margaret Wilson, Tumulty, and Mrs. McAdoo, to attend the Army-Navy football game at the Polo Grounds. After dinner at the House's they saw "Chin Chin" at the Globe Theater.[31] Then, at Mrs. Galt's request, Wilson had his Princeton classmates to dinner on November 30. This was apparently their last appearance together in public before their marriage.

Meanwhile, the nation had been following the courtship with avid interest and gratitude for relief from news of the war in Europe. Outwardly it seemed that everyone approved. But underneath a tide of criticism was beginning to swell. The courtship also furnished new grist for the mill of gossips and backbiters. Many women were outraged by what they thought was disloyalty to Ellen Wilson's memory. Rumors circulated that Wilson had neglected her tomb at Rome, Georgia, and an investigator from the Hearst newspapers found that Wilson had not yet put up a tombstone.[32] "The most surprising thing," the chairman of the board of directors of the Union Pacific Railroad reported to Colonel House, "is the effect produced by the announcement of the President's [impending] remarriage. This is creating quite a stir throughout the West and is extremely unpopular. In several places I am told the women have held indignation meetings; and disapproval seems to be quite as general among the men. As near as I can analyze the feeling from the expressions heard, it is a revulsion from the generally accepted notion that the President was weighed down with the combination of sorrow from the loss of his wife and the great responsibilities resting upon him as a result of the War. It seems to have been something of a shock to the people to suddenly realize that, instead of this weight of sorrow, he was falling in love so soon after the death of his wife; and it apparently is regarded as an evidence of selfishness and a certain lack of propriety on the part of the President."[33]

Worse still was the flood of ugly, malicious rumors about earlier alleged affairs. "[Robert W.] Woolley [Director of the Mint] told much of the Washington scandal mongers' talk of the President," House wrote in his diary in November. "He thinks something should be done to counteract it. There is a deliberate purpose to make the President appear before the country as a thoroughly immoral man. The most exaggerated stories are being told of him, none of them having the

[31] *ibid.*, November 28, 1915.
[32] E. S. Griffith to W. J. Harris, October 23, 1915, Wilson Papers.
[33] R. S. Lovett to E. M. House, November 1, 1915, House Papers.

slightest foundation."[34] One of them, telephoned anonymously to the important newspaper bureaus in Washington on November 26, falsely reported that Mrs. Hulbert had instituted breach of promise proceedings against the President.[35] There were, besides, scores of dirty jokes about Wilson's relations with Mrs. Galt.

Frank P. Glass, publisher of the *Birmingham News* and an old friend of Wilson's from undergraduate days at Princeton, talked to a number of Democratic leaders in Washington about the political effects of the slanders. He thought that the President should be informed. No one volunteered; one of the conferees, a member of the Cabinet, finally persuaded Glass to go. He was embarrassed and talked vaguely, but Wilson questioned him closely, saying that Glass was doing him a great service and that he was astonished that he had been kept in ignorance. "Before he got all of my story, tears came into his eyes, while his voice and demeanor showed that he was profoundly moved. He had not imagined that his enemies could be so unjust, so cruel." He asked Glass what could be done to combat such a campaign of filth, and Glass could only suggest that he hasten his marriage to Mrs. Galt. "When I was parting from him," Glass afterward wrote, "he took both my hands in his, and thanked me in the warmest way for what he regarded as a service of personal friendship."[36]

There was little that Wilson could do without dignifying the rumors. Perhaps the desire to assuage indignant women affected his decision to support a woman suffrage amendment to the New Jersey constitution in a special election on October 19.[37] "I intend to vote for woman suffrage in New Jersey," he declared in a statement to the press on October 6, the same day on which he announced his engagement, "because I believe that the time has come to extend that privilege and responsibility to the women of the State, but I shall vote, not as the leader of my party in the nation, but only upon my private conviction. . . . My position with regard to the way in which this great question should be handled is well known. I believe that it should be settled by the States and not by the National Government and that in no circumstances should it be made a party question."[38] He told the Daughters

---

[34] House Diary, November 22, 1915.

[35] David Lawrence, *The True Story of Woodrow Wilson*, p. 134, alludes to this incident.

[36] F. P. Glass, undated memorandum in the Baker Collection.

[37] For Wilson's earlier opposition to woman suffrage, see A. S. Link, *Wilson: The New Freedom*, pp. 257-259; hereinafter cited as *Wilson*, II.

[38] *New York Times*, October 7, 1915.

of the American Revolution a few days later in Washington: "I know of no body of persons comparable to a body of ladies for creating an atmosphere of opinion. I have myself in part yielded to the influences of that atmosphere, for it took me a long time to observe how I was going to vote in New Jersey."[39]

It was not possible to please everyone. "I observe," former President William Howard Taft commented, "that Wilson has come out for female suffrage, and has followed it with an announcement of his intended marriage. I went over to see Arthur Hadley [president of Yale University] yesterday. . . . Wilson's name came up, and I said to him that in my judgment, having known a good many Presidents, I thought he was the most unblushing and most ruthless opportunist that I had ever met."[40] Opportunism or not, Wilson's change of mind on woman suffrage did not help the cause in New Jersey. The voters rejected the suffrage amendment by a majority of 51,194.[41] "I greatly enjoyed the result of the New Jersey election," Taft chortled. "It hit Wilson right on the nose where he ought to be hit."[42]

The scattered local and state elections held on November 2, 1915, gave no clue to the political effect of the engagement. But there was no doubt that a Republican tide was running strongly. The G.O.P. swept back into control of the legislatures of New York and New Jersey, and Democrats suffered heavy losses in Maryland, although they retained the governor's office and legislature in that state. Only in Massachusetts did Democrats make significant gains, and even there they failed to capture any state office. Analysts could agree only that the elections showed that Theodore Roosevelt's Progressive party was disintegrating, and that Democrats would need Wilson more than ever if they hoped to win in 1916.[43]

Discovery of the campaign of vilification only strengthened Wilson's determination for an early marriage. He convinced Mrs. Galt, and they announced the date on December 4. They were married at Mrs. Galt's home in the evening of December 18. Her minister, Herbert Scott Smith of St. Margaret's Episcopal Church, read the ceremony from the *Book of Common Prayer*, and Doctor James H. Taylor, pastor

[39] *ibid.*, October 12, 1915.

[40] W. H. Taft to H. D. Taft, October 8, 1915, the Papers of William Howard Taft, Library of Congress; hereinafter cited as the Taft Papers.

[41] *New York Times*, October 21, 1915.

[42] W. H. Taft to G. J. Karger, October 23, 1915, Taft Papers.

[43] *New York Times*, November 4, 1915.

of Central Presbyterian Church of Washington, which Wilson had joined after coming to the White House, offered prayer. Only members of both families, a few intimate friends, and the Bolling house servants attended.[44] A buffet supper followed the ceremony, and Mrs. Wilson cut the wedding cake. Then, shortly before ten o'clock, the couple drove to Alexandria to take the train to Hot Springs, Virginia, for a honeymoon at the Homestead Hotel.

The next two weeks sped by quickly. The Wilsons occupied a suite with a private dining room on the third floor, overlooking the golf course. Pleasure was not unalloyed, for White House staff members had established direct communications with Washington, and affairs of state did not wait. But the President and Mrs. Wilson had many hours together on the golf course and in the mountains. "We are having a heavenly time here," Wilson wrote on December 27. "Edith reveals new charms and still deeper loveliness to me every day and I shall go back to Washington feeling complete and strong for whatever may betide. I am indeed blessed beyond my (or any other man's) deserts. . . . There is little to do here but walk and ride and play golf and loaf and spice it all with a little work, not to forget that there *are* duties as well as pleasures in the world. Every day we feel fresher and fitter."[45] They returned to Washington—and reality—on January 3, 1916.

Mrs. Wilson stood always at her husband's side until his death. He believed that God had given her to him for companionship, strength, and joy. She filled the need that became almost paralyzing after Ellen Wilson's death. Her love made him whole again.

[44] *ibid.*, December 19, 1915.
[45] W. W. to Lucy and Mary Smith, December 27, 1915, Baker Collection.

The Preparedness Controversy

EVENTS did not relent during the late summer and early autumn of 1915, not even for a President in love. Wilson and Secretary Lansing settled the *Arabic* case by exacting what seemed to be a satisfactory apology from the German government on October 5, accompanied by a new pledge that submarines would hereafter spare passenger ships. Then, on October 19, the President cut the vexatious Mexican knot by extending *de facto* recognition to the government of Venustiano Carranza. The most important and pressing unfinished business now was expansion of the armed forces.

Wilson, responding to growing public clamor and his own conviction that the nation's defenses were inadequate, had asked Secretary Daniels and Secretary of War Lindley M. Garrison on July 21, 1915, to prepare programs that would assure reasonable security. The General Board, the navy's planning agency, presented its first recommendation to Daniels on July 30. It envisaged a six-year building program costing approximately $1,600,000,000 and providing, among other things, forty-eight dreadnoughts, to give the United States naval equality with Great Britain by 1925.[1] Daniels and Wilson discussed this report on August 12 and must have agreed that its sights were too high. In any event, the General Board came back on October 12 with a more modest proposal. It envisaged expenditure during the next five years of some $500,000,000 to construct ten battleships, six battle cruisers, ten cruisers, fifty destroyers, one hundred submarines, and sundry other vessels. Wilson approved it in conference with Daniels three days later, without altering a single important item.[2]

It was not so easy to persuade Garrison to work in harness. The Secretary of War sent an "Outline of Military Policy," the chief feature of which was a new national reserve force of citizen soldiers, to Wilson on August 12. Garrison added that the administration would have to

---

[1] The General Board's report of July 30, 1915, was published in the *New York Times,* December 25, 1915. See A. S. Link, *Wilson,* III, 588-593, for the background of the preparedness movement and Wilson's response.

[2] New York *World,* October 16, 1915; *New York Times,* October 20, 1915.

be guided by public opinion, and that he intended to publish the gist of his plan in order to test reaction.[3] Wilson was shocked both by the inadequacy of the outline and by Garrison's assertion of need for public guidance. "It was," he wrote to Mrs. Galt, "evidently prepared with a view to publication. What I want is a businesslike statement of actual plans and as full figures of cost as possible. This is a most superficial paper. I am surprised he should have thought to put it off on me. But it is interesting and the idea is not bad."[4] He promptly warned Garrison against premature disclosures.[5] And when the Secretary replied that leaks were inevitable,[6] Wilson made his wishes clear in two letters that said much about his concept of leadership and proper administrative procedure:

"Mr. [Henry] Breckinridge [Assistant Secretary of War] handed me, as I wrote you, the paper containing an outline of military policy and I have now read it with very studious attention. I am sorry to say that it does not contain what I hoped it would. In view of what you wrote me in your letter, it is evident that you were thinking chiefly while preparing it of making the test of public opinion to which you referred. The paper is, therefore, lacking in the detail which is necessary before I can readily form a personal judgment about it.

"I want to say that the general idea contained in it interests me very much and seems to me a feasible one, but the method by which the thing could be done, I mean by which the training of the citizen soldiery could be carried out, and also the cost, it is of the first importance that I should know.

"I learn from Mr. Breckinridge that the War College is now at work on the figures of cost. I hope that it will be possible for you to get them to finish these reckonings at as early a date as possible, and I am going to ask that you will be good enough to have drawn out for me a succinct plan in definite items summing up this paper that I have and sufficiently developing the method of administration to enable me to form a practical as well as a general judgment."[7]

Wilson wrote in the second letter:

"I have your letter of the seventeenth in reply to mine of the day before. You always have such good reasons to give for your opinions that

[3] L. M. Garrison to W. W., August 12, 1915, Wilson Papers.
[4] W. W. to Edith B. Galt, August 18, 1915, *ibid.*
[5] W. W. to L. M. Garrison, August 16, 1915, *ibid.*
[6] L. M. Garrison to W. W., August 17, 1915, *ibid.*
[7] W. W. to L. M. Garrison, August 18, 1915, *ibid.*

I invariably find it difficult to disagree with you, and yet in this instance I do disagree. I think the method of preparedness is something which the country is not prepared to discuss. The demand for reasonable preparedness is clear enough and our own judgments go with it. We are not being driven, but are going of our own accord. It seems to me a very serious matter that there should be leakages of any kind in the War Department with regard to official information, but if that is inevitable, we must endure it and act upon our best judgment notwithstanding. My own judgment is that it is not the best way to go about our difficult job to try our suggestions out before public opinion of their practical and professional side.

"That is the reason I took the liberty of suggesting to you in the letter that followed mine of the sixteenth that you send me a different sort of memorandum. I am anxious to get the whole thing into a very definite basis as soon as possible and to embody it in concrete plan, not only, but also in definite estimates."[8]

Wilson did not know—and Garrison did not tell him!—that the Secretary had already published his plan for a national reserve army in a prominent weekly magazine.[9]

The Army War College set to work at once, or, more accurately, intensified work that it had begun in the spring.[10] "We are all working very hard on the reorganization plan," the Chief of Staff wrote three weeks later. "[General Tasker H.] Bliss, the Assistant Secretary and I were from ten until four last Sunday working on it, and all the morning of Labor Day. This is about the 8th meeting we have had, five hours long."[11]

Work was substantially completed by early October, and what was soon called the Garrison plan was submitted to the President informally on October 14, formally on October 28, and published on November 6.[12] It called for expansion of the Regular Army from a total of 108,008 officers and men to 141,707. They would remain the cornerstone of the

[8] W. W. to L. M. Garrison, August 19, 1915, *ibid.*

[9] L. M. Garrison, "Reasonable Preparation," *The Independent*, LXXXIII (August 16, 1915), 226-227.

[10] See Adjutant General H. P. McCain to H. L. Scott, March 22 and April 13, 1915; H. L. Scott to F. R. McCoy, April 30, 1915; H. L. Scott to J. H. Reaves, May 5, 1915; L. M. Garrison to H. Breckinridge *et al.*, April 21, 1915, all in the Papers of Hugh L. Scott, Library of Congress; hereinafter cited as the Scott Papers.

[11] H. L. Scott to E. St. John Greble, September 8, 1915, *ibid.*

[12] New York *World*, October 15, 1915; H. Breckinridge to J. P. Tumulty, October 28, 1915, Wilson Papers; *New York Times*, November 6, 1915.

military structure—the cadre of any future larger army. The main problem was an effective ready reserve. The Army War College, following conclusions expressed earlier by Major General Emory Upton in *The Military Policy of the United States* (published in 1904), agreed that the National Guard, or state militias, had been useless in the past and could not, in any event, be effectively integrated into a national defense system because of constitutional limitations. The Garrison plan did not abolish the National Guard; that would have been constitutionally impossible and politically suicidal. It simply provided a slight increase in the already minute federal assistance to state forces, on the assumption that the National Guard would be used primarily for local police purposes. It then went on to create a new reserve Continental Army of 400,000 men as a first line of defense. They would serve on active duty two months a year for three years, and in a ready reserve for an additional three years.

Wilson and the defense departments made these plans in the confidence that public opinion had turned massively behind what the President was fond of calling reasonable preparedness. To be sure, Wilson's publication on September 3 of his letters of July 21 to Daniels and Garrison, and subsequent press reports that work was going forward, evoked anguished protests from some pacifists and progressives. For example, one old friend wrote: "You are sowing the seeds of militarism, raising up a military and naval caste, and the future alone can tell what the further growth will be and what the eventual blossoms."[13] Some Republican champions of preparedness did not fail to comment on Wilson's opportunism in espousing the preparedness cause.[14] But the outcry was not loud or widespread, and there seemed to be fully as much approval as criticism.[15]

[13] O. G. Villard to W. W., October 30, 1915, Wilson Papers. See also G. F. Peabody to W. W. Bailey, October 19 and 28, 1915, the Papers of Warren Worth Bailey, Princeton University Library, hereinafter cited as the Bailey Papers; T. H. Ball to W. W., October 4, 1915, Wilson Papers; W. L. Walters to W. W., October 23, 1915, *ibid.*; Jane Addams *et al.* to W. W., October 29, 1915, *ibid.*; *Johnstown* (Pa.) *Democrat*, September 10 and October 9, 1915; *The Public*, xviii (September 17 and November 5, 1915), 897-899, 1066; *Congregationalist and Christian World*, c (September 23 and October 28, 1915), 399, 612; New York *Nation*, ci (October 21, 1915), 485; R. M. La Follette, "Patriots," *La Follette's Magazine*, vii (November 1915), 1.

[14] e. g., H. C. Lodge to T. Roosevelt, August 5, 1915, the Papers of Theodore Roosevelt, Library of Congress, hereinafter cited as the Roosevelt Papers; W. H. Taft to Mabel T. Boardman, November 8, 1915, Taft Papers.

[15] e. g., *Collier's*, LV (August 28, 1915), 14; *New Republic*, IV (October 23, 1915),

Most encouraging to Wilson were the signs that Democratic leaders in Congress seemed to approve heartily. He had taken special care to keep the chairmen of the House and Senate military and naval affairs committees informed about planning in the defense departments.[16] In addition, he conferred with Lemuel P. Padgett of Tennessee, chairman of the House naval affairs committee, on October 4 and with James Hay of Virginia, chairman of the House military affairs committee, ten days later and again on October 25.[17] All congressional leaders immediately concerned had announced general support by October 25, and the majority leader in the Senate had added private reassurances.[18] So heartening was the alignment that Wilson told newspapermen on October 15 that he believed that three fourths of the Democrats and many Republicans would support his preparedness program when it went to Congress.[19] Only Claude Kitchin of North Carolina, who would succeed Oscar W. Underwood as majority leader in the House of Representatives when Congress met in December, had refused to give his blessing. He came to Washington in early October but rather pointedly refused to call at the White House.[20]

Wilson paid slight heed to what seemed to be the very minor groundswells of public opinion on either side of the preparedness question, so confident was he that the preponderant majority wanted reasonable increases in the armed forces and would approve the administration's

---

293-294; R. B. Strassburger, director, Navy League, to W. W., August 14, 1915, Wilson Papers; American Defense Society to W. W., September 3, 1915, *ibid.*; Council of Jewish Women, Savannah, Ga., to W. W., October 12, 1915, *ibid.*; F. M. Jencks *et al.*, Maryland League for National Defense, to W. W., October 18, 1915, *ibid.*; W. S. Davis to W. W., October 20, 1915, *ibid.*; V. Murdock to C. Kitchin, October 6, 1915, the Papers of Claude Kitchin, University of North Carolina Library, hereinafter cited as the Kitchin Papers; T. Stout to C. Kitchin, October 11, 1915, *ibid.*

[16] "I am sure," he wrote to them on August 2, "you have had as much in mind as I have the whole matter of what it is wise and necessary to do in the matter of national defence. I have been taking steps to get full recommendations from the War and Navy Departments and I am hoping that after I get back to Washington it may be convenient for you to come up and have a talk with me as to the best way in which the whole thing can be handled, so that we shall all have a single judgment in the matter and a single programme of action. I shall value your advice in the matter very much indeed." W. W. to J. Hay, August 2, 1915, Wilson Papers; the same letter, *mutatis mutandis*, to G. E. Chamberlain, B. R. Tillman, and L. P. Padgett, August 2, 1915, *ibid.*

[17] *New York Times*, October 5, 1915; New York *World*, October 15 and 26, 1915.

[18] J. W. Kern to J. P. Tumulty, September 9, 1915, Wilson Papers.

[19] New York *World*, October 16, 1915.

[20] W. W. to C. Kitchin, October 27, 1915, Wilson Papers, expressing Wilson's disappointment that Kitchin had not been able to see him.

plans. To friends in both camps he appealed for calmness and under-standing. "There is no need to stir the nation up in favor of national defense," he wrote to one excited preparedness champion. "It is already soberly and earnestly aware of its possible perils and of its duty, and I should deeply regret seeing any sort of excitement stirred in so grave a matter."[21] Addressing the Civilian Advisory Board of the Navy De-partment at the White House on October 6, he added: "I do not have to expound it to you; you know as well as I do the spirit of America. The spirit of America is one of peace, but one of independence. It is a spirit that is profoundly concerned with peace, because it can express itself best only in peace. It is the spirit of peace and good-will and of human freedom; but it is also the spirit of a nation that is self-con-scious, that knows and loves its mission in the world and that knows that it must command the respect of the world."[22] He wrote trying to quiet alarm on the antipreparedness side, "I do not think there need be any fear that the country will go too far in the policy to be adopted. I think its thought is, on the whole, very self-restrained and judicial and that it will wish to see a course pursued that lies between the extremes in every particular."[23] A group representing the National Council of Congregational Churches came to the White House on October 28 to remind Wilson that it was more important to work for peace than to prepare for war. "You bring to me, I may say," he responded, "that which is more deeply upon my heart than anything else."[24]

Plans were fairly complete, and there now remained the larger and more vital task of leadership—to rally the people behind right goals. Wilson launched this campaign in an address before the Manhattan Club in the Biltmore Hotel in New York City on November 4, 1915. He had not come, he began, to talk of domestic questions, but of Ameri-ca's relations with the world. "Our principles are well known. . . . We believe in political liberty and founded our great government to ob-tain it. . . . If we have had aggressive purposes and covetous ambitions, they were the fruit of our thoughtless youth as a nation and we have put them aside. We shall, I confidently believe, never again take an-other foot of territory by conquest. We shall never in any circumstances

[21] W. W. to T. Dixon, September 7, 1915, *ibid.*

[22] *New York Times*, October 7, 1915. See also the report of Wilson's remarks to mem-bers of the Conference on National Defense on October 21, in *ibid.*, October 22, 1915.

[23] W. W. to O. G. Villard, September 7, 1915, the Papers of Oswald Garrison Villard, Houghton Library, Harvard University; hereinafter cited as the Villard Papers.

[24] *Congregationalist and Christian World*, c (November 11, 1915), 705. See also W. W. to Jane Addams, November 2, 1915, Wilson Papers.

seek to make an independent people subject to our dominion; because we believe, we passionately believe, in the right of every people to choose their own allegiances and be free of masters altogether." It was with full consciousness of these principles, he continued, that Americans were beginning to consider the state of their armed forces. They had no intention of attacking anyone: "We have it in mind to be prepared, not for war, but only for defense; and with the thought constantly in our minds that the principles we hold most dear can be achieved by the slow processes of history only in the kindly and wholesome atmosphere of peace, and not by the use of hostile force."

Wilson then explained the plans that he had already approved and would submit to Congress in December, taking care to add a special word of reassurance to the National Guard. The administration's program, he said, had not been conceived in haste or panic. The United States was not threatened from any quarter. Was the plan proposed sane and reasonable? Did it conform to American traditions? Did anyone have a better solution? He took high ground in commending the project to the American people:

"In the fulfillment of the program I propose I shall ask for the hearty support of the country, of the rank and file of America, of men of all shades of political opinion. For my position in this important matter is different from that of the private individual who is free to speak his own thoughts and to risk his own opinions in this matter. We are here dealing with things that are vital to the life of America itself. In doing this I have tried to purge my heart of all personal and selfish motives. For the time being, I speak as the trustee and guardian of a Nation's rights, charged with the duty of speaking for that Nation in matters involving her sovereignty—a Nation too big and generous to be exacting and yet courageous enough to defend its rights and the liberties of its people wherever assailed or invaded. I would not feel that I was discharging the solemn obligation I owe the country were I not to speak in terms of the deepest solemnity of the urgency and necessity of preparing ourselves to guard and protect the rights and privileges of our people, our sacred heritage of the fathers who struggled to make us an independent nation."[25]

Further to point the moral, Wilson a few days later gave to the press a letter he had just written to Seth Low of New York. Low had com-

[25] Ray S. Baker and William E. Dodd (eds.), *The Public Papers of Woodrow Wilson, The New Democracy* (2 vols.), I, 384-390; hereinafter cited as *The New Democracy*.

mended the Manhattan Club address. Wilson replied that he had had Ezekiel 33:2-6 much in mind recently, and he quoted it as follows:

"2. Son of man, speak to the children of thy people, and say unto them, When I bring the sword upon a land, if the people of the land take a man of their coasts, and set him for their watchman:

"3. If when he seeth the sword come upon the land, he blow the trumpet, and warn the people;

"4. Then whosoever heareth the sound of the trumpet, and taketh not warning; if the sword come, and take him away, his blood shall be upon his own head.

"5. He heard the sound of the trumpet, and took not warning; his blood shall be upon him. But he that taketh warning shall deliver his soul.

"6. But if the watchman see the sword come, and blow not the trumpet, and the people be not warned; if the sword come, and take *any* person from among them, he is taken away in his iniquity; but his blood will I require at the watchman's hand."[26]

Some friends and editorial defenders of the administration were delighted. "Will any member of Congress publicly challenge the wisdom and the patriotism of the President in his plea . . . ," the foremost eastern Democratic editor asked on the day after the Manhattan Club speech. "Will any leader of public opinion assume the grave moral responsibility of seeking to defeat the programme of preparedness which the President has presented for the protection of the American people?"[27] Many eastern editors thought not. The President, they said, stood on the "middle ground where the average man proverbially stands";[28] his program was "sane, moderate and in consonance with American spirit and American traditions."[29] Three leading editorial spokesmen of American Protestantism agreed. "We are glad," one of them said, "that we can see that it is possible to believe in a larger national policy of preparedness without having any conquest of nation or nations in view and without denying that the chief bulwark of a nation is in the character of its citizenship and without having dimmed

---

[26] W. W. to S. Low, November 8, 1916, *New York Times*, November 9, 1915.

[27] New York *World*, November 5, 1915.

[28] *Springfield* (Mass.) *Republican*, November 7, 1915.

[29] *The Independent*, LXXXIV (November 15, 1915), 250. For other editorial comment, see "Preparedness and Politics," *Literary Digest*, LI (November 20, 1915), 1143-1145.

before our eyes the vision of a whole world at peace."[30] Businessmen, college presidents, public leaders, and a number of governors gave endorsement in a poll published by the New York *World* soon afterward.[31] The White House mail supporting the President's stand indicated substantial approval among business and patriotic groups.[32]

Most preparedness champions who thought that the administration's program was inadequate held their fire in anticipation of developments in Congress. But Herbert Croly, editor of *The New Republic*, had one word of candid advice:

"Careful study was said to have gone into the President's speech of November 4th on preparedness. The only result of this study seems to have been to eliminate from the utterance every point that could enlighten the country in any way. A speech more resolutely confined to platitudes, to large and dull abstractions, has rarely been offered to an anxious nation. Not a single issue faced, not a doubtful point cleared up. . . . It leaves us in the dark; it will leave other nations in the dark. . . . The President must lead. It is his task to educate opinion, and to crystallize it on all these points. To do anything less is to make the insecurity of the United States greater than it is at present. For on top of our actual physical unpreparedness we shall have developed the illusion that because we have a few more ships and a few more soldiers we are ready to carry out our purposes. Never was there a time when shopworn abstractions had greater potentiality for evil."[33]

The Manhattan Club address crystallized public opinion, to be sure, but not as Croly wanted. It set off a storm of opposition and marked the beginning of one of the fiercest legislative controversies of the decade, one that would severely tax Wilson's powers of leadership.

This reaction and what it signified requires more than a cursory word. The convictions that had spurred humanitarian and progressive reforms since the 1890's included definite beliefs about America and

[30] Nashville *Christian Advocate*, LXXVI (December 24, 1915), 1675; also *The Living Church*, LIV (December 18, 1915), 239-240; *The Churchman*, CXII (December 25, 1915), 846-847; and the sermon preached by the Rev. Dr. L. G. Broughton in the First Baptist Church of Knoxville on November 14, cited in Knoxville *Journal and Tribune*, November 15, 1915.

[31] New York *World*, December 6, 1915.

[32] e. g., Spokane Chamber of Commerce, resolution adopted November 27, 1915; National Security League, resolution adopted November 27, 1915; and Executive Committee of the United Spanish War Veterans to W. W., December 5, 1915, all in the Wilson Papers.

[33] *New Republic*, V (November 13, 1915), 29-30.

her role in the family of nations. First, progressives were concerned, almost exclusively and self-consciously, with matters of economic and social justice at home. Like most Americans of their time, they cared little and thought less about European diplomatic rivalries and what they portended for the United States. True, a small minority led by Roosevelt and his friends did care. But the great majority of progressives, particularly in the South and Middle West, believed that America's unique mission was to purify herself in order to provide an example of democracy triumphant over social and economic injustice and a model of peaceful behavior. Such, in fact, was Wilson's own view before 1916. This self-purification demanded an end to America's reluctant ventures overseas and a halt to her naval building. A second major progressive conviction was the belief that wars in the modern world were mainly imperialistic and economic in origin and, perforce, evil. Bankers with money to lend, munitions-makers with goods to sell, and industrialists with markets to win were the chief promoters and beneficiaries of war. This, also, was the view of Socialists, most of organized labor, and many farmers, all of whom had long nursed grievances and resentments against the alleged eastern industrial and money powers.

It thus followed that the path of progressive righteousness led straight to a limitation of armaments, an international system based on arbitration, and an emphatic repudiation of war as an instrument of national policy. The progressives' old domestic enemies since 1898—big navy advocates, industrialists and bankers, and the armor-plate monopoly—were arrayed fairly solidly behind the preparedness movement by the autumn of 1915. This fact alone probably would have been enough to align progressives on the other side. But progressives, humanitarians, Socialists, and labor and farmer radicals had abundant ideological reasons for opposition to preparedness. To them it meant turning America into an armed camp like Europe, glorification of force, and, worst of all, an end to reform at home. The latter, they were sure, was one of the principal objectives of men financing the preparedness propaganda.

Antipreparedness spokesmen had not been inactive during the months when the preparedness movement was gaining strength. A group of eastern pacifists, including Oswald Garrison Villard, George Foster Peabody, Jane Addams, Lillian D. Wald, and the Reverend Doctor Charles E. Jefferson, had formed the League to Limit Armament in December 1914. Miss Addams and Carrie Chapman Catt, the great woman suffrage leader, had organized the Woman's Peace Party a few weeks later. Along with the older peace societies, they had maintained steady opposition to preparedness propaganda. They had also enjoyed direct access to the White House and strong support from the President all through the early months of 1915.[34]

To the United States
"Did You Call?"
Kempf in *The Masses*

Wilson's espousal even of moderate preparedness had been a shocking blow to these crusaders. "It makes me mentally sick," one of them wrote. "War preparations and emphasis upon militarism is national suicide to all the things I am interested in. I could stand the financial cost if it were equitably distributed, but I can't stand the social cost. It is . . . taking poison into the system."[35] A Chicago pastor wrote to Wilson after his address before the Manhattan Club, "Profound then is our disappointment in your recent utterances and your espousal of what seems to us a vast non-democratic scheme for an uncalled for enlargement of our army and navy and what is still more repugnant to the spirit of Democracy, the militarizing of our youth in schools,

[34] *The Survey*, XXXIII (January 9 and 23, 1915), 394-395, 433-434; A. S. Link, *Wilson*, III, 137-143, 588-593.
[35] F. C. Howe to O. G. Villard, October 1, 1915, Villard Papers.

colleges and civil life. . . . It is time that the alleged followers of the
'Prince of Peace' should give him their belated allegiance in this matter or else cease their weak-kneed hypocrisy."[36] An Iowa minister,
sending Wilson a copy of resolutions adopted by a mass meeting held
by the Iowa Peace Society at Grinnell College, felt impelled to express
his own "great grief" at Wilson's "change of attitude on this matter,
which means so much for democracy and Christianity."[37] Peabody
expressed the hurt reactions perhaps most poignantly: "I confess
I can not understand at all the President's position. I can not at
all get out of my mind the thought of Jeroboam 'who made Israel
to sin' by leading them to false gods. . . . When one thinks of the spir-
itual leadership and the response which followed in the case of the
Mobile speech and the Swarthmore speech and others, one can not but
think that this is a setting up of false gods in a more subtly deadly
fashion than was the case with a man of Theodore Roosevelt's type."[38]

The sharpest crisis within the larger progressive movement since
1912 was now at hand. Whether to follow Wilson and attempt to moderate his program, or to oppose him in a battle that might fatally divide
the forces of reform—these were the alternatives facing church leaders,
farm and labor spokesmen, urban social justice champions, and humanitarians who were important components of the progressive coalition in late 1915. As the leading single tax journal put it: "Some [of
Wilson's supporters] are asking themselves if this is the parting of the
ways. To break with this man who has been the embodiment of so
much hope is hard; yet to follow him in the new course he has laid
may be harder. . . . The pathos of it all is that this monstrous military
plan is proposed by a man of peace."[39] For many agonized progressives
there was only one answer: Fight the President. They met Wilson's
appeal of November 4 with thundering opposition in mass meetings,
councils and committees, and editorial pages. It was soon echoed up
and down the land by clergymen, farmers' unions, and Socialist party
locals.[40] No one knew then, or later, exactly what proportion of public

[36] J. L. Jones to W. W., November 10, 1915, Wilson Papers.

[37] D. P. Breed to W. W., November 6, 1915, *ibid.*

[38] G. F. Peabody to W. W. Bailey, November 15, 1915, Bailey Papers.

[39] *The Public*, XVIII (November 12, 1915), 1092.

[40] The following are typical of general press editorials and comments critical of the
administration's preparedness program during the late autumn and early winter of
1915-1916: *Johnstown Democrat*, November 6 and 20, December 4 and 11, 1915, January 1 and 31, 1916; *New York Evening Post*, November 6, 1915; New York *Nation*, CI
(November 11 and December 9, 1915), 561-562, 677.

For opposition from religious leaders and journals see, e. g.: *Congregationalist and*

opinion this opposition represented, but it was surely articulate, and it would be heard.

It was heard most approvingly by a group of some fifty congressmen who were emerging by mid-November as the crucial leaders in the fight against any increases in the armed forces. The core of this group

---

Christian World, c (November 25, December 9, 16, and 23, 1915), 761-762, 838-839, 879-880, 915; *ibid.,* ci (February 3, 1916) 169; *The* (Chicago) *Standard,* LXIII (December 4, 1915), 419; *ibid.,* February 19 and 26, 1916, pp. 772, 803; *The Churchman,* CXII (December 11 and 18, 1915), 779, 813; New York *Christian Advocate,* XC (December 23, 1915), 1728; *Lutheran Church Work and Observer,* IV (January 6, 1916), 3; *Missionary Voice,* quoted in *The Commoner,* XVI (February 1916), 29; C. E. Jefferson to C. Kitchin, November 10, 1915, Kitchin Papers; J. L. Jones to W. W. Bailey, November 11 and 18, 1915, Bailey Papers; S. S. Wise to W. W., November 12, 1915, Wilson Papers; Zanesville, Ohio, Ministerial Association to W. W., November 15, 1915, *ibid.*; Bishop W. M. Weekly, United Brethren Church, to W. W., November 24, 1915, *ibid.*; J. F. Smith, for Dallas Presbyterian Pastor's Association, to W. W., November 30, 1915, *ibid.*; Women's Fellowship of the First Baptist Church of Los Gatos, Calif., to W. W., January 20, 1916, *ibid.*; Rev. Benedict English, president, St. Francis College, Loretto, Pa., to W. W. Bailey, November 30, 1915, Bailey Papers; W. Gladden to W. W., December 11, 1915, Wilson Papers; S. E. Nicholson, editor, *The American Friend,* to C. Kitchin, November 23, 1915, Kitchin Papers; James Wood, president, American Bible Society, to C. Kitchin, November 30, 1915, *ibid.*; E. C. Wareing, associate editor, Cincinnati *Western Christian Advocate,* to C. Kitchin, December 18, 1915, *ibid.*; Rev. W. P. Merrill, Brick Presbyterian Church, New York City, to C. Kitchin, January 10, 1916, *ibid.*; Ministerial Union of Los Angeles, resolution adopted January 24, 1916, copy in *ibid.*; Monthly Meeting of Friends of Philadelphia to W. W. Bailey, November 25, 1915, Bailey Papers; "A Memorial to the Members of the Senate and the House of Representatives of the United States of America from the Religious Society of Friends of Pennsylvania, New Jersey, Delaware and Parts of Maryland," dated December 10, 1915, copy in *ibid.*

The following are representative of an almost unanimous opposition to preparedness on the part of farmers' organizations and farm leaders: Governor Arthur Capper, speech at Topeka, November 1, 1915, *Kansas City Times,* November 2, 1915; Topeka *Capper's Weekly,* February 26, 1916; *The Public,* XIX (February 4, 1916), 110, quoting *The Farmers' Open Forum;* North Carolina State Farmers' Union, resolution adopted November 18, 1915, *New York Times,* November 19, 1915; W. Starr, Maryland State Grange, to W. W. Bailey, December 19, 1915, Bailey Papers; Tri-State Grain Convention at Fargo, N.D., resolutions, n.d., printed in *La Follette's Magazine,* VIII (February 1916), 3; "petitioners of the rural communities of Hill County, Texas," in W. R. Kimmons to W. W., November 27, 1915, Wilson Papers.

Labor unions, Socialists, and various radical groups expressed their opposition in the following: Local No. 245, International Brotherhood of Electrical Workers, Toledo, to W. W., November 29, 1915, *ibid.*; Ohio Valley Trades and Labor Assembly, Wheeling, to W. W., December 3, 1915, *ibid.*; I. R. Sherwood to W. W. Bailey, November 5 and 12, 1915, Bailey Papers; resolution of Central Labor Union, Toledo, November 5, 1915, New York *World,* November 6, 1915; *American Federationist,* XXIII (January 1916), 23, reporting resolutions adopted by the American Federation of Labor's annual convention at San Francisco, November 8-22, 1915; *American Socialist,* December 4, 1915; National Convention of Unemployed and Migratory Workers to W. W., February 3, 1916, Wilson Papers; *The Survey,* XXXV (January 29, 1916), 505-506.

were some thirty-odd Democratic representatives from rural districts in the South and West—inheritors of Populist traditions and prejudices and followers of former Secretary of State William J. Bryan so long as he was true to agrarian causes. Their leader in the preparedness controversy was Claude Kitchin, a farmer-lawyer from Scotland County, North Carolina. Around the agrarian radicals clustered an ill-defined number of momentary allies like Warren Worth Bailey of Pennsylvania, single taxer and publisher of the *Johnstown Democrat*, Edward Keating of Colorado, child labor reformer, Isaac R. Sherwood of Ohio, who represented a labor constituency in Toledo, Clyde H. Tavenner of Illinois, whose *bête noir* was what he called the World Wide War Trust, and James L. Slayden of Texas, prominent in the American peace movement. They knew that they could also count on the support of a number of midwestern Republicans and ordinarily faithful administration Democrats when preparedness measures came to a vote. Through Kitchin they would have large influence in the appointment of members of the military and naval affairs committees.

They were dedicated, almost fanatical, in their passion against preparedness in any form, and they entered the fight as soon as Wilson's intentions became clear in the summer of 1915. They shared the convictions and apprehensions which inspired the entire antipreparedness movement—that the United States had no vital stake in the European war; military increases were unnecessary; the preparedness movement was a sinister plot against the people by eastern manufacturers, jingoes, militarists, and international bankers; and Wilson had been stampeded into surrendering to these, his old enemies. They speak for themselves in the following excerpts from their correspondence and statements:

It seems incredible that our party should fall so easy a victim to the wiles of the patriots for profit as some of the stories lately appearing in print indicate it is about to do. Talk of the "national defense" is the sheerest rot. Who is threatening invasion? Who is coveting our territory? Who is seeking the overthrow of our institutions? Who is manifesting a desire to bring us under subjugation? When you arm yourself for defense you do so in anticipation of an attack. But we are proposing to arm the United States against an attack that is not threatened—from an attack the reason for which no one is able to give—from an attack that can have no occasion unless we deliberately furnish it by some unthinkable stupidity of our own.[41]

This sudden, radical, and stupendous move for war preparations is going to shock the civilized world, and . . . will force the world again into an

[41] W. W. Bailey to J. W. Kern, August 31, 1915, Bailey Papers.

armed camp. The militarists and war traffickers of every nation will point to our conduct as a reason why they should renew war preparations on a larger scale than ever before. . . . However our own people may remain in ignorance of the terrible seriousness of the preparedness program, every other country will feel convinced that in this tremendous self-imposed burden upon our resources we have other designs than mere self-defense.[42]

The large city newspapers do not reflect the feeling of the masses of the people on the war situation. It is a strange fact that only the rich people tolerate the thought of war.

I believe that nine out of every ten persons are in favor of the government manufacturing its war materials of every character. As long as there is profit in war and preparation for war it means staggering profits to a very powerful group of men to keep us on the verge of war continuously, so that we will always be preparing.[43]

It may be that our admirals and our generals, our armor-plate manufacturers and our powder makers, and all the tribe of munition sellers, our Plattsburg amateurs who see in the future a military title in reward for a week or two of arduous military service in the news columns, and our paid secretaries and publicity experts, led by all the swarm of defence leagues and clubs and militaristic agencies, are deluded by their own mouthings into believing that the American people, at this late day, desire to take up the same incubus of militarism which has so long burdened the nations of Europe and, today, is rushing them to destruction. . . . I have been immensely gratified to find that the people of this district [Seventh Michigan], at least, have not been rushed off their feet by the hysterical propaganda of the militarists; that they still believe that the great mission of this nation lies in ways of peace; and that its safety, as well as its opportunity for the fulfillment of its destiny, lies in the maintenance of a peace, rather than a war footing.[44]

The gross inconsistency between the utterances of President Wilson in his message to Congress, and what he said to a little bunch of grafters is humiliating. The truth is, that Wilson is a [*sic*] part opposed to all this devilment, but he is crazy to be reelected President of the United States, and he thinks he cannot succeed without the support of the Metropolitan Press.[45]

[42] C. Kitchin, interview in the *New York Evening Post*, November 18, 1915.

[43] C. H. Tavenner to C. Kitchin, September 11, 1915, Kitchin Papers.

[44] Representative L. C. Crampton to W. W. Bailey, October 15, 1915, published in the *Johnstown Democrat*, October 20, 1915.

[45] Representative S. A. Witherspoon of Mississippi to W. W. Bailey, October 18, 1915, Bailey Papers. See also the following letters to C. Kitchin, all in the Kitchin Papers: Representative E. W. Saunders (Virginia), August 28, October 6 and 14, November 24, 1915; Representative E. Y. Webb (North Carolina), September 2, 1915; Representative

For men with convictions so deep, the call of conscience was also clear from the moment that Wilson published his letters to Daniels and Garrison. Antipreparedness congressmen, led by Kitchin and Bailey, corresponded and conferred in the late summer and autumn of 1915 to lay plans to defeat the administration program. Kitchin was not optimistic. "If the President had taken no stand one way or the other, but would leave it to the judgment of Congress, there would be no trouble in defeating such a program, or any increase in appropriation for armaments," he wrote in late October. ". . . My fear is that the advocates of the Administration program will insist on a caucus, in the hopes of apparently binding Members who are opposed to the program and give them an excuse to vote for it because the caucus endorsed it."[46] It would not, other antipreparedness congressmen agreed, be easy for the average representative to resist the President.[47] The insurgents could only stand and fight in the conviction that "a member of Congress is bound by his own conscience, by his own sense of right, by his conception of duty and responsibility and by the sentiments of those whose commission he bears."[48]

Democratic insurgents could take courage from the knowledge that one greater than they now fought at their side. He was Bryan, the Great Commoner and apostle of peace, who had given his boundless energy and matchless oratory to the peace crusade since his resignation as Secretary of State on June 8, 1915.[49] He had toured California in

W. L. Hensley (Missouri), September 8, 1915; Representative Frank Buchanan (Illinois), October 4, 1915; Representative J. A. Moon (Tennessee), October 5, 1915; Representative D. J. Lewis (Maryland), October 5, 1915; Representative S. A. Witherspoon (Mississippi), October 6, 1915; Representative J. L. Burnett (Alabama), October 11, 1915; Representative T. W. Sims (Tennessee), October 31, 1915; Representative C. H. Tavenner (Illinois), November 1, 1915; Representative J. L. Slayden (Texas), November 9, 1915; Representative I. R. Sherwood (Ohio), November 13, 1915; Representative J. H. Davis (Texas), November 18, 1915; Representative Robert N. Page (North Carolina), November 18, 1915; Representative R. L. Doughton (North Carolina), November 23, 1915; Representative H. L. Godwin (North Carolina), November 24, 1915; also the following letters to W. W. Bailey, all in the Bailey Papers: Representative E. Keating (Colorado), August 21, 1915; Representative D. V. Stephens (Nebraska), October 8 and 23, 1915; I. R. Sherwood, October 15, 1915; J. L. Slayden, October 24, 1915.

[46] C. Kitchin to W. J. Bryan, October 20, 1915, Kitchin Papers.

[47] E. W. Saunders to C. Kitchin, October 14, 1915, *ibid.*; J. Hay to C. Kitchin, October 15, 1915, *ibid.*

[48] W. W. Bailey to D. V. Stephens, October 26, 1915, Bailey Papers.

[49] A. S. Link, *Wilson*, III, 422-425.

July, calling for peace at any price,[50] and announced his intention to press for legislation to prevent Americans from traveling on belligerent ships in general and on American ships carrying contraband into the war zone.[51] Announcement that the administration was planning for enlarged defenses stunned the Great Commoner. He, too, had no choice but to fight the President. "One can not . . . be governed by fear of losing or hope of winning friends," he wrote. "He must find his reward in doing his duty as he sees it. I am satisfied that I am right—that is enough."[52]

Even before the administration had published its plans, Bryan entered the fight with a call to arms in his monthly magazine, *The Commoner*, in October. "Another fight is on between the people and the special interests, and the Democratic party is the only party in position to take the people's side," he said, ignoring the rather obvious fact that some prominent Democrats were on the other side. ". . . No time is to be lost; immediate action is necessary. Congress will soon meet, and when it meets this issue will confront it. Write to your congressman—write to both your senators. Tell them that this nation does not need burglars' tools unless it intends to make burglary its business; it should not be a pistol-toting nation unless it is going to adopt pistol-toters' ideas. Don't let the jingoes confuse the issue. It is not a question of defense—this country will defend itself if it is ever attacked."[53]

Bryan next took to the field, with speeches in Texas, New York, and Virginia, among other places.[54] Then, from his home in Washington, he issued such a passionate reply to the President's Manhattan Club address that observers were certain that an open break between the two

[50] See, e. g., his speech at Los Angeles on July 16, 1915, *New York Times*, July 17, 1915; also the review of his campaign in California in *The Commoner*, xv (August 1915), 22.

[51] As he told Secretary of the Interior Franklin K. Lane on September 16, 1915, F. K. Lane to W. W., September 16, 1915, Wilson Papers. Bryan opened his campaign with "Two Laws Needed," *The Commoner*, xv (December 1915), 5.

[52] W. J. Bryan to "Dickinson," September 9, 1915, the Papers of William Jennings Bryan, Library of Congress; hereinafter cited as the Bryan Papers, LC.

[53] W. J. Bryan, "The People VS. the Special Interests," *The Commoner*, xv (October 1915), 1.

[54] T. H. Ball to W. W., October 4, 1915, Wilson Papers, reporting on Bryan's speech in Houston on October 3; S. A. Witherspoon to C. Kitchin, October 6, 1915, Kitchin Papers, reporting on Bryan's speech in Meridian, Miss., on October 5; *The Commoner*, xv (October 1915), 22-23, printing various press reports of Bryan's southern tour; *New York Times*, October 18, 1915, reporting on Bryan's speech in New York City on October 17; *The Commoner*, xv (November 1915), 29, reporting on Bryan's speeches in Virginia.

Not Wishing Anybody Any Bad Luck, of Course
Darling in the Des Moines *Register and Leader*

leaders impended. Wilson's program, the former Secretary of State said, was "not only a menace to our peace and safety, but a challenge to the spirit of Christianity which teaches us to influence others by example rather than by exciting fear." He hoped that the President would not be deceived by the atmosphere of the Manhattan Club. It was the one place where the "Mammon-worshipping portion of the Democratic

Party" met to exchange compliments.[55] "When did it become unpatriotic for a citizen to differ from a President," he asked in another statement on November 6. "When did it become disloyal for a Democrat to differ from a Democratic President on an issue which the President declares to be non-partisan?"[56]

Enormous crowds shouted their approbation wherever Bryan spoke. At Houston, for example, some eight thousand persons filled the auditorium, and about the same number were turned away, when he spoke on October 3. The Democratic insurgents watched with growing wonder and hope. "I listened to your address at the Dallas Fairgrounds auditorium last Saturday evening [October 2]," one of them wrote to the Commoner. "My hope is realized. Your Knightly crusade is nobler than that of Peter the Hermit."[57] Warren Worth Bailey was equally enraptured. "Mr. Bryan still has a wonderful hold on the people," he reported to Oswald Garrison Villard. "He spoke the other night in my town . . . and he held that audience in the hollow of his hand from the opening sentence to the last word. It was more like a campaign audience than a lecture audience. . . . He told me that his meeting in Johnstown was a type of all those which he had addressed throughout the country, north, south, east and west."[58] Bryan was not fainthearted. "I won't give up hope of beating this scheme until the vote is counted," he promised Kitchin after the battle had shifted to Congress.[59]

There was not much that Wilson could do to quiet the storm until Congress met. "I can't help being disturbed that Mr. Bryan should see things as he does," he admitted to a friend in Alabama. "My own feeling towards him remains of the most cordial sort, but evidently everything must be worked out by contest, and I dare say it is best so. Only in that way are things threshed to the bottom."[60] He could wait, serene in the confidence that the tumult would subside once the people knew the facts, and not caring, in any event, about particular preparedness plans so long as Congress approved some reasonable measures.

Meanwhile, he did what he could to align his forces in Congress for the coming fight. He wooed the Speaker of the House of Representa-

[55] W. J. Bryan, statement in the *New York Times*, November 6, 1915.
[56] W. J. Bryan, statement in *ibid.*, November 7, 1915.
[57] Representative R. Hardy to W. J. Bryan, October 6, 1915, Bryan Papers, LC.
[58] W. W. Bailey to O. G. Villard, November 10, 1915, Bailey Papers.
[59] W. J. Bryan to C. Kitchin, December 30, 1915, Kitchin Papers.
[60] W. W. to F. P. Glass, November 10, 1915, Wilson Papers.

tives, Champ Clark of Missouri, with honeyed words.[61] Clark came to the White House on November 19 and left endorsing the entire administration program, including the Continental Army.[62] It was rumored, moreover, that the President would try to defeat Kitchin's election as majority leader because of his opposition to administration plans. Tumulty promptly scotched this gossip by declaring that it was "a lie which had no foundation in fact."[63] Then Wilson welcomed Kitchin to the White House on November 8 and appealed once more for his support. "I had a most pleasant and cordial interview with the President," the North Carolinian wrote a few days later. "I worked the whole matter out with him, telling him plainly that he had been badly advised by his military and naval experts; that he had been imposed upon, and tried to show him that his whole program was based upon misconception of facts. The President expressed regret that he could not persuade me to the support of his program, but expressly declared that he fully appreciated my position and the depth and sincerity of my convictions and, under the circumstances, could not insist upon my support of his program. I told him that I felt it my duty, knowing the facts as I do, to fight it. He assured me that, in spite of my opposition to his program, it would not interrupt our cordial relations, etc."[64] Wilson next announced somewhat ostentatiously that he would welcome Republican support[65] and invited the minority leaders to give him their advice.[66]

The first session of the Sixty-fourth Congress opened at noon on December 6, and the next day Wilson went before a joint session in the chamber of the House of Representatives to deliver his third Annual Message. He began by remarking how the European war had drawn the nations of the western hemisphere into closer fellowship. It was more than ever American policy to respect the "genuine equality and unquestioned independence" of neighbors and to encourage the movement for Pan-Americanism under the shield of the Monroe Doctrine.[67] He

[61] W. W. to C. Clark, October 27, 1915, *ibid.*

[62] *New York Times*, November 20, 1915.

[63] L. A. Brown to C. Kitchin, November 3, 1915, Kitchin Papers.

[64] C. Kitchin to C. L. Coon, November 11, 1915, *ibid.*; also *New York Times*, November 9, 1915.

[65] *ibid.*, November 12, 1915.

[66] W. W. to Representative J. R. Mann, November 18, 1915, Wilson Papers; W. W. to Senator J. H. Gallinger, November 18, 1915; *ibid.*; *New York Times*, November 21, 1915. Gallinger came to the White House on December 8, Mann, on December 9. Both promised Republican support for a nonpartisan defense program. New York *World*, December 9, 1915; *New York Times*, December 10, 1915.

[67] This section was written, apparently, in response to J. P. Tumulty, "NATIONAL DEFENSE," undated memorandum, but c. December 1, 1915, Wilson Papers.

then turned abruptly to the need for military preparedness. Once again, as in the Manhattan Club address, he answered his antipreparedness critics by reaffirming their own deeply felt assumptions about the military establishment and America's mission in the world. The American

A Hard Pull
Kirby in the New York *World*

people, he said, had a passion for peace and liberty. They viewed just war "merely as a means of asserting the rights of a people against aggression." But defensive war, if ever it should come, was a thing of disciplined might. Hence the War Department was submitting plans to strengthen the army. Wilson described them in detail, adding that they were "the essential first steps," and "absolutely imperative now." Next came details of the Navy Department's five-year program to give the country a navy "fitted to our needs and worthy of our traditions."

National self-sufficiency and security, Wilson went on, demanded more than "armies and instruments of war." America could never enjoy true economic and political independence until she had her own merchant marine. Hence the necessity for some such shipping bill as had failed to pass in the last Congress.[68] America also had to prove the sincerity of her professions about democracy. Hence, too, the need for legislation to enlarge the self-government of the Philippines and Puerto Rico. Finally, there would have to be new taxes to provide revenue for increases in the military establishment. "I have had in my mind," Wilson went on, "no thought of any immediate or particular danger arising out of our relations with other nations. We are at peace with all the nations of the world; and there is reason to hope that no question in controversy between this and other Governments will lead to any serious breach of amicable relations, grave as some differences of attitude and policy have been and may yet turn out to be."

His listeners thought that this was the end, but Wilson went on to denounce those citizens of foreign birth, obviously German Americans, who had "poured the poison of disloyalty into the very arteries of our national life," brought the good name of the government into contempt, and assisted foreign intrigues. His voice became almost emotional as he called for legislation to save the nation's honor and self-respect. "Such creatures of passion, disloyalty, and anarchy must be crushed out." Then he turned to the necessity for industrial, scientific, and agricultural preparedness to fit the entire nation "to play its

[68] Wilson's decision to press for a shipping measure was in large part due to the campaign that Secretary McAdoo had been waging since the defeat of the ship purchase bill by the lame-duck session of 1914-1915. For an account of this controversy, see A. S. Link, *Wilson*, III, 137-161. McAdoo's campaign during the summer and autumn of 1915 is revealed in the following: W. G. McAdoo to E. M. House, July 8, 1915, House Papers; W. G. McAdoo to C. W. Gold, president, Chamber of Commerce, Greensboro, N.C., August 1, 1915, copy in Wilson Papers, summarized in the *New York Times*, August 5, 1915; W. G. McAdoo to W. C. Redfield, August 20, 1915, copy in the Wilson Papers; W. G. McAdoo, address at Indianapolis, October 13, 1915, copy in *ibid.*; W. G. McAdoo, addresses in St. Louis, October 14, and in Kansas City, October 15, *New York Times*, October 15 and 16, 1915; W. W. to W. C. Redfield, November 9, 1915, Wilson Papers; New York *World*, November 28, 1915. For general and business comment, which revealed that businessmen were still strongly opposed to direct governmental participation and wanted subsidies to shipping companies instead, see the *New York Journal of Commerce*, October 14, 1915. However, the American Federation of Labor's annual convention at San Francisco, November 8-22, 1915, approved creation of a government-owned merchant fleet. Copy of resolution in the Wilson Papers.

part with energy, safety, and assured success." He concluded, "In this we are no partisans but heralds and prophets of a new age."[69]

The address was too long—its reading took a little more than an hour—, detailed, and badly organized to excite much enthusiasm. Some senators ungenerously said that they found Wilson's references to Pan-Americanism incongruous in light of the State Department's recent treaties with Nicaragua and Haiti.[70] "The reception of the President's message by Congress today," one observer wrote, "could not by any means be called an enthusiastic demonstration. There was only perfunctory applause for the preparedness program, and when the question of taxation came up, there was a noticeable shiver on the Democratic side. The most enthusiastic applause was at the beginning of his attack on hyphenated Americans. I have heard him speak many times, but never less effectively."[71]

It was, indeed, evident from the start of the session that the President's program was in trouble. The fundamental danger was massive and implacable Democratic opposition or indifference to the Continental Army scheme. Antipreparedness congressmen were now exploiting the groundswell of popular opposition and playing upon fear of tax increases in an election year. Most Democrats were simply unconcerned,[72] mainly because Wilson had played into the hands of his antipreparedness critics by saying over and over that there were no threats to national security. In addition, a powerful National Guard lobby was hard at work to persuade the military affairs committee to reject the Continental Army plan and rely for defense upon a vastly strengthened National Guard.[73]

[69] *The New Democracy*, I, 406-428.

[70] *New York Times*, December 8, 1915.

[71] O. G. Villard to R. Ogden, December 7, 1915, Villard Papers. For general press comment, see "A Presidential Peace Message in War-Time," *Literary Digest*, LI (December 18, 1915), 1411-1414; *New York Times*, December 8, 1915; *New Republic*, V (December 11, 1915), 130-131. London newspapers had some interesting things to say about Wilson's references to Pan-Americanism and hyphenated Americans. For their comment, see the *Daily News, Daily Chronicle, The Times, Daily Graphic*, and *Daily Telegraph*, all dated December 8, 1915.

[72] As pointed out in the *New York Times*, December 12, 1915, and January 8, 1916; New York *World*, January 11, 1916; H. L. Scott to W. S. Scott, December 27, 1915, Scott Papers; and H. L. Scott to E. St. J. Greble, December 27, 1915, *ibid.*

[73] Garrison and army leaders conferred with officers of the National Guard Association in Washington in late October and thought that they won their support for the Continental Army plan. (H. L. Scott to R. K. Evans, November 1, 1915, Scott Papers;

More ominous still for the future of Garrison's plans was the attitude of the Democratic members of the military affairs committee. They included not a single advocate of the Continental Army plan, and several of them were sympathetic to the agrarian radical group. The committee's chairman, James Hay of Madison, Virginia, had favored the National Guard from the beginning and promised to support Garrison's plan only out of loyalty to Wilson as party leader.[74] He and other members of the committee thought that Garrison was domineering, arrogant, and contemptuous of Congress. Garrison in turn despised Hay as a Southerner who still hated the North.[75] Hay's and the committee's worst suspicions were confirmed when they opened hearings on January 6, 1916. Garrison led off with a general review of the War Department's plan. Under questioning he admitted that he regarded the Continental Army as the final test of the possibility of raising a volunteer force, and that some system of compulsory training would have to be undertaken if it failed. General Scott, Chief of Staff, came out flatly for universal military training on January 10.[76]

It would be an exaggeration to say that the Continental Army plan was ever much alive,[77] but Garrison's and Scott's testimony made sudden death inevitable.[78] Hay went to the White House on January 11 to tell Wilson that he could not and would not support the Continental

---

H. L. Scott to J. F. McGee, November 2, 1915, *ibid.*) Actually, the National Guard leaders left this meeting convinced that Garrison intended to abolish the National Guard. (W. F. Sadler, Adjutant General of New Jersey, to W. W., October 30, 1915, Wilson Papers.) They lost no time in appealing to members of Congress. See, e. g., L. W. Young, Adjutant General of North Carolina, to C. Kitchin, November 30, 1915, Kitchin Papers, enclosing a copy of the report of the legislative committee of the National Guard Association, approved by the Association in national convention on November 11, 1915; and Gardner Harding, " 'Hay Foot! Straw Foot!' " *Everybody's Magazine*, xxxv (July 1916), 1-13, for a long review of the National Guard's fight to defeat the Continental Army plan.

[74] J. Hay to C. Kitchin, October 15, 1915, Kitchin Papers.

[75] J. Hay, "Woodrow Wilson and Preparedness," MS. in the Baker Collection; R. S. Baker, memorandum of interview with L. M. Garrison, November 30, 1928, *ibid.*

[76] *New York Times*, January 7, 9, 11, 1916.

[77] As *The New Republic*, v (December 25, 1915), 183, had already pointed out.

[78] General Leonard Wood and Garrison did not help the situation by their speeches before a thousand bankers at the Hotel Astor in New York on January 17. Wood declared that an adequate defensive force could never be raised by the volunteer system. Garrison denounced plans to create a national reserve force out of the National Guard as "a mockery and not honest." *New York Times*, January 18, 1916. Wood reiterated his plea for universal military service before the Senate military affairs committee on January 19. *ibid.*, January 20, 1916.

Army plan. It could not possibly pass, Hay added, for a large majority of House Democrats opposed it, and only three out of the twenty-two members of the military affairs committee were willing to support it. The President could get army expansion only through the National Guard.[79] "Between us, confidentially," Kitchin boasted a short time later, "we have already practically defeated . . . [the President's] army program; that is, it seems that we will certainly knock out his Continental army."[80] The Army Chief of Staff lamented, "We find . . . apathy . . . everywhere. I do not see that anything is going to galvanize Congress, unless the President comes out with some strong action, or unless the voters make a back-fire against every one of the recalcitrants. Nobody up in Congress takes any interest in the hearings in committees."[81] Garrison warned Wilson on the day after his interview with Hay, "In my judgment we are facing a critical juncture."[82]

It was true, but what could Wilson do to reconcile absolutely irreconcilable points of view and, worse still, men who were barely speaking to each other? Nothing but get the best legislation possible. Accordingly, he told Hay on January 11 that he was not committed to any particular plan and would accept legislation to enlarge the National Guard, if it was constitutionally possible to subject the Guard to effective federal control.[83] He also made it clear to the military affairs committee on January 12, through Assistant Secretary of War Breckinridge, that he was "opposed to the idea of compulsory military service and . . . flatly opposed to any move in that direction."[84] Garrison refused to retreat an inch. He warned the President on January 12 that state troops could not be effectively "federalized" and called for courageous leadership and firm adherence to principle. Wilson then told Garrison on January 14 what he had said to Hay three days before. Garrison returned to his office and dictated a letter that concluded threateningly:

"Those who are conscientiously convinced that nothing but National forces can properly be the basis of a policy of national defense, cannot possibly accept a policy based upon State forces. It not only does not

[79] *ibid.*, January 12, 1916; New York *World*, January 12, 1916.
[80] C. Kitchin to C. O. McMichael, January 26, 1916, Kitchin Papers.
[81] H. L. Scott to C. King, January 22, 1916, Scott Papers.
[82] L. M. Garrison to W. W., January 12, 1916, Wilson Papers.
[83] L. M. Garrison to W. W., January 14, 1916, *ibid.*, repeating Wilson's report to Garrison of his conversation with Hay.
[84] *New York Times*, January 13, 1916.

in itself offer an acceptable solution, but acts to prevent any proper solution.

"If those who are thus convinced are faced with the necessity of declaring their position on the matter, they can only show their sincerity and good faith by declining to admit the possibility of compromise with respect to this essential, fundamental principle.

"I am thus convinced.

"I feel that we are challenged by the existing situation to declare ourselves promptly, openly and unequivocally, or be charged properly with lack of sincerity and good faith. . . .

"Yours is the ultimate responsibility; yours is the final determination as to the manner in which the situation shall be faced and treated. I fully realize this and I do not desire to cause you the slightest embarrassment on my account; if, therefore, my withdrawal from the situation would relieve you, you should not hesitate for a moment on that account."[85]

What Garrison really meant, Wilson understood, was that he would resign if Wilson surrendered to the military affairs committee. The President had suffered Garrison's pretensions to superior righteousness for two years, and his tart reply[86] gave no ground:

"I am very much obliged to you for your letters of January twelfth and January fourteenth. They make your views with regard to adequate measures of preparation for national defense sharply clear. I am sure that I already understood just what your views were, but I am glad to have them restated in this succinct and striking way. You believe, as I do, that the chief thing necessary is, that we should have a trained citizen reserve and that the training, organization, and control of that reserve should be under immediate federal direction.

"But apparently I have not succeeded in making my own position equally clear to you, though I feel sure that I have made it perfectly clear to Mr. Hay. It is that I am not irrevocably or dogmatically committed to any one plan of providing the nation with such a reserve, and am cordially willing to discuss alternative proposals.

"Any other position on my part would indicate an attitude towards the Committee on Military Affairs of the House of Representatives

---

[85] L. M. Garrison to W. W., January 14, 1916, Wilson Papers.

[86] Completed after asking Tumulty to read a draft of the letter and benefiting from the Secretary's suggestions. See W. W. to J. P. Tumulty, January 15, 1916, and J. P. Tumulty, "Memorandum for the President," January 15, 1916, both in the Papers of Joseph P. Tumulty, Library of Congress; hereinafter cited as the Tumulty Papers.

which I should in no circumstances feel at liberty to assume. It would never be proper or possible for me to say to any committee of the House of Representatives that so far as my participation in legislation was concerned they would have to take my plan or none.

"I do not share your opinion that the members of the House who are charged with the duty of dealing with military affairs are ignorant of them or of the military necessities of the nation. On the contrary, I have found them well informed and actuated by a most intelligent appreciation of the grave responsibilities imposed upon them. I am sure that Mr. Hay and his colleagues are ready to act with a full sense of all that is involved in this great matter both for the country and for the national parties which they represent.

"My own duty towards them is perfectly plain. I must welcome a frank interchange of views and a patient and thorough comparison of all the methods proposed for obtaining the objects we all have in view. So far as my own participation in final legislative action is concerned, no one will expect me to acquiesce in any proposal that I regard as inadequate or illusory. If, as the outcome of a free interchange of views, my own judgment and that of the Committee should prove to be irreconcilably different and a bill should be presented to me which I could not accept as accomplishing the essential things sought, it would manifestly be my duty to veto it and go to the country on the merits. But there is no reason to anticipate or fear such a result, unless we should ourselves take at the outset the position that only the plans of the Department are to be considered; and that position, it seems to me, would be wholly unjustifiable. The committee and the Congress will expect me to be as frank with them as I hope they will be with me, and will of course hold me justified in fighting for my own matured opinion.

"I have had a delightfully frank conference with Mr. Hay. I have said to him that I was perfectly willing to consider any plan that would give us a national reserve under unmistakable national control, and would support any such scheme if convinced of its adequacy and wise policy. More he has not asked or desired."[87]

It was just as necessary to maintain lines of communication with the military affairs committee as it was to prepare for Garrison's resignation. Thus Wilson wrote to Hay on January 18, summarizing his recent correspondence with Garrison. "Frankly," he concluded, "as I told you, I do not believe that such a [national] reserve can be

[87] W. W. to L. M. Garrison, January 17, 1916, Wilson Papers.

supplied through the National Guard because of the apparently insuperable constitutional obstacles to a direct control of training and
organization by the National Government. I feel certain that the
country will demand of us imperatively a genuine nationalization of
the reserve forces which we are about to create. But it would, of course,
be ridiculous for me to say that I would not consider methods which
men thoroughly acquainted with the subject matter felt ready to propose. I wish with all my heart that the Committee could see its way to
a direct and immediate acceptance of the plan for a Continental Army
and I believe that it will ultimately find that it must turn in that
direction."[88]

There was sound method in Wilson's seeming madness, but it
appeared otherwise to a large segment of opinion in the country.
Leaders in Congress had not yet agreed on a general legislative program by mid-January, and Democratic members seemed confused and
paralyzed. It seemed that Wilson, for the first time, had either lost
control or ceased to lead. "I think that Wilson is going down hill,"
Taft wrote with ill-concealed pleasure. "The difficulty he is going to
have over preparedness, with all this hulabaloo about it, and the
ridiculous muss that will come out of it, will greatly affect his prestige."[89] Others said that Wilson was to blame for having gone off on
his honeymoon when he was badly needed in Washington. As Senator
Lodge put it, "We are now having a peaceful vacation, the President's
vulgar marriage requiring an interval of a fortnight before the public
business can be taken up."[90] More important, some leading eastern
editors, including the administration's spokesman, the New York
World, were saying openly that the President had only himself to
blame for the deadlock and demanding that he lead with accustomed
vigor and authority.[91]

There were also numerous signs of disgust with Wilson's allegedly
weak foreign and defense policies among eastern academic, literary,
and upper-class circles. Public eruption came with organization of
the American Rights Committee in New York in December 1915 by
George Haven Putnam, the publisher, Ernest V. and Lawrence F.

[88] W. W. to J. Hay, January 18, 1916, *ibid.*

[89] W. H. Taft to G. J. Karger, January 11, 1916, Taft Papers.

[90] H. C. Lodge to T. Roosevelt, December 20, 1915, Roosevelt Papers.

[91] *Collier's*, LVI (December 11, 1915), 16; *ibid.*, January 29, 1916, p. 14; *New York Times*, January 16, 1916; New York *World*, January 21, 1916.

Don't Know Where They're Going, but They're on Their Way

Darling in the Des Moines *Register and Leader*

Abbott of *The Outlook,* and others. They demanded open moral alignment with the Allies and military might to enforce stern policies against
Germany.[92] "The real Americans that I meet in this part of the country,

[92] See American Rights Committee, form letter dated January 1, 1916, announcing
organization of the group, copy in the Papers of Thomas J. Walsh, Library of Congress,
hereinafter cited as the Walsh Papers; also *The Outlook,* CXII (February 23, 1916),

in New York and the East," wrote the president of the University of Cincinnati, "are bitterly disappointed and are getting more and more disgusted."[93] Senator Lodge wrote to an English friend, "I do not wonder that there should be a feeling in Great Britain about us,—in view of the shuffling attitude of the Administration. . . . Wilson's failure to lead has disintegrated public sentiment. Even with all these dangers staring us in the face it seems unable to get anything done in the way of proper national defense."[94]

Finally, it was evident that Republicans were contemplating a heavy assault on the administration for alleged weakness, in preparation for the coming presidential campaign. Herbert Croly and Walter Lippmann, editors of the outstanding progressive journal, *The New Republic*, believed that Wilson was doomed and were, they told the Canadian Prime Minister's secretary, L. C. Christie, on January 24, attempting "to fix" on a man whom they could support for the presidency against Wilson. Their conversation, Christie continued, "disclosed how many and how divergent are the sectional feelings and purposes and interests. There seemed to be no man and no cause that could command the nation. Unity seems in abeyance. There is something almost like political anarchy."[95]

The extremity of feeling was most strikingly revealed in a sonnet by the novelist, Owen Wister:

To Woodrow Wilson. Feb. 22, 1916.

Not even if I possessed your twist in speech
　　Could I make any (fit for use) fit you;
You've wormed yourself beyond description's reach;
　　Truth if she touched you would become untrue.
Satire has seared a host of evil fames,
　　Has withered emperors by her fierce lampoons;
History has lashes that have flayed the names
　　Of public cowards, hypocrites, poltroons,

403-404, on the organization of the American Rights Committee in New York and the Citizens' League for America and the Allies, a comparable group, in Boston.

[93] C. W. Dabney to W. H. Page, January 8, 1916, the Papers of Walter H. Page, Houghton Library, Harvard University; hereinafter cited as the Page Papers.

[94] H. C. Lodge to M. Frewen, January 13, 1916, the Papers of Moreton Frewen, Library of Congress.

[95] L. C. Christie, "MEMORANDUM for the Prime Minister," January 27, 1916, the Papers of Robert L. Borden, Canadian Public Archives, Ottawa; hereinafter cited as the Borden Papers.

You go immune, cased in your self-esteem;
  The next world cannot scathe you, nor can this;
No fact can stab through your complacent dream;
  Nor present laughter, nor the future's hiss.
But if its fathers did this land control
Dead Washington would wake and blast your soul.[96]

"I cannot impress upon you too forcibly the importance of an appeal to the country at this time on the question of preparedness," Tumulty wrote to the President on January 17, 1916. "No matter what the character of the information is that you are receiving, I get it from all sources that there is no enthusiasm on the 'hill' for preparedness, and that the country itself is indifferent because of the apparent inability of the country to grasp the importance of this question. . . . Our all is staked upon a successful issue in this matter."[97]

Wilson agreed, at least in part. "I do not think that the Congress quite realizes the genuine demand of the country for an adequate plan of preparation for national defense," he wrote the day after receiving Tumulty's letter. "I feel that it is my duty to explain this matter to the country and summon its support."[98] That same day, January 18, he announced his decision to reporters after discussing the situation at a Cabinet meeting. He would go to the country in a "swing around the circle." No diplomatic crisis prompted the decision. At this very moment Lansing was conducting delicate negotiations with Germany for settlement of the *Lusitania* case, and they seemed to be going well. Wilson simply wanted, as he or Tumulty told reporters, to recapture initiative from Bryan and encourage popular support for reasonable preparedness.[99] Perhaps he could persuade the military affairs committee to accept the Continental Army plan. No matter if he could not; he would still be in stronger position in dealing with the committee after his return.

President and Mrs. Wilson slipped away late Friday evening, January 21, for a weekend cruise aboard the *Mayflower* in Chesapeake Bay. He returned to the White House late Sunday evening and conferred on Monday, Tuesday, and Wednesday with Democratic leaders from the House about a legislative program.[100] Then he opened his preparedness

[96] *Springfield* (Mass.) *Republican*, February 24, 1916.
[97] J. P. Tumulty to W. W., January 17, 1916, Wilson Papers.
[98] W. W., to Carter Glass, January 18, 1916, *ibid.*
[99] *New York Times*, January 19, 1916.
[100] *ibid.*, January 25 and 26, 1916; New York *World*, January 26 and 27, 1916.

campaign on January 27 with addresses in New York before the New York Federation of Churches, Railway Business Association, and Motion Picture Board of Trade.[101] He hurried back to Washington late that evening and spent most of the next day in his office. That evening, January 28, he and Mrs. Wilson attended a dinner in their honor at the McAdoos'. They then took the train for Pittsburgh, where the President delivered two addresses at Soldiers' Memorial Hall January 29.[102] In these opening addresses, Wilson repeated the main points of earlier speeches: America needed to prepare, not for aggressive war, but for possible defense of the western hemisphere and its international ideals. Economic and scientific preparation was as important as amassing more obvious military might. He was not committed to a single plan for the army, but he believed that constitutional limitations prevented the National Guard from becoming a reliable instrument of national defense.

Wilson seemed to hit his stride in his next address in the Armory in Cleveland on the evening of January 29. He had just learned that the German government was balking at his terms of settlement of the *Lusitania* controversy.[103] Discarding the text that he had already given to the press, he talked passionately about how extremely difficult it had been to maintain peace; he also spoke ominously about dangers ahead. "The world," he cried, "is on fire and there is tinder everywhere. The sparks are liable to drop anywhere, and somewhere there may be material which we cannot prevent from bursting into flame. The whole influence of passion is abroad in the world, and it is not strange that men see red in such circumstances." People coming to the White House had told him, Wilson continued, that they were counting on him to keep the country out of war and maintain the nation's honor. "Have you ever reflected that a time might come when I could not do both, and have you made yourselves ready to stand behind your Government for the maintenance of the honor of your country?"[104]

The President and Mrs. Wilson were nearly overwhelmed when they arrived in Milwaukee, center of German-American sentiment, in the morning of January 31. Fifteen thousand persons greeted them at the station, and crowds lined the streets as they were escorted to the Pfister Hotel by a troop of cavalry. There was no sudden crisis,

---

[101] *New York Times*, January 28, 1916.
[102] *ibid.*, January 30, 1916.   [103] See below, pp. 73-90.
[104] *New York Times*, January 30, 1916.

Wilson told 8,000 persons in the Auditorium. He knew that the people were depending on him to keep them out of war. "So far I have done so. And I pledge you my word that, God helping me, I will, if it is possible." The great crowd thundered its approval. The applause was not as great when he went on to say that the time might come when he could not preserve both peace and national honor.[105] He spoke in Chicago that same evening to 5,000 persons in the Auditorium and covered familiar ground.[106]

Preparedness to defend both peace and national honor was also his theme as he traveled through Illinois into Iowa on February 1, with brief speeches in Joliet, Rock Island, Davenport, and Iowa City, climaxed by an address before 10,000 persons in the Coliseum in Des Moines in the evening. It was, reporters said, the largest crowd ever assembled in that city. Someone had told him, Wilson said, that the people of the Middle West were indifferent to the cause of national defense. "I said," he continued, " 'I do not believe it, but I am going out to see'; and I have seen. I have seen what I expected to see—great bodies of serious men, great bodies of earnest women, coming together to show their profound interest in the objects of this visit of mine." He had not come to excite apprehensions. He could not understand how some men could actually say that the United States ought to be in the war. He had spent all his thought and energy in keeping the country out of war. But he had to say that there was danger to "our national life from what other nations may do." "I know that there is not a man or woman within the hearing of my voice who would wish peace at the expense of the honor of the United States."[107]

The President and Mrs. Wilson arrived in Topeka in zero weather the next morning, February 2, and drove through snowpacked streets and silent crowds. Wilson spoke in the Auditorium to an audience that included a large number of delegates to a meeting of the Farmers' Elevator and Co-operative Union of America.[108] "President Wilson's visit to Kansas did not change very many of our people on the 'preparedness' issue," the Governor of Kansas reported on the following day. "The state is strongly against his program. The farmers are almost unanimous in their opposition to it. . . . The newspaper correspondents

[105] *ibid.*, February 1, 1916.
[106] *ibid.*
[107] *ibid.*, February 2, 1916; *The New Democracy*, II, 70-82.
[108] *New York Times*, February 3, 1916.

accompanying the train said that the president's reception here was the coldest he received at any place."[109]

It was altogether different in Kansas City that evening. Wilson talked before 18,000 persons packed in Convention Hall of dangers that he could not control, of the need for America's healing help in the postwar era, above all, of the need for disciplined might and self-control so that the United States could stay at peace and play its part in "the redemption of the affairs of mankind." He led the audience in singing "America" at the end of his address. The great crowd surged forward afterward, and hundreds of persons crowded around him on the platform.[110]

The climax of the tour came with Wilson's final speech the next morning, February 3, before another audience of 18,000 persons in the Coliseum in St. Louis. He had been intoxicated by the overpowering approval of the crowd in Kansas City. He was even more on fire in St. Louis. The words poured out in poetic cadences, but they were perfectly controlled to build the single, irresistible argument for preparedness toward which he had been working. It was that the United States was determined to avoid involvement in the war, and that it could defend its neutrality only if properly armed to resist assaults on its rights both by submarines and blockading cruisers. "I am ready to make every patient allowance for men caught in the storm of national struggle," he said. ". . . I am ready to yield everything but the absolute final essential right, because I know how my heart would burn, I know how my mind would be in a whirl if America were engaged in what seemed a death grapple. . . . I want the record of the conduct of this administration to be a record of genuine neutrality and not of pretended neutrality." The American people, he went on, were genuinely neutral; they stood in judgment on neither side in Europe. They were determined only to defend their honor. They would get a good army reorganization bill, and the details were not important. They would strengthen their splendid navy. Indeed, he cried, they should have "incomparably the greatest navy in the world."[111]

The Wilsons were back in Washington in the early afternoon of February 4. Reporters noted that the President was invigorated and in

[109] A. Capper to O. G. Villard, February 3, 1916, Villard Papers.

[110] *New York Times*, February 3, 1916.

[111] *The New Democracy*, II, 106-115. Wilson changed this phrase in this official printed version to read "incomparably the most adequate navy in the world."

fine physical form: giving speeches, Grayson said, was as beneficial to Wilson as a game of golf. He was also immensely pleased. "The Western trip was indeed a most interesting and inspiring experience, much fuller of electrical thrills than I had expected," he wrote soon after his return.[112] An estimated million persons had turned out in bitter cold to greet him or hear him speak; only in Topeka had crowds failed to demonstrate trust and warm approval. He had set off new agitation and demands all over the country for some kind of effective defense legislation. It was confined largely to cities and towns and urban professional and business groups, to be sure, but it was no less strong or significant for that fact.[113] Most important, he had recovered initiative and national leadership. As *The New Republic* said: "He has checked his enemies, reassured his friends, disarmed many of his critics, and resumed control of the situation. It is a wonderful example of that opportunity for aggressive leadership which the Presidency of the United States places in the hands of the bold political strategist and

[112] W. W. to R. Olney, February 7, 1916, the Papers of Richard Olney, Library of Congress.

[113] Polls taken in early February by the *Beaumont Enterprise, Beaumont Journal, Galveston News,* and *Dallas Morning News,* for example, showed 20,942 readers in favor of preparedness and 1,983 opposed. *Galveston News,* February 13, 1916. For an analysis of the impact of Wilson's speeches on the Midwest, see the New York *World,* February 7, 1916; for special reports, W. F. Sapp, Democratic national committeeman from Kansas, to J. P. Tumulty, February 3, 1916, Wilson Papers. There were mass meetings to demonstrate support for preparedness in Bryan, Tex., on February 4; Tyler, Tex., on February 5; Wichita Falls, Tex., and Corsicana, Tex., on February 9; Paris, Tex., and Dallas, Tex., on February 10; Bessemer, Ala., and Amarillo, Tex., on about February 11; McGregor, Tex., on February 12; and Temple, Tex., on February 15, 1916. Wilson received resolutions of approval and support (all in the Wilson Papers) from W. T. Hornaday, vice president of the Army League of the United States, February 5; Englewood, N.J., Board of Trade, February 3; Polish-American Chamber of Commerce, Cleveland, Ohio, February 8; Lemars, Ia., Commercial Club, February 8; Ennis, Tex., Commercial Club, February 9; Steubenville, Ohio, Chamber of Commerce, February 9; Alpine, Tex., Commercial Club, c. February 15; and Long Beach, Calif., Chamber of Commerce, February 17, 1916.

For general editorial comment, see, e. g., "The President Rousing the Nation for Preparedness," *Literary Digest,* LII (February 5, 1916), 269-270; "Effect of the President's Pleas for Preparedness," *ibid.,* February 12, 1916, pp. 359-361; New York *World,* January 28 and February 4, 1916; *The Outlook,* CXII (February 9, 1916), 292, 295; *The Independent,* LXXXV (February 14, 1916), 216-217; for favorable comment by the religious press, *The Presbyterian,* LXXXVI (February 10, 1916), 4, and Nashville *Christian Advocate,* LXXVII (February 18, 1916), 3. Small-town favorable reaction is revealed in the *Armour* (S.D.) *Herald,* February 18, 1916; *Conrad* (Mont.) *Independent,* February 17, 1916; *Sheridan* (Mont.) *Forum,* February 17, 1916; *Oshkosh* (Wis.) *North Western,* February 15, 1916; and *Princeton* (Minn.) *News,* February 18, 1916.

the effective platform speaker."[114] Another editor added: "Mr. Wilson has returned to Washington, after having won the first genuine popular triumph, through personal contact with the people, in his public career. He has been rated hitherto as an austere, intellectual impersonality, incapable of arousing much popular interest or enthusiasm."[115]

It was not all pure gain. Pacifists were pacifists still; indeed, Wilson's speeches only deepened their suspicion that he had deserted to the militarists. "I am utterly discouraged and shocked and have completely lost my faith in Wilson," one of them wrote. ". . . I simply feel that he is no longer to be depended upon, and is what Princeton thought him, and not what we have idealized him to be. 'Twas with the deepest sorrow that my wife and I have come to this conclusion. . . . We are never again going to let our enthusiasm for *any* man run away with us."[116] Many of Wilson's strongest supporters were shocked by his declaration at St. Louis in favor of the greatest navy in the world. "Did the austere and self-controlled Wilson suddenly grow dizzy in that atmosphere . . . ," one eastern journal asked.[117] Did he really mean to announce what could only be a disastrous naval race with Britain, old Senator Benjamin R. Tillman, chairman of the naval affairs committee in the upper house, added.[118]

Most portentous of all, Bryan read Wilson's speeches with growing alarm and suspicion. The Commoner trumpeted in his magazine that they indicated that the President was "actually considering a state of war in which the United States will be the aggressor."[119] "I have been amazed at the slush he has been pouring out upon the West," Bryan wrote to Josephus Daniels. "Is he simply imposing upon the public and trying to *scare* the voters into accepting his policy? . . . If I find that his purpose is to drag this nation into this war I may feel it my duty to oppose his nomination."[120]

In Washington, moreover, the deadlock between Garrison and the

[114] *New Republic*, vi (February 5, 1916), 1-2; also *ibid.*, February 12, 1916, p. 30.

[115] *Springfield* (Mass.) *Republican*, February 5, 1916.

[116] O. G. Villard to G. F. Peabody, February 7, 1916, Villard Papers. In a similar vein, see also the New York *Nation*, cii (February 3, 1916), 123; *The Public*, xix (February 4, 1916), 98-99; S. H. Smith to W. W. Bailey, February 8, 1916, Bailey Papers; *Congregationalist and Christian World*, ci (February 10, 1916), 206.

[117] *Springfield* (Mass.) *Republican*, February 5, 1916.

[118] B. R. Tillman to W. W., February 14, 1916, Wilson Papers. For similar comment, see *New York Journal of Commerce*, February 4, 1916; New York *Nation*, cii (February 10, 1916), 153.

[119] W. J. Bryan, "Do You Want War?" *The Commoner*, xvi (February 1916), 1-2.

[120] W. J. Bryan to J. Daniels, February 4, 1916, the Papers of Josephus Daniels, Li-

House military affairs committee was still as hopeless as ever. "I see no real change in the attitude of the Members since the President's Western tour," Kitchin reported to Bryan on February 9.[121] This was certainly true insofar as it referred to Democratic opposition to the Continental Army. Hay lost no time in telling the plain facts to the President after his return. The military affairs committee, Hay warned, simply could not be persuaded to endorse the plan. It believed that Congress had ample constitutional authority over the National Guard, and that a citizen reserve force of between four and five hundred thousand men could be recruited in a "federalized" National Guard.[122] Hay repeated this advice and discussed the constitutional issues in greater detail in a letter on February 8. He added that he had also canvassed the members of the House and concluded that they were overwhelmingly opposed to the Continental Army. "Many southern members fear it," he wrote, "because they believe it will be the means of enlisting large numbers of negroes."[123]

This, Wilson knew, was the reality of the congressional situation. He had already safeguarded his own avenue of retreat in his western speeches, but what could he do to harness Garrison? The Secretary of War resolved this dilemma himself, as Wilson undoubtedly hoped that he would do. He wrote to the President on February 9, saying that he felt impelled to speak out against two measures that fell within his jurisdiction—the so-called Clarke amendment to the Philippine bill granting independence to the islands within five years, and the National Guard plan. "If, with respect to either matter," Garrison added, "we are not in agreement upon . . . fundamental principles, then I could not, with propriety, remain your seeming representative in respect thereto. Our convictions would be manifestly not only divergent but utterly irreconcilable."[124]

Wilson drafted his reply carefully, after consultation with Tumulty. It read:

"In reply to your letter of today let me say,

"First, that it is my own judgment that the action embodied in the Clarke amendment to the bill extending further self-government to

brary of Congress; hereinafter cited as the Daniels Papers; also W. J. Bryan to C. Kitchin, c. February 5, 1916, Kitchin Papers.

[121] C. Kitchin to W. J. Bryan, February 9, 1916, *ibid.*

[122] J. Hay to W. W., February 5, 1916, Wilson Papers.

[123] J. Hay to W. W., February 8, 1916, *ibid.*

[124] L. M. Garrison to W. W., February 9, 1916, *ibid.*

the Philippines is unwise at this time, but it would clearly be most inadvisable for me to take the position that I must dissent from that action should both houses of Congress concur in a bill embodying that amendment. That is a matter upon which I must, of course, withhold judgment until the joint action of the two houses reaches me in definite form. What the final action of the houses will be no one can at this time certainly forecast. I am now, of course, engaged in conference with Mr. [William A.] Jones [chairman of the House committee on insular affairs] and others with regard to the probable action of the House of Representatives in this matter and do not yet know what it is likely to be. *The one obvious thing, it seems to me, is the necessity for calm and deliberate action on our part at this time when matters of such gravity are to be determined, and not only calm and deliberate action but action which takes into very serious consideration views differing from our own.*

"Second, as I have had occasion to say to you, I am not yet convinced that the measure of preparation for national defence which we deem necessary can be obtained through the instrumentality of the National Guard under federal control and training, but I feel in duty bound to keep my mind open to conviction on that side and think that it would be most unwise and most unfair to the Committee of the House, which has such a plan in mind, to say that it cannot be done. The bill in which it will be embodied has not yet been drawn, as I learned today from Mr. Hay. *I should deem it a very serious mistake to shut the door against this attempt on the part of the Committee in perfect, good faith to meet the essentials of the programme set forth in my message but in a way of their own choosing.*

"As you know, I do not at all agree with you in favoring compulsory enlistment for training, and I fear the advocacy of compulsion before the Committee of the House on the part of representatives of the Department of War has greatly prejudiced the House against the proposal for a continental army, little necessary connection as there is between the plan and the opinion of the Chief of Staff in favor of compulsory enlistment.

"I owe you this frank repetition of my views and policy in this matter, which we have discussed on previous occasions, in the letters which we have exchanged and in conversation. I am very much obliged to you for your own frank avowal of your convictions. I trust that you will feel no hesitation about expressing your personal views on both these subjects on the two occasions to which you refer, but I hope that you will be kind enough to draw very carefully the distinction between your own individual views and the views of the administration.

"You will, of course, understand that I am devoting my energy and attention unsparingly in conference with members of the various committees of Congress to an effort to procure an agreement upon a workable and practicable programme. This is a time when it seems to me patience on the part of all of us is of the essence in bringing about a consummation of the purpose we all have in mind."[125]

Garrison replied at once, saying that he and Wilson hopelessly disagreed upon fundamental principles and offering his resignation, to take effect at Wilson's convenience.[126] Wilson feigned surprise, but did not let opportunity pass to speed Garrison's departure. He wrote:

"I must confess to feeling a very great surprise at your letter of today offering your resignation as Secretary of War. There has been no definite action taken yet in either of the matters to which your letter of yesterday referred. The whole matter is under debate and all the influences that work for clarity and judgment ought to be available at this very time.

"But since you have felt obliged to take this action and since it is evident that your feeling in the matter is very great indeed, I feel that I would be only imposing a burden upon you should I urge you to retain the Secretaryship of War while I am endeavoring to find a successor. I ought to relieve you at once and do hereby accept your resignation because it is so evidently your desire that I should do so.

"I cannot take this important step, however, without expressing to you my very warm appreciation of the distinguished service you have rendered as Secretary of War, and I am sure that in expressing this appreciation I am only putting into words the judgment of our fellow citizens far and wide.

"With sincere regret at the action you have felt constrained to take."[127]

Wilson gave his entire correspondence with Garrison since January 12 to the press on the same day that the Secretary resigned, and most newspapers published it in full on the next day, February 11. Army officials in the War Department mourned the departure of "the wisest, most just, most fearless, kindly and courteous man" that they had "ever had the honor of serving with,"[128] and a few editors pummeled

125 W. W. to L. M. Garrison, February 10, 1916, *ibid.* The italicized sentences were suggested in substance as additions in J. P. Tumulty to W. W., February 9, 1916, *ibid.*

126 L. M. Garrison to W. W., February 10, 1916, *ibid.* The Assistant Secretary of War, Henry Breckinridge, also resigned on February 10, 1916.

127 W. W. to L. M. Garrison, February 10, 1916, *ibid.*

128 H. L. Scott to L. M. Garrison, February 11, 1916, Scott Papers.

Wilson for lack of courage in refusing to stand and fight.[129] But reaction was generally calm, and the antipreparedness leaders and members of the military affairs committee were delighted both by Garrison's resignation and Wilson's kind references to them in his correspondence. "I have been instructed by the Committee on Military Affairs of the House of Representatives," Hay wrote to the President on February 11, "to convey to you the very great appreciation which the committee feels for the confidence which you have shown in its good faith and patriotism; and to assure you of its desire to work in harmony with you in perfecting a plan which would be of the greatest benefit to the country."[130] Wilson responded gratefully: "I never at any time have had the least reason to doubt the spirit, the knowledge, or the capacity of the Committee and I want to say that it has given me real pleasure to work with it."[131]

Wilson named General Scott as Acting Secretary of War on Friday, February 11. That evening he and Mrs. Wilson attended a dinner in honor of the Cabinet given by Postmaster and Mrs. Albert S. Burleson and afterward boarded the *Mayflower* for a weekend cruise on the Chesapeake Bay. Wilson wanted time, he told reporters, to think about Garrison's successor.[132] He first considered Secretary of Agriculture David F. Houston and Secretary of the Interior Franklin K. Lane and decided that they were both needed in their posts. Then he thought of Newton D. Baker of Cleveland, whom he had tried to persuade to join the Cabinet in 1913. Subsequent investigation convinced him that Baker was the man for the secretaryship of war, and he offered him the post on March 4, 1916. Baker accepted on March 6, saying that he was at the President's disposal.[133] Only after the appointment had been announced did the press discover that Baker recently had called himself a pacifist and opposed preparedness.[134]

[129] *The Outlook*, cxii (February 23, 1916), 402; *Collier's*, lvi (March 4, 1916), 14; and especially the long and savage editorial in *The New Republic*, vi (February 19, 1916), 56-57, saying that the episode demonstrated Wilson's weakness and incompetence as a leader.

[130] J. Hay to W. W., February 11, 1916, Wilson Papers. Representative Julius Kahn, ranking Republican member of the committee, introduced the resolution thanking the President. *New York Times*, February 12, 1916.

[131] W. W. to J. Hay, February 15, 1916, Wilson Papers.

[132] *New York Times*, February 12, 1916.

[133] *ibid.*, March 7, 1916.

[134] *ibid.*; "A Pacifist Secretary of War," *Literary Digest*, lii (March 18, 1916), 701.

The Second *Lusitania* Crisis

THE happy conclusion of the *Arabic* crisis on October 5, 1915, averted a break in relations with Germany. But it did not restore cordial relations between the American and German governments. Larger differences, symbolized by the *Lusitania* case, still remained unresolved. More immediately important, reports of German-American agitations and German intrigues against American neutrality revived popular suspicions and poisoned the atmosphere of official relations in the early autumn.

German-American and virulently anti-British Irish-American spokesmen had long since recovered from the shock of the *Lusitania* incident and resumed their agitation in pamphlets, editorials, and mass meetings.[1] Leaders of both groups formed a new coalition, the Friends of Peace, in Chicago on September 6 to work for freedom of the seas and an arms embargo, and, they said, to rally 15,000,000 Americans "for political and other action." They were openly subversive. "There can be no doubt," said Francis L. Dorl, editor of the pro-German magazine, *Vital Issue*, and one of the organizers, "that in case of war with Germany many persons, acting privately, will refuse actively to support this Government. Who can blame them?"[2] The two leaders of the Friends of Peace—John Brisben Walker, a former muckraking journalist, and Jeremiah A. O'Leary, president of the American Truth Society—were on the stump all through the autumn of 1915 excoriating Wilson and stirring discontent.[3] They had new allies in their campaign for an arms embargo in the American Embargo Conference, formed by the American journalist in the employ of the German Embassy, William Bayard Hale; the American Independence Union of California, which coordinated German propaganda on the West Coast; the Hearst press; and Senator Robert M. La Follette of Wisconsin.[4] Hearst

---

[1] A. S. Link, *Wilson*, III, 439-440.

[2] *New York Times*, September 7 and 8, 1915.

[3] See, e. g., the account of the meeting at Cooper Union, New York City, on November 19, in the New York *World*, November 20, 1915.

[4] W. R. MacDonald, secretary, the American Embargo Conference, to T. J. Walsh, November 17, 1915, Walsh Papers; Daniel O'Connell, president, American Independence Union of California, to T. J. Walsh, November 30, 1915, *ibid.*; Boston *American*, August

and La Follette aside, they were so obviously paid German agitators that they did not do much more than intensify general anti-German resentments. Wilson, in striking out at them in his Manhattan Club address and his third Annual Message, reflected what was certainly the majority American view.

Most Americans had become accustomed to the rantings of pro-German extremists. The development that convulsed the country in the autumn was revelation by the newspapers of widespread German sabotage, intrigue, and plotting against American neutrality. Actually, the Bureau of Investigation, Secret Service, and other agencies had uncovered most of the details in the preceding summer, and President Wilson and Attorney General Thomas W. Gregory had taken appropriate countermeasures immediately.[5] Public revelations began with a sensational account in the New York *World*, prepared, undoubtedly, with the assistance of the Justice Department, on November 19 and 20. Next came the first public disclosure of the Rintelen affair[6] and trial in New York of officials of the Hamburg-American Line for violating American neutrality during the early months of the war.[7] There followed even more startling reports of sabotage in munitions factories;[8] the arrest of a man who had been making bombs for use against Allied munitions ships;[9] more detailed accounts of Rintelen's incredible intrigues;[10] revelation by a federal grand jury in New York City that German agents had subsidized and directed the formation of Labor's National Peace Council to foment strikes in war factories and conduct pro-German propaganda;[11] and the arrest of another

---

11, 1915; *Chicago Examiner*, August 11, 1915; R. M. La Follette, "Neutrality," *La Follette's Magazine*, VII (September 15, 1915), 1.

[5] See A. S. Link, *Wilson*, III, 558-564.

[6] *New York Times*, November 22, 1915. For the Rintelen affair, see A. S. Link, *Wilson*, III, 561-564.

[7] The trial began on November 23 (*New York Times*, November 24, 1915), and ended in the conviction of four employees of the company on December 2, 1915. (*ibid.*, December 3, 1915.)

[8] New York *World*, December 2, 1915.

[9] "Bringing the War to the United States," *Literary Digest*, LI (November 27, 1915), 1207-1209.

[10] *New York Times*, December 5 and 8, 1915; New York *World*, December 8, 1915.

[11] For the activities of Labor's National Peace Council, see the *New York Times*, June 30, July 9, and August 10, 1915, and New York *World*, July 7, 1915. For reports of the investigation, see *ibid.*, July 10 and December 6, 1915, and *New York Times*, December 6, 7, 8, 11, and 14, 1915. The grand jury indicted Rintelen, Representative Frank Buchanan of Illinois, and six others on December 28, 1915, for various con-

official of the Hamburg-American Line and several other German agents for plotting to destroy the Welland Canal in Canada.[12]

Excitement ran high when the Attorney General, affirming publicly that the Justice Department had received numerous reports "indicating attacks upon lawful American industries and commerce through incendiary fires and explosions in factories, threats to intimidate employes, and other acts of violence," called on state officials to help protect security.[13] Alarm and agitation was intensified most of all when President Wilson and Secretary Lansing demanded the recall of Captain Karl Boy-Ed and Captain Franz von Papen, German Naval and Military Attachés, thus directly implicating the German government in the intrigues.

The case against Boy-Ed was airtight, as the grand jury investigation of the Hamburg-American Line officials revealed conclusively that he had furnished the money to send supply ships to German cruisers in violation of American neutrality laws.[14] Evidence against von Papen was only circumstantial (he afterward privately and publicly declared that he was innocent of any complicity[15]), but it was enough to convince Wilson and Lansing of his guilt, and he had been implicated in Austro-Hungarian plots to disrupt production in American steel and munitions factories.[16] As Lansing wrote to Wilson on November 29, it was high time to expel von Papen, Boy-Ed, and Alexander von Nuber, Austro-Hungarian Consul General in New York, who was also implicated. "The increasing public indignation in regard to these men and the general criticism of the Government for allowing them to remain," the Secretary of State explained, "are not the chief reasons for suggesting action in these cases, although I do not think that such

---

spiracies and intrigues. *ibid.*, December 29, 1915. They were not brought to trial until April 1917.

[12] *ibid.*, December 18, 1915.

[13] *ibid.*, November 22, 1915.

[14] Charles Warren to R. Lansing, November 15, 1915, the Papers of Robert Lansing, Library of Congress.

[15] See, e. g., "Memorandum From the Office of the Assistant Secretary of War," dated December 6, 1915, *Papers Relating to the Foreign Relations of the United States, The Lansing Papers, 1914-1920* (2 vols.), I, 90-93; hereinafter cited as *The Lansing Papers*; and von Papen's testimony before the Reichstag Commission of Inquiry on April 16, 1920, *Official German Documents Relating to the World War* (2 vols.), II, 1308-1316; hereinafter cited as *Official German Documents*.

[16] A. S. Link, *Wilson*, III, 646-647.

reasons should be ignored. We have been over-patient with these people."[17]

Wilson had earlier been eager to expel the whole company of German intriguers, including the Ambassador, Count Johann von Bernstorff. He now approved Lansing's recommendation at once[18] and shortly afterward added his own candidate, Doctor Heinrich Albert, German Commercial Attaché, to Lansing's list. "He," Wilson said, "has been in many ways the head and front of the offending, and it is probable that even the Ambassador is obliged to accept his decisions."[19] Conversation with the Austro-Hungarian Chargé d'Affaires, Baron Erich Zwiedinek, convinced Lansing that von Nuber did not deserve dismissal; and the Secretary had to inform the President that the State Department did not have sufficient grounds to ask for Albert's recall. Wilson concurred reluctantly, although he still believed that Albert was the "king pin" and the "directing and the most dangerous mind in all these unhappy intrigues which are now so deeply exciting the resentment of this country."[20]

Lansing called Bernstorff to the State Department on December 1 to tell him formally that Boy-Ed and von Papen had to go on account of their "violations of our laws" and "fraudulent practices." Bernstorff was most concerned about his own status and relieved when Lansing said that he was not being accused.[21] "I found him visibly shaken," Colonel House recorded in his diary after talking with the Ambassador in New York on the following day. "It is the first time I have seen his equanimity disturbed. . . . [He was] evidently nervous about himself. I assured him there was no intention to make complaint against him."[22] "Bernstorff," House advised Lansing, "was anxious that you should not make the announcement for a few days and he was also anxious that you should make it clear that he was in no way involved mentioning him by name. He thinks if this is not done there will be a hue and cry in the press to have him also go."[23] Lansing gave the announcement to the press on December 3, but he did not exonerate Bernstorff, and he also intimated that von Nuber and Albert were

[17] R. Lansing to W. W., November 29, 1915, *The Lansing Papers*, I, 83.
[18] W. W. to R. Lansing, November 29, 1915, *ibid.*, p. 84.
[19] W. W. to R. Lansing, December 2, 1915, *ibid.*, p. 87.
[20] R. Lansing to W. W., December 1, 2, and 3, 1915, *ibid.*, pp. 85, 87-88, 89; W. W. to R. Lansing, December 5, 1915, *ibid.*, p. 90.
[21] R. Lansing, "Memorandum . . . ," December 1, 1915, *ibid.*, pp. 86-87.
[22] House Diary, December 2, 1915.
[23] E. M. House to R. Lansing, December 2, 1915, *The Lansing Papers*, I, 88.

in serious danger.[24] Von Papen and Boy-Ed left for home as soon as Lansing arranged safe passage for them with the British and French governments.

Public indignation was ominously high by December, high enough, actually, to cast a pall over official relations between the United States and the Central Powers. It also contributed to resentments that erupted in formation of organizations like the American Rights Committee, of which we have already written.[25] "The further disclosures connecting the German Government with deliberate violations of American law are making the situation almost unbearable," the usually forbearing Louis D. Brandeis wrote in late November, for example.[26] The British Ambassador in Washington, Sir Cecil Spring Rice, described the rising anti-German sentiment in a dispatch to Sir Edward Grey, British Foreign Secretary:

"There has been a great change in the situation since I last wrote. The continued publications as to German plots and German outrages have gradually aroused public opinion and the excitement appears to be growing. I cannot tell how far this feeling, which certainly exists in the east, extends in the centre and the west. But it is generally understood that the sentiment against Germany is growing stronger and the President will follow with the sentiment of the country. Of course anti-German does not mean pro-English. If this country has trouble with another country, it will be for its own reasons and not for ours. But there are reasons of its own why this Government should take action hostile to Germany. I have again and again enumerated the outward and visible signs of the German organization here. . . . The President himself has been the object of the most savage personal attacks and it is generally believed that these attacks have been of the most vindictive and intimate character. Politically, the German-Americans have denounced the President and have arrayed all their forces against him. For a long time he appears to have hesitated, and to have done all he could, not to conciliate them, but to suppress open and visible signs of anything like disunion among American citizens. . . .

"The passage in the President's speech denouncing the disloyal action of the hyphenated citizen was greeted with great applause and is now

[24] *New York Times*, December 4, 1915.
[25] See above, pp. 42-43.
[26] L. D. Brandeis to N. Hapgood, November 24, 1915, the Papers of Louis D. Brandeis, University of Louisville Library; hereinafter cited as the Brandeis Papers.

the predominant element in the present situation. It is believed that the President, having written this passage thought for some time of withdrawing it, but finally he determined to read it as it had stood originally. He has thus crossed the Rubicon. He has openly attacked the German-Americans who have as openly attacked him."[27]

The German government was enough concerned about hostile American sentiment to try to allay it. Ambassador von Bernstorff announced on December 12 that Rintelen had had no instructions to commit acts in violation of American laws,[28] and the German Foreign Office added private assurances two days later.[29] Then the Foreign Office gave an unprecedented statement to American reporters in Berlin on December 18. It read in part:

"The German Government naturally has never knowingly accepted the support of any person, group of persons, society or organization seeking to promote the cause of Germany in the United States by illegal acts, by counsels of violence, by contravention of law, or by any means whatever that could offend the American people in the pride of their own authority. . . .

"Apparently the enemies of Germany have succeeded in creating the impression that the German Government is in some way morally or otherwise responsible for what Mr. Wilson has characterized as anti-American activities, comprehending attacks upon property and violations of the rules which the American Government has seen fit to impose upon the course of neutral trade. This the German Government absolutely denies. It cannot specifically repudiate acts committed by individuals over whom it has no control, and of whose movements and intentions it is neither officially nor unofficially informed. It can only say, and does most emphatically declare to Germans abroad, to German-American citizens of the United States, to the American people, all alike, that whoever is guilty of conduct tending to associate the German cause with lawlessness of thought, suggestion, or deed against life, property, and order in the United States is in fact an enemy of that very cause, and a source of embarrassment to the German Government, notwithstanding anything he or they may believe to the contrary."[30]

[27] C. A. Spring Rice to E. Grey, December 9, 1915, Stephen Gwynn (ed.), *The Letters and Friendships of Sir Cecil Spring Rice* (2 vols.), II, 301-302; hereinafter cited as *Letters of Spring Rice*.

[28] *New York Times*, December 13, 1915.

[29] Ambassador James W. Gerard to the Secretary of State, December 14, 1915, Wilson Papers.

[30] *New York Times*, December 19, 1915.

It would have been interesting if true. It was hard to change old habits. Within less than a month the Berlin Foreign Office informed Bernstorff that an Indian nationalist, Doctor Chauracanta Chakrabarty, was on his way to the United States from Mexico, and that $10,000 should be put at his disposal.[31] This marked the beginning of a German intrigue on American soil to stimulate a revolt against British authority in India by propaganda and shipment of arms and ammunition.[32] At the same time, German agents in New York, particularly Wolf von Igel, were working hand in glove with Irish-American leaders planning a rebellion against British authority in Ireland. These were only two examples of continuing German violation of American hospitality and law.

It was in this atmosphere of growing tension that Lansing embarked upon a new diplomatic campaign to obtain satisfaction from the German government for loss of American lives on the *Lusitania*. Lansing broached the matter informally and personally with Bernstorff on November 2, 1915. The Ambassador again offered a draft note that he had sent to the State Department on October 2. It justified the sinking of the *Lusitania* as a reprisal against British illegality, expressed regret that American lives had been lost, and offered, without admitting any liability, to submit the question of liability for monetary damages to The Hague Tribunal.[33] This, Bernstorff said, was as far as his government could or would go. Lansing replied that although he would give Bernstorff's draft further study, he was sure that it would not do. He could understand why the German government was reluctant to admit that it had committed an illegal act, but the American government would have to insist upon a settlement very soon.[34] Bernstorff was not impressed by Lansing's warning, for Colonel House had told him only three days before that the administration preferred to let the *Lusitania* case drift.[35] "I took up matters of Lusitania and freedom of seas with Mr. Lansing according to my instructions," the Ambassador

[31] Foreign Office to Ambassador von Bernstorff, January 13, 1916, "Bernstorff Wireless Despatches—1916," a notebook of deciphered communications between Bernstorff and the German Foreign Office in the Page Papers; hereinafter cited as "Bernstorff Wireless Despatches—1916."

[32] See R. Lansing to W. W., March 30, 1917, Wilson Papers.

[33] J. von Bernstorff to R. Lansing, tentative letter, October 2, 1915, *The Lansing Papers*, I, 484-485.

[34] R. Lansing to W. W., November 2, 1915, *ibid.*, pp. 488-489.

[35] House Diary, October 30, 1915. House did not disclose this part of his conversation in his report to Lansing. See E. M. House to R. Lansing, October 30, 1915, *The Lansing Papers*, I, 487-488.

reported to the Foreign Office in Berlin. "Mr. Lansing suggested putting off discussion for some days, as he thought the note addressed to English Government might influence the attitude of the German Government toward the mentioned matters."[36] "As I have reported several times, the Lusitania matter is not acute any more," he added in a private dispatch to the Imperial Chancellor, Theobald von Bethmann Hollweg. ". . . The Government over here would prefer to let the whole matter drop, except for later settlement."[37]

Events took an ugly turn, and the necessity for definitive settlement of the *Lusitania* case became all the more urgent in Lansing's view, when news came to Washington on November 9 and 10 that a submarine flying the Austrian ensign had sunk the Italian liner *Ancona*, 8,210 tons, bound from Naples to New York, in the northwestern part of the Sicilian Channel on November 7, with heavy loss of life. First reports accused the submarine commander of particularly brutal behavior—of firing numerous volleys into the ship while debarkation was in progress, and of torpedoing her while many passengers remained aboard.[38] It was, the *New York Times* exclaimed, "savage cruelty for the joy of slaughter, for the lust of killing, because of an unquenchable thirst for blood." It was, moreover, this newspaper and others affirmed, further proof of *German* perfidy, for a German submarine had obviously done the deed, and Germany had stubbornly refused to make amends for destruction of the *Lusitania*.[39]

Another major crisis impended, and Lansing moved at once to get the *Lusitania* negotiations with Germany under way. He wrote out the draft of a German note of apology for Wilson's perusal on November 11. It did not use the word "disavow," but it did specifically admit the illegality of the *Lusitania's* destruction and offered suitable indemnity for the loss of American lives.[40] Wilson agreed that it was probably the most that the United States could hope to obtain,[41] and Lansing gave Bernstorff the new draft on November 17. The *Ancona* affair,

[36] J. von Bernstorff to the Foreign Office, November 3, 1915, Archives of the German Foreign Office, microfilm copies in the National Archives; hereinafter cited as German F. O. Archives.

[37] J. von Bernstorff to T. von Bethmann Hollweg, November 3, 1915, *ibid.*

[38] *New York Times*, November 10, 11, 12, and 13, 1915.

[39] *New York Times*, November 12, 1915. For other editorial comment, see "Another 'Lusitania' Case in the Mediterranean," *Literary Digest*, LI (November 20, 1915), 1139-1140.

[40] R. Lansing to W. W., November 11, 1915, enclosing the draft of a German note, *The Lansing Papers*, I, 489-490.

[41] W. W. to R. Lansing, November 17, 1915, *ibid.*, p. 490.

Lansing warned, had aroused as much resentment against Germany as Austria-Hungary. "I told him," Lansing recorded, "that I hoped this [*Lusitania*] matter could be settled satisfactorily to this Government before the assembling of Congress, as the present resentment of public

"I Just Can't Make My Feet Behave"
Evans in the Baltimore *American*

opinion in this country might cause a serious situation of affairs if the matter was discussed in Congress; that it was even possible that Congress, with whom the power rested, might declare war."[42] Bernstorff feigned concern and sympathy for the American point of view, but he

[42] R. Lansing, "Memorandum by the Secretary of State . . . ," November 17, 1915, *ibid.*, pp. 490-491.

was not frightened by such grim talk. He did not send a report of this conversation to Berlin until November 23. Then he said that Lansing had brought the *Lusitania* question up only because he was afraid of congressional criticism. President Wilson, Bernstorff added, did not believe that a settlement was possible and hoped to drag out negotiations until the end of the war, assuming that there were no new incidents. Wilson's great objective was peace in Europe.[43]

Lansing waited for a week for some word from the German Embassy. Then he wrote an urgent personal letter warning Bernstorff that speedy settlement of the controversy, perhaps within a few days, was imperative.[44] The Ambassador was dilatory in reply, pointing out that he had to use the mails for confidential correspondence with his government, and that he would not be able to give an answer for several weeks.[45] He was not really worried. Sending Lansing's letter and his reply to the Imperial Chancellor, he wrote: "I have the honor to submit the enclosed copy of a *purely private correspondence* with Secretary of State Lansing. So far, I believe that the action has been merely started by him alone, since he has never mentioned the President to me, and since I have been informed by other strictly confidential sources [Colonel House] that Mr. Wilson does not pursue the Lusitania incident seriously any more."[46]

Bernstorff did not know it, but Lansing was in a dangerous mood, determined to press for German admission of wrongdoing even to the point of threatening to break diplomatic relations. Germany, he thought, had done great wrong to the United States; now she had to make amends to vindicate the American government's honor. Lansing wanted a settlement, moreover, because he feared that Republicans would mount a violent attack against the administration, once Congress convened, for failing to settle the *Lusitania* controversy. It is also possible that the Secretary of State *wanted* a break with Germany and undertook his campaign with this objective in view. Colonel House later told the British Foreign Secretary that Lansing was insisting on a break

[43] J. von Bernstorff to T. von Bethmann Hollweg, Telegram No. 557, November 23, 1915, German F. O. Archives, including copies both of Bernstorff's draft note and Lansing's.

[44] R. Lansing to J. von Bernstorff, November 24, 1915, *The Lansing Papers*, I, 496.

[45] J. von Bernstorff to R. Lansing, November 25, 1915, *ibid.*, pp. 496-497.

[46] J. von Bernstorff to T. von Bethmann Hollweg, November 25, 1915, German F. O. Archives; italics Bernstorff's.

with Germany in "the belief that if the Central Powers win, we would have to reckon with them later."[47]

The Secretary of State wrote to Wilson on November 19, two days after his last interview with Bernstorff, warning that a total impasse with Germany was possible. Delay would only cause criticism of the administration for being supine. If the Germans refused to give satisfaction, he went on, the administration would have only two choices—either to break diplomatic relations, or to lay the entire matter before Congress with the request that it make the decision for war or peace. Probably the second alternative was best. "From the selfish standpoint of politics," Lansing went on, "I think that the people generally are very much dissatisfied with a continuance of negotiations, that, if our demands are not acceded to, they desire action in asserting our rights, and that if there is further delay, they will turn against the Administration. I believe the pro-German vote in this country is irrevocably lost to us and that, no matter what we do now, we can never win back any part of it. If this view is correct, we ought not from the political standpoint lose the support of the Americans hostile to Germany. And I am afraid that we will do so if we are not rigid in our attitude on the *Lusitania* case. . . . I notice a growing spirit of complaint at what they consider inaction by the Government. The country newspapers as well as letters coming in voice this increasing dissatisfaction." He needed to have the President's views, Lansing concluded, in order to know how to deal with Bernstorff.[48]

Wilson did not comment on Lansing's suggestion that considerations of domestic expediency ought to govern the determination of high foreign policy. The President was obviously determined to press the Germans hard, but only because he did not want to lose all the diplomatic ground gained at so much effort since the *Lusitania* incident. As he explained in a letter that he wrote on his own typewriter on November 21:

"I am quite clear that the position we should take, in conversations with the German Ambassador and in all future dealings with his government in regard to the matters in controversy between us, is

"First, that the matter of the *Lusitania* is just as important and just as acute now as it was the day the news of her sinking arrived, and that a failure to secure a satisfactory settlement will disclose the same questions of future action that then lay in the background;

---

[47] House Diary, January 6, 1916.
[48] R. Lansing to W. W., November 19, 1915, *The Lansing Papers*, I, 491-493.

"Second, that we now know, as a result of the various communications that have passed between that government and this, that the commander of the submarine which sank the *Lusitania* acted contrary to the instructions which had been given by the Imperial German Admiralty;[49] and

"Third, that we should regard a failure to settle this question in the same frank way that the sinking of the *Arabic* was settled would be little less than a repudiation of the assurances then given us and seem to lead back to the very crisis in our relations that was then so happily avoided.

"I think the Ambassador cannot be too explicit with his government in this matter. . . ."[50]

Lansing saw Colonel House in New York on November 28 and finally brought him up to date on negotiations, or lack of them, to this point. House had been profoundly affected by recent revelations of German intrigues and plots and was in a violently anti-German mood. "I tried to impress upon Lansing," he wrote in his diary, "the necessity of the United States making it clear to the Allies that we considered their cause our cause, and that we had no intention of permitting a military autocracy to dominate the world, if our strength could prevent it. We believed this was a fight between democracy and autocracy and we would stand with democracy. . . . Lansing agreed to this and we discussed the best means of reaching an understanding [with the Allies]."[51] Did they also talk about the possibility, even desirability, of a break with Germany? Perhaps, for House was at this very moment hard at work to persuade the President to approve a plan for Anglo-American collaboration in a peace drive that carried at least the risk of war with Germany.[52] "Things are moving rapidly," House reported soon to Walter Page, American Ambassador in London. "We are much nearer a break with the Central Powers than at any time before. It would be well for you to call to the attention of our friends in England the fact that the lower their fortunes seem the more ready we are to help."[53]

Wilson and Lansing were absorbed during the first two weeks of December, and Bernstorff gained a breathing spell, by the rapid develop-

[49] Wilson was mistaken in this statement.
[50] W. W. to R. Lansing, November 21, 1915, *The Lansing Papers*, I, 493.
[51] House Diary, November 28, 1915.
[52] See below, pp. 101-108.
[53] E. M. House to W. H. Page, December 12, 1915, House Papers.

ment of a crisis with Austria-Hungary over the *Ancona* incident. Some of the facts were clarified once the Austro-Hungarian authorities had received a report from the submarine commander involved in the attack. The naval office in Vienna reported on November 14 that the *Ancona* had tried to escape after being warned and had stopped only after being hit several times; that the submarine commander had given the crew forty-five minutes to evacuate the ship and fired his torpedo, even though he knew that passengers remained on board, because another steamer was approaching; and that there had been great loss of life only because the crew had jumped in life boats and abandoned the passengers.[54] What the Austrian report did not disclose, and the American government never knew, was that a German submarine flying the Austrian flag—*U38*, Commander Max Valentiner—had done the deed, and that, moreover, the Austro-Hungarian government had agreed to take full responsibility.[55]

There was, Lansing thought, sufficient evidence from the Austro-Hungarian side alone to justify a stern note. As he explained on submitting his draft to the President on December 3, "The essential fact, that the vessel was shelled and torpedoed while persons were still on board—one of whom, at least, is an American[56]—is amply proven."[57] His note was brief and extraordinarily severe, perhaps because it was safer to speak harshly to Vienna than to Berlin. After reviewing the

[54] The Austro-Hungarian Chargé to the Assistant Secretary of State, November 15, 1915, enclosing the Naval Ministry's statement, *Papers Relating to the Foreign Relations of the United States, 1915, Supplement, The World War,* p. 614; hereinafter cited as *Foreign Relations, 1915, Supplement*; the statement was also printed in the *New York Times,* November 15, 1914.

This report was correct. See Arno Spindler, *La Guerre Sous-Marine* (3 vols.), III, 36-38, for the submarine commander's log entry describing the *Ancona* incident.

[55] H. von Holtzendorff, head of the German Admiralty, to Foreign Secretary G. von Jagow, November 15, 1916; K. von Treutler to the Foreign Office, November 15, 1915; Chief of the Navy Section, Austrian War Ministry, to the Imperial German Admiralty, December 1, 1915, all in the German F. O. Archives.

[56] It was impossible to know how many, if any, American lives had been lost on the *Ancona* when Lansing drafted his note. First reports told of the probable death of twenty-seven Americans; then press reports on November 14 said that nine Americans had lost their lives. The State Department had not received precise information when Lansing drafted this note, and he merely said that a "large number" of persons, "among whom were citizens of the United States," had lost their lives or been injured during the attack. A later report from the American Ambassador in Italy revealed that twelve Americans had been aboard the *Ancona,* and that nine had lost their lives. Ambassador T. N. Page to the Secretary of State, December 18, 1915, *Foreign Relations, 1915, Supplement,* p. 646.

[57] R. Lansing to W. W., December 3, 1916, *The Lansing Papers,* I, 497-498.

A Matter of Routine
President Wilson—"This calls for a note—Mr. Secretary, just bring
me in a copy of our usual No. 1 Note to Germany—'Humanity' Series."

Punch (London)

facts in the case as disclosed mainly by the Austro-Hungarian naval authorities, Lansing maladroitly said that the Hapsburg government had been advised, through correspondence between the Washington and Berlin governments, of the American attitude toward the use of submarines against merchantmen. The conduct of the submarine commander in attacking the *Ancona*, he went on, could "only be characterized as wanton slaughter." The American government preferred to believe that the commander "committed this outrage without authority and contrary to the general or special instructions which he had received." Moreover, it expected prompt disavowal of "an act which is condemned by the world as inhumane and barbarous, which is abhorrent to all civilized nations, and which has caused the death of innocent American citizens," along with punishment of the commander responsible and payment of appropriate indemnity.[58]

It was, Wilson agreed, a peremptory note, but he approved it unthinkingly, as events later proved, on December 5,[59] and it was dispatched to Vienna as soon as it could be coded on the following day. It was delivered to the Austrian Foreign Office on December 10 and published in American newspapers on December 13 and the Viennese press two days later.[60] Lansing added a personal appeal and explanation through the Austro-Hungarian Chargé, Baron Zwiedinek, on December 11. He had great respect and appreciation for the bravery and chivalry of the Austro-Hungarian army and navy, Lansing said, and had not meant his note to be offensive. He and the other members of the Washington government would be painfully surprised if Austria-Hungary defended an action so contrary to her proud traditions and the laws of humanity.[61]

Baron Stephan Burián, Austro-Hungarian Foreign Minister, replied quickly, saying politely but ironically that surely such a severe indictment as Lansing's needed more legal proof and discussion of the points of law than the Secretary of State had furnished. It would also be interesting, Burián went on, to know precisely how many Americans were aboard the *Ancona* and what their fate had been. Finally, the note

[58] The Secretary of State to Ambassador Penfield, December 6, 1915, *Foreign Relations, 1915, Supplement*, pp. 623-625.

[59] W. W. to R. Lansing, December 5, 1915, *The Lansing Papers*, I, 498.

[60] See the *New York Times*, December 17 and 18, 1915, for Austrian and German press reaction.

[61] The Secretary of State to Ambassador Penfield, December 13, 1915, transmitting Baron Zwiedinek to Baron S. Burián, December 11, 1915, *Foreign Relations, 1915, Supplement*, pp. 626-627.

concluded, the Austro-Hungarian government felt obliged to remind the American authorities that it had never been informed of correspondence between Berlin and Washington, and that, in any event, it preferred to conduct its own foreign relations.[62]

The Austrian reply was decoded at the State Department early in the morning of December 17. Lansing was plainly irritated. The note, he advised President Wilson, was "special pleading consisting of technicalities and quibbles." The American government should refuse to debate the principles of law and humanity involved. Then he drafted a harsh reply saying that details of the incident were not necessary to prove the guilt of the submarine commander, and that the American government held the Austro-Hungarian government responsible and repeated its demands of December 6.[63] Wilson reworked Lansing's note on the day of his marriage to Mrs. Galt, December 18, softening its harsh phrases and adding courteous references, and it was sent to Vienna on December 19.[64]

Tedious discussions about the nature of the evidence and the law now followed between Washington and Vienna, and it seemed for a moment that Burián would suggest arbitration as a way out.[65] Wilson followed these exchanges from Hot Springs with growing conviction that his Secretary of State was going too far too fast, especially after Lansing wrote on December 28 that the United States might soon have to break relations, this would *probably* mean war, and Wilson ought to consider the possibility of laying the facts before Congress to obtain its approval before severing relations with the Hapsburg government.[66] Wilson's reply indicated that he was having many second thoughts:

"I have your letter of yesterday about our relations with Austria-Hungary.

"What new elements in the case make you feel now, what, I remember, you did not feel at the outset of this matter, that a breach of diplomatic relations would *probably*, rather than possibly, mean war? I do not now recall any new influences that have recently come into the

[62] Ambassador Penfield to the Secretary of State, December 15, 1915, *ibid.*, pp. 638-639.

[63] R. Lansing to W. W., two letters, December 17, 1915; R. Lansing, "Draft Telegram . . . ," all in *The Lansing Papers*, I, 499-500.

[64] The Secretary of State to Ambassador Penfield, December 19, 1915, *Foreign Relations, 1915, Supplement*, pp. 647-648.

[65] See the memoranda and notes printed in *The Lansing Papers*, I, 501-505.

[66] R. Lansing to W. W., December 28, 1915, *ibid.*, pp. 507-508.

field, and I would very much like to know what has made this impression on your mind.

"You may of course be right. All along there has been reason to fear that such might be the outcome. And I quite agree with you that we ought to think our course out very frankly and carefully, blinking nothing.

"I do not think that it would be wise in any case to lay the matter publicly before Congress. The most that I could do would be to consult with the leaders on the hill. To lay the matter publicly before Congress would in effect be to announce that we expected war and might be the means of hastening it.

"There are some wise and experienced men on the Senate Committee on Foreign Relations and it is quite possible that we might get useful guidance from them. For myself I do not doubt the constitutional powers of the Executive in this connection; but power is a different matter from wise policy.

"Your answer to some of the questions I raised or suggested in my last brief note to you on the news from Vienna[67] will necessarily form a part and a very fundamental part of our discussion of the whole situation. If the Imperial and Royal Government thinks that it can put a very different face upon the *Ancona* case by representations which it thinks us bound in fairness to it to consider, how can we refuse to discuss the matter with them until all the world is convinced that rock bottom has been reached?"[68]

There were, indeed, many signs that Lansing had grossly misjudged public, and particularly congressional, sentiment. Prominent Democratic senators, so Washington correspondents reported on the same day that Wilson wrote the above letter, believed that the first *Ancona* note had been much too severe and could not understand why the United States should refuse to arbitrate the controversy. They also intimated that Wilson had promised Senator William J. Stone of Missouri, chairman of the foreign relations committee, that there would be no rupture with Austria-Hungary until Democratic members of the committee had had an opportunity to talk to the President.[69] The records do not reveal the fact, but it is possible that Stone called Wilson

[67] This was W. W. to R. Lansing, December 27, 1915, *ibid.*, pp. 506-507, asking how the American government could refuse to consider arbitration if the Austrian government proposed it.

[68] W. W. to R. Lansing, December 29, 1915, *ibid.*, pp. 508-509.

[69] *New York Times*, December 30, 1915.

by telephone on December 29 and their conversation influenced Wilson's letter to Lansing on the same day.

Burián saved the President the necessity of a showdown with his Secretary of State by sending a full and responsive reply on the *Ancona* affair to Washington on December 29. It reaffirmed the Hapsburg government's respect for the "sacred demands of humanity" and promised that Austrian submarines would not sink passenger vessels or merchantmen without making provision for the safety of passengers and crews, provided that they did not resist attack or attempt to escape. It recounted the details of the attack on the *Ancona*, emphasizing that the submarine commander had been certain when he fired the torpedo that the ship would not sink rapidly, and that she had in fact stayed afloat forty-five minutes after being hit. Even so, the note went on, the commander had grievously erred and been punished for violating his instructions. Moreover, the Austro-Hungarian government also recognized its liability to indemnify American citizens affected by the attack.[70]

It was more than Lansing had hoped for—a complete vindication of the American position on submarine warfare. He sent a copy of Burián's note by special messenger to Hot Springs on the night of December 30. He also gave a copy to reporters on the following day, adding that Burián had met American demands squarely and in a manly way, and that the settlement would facilitate agreement between Germany and the United States in the *Lusitania* controversy.[71] Wilson must have called Lansing to congratulate him on the victory, for he did not write a personal note, although he later told the Austro-Hungarian government that Burián's "friendly and reasonable" and frank note had made an "amicable and satisfactory settlement" of the *Ancona* case easy to achieve.[72] Most editors agreed and were fulsome in congratulations.[73]

[70] Ambassador Penfield to the Secretary of State, December 29, 1915, *Foreign Relations, 1915, Supplement*, pp. 655-658.

[71] *New York Times*, January 1, 1916.

[72] Wilson's note to Ambassador Penfield, quoted in W. W. to R. Lansing, January 2, 1916, *The Lansing Papers*, I, 512-513, and transmitted in the Secretary of State to Ambassador Penfield, January 3, 1916, *Papers Relating to the Foreign Relations of the United States, 1916, Supplement, The World War*, pp. 143-144; hereinafter cited as *Foreign Relations, 1916, Supplement*.

[73] e. g., *New York Evening Post, Chicago Herald, St. Louis Republic, Pittsburgh Dispatch, Baltimore American*, Baltimore *Sun*, and *Hartford Courant*, all dated January 1, 1916; also "Apology for the 'Ancona'; Torpedo for the 'Persia,'" *Literary Digest*, LII (January 15, 1916), 101-103.

The *Lusitania* negotiations had meanwhile suddenly taken a serious turn at the very moment when it seemed that a break with Austria-Hungary was possible. Lansing reminded Bernstorff on December 1 of the need for some progress and even offered to send a cipher dispatch to Berlin for him.[74] Two weeks passed without any word from the German Embassy, and Lansing's patience snapped. "I feel that continued delay in reaching an agreement in this matter," he wrote to Bernstorff on December 15, "may precipitate a situation which both of us would seriously regret."[75] Boy-Ed's and von Papen's dismissal, Wilson's denunciation of German-inspired intrigue in his Annual Message, and dispatch of the first *Ancona* note had all recently unnerved the German Ambassador. Receipt of Lansing's letter of December 15 on that same day confirmed his fears. He rushed to Colonel House's apartment in New York on the following morning and complained bitterly that the United States was deliberately seeking to break diplomatic relations with both Central Powers. "He thought, too, that the President was largely influenced by his belief that Germany was instigating plots in the United States."[76] He also pleaded strongly against sending a sharp note to Berlin and said that he thought that he could obtain an apology and indemnity from his government if only he had time.[77]

Bernstorff sent Lansing's letter, this time by wireless, to the Foreign Office in Berlin as soon as he received it.[78] It arrived at Wilhelmstrasse on December 17. Bernstorff's long Telegram No. 557, of November 23, which he had sent by mail, had reached the Foreign Office on December 16. Chancellor von Bethmann Hollweg and Foreign Secretary Gottlieb von Jagow were startled but did not miss the signs of crisis. Bethmann set to work on a reply, and Jagow sent a wireless message asking Bernstorff to let him know if there was danger in further postponement. If there was, he added, he would have to send instruction by wireless even though he was reluctant to do so.[79]

Bethmann was determined that His Imperial Majesty's Ambassador in Washington should not have any opportunity for such freewheeling diplomacy as he had practiced in the *Arabic* crisis. With Lansing's pro-

[74] R. Lansing, "Memorandum by the Secretary of State . . . ," December 1, 1915, *The Lansing Papers*, 1, 86-87.

[75] R. Lansing to J. von Bernstorff, December 15, 1915, *ibid.*, p. 498.

[76] House Diary, December 16, 1915.

[77] E. M. House to W. W., December 16, 1915, Wilson Papers.

[78] Ambassador von Bernstorff to the Foreign Office, December 15, 1915, German F. O. Archives.

[79] G. von Jagow to the German Embassy, Washington, December 18, 1915, *ibid.*

posed draft before him, the Chancellor laboriously wrote out detailed instructions and three counterproposals by hand. The first said that Germany's submarine campaign was being conducted in reprisal against England's illegal blockade; declared that neutrals suffered from the submarine campaign mainly because they acquiesced in English measures; claimed that Germany was under no obligation to pay indemnity for loss of American lives on the *Lusitania*, as much as she regretted this loss of life; and offered to submit the specific issue (but not the question of the legality of the submarine war) to an international court of arbitration.[80] Bethmann's second counterproposal was identical with the first until the last paragraph. It then omitted the reference to arbitration and read: "However, the German Government, without recognizing any obligation under international law, but out of a spirit of friendship, is willing to pay an indemnity for the death of American citizens on account of the sinking of the Lusitania." The third counterproposal also omitted the reference to arbitration and substituted a new concluding paragraph as follows: "The German Government, on the other hand, recognizes from the course which the negotiations so far have taken, the difficulty of reconciling in principle the American and German points of view. . . . A perpetuation of this difference of opinion would not, however, be conducive to the friendly relations between the United States and Germany which have never been disturbed and the continuation of which is so sincerely desired by both Governments. Actuated by this spirit the Imperial German Government repeats its deep regrets over the death of American citizens caused by the sinking of the Lusitania and, in order to settle this case amicably, declares its readiness to pay indemnity for the losses incurred."[81]

Bethmann added precise instructions for each step, adding: "Any changes, except stylistic ones, have to be authorized over here."[82] He then put the dispatch in the mail. Jagow had already informed Bernstorff by wireless that explicit instructions were on their way by mail.[83]

Bernstorff passed this message on to Lansing on December 20. The Secretary of State replied that further delay would only imperil a settlement and suggested that the Foreign Office repeat its instructions in

[80] This is printed in *The Lansing Papers*, I, 511-512.

[81] This third counterproposal is also printed in *ibid.*, pp. 514-515.

[82] The Imperial Chancellor to Count von Bernstorff, December 19, 1915, German F. O. Archives.

[83] Foreign Office to German Embassy, Washington, December 18, 1915, repeated December 21, 1915, *ibid*.

the German code over the State Department wire from Berlin.[84] Bernstorff relayed Lansing's message to Berlin by wireless;[85] Lansing, taking no chances, repeated the suggestion to the Chancellor through James W. Gerard, American Ambassador in Berlin.[86]

The Foreign Office sent no reply immediately, and Bernstorff became almost frantic. "Request urgently as soon as possible detailed instructions through mediation of Gerard. Hysteria here grows daily," he wrote in a telegram on December 24.[87] "Pressure here for settlement of Lusitania question increases more and more due to nervousness because of Congress, so-called German conspiracy, and Ancona affair," he warned by wireless on the same day. "As I have reported, the situation is very serious. Break with Austria-Hungary seems almost unavoidable, since the abruptness of the American tone makes yielding extremely difficult."[88] "Secretary of State renewed his request to have instructions sent telegraphically," Bernstorff urged again on December 25. "Gerard instructed to forward any message regarding Lusitania."[89] Jagow had waited to repeat the instructions to Bernstorff only because he knew that the Austrians were about to yield in the *Ancona* controversy, and he wanted to exploit the good feeling that would follow reception of the Austrian note in the United States.[90] But under Bernstorff's and Lansing's prodding he repeated Bethmann's instructions by cable on December 26.[91]

Bernstorff went through the motions of presenting Bethmann's first counterproposal to Lansing on December 31, adding that he expected other instructions and realized that Berlin's statement covered old ground. Following the Chancellor's instructions, he said that his government would like to know the reasons why the American government rejected arbitration of the *Lusitania* dispute, if, indeed, it did still

---

[84] J. von Bernstorff to R. Lansing, December 20, 1915; R. Lansing to J. von Bernstorff, December 20, 1915, *The Lansing Papers*, I, 502.

[85] J. von Bernstorff to the Foreign Office, December 21, 1915, *Foreign Relations, 1915, Supplement*, 648-649. The Foreign Office received this dispatch on December 23.

[86] J. W. Gerard to T. von Bethmann Hollweg, December 23, 1915, German F. O. Archives.

[87] Ambassador von Bernstorff to the Foreign Office, Telegram No. 661, December 24, 1915, *ibid.*

[88] Ambassador von Bernstorff to the Foreign Office, Wireless No. 274, December 24, 1915, *ibid.*

[89] Ambassador von Bernstorff to the Foreign Office, Wireless No. 281, December 25, 1915, *ibid.*

[90] As he said in G. von Jagow to Ambassador von Bernstorff, December 28, 1915, *ibid.*

[91] Foreign Office to Ambassador von Bernstorff, Telegram No. 534, December 26, 1915, *ibid.*

reject it. Then, very much on his own, he added "that he believed that his Government, if a fairly good case could be made out against arbitration, would follow the course which had been adopted apparently by Austria in their *Ancona* case." Lansing replied that there was nothing in the fundamental issues to arbitrate, *even though the American government was prepared to arbitrate the amount of the indemnity.* The German government, he went on, had conceded in a recent note that *no* merchant ship should be sunk until all persons on board had been placed in safety.[92] *It would not, Lansing added, be necessary to mention the matter of liability in a published statement; liability could be passed over as had been done in the Arabic statement.* Bernstorff said that he "would communicate with his Government at once in regard to the matter and see if they would not follow out a course which they had so plainly set forth as to the illegality of retaliatory measures, and as to the duties imposed upon the commander of a submarine in sinking a merchant vessel." He was hopeful that agreement could be reached along these lines.[93]

This good beginning was briefly interrupted by receipt in Washington on January 1, 1916, of news that a British liner, *Persia*, 7,964 tons, of the Peninsular and Oriental Line, had been torpedoed off Crete on December 30, 1915, with the loss, among others, of two American lives.[94] A report on the following day from the American Consul at Alexandria said that the *Persia* had carried a 4.7-inch gun and raised doubt as to whether she had actually been torpedoed.[95] "Are we sufficiently informed as to the facts in the case of the *Persia* to form a judgment and plan for a course of action," Wilson wrote in a telegram to Lansing on that same day, after reading the Consul's report. "I would very much like your candid advice as to whether you think it best that I should return to Washington." Meanwhile,

[92] Lansing was referring here to the latest note (Ambassador Gerard to the Secretary of State, December 2, 1915, *Foreign Relations, 1915, Supplement*, pp. 644-646) in the *Frye* case involving German treatment of American shipping under the terms of the Prussian-American treaties of 1785 and 1799, for the background of which see A. S. Link, *Wilson*, III, 454. Lansing was rather grossly misinterpreting the statement in the German note. It referred specifically to *American* ships, not to merchant ships in general, and certainly not to belligerent merchant ships.

[93] R. Lansing, "Memorandum by the Secretary of State . . . , December 31, 1915," *The Lansing Papers*, I, 510-511. The italicized portions of this account are taken from J. von Bernstorff to the Foreign Office, January 3, 1916, German F. O. Archives.

[94] *New York Times*, January 2, 1916.

[95] *ibid.*, January 3, 1916.

he continued, Lansing should dispatch a note of inquiry (the text of which he suggested) to the Austro-Hungarian government.[96] Lansing replied in considerable excitement, saying that he was afraid that popular excitement might manifest itself in Congress and he thought that Wilson should return at once.[97]

There was, indeed, much commotion in Washington on the following day, January 3, when reporters learned that the President was returning to the city by special train.[98] It did not survive very long once Wilson arrived on January 4. Review of dispatches soon convinced him that there simply was not enough evidence for a judgment. He canceled a Cabinet meeting scheduled for the morning and then gave out a statement saying that the President and Secretary of State were trying to obtain the facts "in this grave matter" and would act as soon as information was available.[99]

Tumulty saw Wilson on the same day and wrote the following memorandum of a memorable conversation:

"About ten minutes to ten o'clock this morning I had a very interesting conversation with the President at the White House, my purpose being to bring to him the atmosphere of Washington and the country as far as I could ascertain with reference to the sinking of the *PERSIA* by a submarine. The other purpose of my visit was to warn him that Senator Stone might induce him to make some admission with reference to his attitude which might embarrass the President in the future.

"The President looked very well after his trip and seemed to be in a fine mood, although it was plainly evident that the *PERSIA* affair rested heavily upon him. My attitude toward this matter was for action, and action all along the line. This did not seem to meet with a very hearty response from the President. He informed me that it would not be the thing for us to take action against any government without our government being in possession of all the facts. I replied that that was my attitude, but I thought there should be action and vigorous action as soon as all the facts were ascertained. He agreed with me in this. When I began to tell him about the attitude of the country and the feeling that there was a lack of leadership, he stiffened up in his chair and said, 'Tumulty, you may as well understand my position right now.

[96] W. W. to R. Lansing, January 2, 1916, *The Lansing Papers*, I, 512-513.
[97] R. Lansing to W. W., January 3, 1916, Wilson Papers.
[98] New York *World*, January 4, 1916; *New York Times*, January 4, 1916.
[99] *ibid.*, January 5, 1916.

If my re-election as President depends upon my getting into war, I don't want to be President. I have been away and I have had lots of time to think about this war and the effect of our country getting into it, and I have made up my mind that I am more interested in the opinion that the country will have of me ten years from now than the opinion it may be willing to express today. Of course, I understand that the country wants action, and I intend to stand by the record I have made in all these cases, and take whatever action may be necessary, but I will not be rushed into war, no matter if every damned congressman and senator stands up on his hind legs and proclaims me a coward.' He continued, speaking of the severance of diplomatic relations,—'You must know that when I consider this matter, I can only consider it as the forerunner of war. I believe that the sober-minded people of this country will applaud any efforts I may make without the loss of our honor to keep this country out of war.' He said that if we took any precipitate action right now, it might prevent Austria from coming across in generous fashion."[100]

Criticism broke out sharply in the Senate on January 5, but most of it, in fact, was aimed at the administration for permitting Americans to travel on belligerent ships.[101] Excitement died entirely when the American Consul at Alexandria telegraphed a summary of the affidavits of survivors on the following day, January 6. No one had seen a submarine, and no one was willing to swear that he had seen either a torpedo or its track.[102] Later reports from Vienna and Berlin affirmed that no Austrian or German submarine had been involved[103] and suggested that an internal explosion might have caused the disaster.[104]

Officials in the German Foreign Office had meanwhile been mystified and alarmed lest misunderstanding over the *Persia* imperil the *Lusitania* negotiations. The German Admiralty had stationed a flotilla of submarines at the Austro-Hungarian naval base at Pola on the Adri-

[100] Memorandum dated January 4, 1916, Tumulty Papers.

[101] *New York Times*, January 6, 1916. *Congressional Record*, 64th Cong., 1st sess., pp. 495-496, 505-510.

[102] *New York Times*, January 7, 1916.

[103] Ambassador Penfield to the Secretary of State, January 22, 1916, *Foreign Relations, 1916, Supplement*, pp. 148-149; Ambassador Gerard to the Secretary of State, January 17, 1916, *ibid.*, p. 145, summarizing H. von Holtzendorff to G. von Jagow, January 17, 1916, German F. O. Archives.

[104] *New York Times*, January 12, 1916. There was a report from Amsterdam on January 23, 1916, that a Turkish submarine had sunk the *Persia. ibid.*, January 24, 1916. The Turkish government denied the allegation. The Chargé in Turkey to the Secretary of State, March 8, 1916, *Foreign Relations, 1916, Supplement*, pp. 214-215.

atic, but they were operating under orders to observe the rules of cruiser warfare except when dealing with armed merchantmen, and not to sink liners, even when they were armed.[105] Officials in the Foreign Office thought some reassurance had to be sent to Washington after receiving the following warning from Bernstorff on about January 5: "Attitude here due to the Persia incident again worse and speed necessary. Situation as difficult as my reports emphasize. Congress and administration wish to go ahead against England but repeatedly kept from it since the anti-German clique has pushed the submarine question into the foreground."[106]

Jagow, with the approval of the head of the Admiralty, Admiral Henning von Holtzendorff,[107] telegraphed a detailed summary of instructions governing submarine operations in the Mediterranean to Bernstorff on January 5 or 6 (omitting, however, any reference to armed merchantmen), and Bernstorff gave the dispatch to Lansing on January 7, with the request that the Secretary of State hand it to the press.[108] It was, the newspapers said, a second notable diplomatic triumph within scarcely more than a week,[109] and a good augury, administration leaders thought, for the success of the *Lusitania* negotiations.[110] Both conclusions were accurate, but, as we will see later,[111] the *Persia* incident had its most significant impact in causing Wilson and Lansing to undertake a new diplomatic campaign to disarm all liners and merchant ships.

Bernstorff resumed the *Lusitania* negotiations on January 7, 1916, at the same time that he disclosed instructions to German submarine

---

[105] A. Spindler, *La Guerre Sous-Marine*, III, 12, 29-30.

[106] J. von Bernstorff to the Foreign Office, January 4, 1916, German F. O. Archives.

[107] Von Holtzendorff told Grand Admiral Alfred von Tirpitz, Naval Secretary, and General Erich von Falkenhayn, Chief of the Army General Staff, and others on January 5, 1916, that he had given his approval. "General v. Falkenhayn and the War Minister [Wild von Hohenborn] said that in this case one shouldn't be surprised if America became still more insolent, since she had already received a guarantee in advance that her biggest demands had been granted." "Notes on the Conference of January 5, 1916," Alfred von Tirpitz, *Politische Dokumente von A. von Tirpitz, Deutsche Ohnmachtspolitik im Weltkrieg* (2 vols.), II, 458; hereinafter cited as *Politische Dokumente*.

[108] Ambassador von Bernstorff to the Secretary of State, n. d., delivered on January 7, 1916, *Foreign Relations, 1916, Supplement*, pp. 144-145; R. Lansing to W. W., January 7, 1916, *The Lansing Papers*, I, 513; *New York Times*, January 8, 1916.

[109] *New York World*, January 8, 1916; *New Republic*, V (January 15, 1916), 260-261; "American Law for the Submarine," *Literary Digest*, LII (January 22, 1916), 161-163.

[110] R. Lansing to W. W., January 7, 1916, *The Lansing Papers*, I, 513-514.

[111] See below, p. 142.

commanders in the Mediterranean, by handing Bethmann's third counterproposal to Lansing. Lansing was much encouraged. "There is lacking any recognition of liability since the indemnity which they proposed to pay is, in fact, on the basis of comity and not on the basis of right . . . ," he wrote to Wilson on that day. If in any way the agreement to pay the indemnity can be construed into a recognition of liability it would seem as if a final settlement of the case was very near."[112] Perhaps the two governments were not so far apart. As Wilson observed in reply on January 10:

"I have tried hard to find something in this note about the *Lusitania* out of which a satisfactory answer to our demands could be made, but must admit that I have failed. It is a concession of grace, and not at all of right.

"And yet I do not see that it would be essentially out of tune with it if the Imperial Government were to say that, even while it was arguing and without abatement insisting on the necessity for retaliation and even the right to retaliate, it was not willing to make that necessity an excuse for abbreviating the rights of neutrals or for unnecessarily imperiling the lives of non-combatants, and that, therefore, while wishing to make very plain the imperative grounds for its recent policy, it was ready to recognize very frankly the justice of the contentions of the United States with regard to the rights of American citizens and assume the responsibility which she (the Imp. Gov.) had incurred by the incidental ignoring of those rights on the occasion referred to.

"She could in this wise put Great Britain more obviously in the wrong as compared with herself, by showing that she, in contrast with Great Britain, was willing to make good for the damage done neutrals.

"I understand you had a conference with Bernstorff to-day. Do you think from the present aspect of the situation that a suggestion such as I have outlined would set the settlement a step forward, or not?"[113]

Lansing had anticipated Wilson's own reactions in an interview with Bernstorff in the morning of January 10. The trouble, the Ambassador replied, was that the German public and many leaders in the Imperial government were not willing to abandon a policy of reprisals so long as Great Britain continued her illegal blockade. He handed Lansing a statement that he had just received from the Foreign Office saying that the German government would be gratified if the United States took

[112] R. Lansing to W. W., January 7, 1916, *The Lansing Papers*, I, 513.
[113] W. W. to R. Lansing, January 10, 1916, *ibid.*, pp. 515-516.

energetic steps to establish "real freedom of the seas."[114] Lansing replied that it was not necessary for Germany to give up reprisals. Retaliation against Great Britain might indeed be justified, but it was necessarily illegal in a strict sense. All that Germany had to do was to admit that this retaliation was illegal and imposed liabilities on the German government when neutrals suffered in consequence. "I said, to him," Lansing recorded, "that that was the same course we were taking with regard to Great Britain—that Great Britain's interruption of trade to Germany was admittedly retaliatory and that it, therefore, was illegal and so far as neutrals were concerned it imposed liability on Great Britain; and that I could not see how we could treat the matter differently with the two Governments."[115]

Bernstorff cabled a long résumé of this conversation to the Foreign Office on January 13, but he failed to convey Lansing's essential point —admission of German liability that would amount to a disavowal— and suggested only a redrafting of the third counterproposal by deletion of its second paragraph which asserted that neutrals had no right to complain when they suffered from German retaliatory measures.[116] This, Jagow replied, was agreeable if it would satisfy Lansing's worries. Indeed, the Foreign Secretary went on, if a shortened third counterproposal was unacceptable, then Bernstorff as a last resort might resubmit the draft note that he had sent to Lansing on October 2, but with a few textual changes, elimination of its last paragraph, and substitution almost verbatim of the concluding paragraph of Bethmann's third counterproposal.[117] The shortened third counterproposal and revised Bernstorff draft read as follows:

SHORTENED THIRD COUNTERPROPOSAL

The German submarine war against England's commerce at sea, as announced on February 4, 1915, is conducted in retaliation of England's inhuman war against Germany's commercial and industrial life. It is an acknowledged rule of international law that retaliation may be employed against acts committed in contravention of the law of nations. Germany is enacting such a retaliation, for it is England's endeavor to cut off all imports from Germany by preventing even legal commerce of the neutrals

[114] It was G. von Jagow to the German Embassy, January 7, 1916, German F. O. Archives. It is published in *The Lansing Papers*, I, 517.

[115] R. Lansing, "Memorandum by the Secretary of State . . . ," January 10, 1916, *ibid.*, pp. 516-517.

[116] J. von Bernstorff to the Foreign Office, January 13, 1916, German F. O. Archives.

[117] G. von Jagow to J. von Bernstorff, January 18, 1916, *ibid.*

with her and thereby subjecting the German population to starvation. In answer to these acts Germany is making efforts to destroy England's commerce at sea, at least as far as it is carried on by enemy vessels. If Germany has notwithstanding limited her submarine warfare this was done in view of her long standing friendship with the United States and in the expectation that the steps taken by the American Government in the meantime aiming at the restoration of the freedom of the seas would be successful.

The German Government, on the other hand, recognizes from the course which the negotiations so far have taken the difficulty to reconcile in principle the American and the German point of view, as the interests and legal aspects of the neutrals and belligerents naturally do not agree in this point and as the illegality of the English course of procedure can hardly be recognized in the United States as fully as it is in Germany. A perpetuation of this difference of opinion, however, would not tend to further the amicable relations between the United States and Germany which have never been disturbed and the continuation of which is so sincerely desired by both Governments. Actuated by this spirit the Imperial Government again expresses its deep regret at the death of American citizens caused by the sinking of the *Lusitania* and, in order to settle this question amicably, declares its readiness to pay indemnity for the losses inflicted.

REVISED BERNSTORFF DRAFT NOTE

The attack on the *Lusitania* formed part of the reprisals enacted by the Imperial Government against Great Britain on account of her illegal starvation policy. According to the German opinion such reprisals were amply justified by the inhuman British warfare. At that time the Imperial Government had not yet issued the instructions which now regulate the German submarine warfare and according to which the *Arabic* case was settled. These instructions were issued with regard to the friendship of many years' standing between Germany and the United States and in expectation that the steps the American Government has undertaken in the meantime to reestablish the freedom of the seas would be successful. Even before these instructions were issued it was, however, not the intention of the Imperial Government that our reprisals should lead to the loss of the lives of noncombatants. My Government has, therefore, on previous occasions expressed its deep regret that American lives should have been lost on the *Lusitania*.

As for the question whether the Imperial Government is obliged to grant an indemnity in this case, it appears from the negotiations which have hitherto taken place that a further accentuation of the difference of opinion which has arisen on this point would not be apt to promote the friendly relations between Germany and the United States which both Governments have at heart and which so far have never been troubled. In a spirit of friendship and conciliation, therefore, the Imperial Government in order to settle definitely the *Lusitania* incident, declare themselves willing to grant an indemnity for the lives of American citizens which were lost by the sinking of the boat.[118]

Jagow's new instructions arrived in Washington on Saturday, January 22, and Bernstorff at once drafted the two new counterproposals and sent them to Lansing that same night. The new drafts, the Secretary of State wrote when sending copies to the President on January 24, were no improvement at all over the old ones. He would not talk with Bernstorff until he had heard from Wilson, Lansing said, but he could only conclude that there was nothing to do but make a formal demand for admission of illegal conduct upon the German government and break diplomatic relations if Germany did not yield.[119] Wilson agreed that the new counterproposals would not do. But he reminded Lansing of the cable message he had received from Colonel House on January 15, advising that it was of *"utmost significance"* to continue relations with Germany and Austria-Hungary until the President had received a letter which House was writing and would mail on January 19.[120] Would it not be better, Wilson wondered, to postpone final steps until House's letter had arrived?[121]

Lansing and Wilson agreed on Tuesday morning, January 25, that the Secretary of State should at least prepare the way for a final break in negotiations, but also give authorities in Berlin one final opportunity to yield. In any event, Lansing should wait until the President's return from his preparedness tour before making any final moves. Lansing was, consequently, ominous in tone when he talked to Bernstorff in the afternoon. There was no good reason to continue conversations, he said, unless the German government was prepared to admit the illegality of the destruction of the *Lusitania*. What would the American government do, the Ambassador asked, if Germany refused to accede

[118] As printed in *The Lansing Papers*, I, 519-520.

[119] R. Lansing to W. W., January 24, 1916, *ibid.*, pp. 521-522.

[120] The cablegram was E. M. House to W. W., January 15, 1916, Wilson Papers. The letter was E. M. House to W. W., January 15, 1916, *ibid.* It expressed high hopes for the possibility of Wilson's mediation if only he could avoid major difficulties with *both* rival alliances. Wilson had repeated the cablegram to Lansing in W. W. to R. Lansing, January 17, 1916, the Papers of Robert Lansing, Princeton University Library.

[121] W. W. to R. Lansing, January 24, 1916, *The Lansing Papers*, I, 522.

to such harsh terms? It would have no choice but to break diplomatic relations, Lansing replied. "I do not see how the matter could stop with the breaking off of diplomatic relations. It would go further than that," Bernstorff said. Lansing agreed, adding that the President and he would not hesitate to assume responsibility. He suggested that Bernstorff return the next day with a memorandum meeting the American terms, with the understanding that he should have one last chance to persuade his government to yield. Bernstorff agreed but said that he thought the situation was hopeless.[122]

The Ambassador returned to the State Department on the following morning, January 26, at 11:45. He had a revised memorandum in hand; Lansing said that it was unacceptable. Would Lansing, then, suggest necessary changes? Lansing did so gladly, and Bernstorff dictated a new memorandum. It repeated the first paragraph of the shortened third counterproposal through the words "if Germany has notwithstanding limited her submarine warfare this was done in view of her longstanding friendship with the United States," and then substituted the following new text to the end:

> and in view of the fact that the sinking of the *Lusitania* caused the death of citizens of the United States. Thereby the German retaliation affected neutrals, which was not the intention as retaliation becomes an illegal act if applied to other than enemy subjects.
>
> The Imperial Government, having, subsequent to the event, issued to its naval officers the new instructions which are now prevailing, expresses profound regret that citizens of the United States suffered by the sinking of the *Lusitania* and, recognizing the illegality of causing their death, and admitting liability therefor, offers to make reparation for the lives of the citizens of the United States who were lost by the payment of a suitable indemnity.
>
> In the note of the American Government, July 21, concerning the *Lusitania* incident, the Government of the United States invited the practical cooperation of the Imperial German Government in contending for the principle of the freedom of the seas, and added that this great object could, in some way be accomplished before the present war ends. The Imperial Government will at all times gladly cooperate with the Government of the United States for the purpose of accomplishing this common great object.

Lansing called the President and read this draft to him as soon as Bernstorff left. Wilson approved it, and Lansing telephoned Bernstorff

[122] R. Lansing, "Memorandum by the Secretary of State . . . , January 25, 1916," *ibid.*, pp. 523-525.

to say that the President thought that the memorandum was now satisfactory.[123] Lansing then sent a long cablegram to Gerard and House in Berlin reviewing his recent conversations with Bernstorff and repeating the new *Lusitania* memorandum.[124]

Lansing now set about to prepare the public, which had been almost entirely in the dark about negotiations to this point, for a diplomatic rupture.[125] A high official, undoubtedly the Secretary of State, told reporters on January 28 that the *Lusitania* negotiations were going badly and the President and Secretary of State were determined to end them soon if the Imperial government did not make a satisfactory disavowal. Reporters concluded that this would mean a break in relations.[126] "The situation," this "high official" told reporters again on January 29, "is now graver than it has been for some time—and the country has a right to know."[127]

Bernstorff's dispatch enclosing a copy of the "last chance" *Lusitania* memorandum and the Ambassador's own alarming report of Lansing's threatening conversation, sent on January 26, arrived in Berlin in the morning of January 29. It was bad enough, but a rumor was running through high political circles that Lansing had just told a prominent person: "I am too busy to take up your matter. I have more important work just now. We may be in a war with Germany within the next few days."[128]

These developments found the Imperial Chancellor already deeply involved in a desperate struggle over submarine policy. It began in December 1915, when General Erich von Falkenhayn, Chief of the Army General Staff, requested a conference of high military and naval chieftains to review the general situation on the eve of a new year. Consequently Falkenhayn, Holtzendorff, Grand Admiral Alfred von Tirpitz, Imperial Naval Secretary, Vice Admiral Reinhard Koch, deputy Chief of the Admiralty, and General Wild von Hohenborn, Prussian Minister of War, met at the War Ministry in Berlin on December 30.

---

[123] R. Lansing, "Memorandum by the Secretary of State . . . , January 26, 1916," *ibid.*, p. 525.

[124] The Secretary of State to Ambassador Gerard, January 26, 1916, *ibid.*, pp. 525-527.

[125] He also drafted a note embodying a formal demand for disavowal by the German government, to be used in the event that the informal negotiations had to be terminated. "Draft Note from the Secretary of State . . . ," January 26, 1916, *ibid.*, pp. 527-529.

[126] *New York Times*, January 29, 1916; New York *World*, January 29, 1916.

[127] *New York Times*, January 30, 1916.

[128] Karl von Wiegand in the New York *World*, February 11, 1916.

Falkenhayn opened the discussion with the statement that he had opposed risking a break with America during the preceding summer because of the desperate situation in the Balkans and Turkey. That situation had meanwhile wonderfully improved: Bulgaria had joined the Central Powers, Serbia was prostrate, and the route to Constantinople was secure. From a *military* point of view America would be no more dangerous to Germany as a belligerent than as a so-called neutral. Consequently, he no longer maintained his old objections against an unlimited submarine campaign. Moreover, Germany had to win the war in 1916, and she could win it only by striking at England. Did the navy believe, Falkenhayn asked, that the benefits to be derived from all-out submarine warfare were great enough to justify a rupture with America, and could it force England to consent to peace before the end of 1916?

Holtzendorff replied confidently that an energetic submarine campaign would bring England to her knees before the end of 1916. Then Tirpitz broke in with an impassioned diatribe. What difference would American belligerency make? The United States had a huge economic stake in an Allied victory. It had become an Allied arsenal, a belligerent directly participating in the war against Germany. Of course America would break relations if Germany hit England in a vital spot. But American intervention would make no material or military difference. The submarine campaign would succeed only if it destroyed all maritime commerce going to England, but it could succeed if prosecuted vigorously. General von Hohenborn agreed that there was no need to fear America as an enemy.

Holtzendorff spoke again, more cautiously. He hoped that a break with America might be avoided, for the political consequences of a rupture were not to be desired. Even so, he concluded, one had to balance them against the possibility of resorting to the only means of bringing the war to a satisfactory conclusion within a bearable time. On balance he preferred taking the risks that accompanied an all-out effort.[129]

Falkenhayn talked with Bethmann immediately after this conference and with Karl Helfferich, Treasury Secretary, on January 2, repeating on both ocasions that it was a matter of complete indifference to him

[129] The above account is based on A. Spindler, *La Guerre Sous-Marine*, III, 94-99, and A. von Tirpitz, memorandum dated January 2, 1916, printed in A. von Tirpitz, *Politische Dokumente*, II, 450-455.

whether the United States declared war on Germany.[130] The military and naval chieftains met again on January 5. It was clear, they agreed, that Bethmann, Jagow, and Helfferich were opposed to any action that might lead to disagreement with America. They discussed the best form to adopt for the U-boat campaign and when it should begin. Then Tirpitz, turning fiercely to Falkenhayn, warned that Germany would lose the war if the submarines were not unleashed, and that Falkenhayn, the Emperor's adviser on the entire conduct of the war, would have to bear responsibility for defeat if he did not press the issue. That decision, Falkenhayn said with a bow, belonged to His Majesty.[131]

Conferences between military and civilian leaders and exchanges of prolix notes and memoranda followed furiously during the balance of January.[132] Bethmann remained skeptical if not altogether adamant, wanting if possible to avoid a final showdown. As he told Holtzendorff on January 8, he regarded the submarine war as an *ultima ratio*, since it would be such a provocation to the entire world that it must end in *finis Germaniae* if it failed. He could approve unlimited submarine warfare only if convinced that it was in fact impossible to obtain an honorable peace by other means, or that Germany was bound to be defeated in a long war. It was, he conceded, opportune and necessary to begin preparations; but the undersea campaign could not be resumed before necessary negotiations with America, and it must not begin in any event before March 1.[133]

Bethmann entertained the Emperor's naval adviser, Admiral Georg A. von Müller, at dinner on January 11. "After the meal," von Müller wrote in his diary, "he spoke very seriously about the critical decision of the sharpened submarine war. It could result in the condemnation of the entire civilized world—a kind of crusade against Germany. It was like a second decision for war. Not only were the neutrals fully uncertain, but our allies were also doubtful. . . . Our situation is not so

---

[130] T. von Bethmann Hollweg, memorandum dated January 4, 1916, *ibid.*, pp. 455-456.

[131] From Tirpitz's notes of the conference of January 5, 1916, in *ibid.*, pp. 456-459.

[132] e. g., H. von Holtzendorff to the Imperial Chancellor, January 7 and 21, 1916, *ibid.*, pp. 460-461, 466-468; A. von Tirpitz to the Imperial Chancellor, January 20, 1916, *ibid.*, p. 463; Hans Peter Hanssen, *Diary of a Dying Empire*, pp. 123-126; and Kuno F. V. von Westarp, *Konservative Politik im Letzten Jahrzent des Kaiserreiches* (2 vols.), II, 115 (hereinafter cited as *Konservative Politik*), for debates among party leaders.

[133] A. Spindler, *La Guerre Sous-Marine*, III, 100-101. See also Bethmann's memorandum drafted January 10, 1916, and circulated in the Foreign Office, the German text of which is printed in Karl E. Birnbaum, *Peace Moves and U-Boat Warfare*, pp. 345-347.

bad that we must grasp at the last straw. Strong bitterness against 'the gambler,' Falkenhayn."[134] Bethmann was even more alarmed a few days later. He "saw in his imagination many united neutral peoples rising against us, the mad dog among nations. That would be, then, Finis Germaniae."[135]

Holtzendorff, getting no encouragement from the Emperor in an audience on January 6,[136] sent an Imperial order to the fleet on January 8 explaining that political negotiations in progress required extreme caution and ordering a complete cessation of submarine and air attacks against England.[137] But Holtzendorff came back to see the Emperor again at Bellevue Castle in Berlin on January 15 to argue that a sharpened submarine war would force England to sue for peace within six to seven months. William replied indecisively. He was, he said, revolted by the thought of killing innocent passengers. He bore responsibility to God for the way he waged war. On the other hand, could he, against the opinions of his military advisers, take responsibility for prolonging the war for humane reasons? He stood before the most critical decision of his life. He could not, he concluded, ignore the political consequences and underestimate the participation of a hostile America.

William consequently sought the middle road—by asking the navy to take a new look at the possibility of resuming submarine warfare while still sparing neutral shipping, and by asking Bethmann to take all initial diplomatic steps to prepare the way for a submarine campaign to begin on March 1.[138] The Emperor on January 18 approved at Holtzendorff's request the following orders: "*Enemy merchant ships* are to be destroyed by all means possible. Merchant ships under *neutral* flags are to be treated as enemy vessels unless they can be *positively* identified as neutral—even by *surfaced* submarines." No date was set for resumption of this nearly all-out submarine campaign, but it was assumed that March 1 would be the fateful day.[139]

This, then, was the threat that hung over Bethmann's head as he studied Bernstorff's dispatch of January 26 and the "last chance" *Lusi-*

[134] Walter Görlitz (ed.), *Regierte der Kaiser? Kriegstagebücher, Aufzeichnungen und Briefe des Chefs des Marine-Kabinetts Admiral Georg Alexander von Müller, 1914-1918*, p. 146; hereinafter cited as *Regierte der Kaiser*.

[135] *ibid.*, p. 147, entry for January 12, 1916.

[136] *ibid.*, p. 146.

[137] A. von Tirpitz, *Politische Dokumente*, II, 461.

[138] W. Görlitz (ed.), *Regierte der Kaiser*, pp. 147-148, entry for January 15, 1916.

[139] A. von Tirpitz, *Politische Dokumente*, II, 462.

tania memorandum. If he refused to yield the vital demand, he faced, it seemed, the rupture with the United States that he had risked so much to avert. If, on the other hand, he admitted that the attack on the *Lusitania* had been illegal, he would give Germany's legal case away, dishonor the German nation, and perhaps so excite public opinion that the furor would drive him from office and give complete control of policy to the submarine extremists. There was really not much choice, Bethmann concluded. He would have to stand firm against the United States and accept the consequences.

First, however, he had to prepare the way at home for the sudden collapse of his American policy and also, incidentally, to quiet fears, raised by Colonel House's visit to Berlin, that the Imperial government intended to yield completely. Bethmann saw Matthias Erzberger, head of the powerful Catholic Centre Party, on February 1, explained the American demands, and asked him what the German people would say to a break with America over the *Lusitania* disavowal. Erzberger urged him to convene the Reichstag, submit the *Lusitania* correspondence to it, and announce inauguration of the submarine campaign at the same time.[140] On the following day the Chancellor sent Arthur Zimmermann, Undersecretary at the Foreign Office, to break the news to Count Kuno von Westarp, head of the right-wing, pro-submarine Conservative Party. The Chancellor, Zimmermann added, was leaning toward unlimited submarine warfare.[141]

Meanwhile, Zimmermann had also been working on Gerard and House in the hope of somehow lessening the American pressure. Zimmermann had lunch with the two envoys on January 29, only a few hours after Bernstorff's dispatch arrived, and said unequivocally that the Imperial government could not yield. He hoped that Colonel House would make this clear to the President. House said that he would, and that he would be glad to convey anything that Zimmermann wanted the President to know.[142] Later in the afternoon, Zimmermann sent a letter to House for direct transmission to Wilson. It reiterated that Germany would accept a break in relations rather than admit that the submarine campaign was illegal.[143] Gerard and House

[140] K. von Westarp, *Konservative Politik*, II, 116.

[141] *ibid.*

[142] Ambassador Gerard to the Secretary of State, January 29, 1916, 7 p.m., *Foreign Relations, 1916, Supplement*, p. 153; "Report of the Intelligence Bureau [of the Naval Ministry], January 31, 1916," A. von Tirpitz, *Politische Dokumente*, II, 468.

[143] A. Zimmermann to E. M. House, January 29, 1916, in Ambassador Gerard to

made it plain both to Lansing and Wilson that they agreed entirely with the German argument that something less than an explicit admission of wrongdoing would have to suffice, and should suffice.[144]

Lansing was much annoyed. As he wrote on January 31 in a letter destined to reach Wilson in Kansas City on February 2, Gerard and House did not appreciate the "real point at issue—namely, that the German Government should admit the wrongdoing of the submarine commander who torpedoed the vessel." They had probably encouraged Zimmermann to believe that Wilson would accept one of the earlier German proposals. "It shows the danger of attempting to negotiate at two ends of the line." Would the President like him to frame a reply to Gerard, disabusing Zimmermann of the idea that anything less than outright admission of illegality would do?[145] Wilson immediately wired Lansing to send the message "explaining the point at issue."[146]

The President began to change his mind and policy as he traveled between Kansas City on February 2 and Terre Haute, Indiana, on the following day. Perhaps the change was not as sudden as the cryptic records suggest. Wilson's affirmations, made repeatedly during his preparedness tour, that there was then no specific crisis in foreign relations, and that he did not foresee any crisis in the near future, raise some doubt whether he had ever intended to permit Lansing to push matters to the point of rupture and probable war. It is certainly possible that Wilson had simply been pressing the Germans hard for maximum diplomatic results. We can be more certain that three factors very powerfully caused Wilson to re-examine policy in early February.

The first was that the fierce congressional outburst against Germany and the Washington administration for failing to deal severely enough with her had failed utterly to materialize. There had been criticisms, to be sure, but they had been leveled almost exclusively against the administration's alleged weakness in resisting English, not German, encroachments and its continued insistence upon the right of Americans to travel on belligerent ships. Not one word of criticism of the administration for failing to obtain a satisfactory *Lusitania* settlement had

---

the Secretary of State, January 29, 1916, 9 p.m., *Foreign Relations, 1916, Supplement*, p. 154.

[144] Ambassador Gerard to the Secretary of State, January 29, 1916, 10 p.m., *ibid.*, pp. 153-154.

[145] R. Lansing to W. W., January 31, 1916, *The Lansing Papers*, I, 529-530.

[146] W. W. to R. Lansing, February 2, 1916, *ibid.*, p. 530.

been uttered since Congress assembled.[147] "One of the reasons for public sentiment swing[ing] against Great Britain," the Counselor of the State Department explained to Colonel House, "is the general impression that she (Great Britain) is riding roughshod over the small neutrals. . . . As far as Congress is concerned I think the situation is well in hand. The danger lies in the direction of England, provided Germany settled [the *Lusitania* case]."[148] As the British Ambassador wrote to Sir Edward Grey at this time: "The situation here, so far as politics are concerned, has not improved in favour of the Allies. The spirit of Congress is somewhat menacing. Congress was opened in stormy meetings in which violent attacks were made upon our commercial policy. . . . The general tone of the debate was not favourable to us. The same could be said of the House of Representatives. Violent language was used against the measures in restriction of trade."[149]

A second factor influencing Wilson's shift in policy was the almost overpowering impact of the obvious anti-war temper and mood of the American people at this time. Popular sentiment had been reflected in the opposition to preparedness legislation and in the congressional comments to which we have just referred. Wilson encountered it most immediately and dramatically on his preparedness tour. As we have seen, neutralist feeling was so unmistakable in the Midwest that he had felt himself compelled to argue for preparedness as the best insurance against involvement in the European war.[150] There is no evi-

[147] See the *New York Times*, December 11, 1915, and *Congressional Record*, 64th Cong., 1st sess., pp. 138-145, for speeches by Senator Hoke Smith of Georgia and Senator Thomas J. Walsh of Montana; *New York Times*, January 11, 1916, and *Congressional Record*, 64th Cong., 1st sess., p. 753, reporting the introduction by Senator Thomas P. Gore of Oklahoma of resolutions empowering the President to use force to compel respect for American neutral trading rights; above, p. 78, for congressional discussion after the *Persia* incident; W. J. Stone to W. W., December 13, 1915, Wilson Papers; and particularly R. Lansing to W. W., December 21, 1915, *The Lansing Papers*, I, 221-222, reporting on Lansing's conversation with Senator Stone on the same date. Lansing, in a memorandum written allegedly on January 9, 1916, expressed the conviction that congressional and public opposition to strong measures against Germany made it necessary for him to attempt to come to some understanding with the German government on the submarine question. See the Diary of Robert Lansing, January 9, 1916, Library of Congress, hereinafter cited as the Lansing Diary; and R. Lansing, *War Memoirs of Robert Lansing*, pp. 102-104; hereinafter cited as *War Memoirs*. It is very dubious that Lansing wrote this memorandum on January 9, 1916, or anywhere near this date. See the comment below, pp. 143-144, n. 4.

[148] F. L. Polk to E. M. House, January 21, 1916, House Papers.

[149] C. Spring Rice to E. Grey, January 13, 1916, S. Gwynn (ed.), *Letters of Spring Rice*, II, 308.

[150] See above, pp. 46-48.

dence that Wilson ever intended to push the *Lusitania* negotiations to the point of war, but he would probably have drawn back from such a policy even had he once contemplated it in view of public sentiment. As the British Ambassador explained earlier, in commenting on his philosophy and methods of leadership:

"As I have often said, the President feels that he is not Woodrow Wilson but the President of the United States, and that he can take no action unless he is supported by the American people. He has continually waited for an indication of what is the popular will. When the popular will has been expressed he has done what the popular will seemed to demand. Until then he has held back. He is known to be of a very determined character, not prone to yield or to forgive an injury or an insult. But he is not supposed to carry personal feelings into public affairs. His policy from the first was to maintain absolute neutrality and he certainly did his best to keep the straight line. If the people desire action in regard to foreign affairs inconsistent with neutrality, and this desire is clearly expressed, he will no doubt take it; but not until the expression is clear and definite. There is an impression that he once bitterly complained that the people of the United States demanded energetic words but would not consent to energetic action. He is believed to have said that he would not approve drawing cheques which the people would not honour. Hence a policy of extreme caution."[151]

Finally, there was the decisive influence of Colonel House's advice to avoid a break over the single issue of a *Lusitania* disavowal. House repeated this advice in two cablegrams that reached the President at St. Louis on February 2 and on his train the next day, as follows:

The situation is like this. A great controversy is going on in Germany regarding undersea warfare. The navy, backed more or less by the army, believe that Great Britain can be effectively blockaded, provided Germany can use their new and powerful submarines indiscriminately and not be hampered by any laws whatsoever. They also believe failure has resulted from our interference and Germany's endeavor to conform to our demands. They think war with us would not be so disastrous as Great Britain's blockade. The civil Government believe that if the blockade continues, they may be forced to yield to the navy; consequently they are unwilling to admit illegality of their undersea warfare. They will yield anything but this. If you insist upon that point, I believe war will follow. Gerard under-

---

[151] C. Spring Rice to E. Grey, December 9, 1915, S. Gwynn (ed.), *The Letters of Spring Rice*, II, 302-303.

stands the question and I would suggest letting him try to arrange something satisfactory direct. I hope final action may not be taken until I have had an opportunity of talking with you. . . .[152]

I doubt whether a crisis with Germany can long be avoided. The [English] . . . blockade will make the demand imperative that an attempt be made to break it by the transcendent sea warfare. We will then be compelled to sever relations and our position will be far better than if we do so over a nine months' old issue and largely upon the wording of a suitable apology. I think reference to the freedom of the seas in Bernstorff's proposed apology is unfortunate. It will irritate the Allies and give Germany hope where there is none. The rules of the sea cannot be changed during the war and it will be hurtful to all concerned to encourage such a delusion.[153]

It was as if Wilson had seen a great light. For the first time he understood what Gerard had failed to make clear, even to mention—that severe demands might well tip the balance in Germany against the Chancellor and set engines in fatal motion under the seas. "Please hold message suggested yesterday until I can see you or if it has been sent send word to await further instructions," he instructed Lansing by telegram when his train stopped at Terre Haute on February 3. "Will explain when I reach Washington."[154] He had made his decision firmly by the time he arrived in Washington on the following afternoon. He was too busy to see Lansing immediately, but he sent House's dispatches to him, adding that they would show why he had sent his telegram from Terre Haute. He would see Lansing tomorrow. Meanwhile, he went on, "Do you not think that we could frame a handsome apology from Germany which we could accept without explicit disavowal, and leaving out reference to freedom of the seas. Bernstorff must see that nothing immediate can be done about that."[155]

Bernstorff arrived at the State Department at 3:55 p.m. on February 4, not long after Wilson wrote the above letter, bringing a note that he had just received from Berlin. It was the Foreign Office's redraft of the *Lusitania* memorandum that Bernstorff had sent on January 26. The following excerpt from von Müller's diary sheds some light on the preparation of the new memorandum: "From Berlin I was informed of the shameless demand of the American Government in the 'Lusitania' matter. We should ourselves acknowledge the sinking of

---

[152] E. M. House to W. W., from Geneva, January 30, 1916, Wilson Papers.
[153] E. M. House to W. W., February 2, 1916, *ibid.*
[154] W. W. to R. Lansing, February 3, 1916, *The Lansing Papers*, I, 530.
[155] W. W. to R. Lansing, February 4, 1916, Wilson Papers.

the 'Lusitania' as a 'disloyal act' and thereby—and that is naturally the heart of the matter—bind our hands for the future. In agreement with the Admiralty staff, Jagow has rejected this humiliation as quite unacceptable and has suggested a somewhat moderate statement to which the Emperor gave his approval. The Emperor was, he told me, quite wounded since he had meanwhile entirely forgotten that the 'Lusitania' affair was still hanging fire."[156]

Jagow had made only two changes in Bernstorff's memorandum. One changed the sentence "Thereby the German retaliation affected neutrals which was not the intention as retaliation becomes an illegal act if applied to other than enemy subjects" to read: "Thereby the German retaliation affected neutrals which was not the intention, as retaliation must not aim at other than enemy subjects." The second changed the sentence "The Imperial Government . . . expresses profound regret that citizens of the United States suffered by the sinking of the *Lusitania* and, recognizing the illegality of causing their death, and admitting liability therefor, offers to make reparation . . . ." to read: "The Imperial German Government . . . expresses profound regret that citizens of the United States suffered by the sinking of the *Lusitania*, and assuming liability therefor, offers to make reparation. . . ."[157] The effect was, obviously, to remove all explicit admission of illegality. It was, Bernstorff said, "as far as his Government possibly could go."[158]

Some leaders in Berlin feared that it did not go far enough to prevent a rupture. The Emperor told von Müller on February 1 that he had lain awake half the night thinking about relations with America and whether he would be responsible for a new war further to burden the German people.[159] Zimmermann informed press correspondents of the contents of the note on February 2 and authorized them, for the first time, to break the news of the crisis to the German people. A semiofficial announcement of the dispatch of the note appeared in the German press on February 3. It was followed by a rash of editorial comment during the next few days. Not even the right-wing newspapers were provocative, but all editors, moderate and extremist alike, agreed that the Imperial government had gone the limit in concession, and that the

[156] W. Görlitz (ed.), *Regierte der Kaiser*, p. 151, entry for January 31, 1916.
[157] The German Ambassador to the Secretary of State, memorandum sent from Berlin on February 1, 1916, and delivered to Lansing on February 4, 1916, *Foreign Relations, 1916, Supplement*, p. 157.
[158] R. Lansing to W. W., February 4, 1916, *The Lansing Papers*, I, 530-531.
[159] W. Görlitz (ed.), *Regierte der Kaiser*, p. 151.

Washington government now would have to make the decision for peace or war.[160]

German leaders, using a method that had proved its effectiveness during earlier German-American crises, also appealed directly to the American people. Zimmermann called the Associated Press representative to the Foreign Office on February 4, explained the basic issue in dispute, and gave a statement to appear in the American press along with news of receipt in Washington of the German memorandum. "The Government," he said, "is willing to do everything in its power, and has done everything in its power to meet American wishes, but there are limits beyond which even friendship snaps. I do not understand America's course. We had thought the submarine issue settled and the Lusitania question on the way to arrangement—had agreed to pay indemnity and all that—when the United States suddenly made its new demands, which it is impossible for us to accept. You must not push your demands too far. You must not attempt to humiliate Germany."[161]

Bethmann, four days later, gave an even more impassioned interview to Karl H. von Wiegand, reporter for the New York *World*. The Chancellor after reviewing the *Lusitania* negotiations in some detail, added that "the phraseology of Secretary Lansing's note was such as left him no alternative but to reject it; that no German Government could concede such a humiliation for its people and survive." He then exclaimed:

"What your Government asks is an impossible humiliation. I have gone far to maintain those cordially friendly relations with America which have existed between your country and Germany since the day when, more than 125 years ago, Prussia was the first nation to recognize America's independence in her war with England.

"You know that in this entire question I have shown a fair and conciliatory spirit toward your country and people. I have been and am willing to concede to America everything that Germany can concede within reason and fairness; within the principles of justice and honor.

"But I cannot concede a humiliation of Germany and the German people, or the wrenching of the submarine weapon from our hands,

---

[160] *Berliner Lokal-Anzeiger*, February 4, 1916; Berlin *Kreuz-zeitung*, February 4, 1916; and Berlin *Vossische Zeitung*, cited in the *New York Times*, February 5, 1916; Berlin *Kreuz-zeitung*, February 5, 1916, quoted in *ibid.*, February 6, 1916; review of German press opinion of February 6 and 7, *ibid.*, February 7 and 8, 1916.

[161] *New York Times*, February 5, 1916.

even to placate America and to insure the continuance of those cordial relations with your country which every true German values and sincerely desires, except at the price of national humiliation.

"It is not with a light heart that I tell you this, but in doing so I am conscious of the fact that I am voicing the sentiment of the united German peoples.

"We are battling for our very existence. The German people, in marvellous [sic] solidarity and unity and heroism, in unparalleled sacrifices, are giving their blood and treasures for their country. We are not at war with America, we do not want to be. Certainly no one can credit us with such madness.

"I have done and shall continue to do everything within my power to avoid it, but there are some things I cannot do. If that same spirit of upright sincerity in desire to reach an agreement with honor to both nations prevails in America that exists in the German Government and people, then there will be no break in the century and a quarter of friendly relations between the two countries."[162]

Tension in Washington eased, curiously, at the same time that it began to rise in Berlin. Lansing was enormously pleased by the German government's proposed memorandum, or at least pretended to be now that he knew that the President would not permit him to force the issue of illegality. "It comes so near meeting all our demands that I wish to study it with care to see if it cannot be considered acceptable," Lansing wrote to Wilson on February 4 while sending him a copy of the memorandum. "Of course the word *illegal* and the word *illegality* are omitted, but if we do accept this settlement I believe we could state our understanding of the language in order to show in our acceptance that we consider there is a direct admission of wrong."[163]

Unnamed spokesmen in both the State Department and the White House gave a fairly detailed summary of the German memorandum to reporters on February 4, and a "high authority" announced that the German concessions had removed the danger of a break in relations, even though the situation was grave. Zimmermann's statement, reporters were also told, was for home consumption and intended to cover Germany's retreat.[164] White House and State Department spokesmen

---

[162] New York *World*, February 9, 1916. Von Weigand's dispatch also included interviews in the same vein with Zimmermann, an unnamed officer on the Army General Staff, and Admiral von Holtzendorff.

[163] R. Lansing to W. W., February 4, 1916, *The Lansing Papers*, I, 531.

[164] New York *Times*, February 5, 1916; New York *World*, February 5, 1916.

intimated even more pointedly on February 5 and 6 that the crisis had passed, and that the President and Secretary of State were in no great hurry to confer about the German memorandum.[165]

Lansing finally saw the President at the White House at 10 a.m. on February 8. They went over the German memorandum and read it to the Cabinet when it met an hour later. Afterward they told reporters that its wording, while not exactly what they had wanted, was acceptable, and that there was no longer any danger of a rupture. "A settlement of the Lusitania case is in sight," a "high Administration official" said in a formal statement to reporters, "probably within the next few days. The United States has not increased its demands; it has not reduced them. You can draw your own conclusions as to the basis of the agreement. The wording proposed by Germany appears to cover the position of the United States. It is not fair to assume that there will have to be any further admissions or concessions from Berlin."[166]

It seemed, indeed, almost as if Lansing was saying that there never had been any crisis at all. Certainly the statements that the United States had neither increased nor reduced its demands, and that the German memorandum "covered" the original American demands, were not quite accurate. The truth was that Wilson and Lansing had retreated from a very advanced position both because Wilson did not want a break and because they both had suddenly realized that congressional opinion would not tolerate a rupture over this particular issue.

This came out fairly clearly in the aftermath of Bethmann's appeal of February 8. The correspondent of the semi-official German Wolff Bureau asked various American leaders for replies to send to the German people. Lansing denied that American demands had ever been an "impossible humiliation," adding that "nothing had been asked of Germany which was not reasonable and fair, and with which a nation could not comply without doing violence to its honor and dignity." Vice President Thomas R. Marshall, Senator Stone, and Representative Henry D. Flood of Virginia, chairman of the foreign affairs committee, all declared that the American government had no desire to humiliate Germany. Senator Hoke Smith was even more blunt—and accurate: "I can truthfully say that there is no desire either in the Administration or in Congress to humiliate Germany, with which our people wish to live in peace and friendship. There is no danger of war,

---

[165] *New York Times*, February 6 and 7, 1916.
[166] New York *World*, February 9, 1916; also *New York Times*, February 9, 1916.

not even a danger of a diplomatic break, for Congress would not tolerate it over merely one word."[167]

A strange dénouement unfolded quickly. Lansing, following his conference with the President and the Cabinet meeting in the morning of February 8, saw Bernstorff at the State Department in the late afternoon. The Secretary affirmed that the two governments were in substantial agreement. But, Lansing asked, would not the Berlin authorities be willing to substitute the words "recognizing its liability" for "assuming its liability" in the sentence of its memorandum of February 1? Bernstorff was confident that his superiors would be happy to make this change.[168]

A wave of relief surged through official circles in Berlin upon receipt of Bernstorff's report of this conversation and of reports from Washington to the effect that the *Lusitania* crisis was over. "The deep pessimism over the relations between Germany and America, which has been like a pall for several days, such as I have not experienced here since the beginning of the submarine war," von Wiegand reported from the German capital on February 9, "has lifted considerably since yesterday."[169] Bethmann, still deeply engaged in the larger struggle over submarine policy, was delighted to earn credit so cheaply. He approved the change suggested by Lansing, and the revised German *Lusitania* note was put on the American Embassy's wire probably on February 14. It arrived in Washington on the following day, and Bernstorff delivered it to Lansing at noon on February 16. "This matter," Bernstorff wrote to Bethmann, "which several times has brought us to the brink of war with the United States, now appears to be approaching a definitive resolution."[170]

[167] *New York Times*, February 12, 1916; New York *World*, February 12, 1916.

[168] R. Lansing to W. W., February 8, 1916, *The Lansing Papers*, I, 531; New York *World*, February 10, 1916.

[169] New York *World*, February 11, 1916. See also the *Frankfurter Zeitung*, first and second morning edns. and afternoon edn., February 8, 1916, and second morning edn., February 9, 1916.

[170] "During the last ten months there were numerous times when it seemed that either the American Government or we wanted a dilatory treatment of the issue," Bernstorff continued. "At last relations were such, in my opinion, that it lay in the great interest of both governments to remove the bone of contention entirely, if it was at all possible. We were completely hindered here because at every step that I took, upon every question that I raised—whether from the government or from the press—the Lusitania was always brought up. When an anti-English speech was made in the Senate or the House of Representatives our enemies would render it ineffective by mentioning the Lusitania.

"In brief, this issue blocked every positive action on our side, while the government

Settlement was so near and yet so far away! The German Admiralty on February 10 had announced that, beginning February 29, German submarines would sink all armed merchantmen without warning. Lansing sent Bernstorff's *Lusitania* note, dated February 16, to the President. "In view of the recent manifesto from Berlin in regard to armed merchant vessels," he wrote, "I do not see how we can now accept this answer as a settlement of the *Lusitania* case. . . . The recent declaration is . . . contradictory of their former position and would appear to nullify the assurances which they have given."[171] Wilson agreed, replying:

"I have no hesitation in saying that, but for the recent announcement of the Central Powers as to the treatment to which they purpose subjecting armed merchantmen and those which they presume to be armed, it would clearly be our duty in the circumstances to accept the accompanying note as satisfactory. But that announcement inevitably throws doubt upon the whole future, and makes it necessary that we should think the situation out afresh.

"I would suggest that you have a frank conversation with the German Ambassador and point out to him just our difficulty—the difficulty of interpreting their recent assurances in the light of their new and dangerous policy, and of understanding that new policy in view of the fact that all the circumstances upon which they base their adoption of it were known to them at the time of the *Arabic* note.

"I doubt whether it would be wise to address a note to him. I think that it would be best, all things considered, to make the interchange of explanations oral only, for the present."[172]

Lansing announced the President's decision to reporters on February 16 and conveyed it formally to Bernstorff on the following day.[173] In actual fact, the *Lusitania* case was now agreeably buried, if not for-

---

here was continually attacked by its Republican opponents because it had accomplished nothing in the matter. Roosevelt utilized the situation when at all possible against Wilson. The former's fanaticism no longer knows any bounds. The question now is whether Mr. Roosevelt can still be considered sane. Madness appears to have enveloped his mind. Otherwise, it is scarcely possible to understand his latest remark: 'Wilson fears no one except the Kaiser and myself.' If Roosevelt continues to go on in this manner he will provide the Republican Party with defeat for the second time." J. von Bernstorff to T. von Bethmann Hollweg, February 15, 1916, German F. O. Archives.

[171] R. Lansing to W. W., February 16, 1916, *The Lansing Papers*, I, 531-532.

[172] W. W. to R. Lansing, February 16, 1916, *ibid.*, pp. 532-533.

[173] *New York Times*, February 17, 1916; New York *World*, February 17, 1916; "Memorandum of the Secretary of State . . . , February 17, 1916," *Foreign Relations, 1916, Supplement*, p. 172.

mally settled. As the German Ambassador reported to the Foreign Office on February 18: "So far as the *Lusitania* question itself is concerned, it must be conceded to be settled, but the final formula, which was reached only after untold labor, is, as [Lansing] expressed it, 'acceptable but not satisfactory.' The battle about the word 'illegal' ended in failure on Mr. Wilson's part since he does not desire war. This means that the President has not obtained the diplomatic victory in the *Lusitania* controversy which he wished to have to his credit for election purposes. In the meantime, he is looking around for additional laurel wreaths."[174] "If it had only used a little journalistic skill," Bernstorff wrote ten days later, "the American government might have been able to present the settlement of the *Lusitania* question in the light of a success. Instead, it looks from here as if the President had given in on the fundamental question in order to avoid war."[175]

Wilson and Lansing were content to let the *Lusitania* case remain in limbo,[176] and the American government did not raise the issue again until a German-American Claims Commission settled the matter of financial liability in the 1920's. Meanwhile, in mid-February 1916, the two governments stood on the brink of a new submarine dispute that threatened to engulf them both. We will discuss this dire development in due course, after we have reviewed one of the most astounding episodes in American history—Colonel House's peace mission to Europe and its startling climax.

[174] Ambassador von Bernstorff to the Foreign Office, February 18, 1916, *Official German Documents*, II, 1286. I have changed the translation slightly.

[175] Ambassador von Bernstorff to the Foreign Office, February 28, 1916, *ibid.*, p. 1288.

[176] They did discuss, in late September and early October 1916, the advisability of reopening negotiations with a view to accepting the German note, but they agreed that such a move would not be wise during the presidential campaign then in progress. R. Lansing to W. W., September 21 and October 2, 1916; W. W. to R. Lansing, September 29 and October 6, 1916, *The Lansing Papers*, I, 569-572.

The House-Grey Memorandum

EVENTS of the autumn of 1915 convinced Colonel House that the future was full of perils for the American ship of state. The *Arabic* pledge had brought momentary abatement of high tension with Germany, but the *Lusitania* case still remained unsettled, and other incidents and difficulties were almost bound to arise. There were dangers ahead with the Allies, too, particularly after dispatch of the American note to Great Britain of October 21 denouncing the Anglo-French blockade of Germany as "ineffective, illegal, and indefensible." House did not think that there was any serious danger of rupture with Great Britain. He thought, instead, that American failure (which seemed to him inevitable) to do anything effective to challenge the British blockade would tip the balance in Germany in favor of advocates of an all-out submarine effort. This would drive the United States pell-mell into the war in 1916. He did not necessarily *want* this to happen. He blew hot and cold about the desirability of American participation, depending mainly on the changing circumstance. He simply thought that American participation was unavoidable.

President Wilson, House thought, had two choices, among others, in this perilous situation. As the Colonel's biographer has put it: "He might drift upon events, trusting that the persistent difficulties which arose with each belligerent group could be met separately and safely. He might push the still unsettled dispute with Germany over the disavowal of the sinking of the *Lusitania* to a point where a break would be inevitable, and thus bring the United States into the war on the side of the Entente."[1] A policy of drift meant permitting Germany, as well as the Allies, to determine American policy and could result in a declaration of war for the wrong reason—mere defense of technical neutral rights. And it would be ridiculous, and risky as well, House thought, to break with Germany over the *Lusitania*, an incident that was virtually dead in the American public mind. There was, House knew, another way out of the dilemma—an American *démarche* to end the war.

[1] Charles Seymour (ed.), *The Intimate Papers of Colonel House* (4 vols.), II, 82.

House, like Wilson, had dreamed of various ways of mediation ever since his ill-fated mission to Europe in the early months of 1915.[2] The plan that later found its embodiment in the House-Grey Memorandum took form in House's mind during the critical period when it seemed that a break with Germany over the *Arabic* could not be avoided. To begin with, he received, in late August and early September, two letters from Sir Edward Grey, hinting broadly that the Allies would welcome an American mediation offer provided it was accompanied by a guarantee to join a league of nations and defend a new postwar structure based upon disarmament on land and sea.[3] "All our efforts are of course concentrated on saving ourselves and our Allies by securing victory in the war," Grey wrote in his second letter on August 26. "But it is in my mind continually that the awful sufferings of this war will, to a great extent, have been in vain unless at the end of it nations are set and determined together that future generations shall not fall into such a catastrophe again." Secondly, a chance remark by President Wilson on September 22, at the height of the second *Arabic* crisis, led House to believe that Wilson might view a bold diplomatic project more sympathetically than before. "Much to my surprise," House recorded in his diary, "he said he had never been sure that we ought not to take part in the conflict and if it seemed evident that Germany and her militaristic ideas were to win, the obligation upon us was greater than ever."[4]

House moved quickly to explore the possibilities. "Do you think the President could make peace proposals to the belligerents at this time," he wrote pointedly to Grey on September 3, "upon the broad basis of the elimination of militarism and navalism and a return, as nearly as possible, to the status quo? Will you not advise me?"[5] Then he saw Wilson in New York on October 8 and broached the plan that had been forming in his mind. "I thought," House said, "we had lost our opportunity to break with Germany, and it looked as if she had a better chance than ever of winning, and if she did our turn would come next; and we were not only unprepared, but there would be no one to help us stand the first shock. Therefore, we should do some-

[2] For which, see A. S. Link, *Wilson*, III, 203-231.

[3] E. Grey to E. M. House, August 10 and 26, 1915, House Papers. Grey was writing, specifically, to comment on a peace feeler that Bethmann had put out to him through Raymond Swing, correspondent of the *Chicago Tribune* in Berlin, and Edward Price Bell, London correspondent of the *Chicago News*.

[4] House Diary, September 22, 1915.

[5] E. M. House to E. Grey, September 3, 1915, House Papers.

thing decisive now—something that would either end the war in a way to abolish militarism or that would bring us in with the Allies to help them do it. My suggestion is to ask the Allies, unofficially, to let me know whether or not it would be agreeable to them to have us demand that hostilities cease. We would put it upon the high ground that the neutral world was suffering along with the belligerents and that we had rights as well as they, and that peace parleys should begin upon the broad basis of both military and naval disarmament. . . . If the Allies understood our purpose, we could be as severe in our language concerning them as we were with the Central Powers. The Allies, after some hesitation, could accept our offer or demand and, if the Central Powers accepted, we would then have accomplished a master-stroke of diplomacy. If the Central Powers refused to acquiesce, we could then push our insistence to a point where diplomatic relations would first be broken off, and later the whole force of our Government—and perhaps the force of every neutral—might be brought against them." The President was startled and seemed to approve by silence. They did not have time to discuss the plan.[6]

Five days later, October 13, House explained his plan to Lansing in Washington; he added that "it was clear it would not do to permit the Allies to go down in defeat, for if they did, we would follow in natural sequence." Lansing, agreeing, approved the project.[7] That same day the British Ambassador, Sir Cecil Spring Rice, handed to House Grey's reply to the pointed question that House had posed on September 3. He could not give an answer, the Foreign Secretary wrote, without consulting the British Cabinet and the Allied governments, and it would not be easy to do this unless he knew that the President really was prepared to make his proposal. His personal impression, Grey went on, was that neither side was ready to discuss peace. The great objective of the present war was security against future aggression. "How much are the United States prepared to do in this direction? Would the President propose that there should be a League of Nations binding themselves to side against any Power which broke a treaty; which broke certain rules of warfare on sea or land (such rules would, of course, have to be drawn up after this war); or which refused, in case of dispute, to adopt some other method of settlement than that of war?" Only in some such postwar security system, Grey went on, did hopes for disarmament lie. Only the American government was in

[6] House Diary, October 8, 1915.
[7] *ibid.*, October 13, 1915.

position to make such a proposal. England had to fight on with her allies. She would like to see France recover Alsace-Lorraine and Russia obtain an outlet to the sea, but "the minimum to avoid disaster" was restoration of Belgium and "preservation" of France in the peace treaty.[8]

Greatly excited, House took Grey's letter to the White House on the following day, October 14. Wilson, too, was tremendously encouraged. Grey had certainly not been unresponsive; better still, he had seemed to intimate that Great Britain might be willing to consider a settlement based upon the *status quo ante bellum*. Wilson thought that the only question now was when and how House's plan should be executed; he asked House to draft a reply and send it to him for approval before it was dispatched to London.[9]

House dictated the letter—"one of the most important letters I ever wrote," he called it—on October 17, and Wilson read and returned it on the following day. "I have made one or two unimportant verbal changes in this, but they do not alter the sense of it," Wilson wrote in an accompanying letter. "I do not want to make it inevitable quite that we should take part to force terms on Germany, because the exact circumstances of such a crisis are impossible to determine. The letter is altogether right. I pray God it may bring results."[10] House mailed the letter as a split message in two separate envelopes on October 19. It follows, with Wilson's changes in italics:

"Your letter of September 21st [22nd] was handed me by Sir Cecil when I was in Washington. . . . I have written Sir Cecil that I think it is better that he should know nothing of what you and I are, at the moment, discussing, that it is now merely between friend and friend and that if anything comes of it, it can be brought to his attention officially. Sir Cecil knows nothing excepting what he read in your letter and I will not discuss the matter with him further, or with anyone else.

"It has occurred to me that the time may soon come when this Government should intervene between the belligerents and demand that peace parleys begin upon the broad basis of the elimination of militarism and navalism.

"I would not want to suggest this to the President until I knew in advance that it would meet the approval of the Allies. This approval, of course, would have to be confidential and known only to me.

[8] E. Grey to E. M. House, September 22, 1915, House Papers.
[9] House Diary, October 14, 1915.
[10] W. W. to E. M. House, October 18, 1915, House Papers.

"In my opinion, it would be a world-wide calamity if the war should continue to a point where the Allies could not with the aid of the United States bring about a peace along the lines you and I have so often discussed. What I want you to know is that whenever you consider the time is propitious for this intervention I will propose it to the President. He may then desire me to go to Europe in order that a more intimate understanding as to procedure may be had.

"It is in my mind that after conferring with your Government I should proceed to Berlin and tell them that it was the President's purpose to intervene and stop this destructive war, provided the weight of the United States thrown on the side that accepted our proposal could do it.

"I would not let Berlin know, of course, of any understanding had with the Allies, but would rather lead them to think our proposal would be rejected by *the Allies*. This might induce Berlin to accept the proposal, but if they did not do so, it would nevertheless be the purpose to intervene. If the Central Powers were still obdurate, it would *probably* be necessary for us to join the Allies and force the issue. I have expressed myself badly, and I do not mean to be unfair to Berlin.

"I want to call your attention to the danger of postponing action too long. If the Allies should be unsuccessful and become unable to do their full share, it would be increasingly difficult, if not impossible, for us to intervene. I would have made this proposal to the President last Autumn, but you will remember that it was not agreeable to the Allies.

"It might be well for you to cable me under the code we have between us, unless you prefer to send a letter. The understanding will be that the discussion is entirely between you and me until it is desired that it be broadened further.

"Your letters seem strangely delayed for it has been nearly a month since your last was written, and it has happened so each time."[11]

House's letter, delayed because the steamer which carried it put in at a Canadian port to pick up troops, arrived in London on about November 8, 1915. It found Grey in no mood to think or talk seriously of peace. He certainly had not meant to excite House so greatly. But he could not afford to offend such a good friend at the American court, and he did not dare to give the President the impression that he was not always eager for a reasonable settlement. Hence he resorted to the

[11] E. M. House to E. Grey, October 17, 1915, *ibid.*

same kind of evasion that had proved so satisfactory in dealing with House during the Colonel's first peace mission. He put House off with another question in a cablegram on November 9: "What is the proposal of the elimination of militarism and navalism that you contemplate? Is it that suggested in fourth paragraph of letter to you of September 22?"[12] He also made it plain in a letter two days later that House's plan had little chance at this particular time. "I wish that you were here, so that I could talk things over," Grey concluded amicably, "but the situation at the moment and the feelings here and among the Allies, and in Germany so far as I know, do not justify me in urging you to come on the ground that your presence would have any practical result at the moment."[13]

Receipt of Grey's cablegram on November 9 further excited House's rising hopes. Sending a copy of the cablegram to Wilson, House also proposed a reply: "Yes, the proposal contemplated is, broadly speaking, along the lines mentioned in fourth paragraph of your letter to me of September 21st [*sic*]." "It seems to me," he went on in his letter to Wilson, "that we must throw the influence of this nation in behalf of a plan by which international obligations must be kept, and in behalf of some plan by which the peace of the world may be maintained. We should do this not only for the sake of civilization, but for our own welfare, for who may say when we may be involved in such a holocaust as is now devastating Europe. Must we not be a party to the making of new and more humane rules of warfare, and must we not lend our influence towards the freedom of both the land and sea? This is the part I think you are destined to play in this world tragedy, and it is the noblest part that has ever come to a son of man. This country will follow you along such a path, no matter what the cost may be."[14]

Almost all his life Woodrow Wilson had shared age-old dreams for a universal dominion of peace through law. He had hoped since the beginning of the war that Europe's travail might find reward in a new postwar security system. Who was he to refuse to answer if noble destiny called? "Message approved," he replied to House on November

[12] E. Grey to E. M. House, November 9, 1915, quoted in E. M. House to W. W., November 10, 1915, Wilson Papers. Grey was referring here to the following paragraph in his letter of September 22: "To me, the great object of securing the elimination of militarism and navalism is to get security for future against aggressive war. How much are the United States prepared to do in this direction? Would the President propose that there should be a League of Nations . . . ?"

[13] E. Grey to E. M. House, November 11, 1915, House Papers.

[14] E. M. House to W. W., November 10, 1915, Wilson Papers.

11. "You might even omit words 'broadly speaking' and say merely 'along the lines of .' "[15] "I think the paragraph quoted from . . . [Grey's] letter of September twenty-second contains the *necessary* programme," he added on the following day.[16] The revised message went to Grey by cable on November 11.[17]

Peace was the great topic of public conversation during the autumn of 1915,[18] but Colonel House could not proceed very far until he had received more positive encouragement from Grey. The Colonel saw Bernstorff on November 19 and intimated that the President was contemplating moving for a settlement on a basis of general disarmament. Indeed, House continued, Wilson was prepared to send him to London and Berlin if the German authorities approved. Bernstorff accompanied his report of this interview with some interesting observations on Gerard and House: "It seems to me that the House mission is to be de-

[15] W. W. to E. M. House, November 11, 1915, House Papers.

[16] W. W. to E. M. House, November 12, 1915, *ibid*.

[17] E. M. House to E. Grey, November 11, 1915, House Papers.

[18] e. g., Miss Jane Addams and leaders in the Woman's Peace Party had just participated in a Woman's Peace Congress at The Hague, talked to various European statesmen, and returned home to promote a plan for an early neutral peace congress at the Dutch capital. They called on President Wilson on November 26, 1915. See the *New York Times*, November 27, 1915; New York *World*, November 27, 1915; and Jane Addams to E. M. House, November 23, 1915, House Papers. This campaign culminated in the chartering of the Scandinavian-American liner *Oscar II* by Henry Ford, the automobile manufacturer, to carry delegates from the Woman's Peace Party and others to Europe to try to end the war. "We are going to try to get the boys out of their trenches and back to their homes by Christmas Day," Ford explained. "I want to do the greatest good to the greatest number, and certainly getting the men out of the trenches will be accomplishing that." *New York Times*, November 25, 1915. What the London *Spectator*, December 4, 1915, p. 776, called the "Ship of Fools" sailed from New York on December 4, 1915, for Copenhagen as the band on board played "I Did Not Raise My Boy to Be a Soldier" and "Tell the Boys It Is Time to Come Home." The motley delegation visited the capitals of the northern European neutrals.

Ford returned home early, much less hopeful about prospects for peace. "A marked change has come over my whole viewpoint since I went away," he told reporters in New York on January 2, 1916. "Before going to Europe I held the view that the bankers, militarists, and munition manufacturers were responsible. I come back with the firm belief that the people most to blame are the ones who are getting slaughtered." *New York Times*, January 3, 1916.

House's judgment of Ford was interesting. "I found him," the Colonel wrote in his diary after having dinner with Ford, "crude, ignorant and with very little general information. He cannot discuss foreign affairs because he knows so little about them. He knows even less about politics and the only safe ground was practical mechanics and farming. I think he is a genius along these lines and is an idealist and has many fine qualities. Just how he has succeeded in amassing so large a fortune is something of a mystery to me." House Diary, October 2, 1916.

sired because the United States is unfortunately so poorly represented in Berlin. Colonel House is at least absolutely neutral, very discreet as well as trustworthy, and stands in the very center of the political situation on this side. . . . Up to the present time, he has been of extraordinary value to me."[19]

Grey's discouraging letter of November 11 arrived in New York on about November 25, and House was downcast and irritated. "The offer which I made in my letter [of October 17], which was practically to insure victory to the Allies, should have met a warmer reception," he complained in his diary after reading Grey's reply. "The British are in many ways dull."[20] House and Wilson found an hour and a half in the late afternoon of November 28, on the occasion of Wilson's and Mrs. Galt's weekend visit to New York, for a private conversation. House had just talked to Lansing about the utter necessity of making the Allies understand that "we considered their cause our cause, and that we had no intention of permitting a military autocracy to dominate the world, if our strength could prevent it." House, at least so he wrote in his diary, repeated these same sentiments to Wilson. The President wondered how he and House could convey such a message to the Allies. It was not possible to work through the British and American Ambassadors. Page, Wilson and House agreed, was utterly hopeless. Spring Rice, Wilson said, was a "highly excitable invalid." The only safe way to let the Allies know "how our minds are running," Wilson said, was for House to go to London. "I feel, myself," House afterward wrote, "that it could not properly be done excepting in this way and, if it is done at all, it should be done well, otherwise a hopeless situation might come about. We are now in the most delicate situation that has yet arisen and such negotiations as we have under advisement need the best that we all have in us. It means the reversal of the foreign policy of this Government and no man can foresee the consequences."[21]

It was, of course, still necessary to obtain a change of mind in London, and House worked in every discreet way available. He had a series of conferences with Sir Horace Plunkett in New York in early December. Plunkett had served as House's direct liaison with the

---

[19] Ambassador von Bernstorff to the Foreign Office, November 23, 1915, *Official German Documents*, II, 1278-1279. House's report to the President of this conversation (E. M. House to W. W., November 19, 1915, Wilson Papers) was quite incomplete.

[20] House Diary, November 25, 1915.

[21] *ibid.*, November 28, 1915.

British Cabinet during the preceding summer and had, in fact, come to New York at House's request. "He told me," Plunkett recorded in his diary on December 3, "his (and Wilson's) whole mind upon the war. They are determined to see the Allies through but they cannot go further than public opinion will support them. . . . The chief trouble in the Anglo-American situation was the temperament of Sir Cecil Spring-Rice."[22] The United States, House told Plunkett again three days later, meant to see the Allies through if necessary but would take action in its own way at its own time.[23] "Another long talk with House," Plunkett wrote on December 7. "Unless he is a liar—and I am absolutely satisfied he is the embodiment of truth—the President is seeking to break off diplomatic relations with Austria over the *Ancona* outrage and then to have a single diplomatic (the German) link with the Central Powers. House talks as though the only question about this link is not whether but when it will be snapped."[24] House also asked Plunkett to convey his remarks to Grey and Arthur Balfour, Plunkett's friend and head of the British Admiralty.[25] It was an unnecessary request. House's statements to Plunkett also found their way to the ears of Jean J. Jusserand, French Ambassador in Washington, who cabled them to the Quai D'Orsay. A few days later, House wrote the letter to Page quoted in the preceding chapter, saying that the United States was near a break with the Central Powers and Page should tell English friends that "the lower their fortunes seem the more ready we are to help."[26]

Plunkett, who thought that Britain's salvation lay in firm alliance with America, would gladly cooperate. Grey was not so easily tantalized since he had just received a warning from the British Ambassador in Washington advising "extreme caution in any communications to your

[22] The Diary of Sir Horace Plunkett, Horace Plunkett Foundation, London, December 3, 1915; hereinafter cited as the Plunkett Diary. See also Margaret Digby, *Horace Plunkett, An Anglo-American Irishman*, pp. 190-191.

[23] Plunkett Diary, December 6, 1915.

[24] *ibid.*, December 7, 1915. Compare House's report to Wilson (E. M. House to W. W., December 7, 1915, Wilson Papers) of these conversations. Plunkett said, House wrote, that the great danger to the Allies was German pressure on nearby neutrals, and that there was a general feeling among the Allies that it would help to swing the neutrals away from Germany if the United States took a firm stand. It would in his opinion, House wrote, be better to refrain from decisive action until the process of attrition had continued for some months longer. There was danger, he added, in a decisive Allied success. House did not mention to Wilson his remarks to Plunkett about American determination to see the Allies through to the end.

[25] As House said in E. M. House to E. Grey, December 7, 1915, House Papers.

[26] See above, p. 66.

Friend."[27] House now used all his guile to entice an invitation from Whitehall. He wrote to Grey after his last conversation with Plunkett saying that he had not received an answer to his cable message of November 11. Things had been moving very rapidly in the United States. The President and he had discussed the advisability of his going to London. There were reasons for and against this. Grey was mistaken in thinking that he and Wilson had any desire to weaken British sea power at this time. "It is the one reassuring potential element in the war." His mind, House went on, was not "running towards peace, even upon the broad lines spoken of before. What is needful at present is a better working understanding with you and how this is to be brought about is uppermost in our thoughts. The machinery we are using is not altogether satisfactory. Just why I cannot explain here, and perhaps it may be necessary for me to see you in person."[28] Three days later House wrote again. There were many things that he needed to tell Grey, he said; he also asked whether Grey could send his secretary, Eric Drummond, to Washington at once.[29]

House was at the Executive Mansion again on December 15, before he had had any further word from Grey. Wilson now insisted that House should go to London as soon as arrangements could be made. It was absolutely urgent, he said, to explain the American point of view directly to the British Cabinet. It might help if House went to France earlier than he had planned. Circumstances should determine whether he went to Germany; in any event, he should not go there without an invitation. Wilson then approved House's suggestion that he explain to reporters that he was going to bring American Ambassadors in Europe up to date on their government's policies. Wilson left for an appointment, and Lansing came in and said that House's trip should be delayed because the American government was approaching an impasse with Austria and Germany and might have to break diplomatic relations. Upon Wilson's return, Lansing repeated his statement, but Wilson again insisted that House should go very soon. House then asked the President to read what Gerard had reported about a recent interview with the German Emperor. Wilson took the dispatch from the safe where he kept his most confidential documents. "The upshot of what Gerard wrote," House recorded in

[27] C. Spring Rice to the Foreign Office, November 29, 1915, copy in the Papers of Herbert Asquith, Bodleian Library, Oxford; hereinafter cited as the Asquith Papers.
[28] E. M. House to E. Grey, letter, December 7, 1915, House Papers.
[29] E. M. House to E. Grey, letter, December 10, 1915, *ibid.*

his diary, "was that the Kaiser said 'he would attend to America when this war was over; that President Wilson's attitude regarding Germany eliminated him from any possibility of acting as mediator.' "[30] House pretended to take the matter seriously.

Lansing left, and Wilson and House turned to a more serious matter: the purpose of House's journey. They had apparently been talking all along about different things. House had talked of American support of the Allies, even armed intervention if that was necessary to guarantee Germany's defeat. He had in fact already told Grey and the British Cabinet that the United States meant to see the Allies through to victory. His great mission, as he conceived it, was to obtain Allied approval of an American mediatory effort with firm understanding about the larger terms of a settlement. He was certain that the United States would enter the war in 1916 in any event, and he wanted, not to hasten that entry, but to make it worthwhile when it occurred. A subsidiary objective, House thought, was to persuade the British to respond to the recent American note by taking action to open the channels of peaceful neutral commerce to Germany. But he would urge them to do this only *because such action would lessen anti-British sentiment in the United States and facilitate American diplomatic or military intervention.*

Wilson, it is clear, now had rather different objectives in mind. He was still eager for House to explore the possibilities of an American mediatory effort looking toward general disarmament and a postwar league of nations. But he made it plain that he did not have any thought of risking military involvement in order to achieve this goal. "I found the President not quite as belligerent as he was the last time we were together," House wrote in his diary. "He seemed to think we would be able to keep out of the war. His general idea is that if the Allies were not able to defeat Germany alone, they could scarcely do so with the help of the United States because it would take too long for us to get in a state of preparedness. It would therefore be a useless sacrifice on our part to go in. I called his attention to the necessity of our having the Allies on our side for the reason we would have to undertake the task alone when Germany was ready to deal with us. He admits this, and yet I cannot quite get him up to the point where he is willing to take action. By action, I mean not to declare war, but to let the Allies know we are definitely on their side and that it is not

[30] I have not been able to find this letter in the Wilson Papers.

our intention to permit Germany to win if the strength of this country can prevent [it]. The last time we talked he was quite ready to take this stand,[31] but he has visibly weakened. I am wondering whether it is not the influence of Congressmen and Senators upon him. They know so little of what is happening and think merely in local terms."[32] Wilson also wanted House to press hard for relief of legitimate American commerce with Germany *because the complaints of American shippers and merchants were, he thought, justified, and it was right that the American government should support them.* What he had in mind, and what he must have said to Colonel House in this conversation, were evidenced in the letter that he wrote for House, at House's explicit request, from Hot Springs. It follows:

"You ask for instructions as to what attitude and tone you are to take at the several capitals. I feel that you do not need any. Your own letters (for example, this one in which you report your conversation with Bernstorff)[33] exactly echo my own views and purposes. I agree with you that we have nothing to do with local settlements,—territorial questions, indemnities, and the like,—but are concerned only in the future peace of the world and the guarantees to be given for that. The only possible guarantees, that is, the only guarantees that any rational man could accept, are (a) military and naval disarmament and (b) a league of nations to secure each nation against aggression and maintain the absolute freedom of the seas. If either party to the present war will let us say to the other that they are willing to discuss peace on such terms, it will clearly be our duty to use our utmost *moral* force to oblige the other to parley, and I do not see how they could stand in the *opinion of the world* if they refused.

"The errand upon which you are *primarily* bound you understand as fully and intimately as I do, and the demand in the Senate for further, immediate, and imperative pressure on England and her allies makes the necessity for it the more pressing. About the possibilities in the direction of peace you need no further intimation than that given above. If any particular question arises I know that you will cable me fully, and I shall of course reply at the earliest possible moment.

"I am sure you know how fully my heart goes with you and how deeply grateful I am for the incomparable and inestimable services you

[31] This was, of course, House's understanding. There is no other evidence to support this statement.

[32] This quotation is taken from, and the above account of the conversations of December 15 are based upon, the House Diary, December 15, 1915.

[33] Wilson was here referring to E. M. House to W. W., December 22, 1915, Wilson Papers, for discussion of which see below, pp. 113-114.

are rendering the country and me, your friend. Mrs. Wilson joins me in most affectionate messages to you both. We are having a heavenly time, and I am sure that I am being daily rendered more fit for the winter's work. I shall miss you and your counsel about domestic matters very sorely and very constantly, but the greater must be preferred to the less.

"Please give my most respectful and sincere regards to Sir Edward Grey and to the other troubled and responsible men with whom you will confer in England, France, and Germany. It would make me very happy to cooperate with them in any way for the peace of the world and a perfect understanding between them and this country."[34]

House could not possibly have misunderstood. As we will see, he later grossly misrepresented the President and misinformed him as well. But, presumably, this was because he thought that he was justified in pursuing an independent policy because the stakes were so high and the objectives so noble.

House returned to New York on December 16 in order to put his personal affairs in order. Lansing made the necessary diplomatic arrangements, informing the British, French, and German governments that House had no peace mission in mind and was coming to Europe only in order to confer with American Ambassadors. House wrote to Grey on December 17, explaining that he was coming to London at the President's and Secretary of State's request, and that there would be no need for Drummond to come to Washington.[35] He wrote to Page on the same day, saying that he had absolutely no peace plans, and that Page should let this be known in London.[36] The British Ambassador came to call soon afterward, and House convinced him that he was going to Europe only in order to talk to American Ambassadors.[37] Then reporters asked House on December 21 whether rumors about his trip were true. House admitted that he was going to Europe and repeated the explanation.[38] Wilson issued a confirmatory statement on the following day, adding that his friend's trip was in no way connected with "the peace movement."[39]

One mildly encouraging development occurred before House left. Bernstorff came to his apartment on December 22 to say that he had

[34] W. W. to E. M. House, December 24, 1915, House Papers; italics added.

[35] E. M. House to E. Grey, December 17, 1915, House Papers.

[36] E. M. House to W. H. Page, December 17, 1915, *ibid*.

[37] C. Spring Rice to E. Grey, December 23, 1915, S. Gwynn (ed.), *Letters of Spring Rice*, II, 304-305; House Diary, December 17, 1915.

[38] *New York Times*, December 22, 1915.

[39] *ibid.*, December 23, 1915.

just received a wireless message from the Foreign Office[40] urging House to come directly to Berlin to discuss peace upon the basis of disarmament.[41] House reported the conversation to Wilson at once, adding that he had earlier told Bernstorff that the President "would be willing to throw the weight of this Government into the scales and demand that the war cease" if the Germans would consent to a settlement embracing general disarmament, and that Americans were not concerned about territorial questions and indemnities. "The Allies," House went on, "will take care of the territorial and indemnity questions, and we need not go into that at this time."[42] Wilson was pleased if not excited. "What you tell me of your latest conversation . . . ," he replied, "is . . . most interesting. It makes me feel, as you evidently do, that it is possible that we are on the eve of some real opportunity. I pray it may turn out to be so! At any rate, it is the more clear that you are starting on your present errand at just the right juncture."[43]

House, accompanied by his wife and secretary, sailed aboard the *Rotterdam* of the Holland-America Line on December 28, 1915. They landed at Falmouth on January 5 after an uneventful crossing and were sent on their way to London by naval officers assigned to care for them. House had his first conference with Grey in the afternoon of January 6. The Colonel explained what he "thought should be done toward bringing the democracies of Europe in closer touch with the United States" and intimated that the American government was prepared to join a league of democracies. He also outlined his plan for American intervention "based upon a demand for freedom of the seas and the curtailment of militarism." "I thought it far better," House recorded in his diary, "for the democracies of the world to unite upon some plan which would enable the United States to intervene, than for us to drift into the war by breaking diplomatic relations with the Central Powers." The American people, he went on, had lofty ideals—in spite of what one might think about their businessmen—and would make any sacrifices to achieve these ideals. House also told Grey that he had advised the President against breaking with Germany at this particular time, because he hoped that "we might come to some agreement along the lines now contemplated." House finally mentioned

[40] It was G. von Jagow to Ambassador von Bernstorff, December 20, 1915, *Official German Documents*, II, 1279.

[41] House Diary, December 22, 1915.

[42] E. M. House to W. W., December 22, 1915, Wilson Papers.

[43] W. W. to E. M. House, December 24, 1915, House Papers.

the blockade and urged Grey "to make matters easier" for Wilson. Grey seemed interested; indeed, House reported, he favored the disarmament plan provided the United States would sign a general covenant to sustain it. They agreed to meet again with Arthur Balfour on January 10 to try to formulate some specific plan, and House sent a telegram to Washington asking Wilson to send some assurance of his "willingness to cooperate in a policy seeking to bring about and maintain permanent peace."[44] House had dinner with Arthur Balfour following this conference.

House, Grey, and Balfour met for lunch and further conversation on January 10. House had received Wilson's assurance that he would be "willing and glad when the opportunity comes to cooperate in a policy seeking to bring about and maintain permanent peace among civilized nations."[45] House again explained the "real purpose" of his visit, and both Grey and Balfour were, he thought, full of suppressed excitement. Balfour, however, seemed somewhat analytical and argumentative. He wanted to know how far Wilson would go in an agreement concerning European affairs, and whether the President would really be able to obtain American support for House's plan. The President, House replied, was interested only in broad questions like disarmament that affected the future of every nation. "I told them it would be easier for me to persuade the President to accede to what I . . . [had suggested than it would be] for them to succeed with their colleagues. I had only one man to convince and I knew him sufficiently well to know what he would accept and what refuse."[46] Grey and Balfour ventured the opinion that the Allies had the capacity to win on their own, and House reminded them that it was not impossible that Germany might come to separate terms with Russia and France.[47]

It was, House reported by cable to the President, an entirely satisfactory conference. "We are to meet again Saturday [January 15] to continue discussion. So far there is no disagreement between us. . . . My plan is to come to a tentative agreement with them before going to the Continent on the twentieth and let them bring their colleagues into line before I return. They have agreed to undertake this."[48]

[44] E. M. House to W. W., telegram, January 7, 1916, and letter, January 7, 1916, both in the Wilson Papers; House Diary, January 6, 1916.

[45] W. W. to E. M. House, January 9, 1916, House Papers.

[46] House Diary, January 10, 1916.

[47] E. M. House to W. W., letter, January 11, 1916, Wilson Papers.

[48] E. M. House to W. W., cablegram, January 11, 1916, *ibid*.

Wilson was perhaps encouraged, but he was more concerned at the moment about relief from the blockade, about which House had said very little thus far. "It now looks as if our several difficulties with Germany would be presently adjusted," he replied on January 12. "As soon as they are, the demand here, especially from the Senate, will be imperative that we force England to make at least equal concessions to our unanswerable claims of right. This is just at hand. I send this for your information and guidance."[49]

House had, indeed, already discussed the blockade with some callers, but always as an obstacle to Anglo-American understanding, never as an issue that the United States meant to press as a question of neutral right and duty.[50] He had also made it clear that relatively small things like the blockade would not be permitted to prevent American co-operation with the Allies. Ambassador Page invited McKenna, David Lloyd George, Minister of Munitions, Austen Chamberlain, Colonial Secretary, and Lord Chief Justice Reading to a dinner in House's honor at the American Embassy on January 11. Page opened the conversation by saying that his British friends had asked him what the United States wanted Great Britain to do. "The United States," House replied, "would like Great Britain to do those things which would enable the United States to help Great Britain win the war." One way that Britain could help was to do something to ease the heavy burden that shipping troubles placed on the President.[51]

House had lunch with Page, Grey, and Lord Robert Cecil, Undersecretary of State for Foreign Affairs (he would soon join the Cabinet as Minister of Blockade), at the American Embassy on the following day, January 12. House apparently read the President's cable about relaxation of the blockade to the group. Grey and Cecil both declared that their political careers would end the moment they acceded to Wilson's request. The French authorities, they added, were even more determined than the English to maintain the blockade in all its severity and would not listen to any proposals from London for relaxation. Grey intimated that he would personally be willing to permit foodstuffs to go

[49] W. W. to E. M. House, draft of a cablegram, in Wilson's handwriting, January 12, 1916, *ibid.* The next to the last sentence in the message that House received read simply "This is just." Wilson or Mrs. Wilson coded the message personally, and it is possible that the President shortened the sentence himself while coding it.

[50] e. g., his conversations with Eric Drummond, Grey's secretary, on January 8 and with Reginald McKenna, Chancellor of the Exchequer, and Walter Runciman, President of the Board of Trade, on January 11. House Diary, January 8 and 11, 1916.

[51] *ibid.*, January 11, 1916.

to neutral ports without question if Germany would give up her sub-marine campaign. House did not press the issue and sweetened the conversation by repeating his statement that the United States wanted Britain to do whatever would make it possible for the United States to help the Allies.[52] "I have presented our side of the argument to nearly every member of the Cabinet," he reported to Wilson on January 13. "I have given them the state of public feeling in America and have told them of the danger which the Allies run in doing these things and in creating adverse opinion against them. They know your position now as well as I know it, and they appreciate it. . . . I am giving you the situation as it actually is so you can use your own judgment as to how to proceed."[53] He did not report his statements about the alleged Ameri-can desire to be helpful in every way.

House was greatly excited by a long conversation at dinner with Lloyd George at the Savoy Hotel on January 14. The Colonel apparently did not mention his mediation plan, but the volatile Welshman talked wildly and alluringly anyway. The war could continue almost indefi-nitely, he said, and Britain would grow stronger all the while. Only intervention by the American President could end the conflict. His chance for mediation would come in September, after the British had had a try with their new army on the western front. Then the Presi-dent could dictate terms of peace and demand that Germany evacuate Belgium and France and Russia consent to creation of an independent Poland. Militarism, too, would go at Wilson's command. The peace to be made should be a peace of reconciliation; Germany and England should be friends, not enemies.[54] It was the first positive word in sup-port of American mediation that House had heard in London, and he hastened to send a full report to the President[55] and a special cable mes-sage: "Would suggest not sending any note to England concerning shipping troubles until . . . [my letter] arrives. It is equally of *utmost importance* to continue relations with Germany and Austria until then. There seems to be some day light ahead if fortune favors us."[56]

Hopes so easily inflated were as easily dashed when House conferred again with Grey and Balfour on January 15. House told them about his

[52] The Diary of Walter H. Page, Houghton Library, Harvard University, January 12, 1916; hereinafter cited as the Page Diary; E. M. House to W. W., January 13, 1916, Wilson Papers.

[53] E. M. House to W. W., January 13, 1916, *ibid.*

[54] House Diary, January 14, 1916.

[55] E. M. House to W. W., letter, January 15, 1916, Wilson Papers.

[56] E. M. House to W. W., cablegram, January 15, 1916, *ibid.*

conversation with Lloyd George on the preceding night and asked if they had discussed the matter of Wilson's mediation with him. Not at all, they replied. The three men then turned to House's plan and discussed it for more than an hour. Balfour was argumentative; Grey seemed to agree with House that Britain could find security in a post-war league of nations. But Grey agreed with Balfour that it was not prudent to discuss such matters with their colleagues in the Cabinet, and that it certainly was not wise to broach the matter of American mediation to Britain's allies. Even if they could do both, the British people could not be told. They parted with the understanding that Grey and Balfour should think the matter over further, discuss it with the Prime Minister and Lloyd George, and talk to House again when he had returned from the Continent.[57]

House was profoundly discouraged when he reported on this conversation to Wilson on the following day, recommending virtual abandonment of any immediate plans for American intervention. He wrote in part:

"Grey, Balfour, and [Lloyd] George say if they could tell the country that there was a chance of bringing about a tentative understanding with us, the people would yield to almost any demand we might make. But the opinion is firmly fixed that America will do nothing, and that England must fight the battle alone, with the only weapon that has so far proved effective.

"Nearly every American here, and this includes our entire Embassy I think, would be glad to see us come into the war on the side of the Allies. This feeling is shared, of course, by many Englishmen and by nearly all the French, although one is constantly told that this is not desired.

"I believe I have convinced those to whom I have been able to talk freely, that it is best for all concerned for us to keep out, conserving our strength so at the proper moment, we may lead them out of their troubles.

"I am more and more certain that it would be a mistake from every viewpoint for us to come in, although we should be ready to throw our weight at the right time in the right direction for the good of humanity. We are growing stronger as they grow weaker, consequently our power is increasing in double ratio.

"I am sure that our policy should be to have no serious friction with the Allies over the blockade, and to keep upon such terms with Ger-

[57] House Diary, January 15, 1916.

many that our diplomatic relations may be maintained. If you do this, and I would do it in spite of all the protests at home and abroad, you will find yourself the potential factor in concluding peace. It does not matter how much you are reviled now if the end justifies your course. The criticism, both in Europe and America[,] comes from ignorance and from partisan feeling and can be swept aside by your final action. . . . P.S. Of course, I do not mean to advise that diplomatic relations should not be immediately broken if the Central Powers sink another passenger ship without warning. If this were not done, it would discredit us everywhere, and greatly minimize your influence."[58]

House saw many other British leaders, including Prime Minister Herbert Asquith, during the next four days, but he mentioned the mediation project only to Grey on January 19. They talked about whom they should tell the purpose of House's mission and agreed that Lloyd George, Lord Reading, Spring Rice, and Page would have to be told. House confided to his diary that he was sorry that Page would have to be informed because he was so antagonistic to the American point of view.[59]

Colonel House left London with his wife and secretary for the Continent on January 20, going first to Paris by way of Folkestone and Boulogne. They spent a few quiet days in the French capital and then entrained for Geneva, Basel, and Berlin, arriving in the latter city in the morning of January 26, 1916. Gerard and Bernstorff had prepared the way, and civilian leaders were eager to present the German side to an American with a sympathetic ear. House, in turn, was happy to oblige, in order to plant seeds of peace, without giving his plans away.

There was first a large formal dinner at the American Embassy, where the Houses were staying, in the evening of January 26. Then House saw Wilhelm Solf, Secretary of State for Colonies, at breakfast with Gerard on the following morning. He talked freely and perhaps indiscreetly about the situation in Britain. Grey, he said, was eager for peace negotiations, but his prestige was declining. The King was a "nobody," and there was not a statesman of outstanding capacity and energy in the entire Cabinet. Anti-American feeling was stronger in England even than in Germany. He still hoped, House went on, to

[58] E. M. House to W. W., January 16, 1916, Wilson Papers.
[59] House Diary, January 19, 1916.

put a stop to the insane butchery and violence that was destroying Europe. There were enough farseeing people in England and Germany to end the war if they could only meet on common ground. Indeed, if such a platform could be found people like Grey in England and Solf in Germany could reach an understanding between sunrise and sunset. Grey, for example, was willing to debate the question of blockade and submarine warfare and to make concessions in return for limitations on the submarine campaign.[60]

Gerard entertained Chancellor von Bethmann Hollweg and Foreign Secretary von Jagow, among others, at dinner on January 28, and House had long conversations with both men. Bethmann drank beer copiously and talked bitterly about the origins of the war, saying that the guilt did not lie on him, and that Germany was not yet beaten and did not need to beg for peace. House spoke of his impressions of England, remarking that he had encountered more antagonism against America there than in Germany. Grey as well as Lloyd George, he went on, had not been as negative about peace as he had expected. The latter, at least, wanted a peace of understanding with Germany and was willing to concede extensive colonial possessions and a free hand against Russia to Germany. The trouble was that there was no united view in the English Cabinet. Some way out of the European deadlock would have to be found in the end; at least one could begin to talk about peace. Bethmann replied that he, too, wanted a permanent peace, provided Germany could have security in the future on the Polish and Belgian sides, an indemnity for evacuating northern France, and reparation for English wrongs. The return of Poland and Belgium would have been possible earlier but was not discussable now. The Allies, House said, would not consider such terms for a moment. The two men talked also of the blockade and submarine campaign, and Bethmann said that England could never starve Germany. The conversation lagged, and they joined the other guests.[61] Then House and Jagow went into the Blue Room of the Embassy alone and talked

[60] W. Solf to G. von Jagow, January 28, 1916, German F. O. Archives, also printed in *Official German Documents*, II, 1280-1281.

[61] The above account of this conversation is based on T. von Bethmann Hollweg, "Memorandum of the Imperial Chancellor . . . ," January 28, 1916, German F. O. Archives, printed in *Official German Documents*, II, 1281-1283; House Diary, January 28, 1916; and the Emperor's account of Bethmann's report of the conversation, as recorded in W. Görlitz (ed.), *Regierte der Kaiser*, p. 152, entry for February 4, 1916; see also Fritz Fischer, *Griff nach der Weltmacht*, pp. 262-272, 353-362, for general background and German thinking about the Belgian question at this time.

mainly about the submarine war and its impact on German-American relations.[62]

Additional conversations with Zimmermann and others confirmed House in the belief that the Germans were not ready for any peace talks to which Allied leaders would listen. He also saw enough evidence of the fierce struggle over submarine policy then in progress to cause him to send the cable from Geneva on January 30 printed in the preceding chapter.[63] A few days later he sent Wilson a longer report from Paris, as follows:

"So much has happened since I last wrote that I scarcely know where to begin. I will not try to go into detail, leaving that for a personal conference.

"I was well received in Germany—better than before, if anything. I had many invitations while there, but concluded it would be wiser to see everyone at our Embassy.[64]

"I conferred with the Chancellor alone for an hour and a half, and had conferences with von Jagow, Zimmerman and Solf, besides many other important Germans. The Chancellor, for the moment, is in control with the Emperor. . . .

"I do not believe the Chancellor will be able to hold the first place long, particularly if we do not take measures against the Allies—which, indeed, it would be impossible for us to take in a way that would satisfy Germany.

"When they find that this cannot be brought about, and when the pinch of the blockade becomes even greater than now, a revulsion of feeling will probably take place and a sentiment will develop for any measure that promises relief.

"The Navy crowd are telling the people that an unrestricted undersea warfare will isolate England. I look, therefore, in any event for troublous times with Germany during the next few months, and I am afraid that my suggestion that we remain aloof until the time becomes more propitious for you to intervene and lead them out, is not promising.

"The reason I am so anxious that you do not break with Germany over the *Lusitania* is that any delay may make it possible to carry out

[62] House Diary, January 28, 1916.

[63] See above, pp. 92-93.

[64] Because he feared that he might meet Tirpitz at some affair given by a German. "I feel," House wrote in his diary on January 27, 1916, "that von Tirpitz is almost solely responsible for German frightfulness upon the sea, and if he got his desserts he would be hanged at the end of a yardarm like any pirate of old."

the original plan in regard to intervention. And if this cannot be done because of Germany's undersea warfare, then we will be forced in, in a way that will give us the advantage.

"I discussed peace with the Chancellor, with Zimmermann, and with Solf. The Chancellor was the most unreasonable, coming back always to the point that he was the only one in power amongst the belligerents that had spoken for peace. . . . He is an amiable, well-meaning man, with limited ability. Zimmermann is much abler and my talk with him was more satisfactory.

". . . If the war goes against Germany, when the army is disbanded trouble will surely come for the masters. If victory is theirs, the war lords will reign supreme and democratic governments will be imperilled throughout the world."[65]

The one significant result of House's visit to Berlin, then, was reinforcement of his earlier conviction that submarine extremists would drive Germany to hostilities with the United States in 1916. It was, House thought, no time for despairing submission to blind events. The Allies must be persuaded by hook or crook to approve the mediation plan. Only then could the United States use its power constructively and responsibly for the good of mankind. His immediate, indispensable task, House thought, was to win the confidence of the leaders of France. They had been adamant heretofore against any suggestions of a negotiated peace.[66] He would not excite their suspicions by talking too much of peace. It would suffice if he could persuade them that America was a true and loyal friend. If they believed that, then Grey could perhaps persuade them to cooperate.

House arrived in Paris on February 1, after stopping over briefly in Geneva to talk to Ambassador Frederick C. Penfield who came from Vienna for the conference. He had his first conference with Jules Cambon, former French Ambassador to Germany, at the Foreign Ministry on February 2. Cambon promised to give an exact account of their conversation to Premier and Acting Foreign Minister Aristide

[65] E. M. House to W. W., February 3, 1916, Wilson Papers.

[66] Among other reasons, because they had determined to crush Germany and destroy her offensive power forever. The French (and British) governments had agreed in principle to a program of "*écrasement*" suggested by the Russian government in September 1914. It envisaged Russian annexations on the eastern German frontier, French recovery of Alsace-Lorraine, possible French annexation of the Palatinate, and other drastic territorial changes. See Erwin Hoelzle, "Das Experiment des Friedens im Ersten Weltkrieg, 1914-1917," *Geschichte in Wissenschaft und Unterricht*, 13th Year (August 1962), 468.

Briand. House related his conversations with Bethmann, Jagow, and Zimmermann. Cambon got the impression as the conversation proceeded that House had come to Europe in the hope that a peace based on the *status quo ante bellum* was possible, and that he now realized that it was out of the question. The Allies, House said, must understand the necessity of helping the American government to help them. He could not recommend too urgently, he went on, that they should be manifestly guided by reasons of military necessity in executing measures against Germany that also damaged neutrals. That was essential. America, in spite of all more or less formal declarations, would accept all measures based on military need. But it was essential, House continued, to avoid irritating American public opinion, and France should support American protests against the illegal aspects of the *British* blockade. The naiveté of this statement, the seeming ignorance of the fact that the blockade was an Anglo-French affair, may have been deliberate.

If the Allies followed his advice, House continued, America would inevitably enter the war before the end of the year and range herself on the side of the Allies. Cambon was so startled by this assertion that he asked House to repeat it; Cambon then wrote it down and read it back. But, House went on, American intervention could come only after some incident had rallied public support behind the President. Cambon replied that this seemed unlikely, since the Germans appeared willing to do almost anything to prevent a conflict with the United States. That was true, House replied, but he had left Germany with the conviction that the Germans would wage unrestricted submarine warfare if the British tightened their blockade. In fact, the Germans believed that their powerful new submarines could cut off England and win the war. An unrestricted submarine campaign would force America's hand. Conversation about the larger issues of the war followed, Cambon saying that this was the last conflict between democracy and what remained of feudalism in the world. Those, House replied, were his own sentiments, and this was why American sympathies went out to the Allies. He hoped that the end of the war would see an alliance to maintain peace among France, the United States, and England. It would be indomitable.[67]

House apparently also saw Briand briefly after his conversation with Cambon. He went back to the American Embassy to make his report to the President. Something that Cambon or Briand said, which the

[67] The above is based in part on the House Diary, February 2, 1916.

documents do not reveal, must have greatly encouraged him. "Unless there is a change of government here and in England," he reported in a cablegram, "the situation is now largely in your hands, provided you do not break with Germany. I strongly advise no positive action upon any of the pending questions between our government and that of the belligerents until I confer with you and the Secretary of State."[68] Then he dictated a letter relating—or purporting to relate—his conversation with Cambon, as follows: "I talked to Cambon quite freely, outlining the entire situation as it seems to me, and I am hopeful that the result of what I said will show itself in the immediate future. I took up our shipping troubles with him, and he seemed more readily to understand our difficulties than they do in England. I have told them all that what we wanted most was for them to do those things which would help us to help them best. . . . In my opinion, hell will break loose in Europe this spring and summer as never before and I see no way to stop it for the moment. I am as sure as I ever am of anything that by the end of the summer you can intervene."[69]

The discrepancy between what House reported and what he had actually said to Cambon was, to say the least, remarkable.

Word of House's conversation passed rapidly through high political circles, and the atmosphere was, in contrast to what it had been a year before, positively cordial. Between February 4 and 9 House talked to politicians, editors, and others, including President Raymond Poincaré. Only the British Ambassador, Lord Bertie of Thame, whose chief small pleasure was excoriating Americans in his diary, was less than friendly. He attended a dinner at the American Embassy in honor of Colonel and Mrs. House during the evening of February 4 and left early because he was bored.[70] He later told an official at the Foreign Ministry that House was playing a double game.

House had a final conference with Briand and Jules Cambon at the Quai d'Orsay at 11 a.m. on February 7. House afterward told President Wilson that he had tried in his first conversation with Cambon only to create a "good atmosphere," and that he afterward decided to take the risk and talk plainly in the second conference. He began by assuring Briand and Cambon of America's profound sympathy for the Allies. It was, he said, the American government's intention to intervene, be

[68] E. M. House to W. W., c. February 3, 1916, Wilson Papers.
[69] E. M. House to W. W., February 3, 1916, *ibid.*
[70] House Diary, February 4, 1916; Lady Algernon G. Lennox (ed.), *The Diary of Lord Bertie of Thame, 1914-1918* (2 vols.), I, 297.

it peacefully, be it even militarily, to obtain a peace settlement favorable to the Allies. The lower France's fortunes fell, the stronger would be American friendship. Or, as House recorded it in his diary, "I again told them that the lower the fortunes of the Allies ebbed, the closer the United States would stand by them." His listeners might be assured, House went on, that if the Allies obtained some small military successes during the coming spring or summer, the United States would intervene in favor of peace. If they suffered reverses, the United States would intervene militarily and take part in the war against Germany.[71]

The Allies, House went on, should take care to avoid all small difficulties over shipping in order to facilitate President Wilson's role, and it would be helpful if the French said this to the London Cabinet. He would, on his return home, urge Wilson to speed up military and naval preparations. He repeated that he had advised the President to avoid a break over the *Lusitania* disavowal, but he said that there would be only a delay in American action which, when it did come, would be decisive in the fortunes of the war.

What, Briand and Cambon both asked, did House think about Alsace-Lorraine? The French people would never consent to a peace settlement that did not restore the two lost provinces to *la patrie*. That, too, House replied, "might be accomplished by giving Germany a part of Asia Minor, and compensating Russia in the same way." Cambon exclaimed, "Then you would wipe out Turkey." That, House said, was in his mind; Turkey must disappear. In any event, he continued, France and England must agree in a broad and liberal spirit on the peace terms that they thought were possible. The United States would support them and enter the war if Germany did not accept them.

Cambon, with Briand's approval, remarked that the time for such propositions had not come. Neither the military situation nor public opinion would permit such a peace initiative. Moreover, England and France had allies and could discuss peace only in accord with them. That might be true, House replied, but the United States could not negotiate with all the Allies. It was England's and France's business to determine when the time for American intervention was ripe, to discuss the matter with their allies, and then to approach the Washing-

[71] House's text of this statement is not quite as clear as the above. He wrote it in his diary on February 7, 1916, as follows: "*In the event the Allies are successful during the next few months I promised that the President would not intervene. In the event they were losing ground, I promised the President would intervene.*" (Italics in the original text.)

ton government. "I slowly and emphatically outlined the danger of delay and of too much optimism. I saw nothing in the situation to warrant it," House wrote in his diary. House reiterated Wilson's determination to act on behalf of the Allies, peacefully if possible, militarily if necessary. The American President, he concluded, also wanted these declarations to be secret. If Briand wished to communicate on this subject to Wilson, House concluded, he would do well to write directly to him, Colonel House. Then he asked Cambon to write a summary of the conversation. Cambon read it back to him, and he "affirmed its correctness."[72]

French leaders must have been as excited as they were intrigued. It was significant that the Foreign Ministry, in cabling a summary of House's two principal conversations to the French Ambassadors in London and Washington, emphasized House's prediction that the United States would enter the war on the Allied side before the end of the year on account of an unlimited German submarine attack, as well as his statement that American mediation did not seem possible at the present time.[73] Jules Cambon told Lord Bertie that House had said that "the war will be long, that the Allies will win in the end, and that in a year's time America will be with us."[74] It was significant, also, that the Foreign Ministry, while briefly informing French envoys to prominent European neutral governments of House's visit, announced a major change in American foreign policy, namely, that the United States would henceforth accept all Allied commercial restrictions justified by military necessity.

House for his part was exhilarated by the thought that he had finally won French confidence. The meeting with Briand and Cambon on February 7 was, he wrote in his diary on the same day, "an important— perhaps the most important, conference I have had during this visit to Europe. We had a complete understanding as to the immediate future." He went to the American Embassy to dispatch a brief cable telling President Wilson that he had just talked to Briand and Cambon. "I dare not cable substance," he wrote, "further than to say that it was the most important conference I have had in Europe and that it was along

[72] The above is based in part on the House Diary, February 7, 1916, from which the quotations are taken.

[73] The Foreign Ministry also sent copies of the *texts* of the two conversations to the French Ambassadors in London and Washington.

[74] Lady Algernon G. Lennox (ed.), *The Diary of Lord Bertie of Thame*, I, 301; entry dated February 12, 1916.

the line of my conversation with Lloyd G. before leaving London, but much more gratifying."[75]

One wonders how the Colonel could possibly have arrived at such a conclusion. Lloyd George had seemed to be eager for Wilson's early mediation. The records show that Briand and Cambon said only that Wilson's diplomatic intervention was impossible at this time. House was even more mystifying (to the historian) and incomplete (to Wilson) in the report that he wrote to the President just before he left France. It follows:

"I shall not go into much detail in regard to my conversation with the Prime Minister and Cambon, but will give you a brief outline.

"In the first interview I tried to create a good atmosphere, and I was undetermined whether to leave it at that or go further. Up to the present I have been confidential with the British Government alone, and have left to them the bringing into line of their Allies.

"However, I was never more impressed by their slowness and lack of initiative as upon this trip, and I concluded that we had better take the risk and talk plainly to the French. The result was surprisingly satisfactory.

"I outlined the situation to them as I see it, bringing in all the doubtful elements which might throw the balance against them—their lack of victories, their mistakes, the efficient German organization under an autocracy as against an inefficient organization under democracies, and the danger of separate peace with Russia and Italy. All this I outlined with care. I pictured what was at stake, not only for them, but for the whole world, and, while declaring that we felt able to look out for our own interests in our own way, yet I let them see how deeply concerned we were for the future of democratic government.

"It was finally understood that in the event the Allies had some notable victories during the spring and summer, you would intervene; and in the event that the tide of war went against them or remained stationary, you would intervene. This conversation is to go no further than between Briand, Cambon, and myself, and I promised that no one in America should know of it excepting yourself and Lansing.

"I told them I had had a similar conversation in England and that there it would go no further than a group composed of the Prime Minister, Sir Edward Grey, Balfour, and Lloyd George. This seemed agreeable to them.

[75] E. M. House to W. W., cablegram, c. February 7, 1916, Wilson Papers.

"They are to keep in touch with me by letter and messages, and I, in turn, am to do likewise. This was done to give more freedom, because of its unofficial character.

"Briand and Cambon know and seemed to agree to the advice I gave you concerning the settlement of the *Lusitania* matter. It is impossible for any unprejudiced person to believe that it would be wise for America to take part in this war unless it comes about by intervention based upon the highest human motives. We are the only nation left on earth with sufficient power to lead them out, and with us once in, the war would have to go to a finish with all its appalling consequences. It is better for the Central Powers and it is better for the Allies, as indeed it is better for us, to act in this way; and I have not hesitated to say this to the British and French Governments, and have intimated it to Germany.

"A great opportunity is yours, my friend—the greatest, perhaps, that has ever come to any man. The way out seems clear to me and, when I can lay the facts before you, I believe it will be clear to you also.

"In each government I have visited I have found stubbornness, determination, selfishness, and cant. One continually hears self-glorification and the highest motives attributed to themselves because of their part in the war. But I may tell you that my observation is that incompetent statesmanship and selfishness is at the bottom of it all. It is not so much a breaking down of civilization as a lack of wisdom in those that govern; and history, I believe, will bring an awful indictment against those who were short-sighted and selfish enough to let such a tragedy happen."[76]

Colonel and Mrs. House and House's secretary left Paris for Boulogne in a special car provided by the French government in the morning of February 8, and House visited King Albert of Belgium at his headquarters at La Panne that afternoon. They discussed peace terms, and House suggested that Belgium might make her contribution to world peace by permitting Germany to purchase the Belgian Congo. If Germany could obtain this territory, Portuguese Africa, and a sphere of influence in Asia Minor, he said, she might cede Alsace-Lorraine to France and certain German colonies in Africa to the Union of South Africa. Albert said that sale of the Congo might be arranged. He also eagerly endorsed House's suggestion that all belligerents pay an indemnity to Belgium.[77]

[76] E. M. House to W. W., February 9, 1916, *ibid.*
[77] House Diary, February 8, 1916.

House spent the night in Boulogne and went on to London on the next day, February 9. He had dinner with Ambassador Walter Page at the Ritz Hotel that evening and told him about his mediation plan. It was one of the most unpleasant evenings that House ever spent. Page had already heard something about the project, for he wrote in his diary just before this meeting: "They are laughing at the 'Empty House' here." The Ambassador did not think well of the scheme that House detailed. It was, he thought, "purely academic nonsensical stuff." House told him that the French approved. Then, Page said, the French certainly had misunderstood. The plan, Page thought, was "a morally weak, indirect scheme," "doomed to failure—is wrong, in fact." No one in London would talk peace or accept the President's mediation: "They no longer have confidence in the President."[78] House recorded his own reactions in his diary that same evening. "He frets me to such an extent," the Colonel wrote, "that I fear I talked to him rather roughly. Everything the President was doing was wrong, the contempt of the British and Europe generally for us was growing stronger every day, and the United States was in bad odor everywhere. In reply I literally flayed him, and I was surprised afterward that he took it so kindly. The man hinders me my work because he tries to discourage me, and would totally do so if I were of a different temperament."[79]

Page told House on February 11 that he would prefer not to participate in any discussions that House might have with members of the Cabinet. "He was more depressing than ever, literally damning the President and Lansing for their lack of foresight and policy. He declared it would be ridiculous for him to talk about closer relations with Great Britain, when we were doing everything we could possibly to irritate them."[80] Page vented his feelings even more freely in his diary:

"House is doing a lot of harm here, which I must somehow turn to good—e. g. make it accentuate the crisis as soon as he is gone.

[78] Page Diary, February 9, 1916.

[79] House Diary, February 9, 1916. House dined with Page at the American Embassy on the following evening and had to listen to another severe denunciation. *ibid.*, February 10, 1916.

[80] *ibid.*, February 11, 1916. Page was now terribly upset by the impending *Lusitania* settlement with Germany and by Lansing's recent diplomatic campaign to persuade the Allies to disarm all merchantmen. As House reported to Wilson on February 10: "I arrived here last night and had a conference with Page in which with characteristic pessimism he declared I would not be able to do anything with this Government because of the Lusitania settlement and because of Lansing's proposal in regard to disarming merchantmen. He told me Sir Edward Grey had said as much to him

"My present mood is—not to mention House in any letter or dispatch to Washington, lest I be misunderstood. I must stick by the job now lest the public conclude that House's coming caused my withdrawal as personal pique. But if House proposes to come again, I think I shall simply say—'Well, I go at once, then.'[81]

"All the vain and silly talk about 'intervention,' *i.e.* about submitting proposals to the belligerents, and about standing in waiting for a peace proposal from one belligerent to the other—this is all mere aloof moonshine."[82]

Page might speak frankly to House, but Grey and other British leaders could not afford the luxury. Grey must have had some large doubts about the inevitability of American military intervention in 1916—Spring Rice in Washington had long advised that Wilson and the majority of Americans would do almost anything to avoid involvement. Grey also thought little more of House's mediation scheme than Page. But he did not dare to offend the man whose opinion Wilson seemed to respect the most. He would, therefore, humor House, even to the point of coming to some understanding so long as it was not binding. Such an agreement might be useful, anyway, if the Allies ever were about to lose the war. And Colonel House might, after all, be right in thinking that German submarine extremists would force a German-American crisis in 1916.

Thus British leaders made a point of seeming eager to get on with conversations when House returned. Grey sent him a note on the evening of February 9 saying that he would be pleased to see House the next morning. Lord Reading called after breakfast on February 10 to advise that Lloyd George wished to see House alone within the next day or two. House and Grey came, seemingly, to perfect agreement in their conference that same morning. Grey remarked that a straightforward American belligerency would be the best solution. House argued earnestly and "convinced" Grey that it would be better if the American government settled the *Lusitania* controversy and intervened by demanding a peace conference. "We finally agreed," House wrote in his diary, "it was best for the President not to set any conditions whatever, but merely to demand that war cease, and a conference be held. We decided to take into our confidence, Asquith, Balfour, Lloyd

---

without telling him exactly to what he referred." E. M. House to W. W., February 10, 1916, Wilson Papers.

[81] Page Diary, February 13, 1916.

[82] *ibid.*, February 15, 1916.

George and Reading. It was further decided that I should make the initial talk tomorrow when the Prime Minister, Balfour and myself met at Grey's for lunch. Page, Lloyd George and Reading are to be brought into the discussion at Lord Reading's dinner Monday night."

House by this time had forgotten completely about Wilson's instructions. When Grey said that he wondered whether it would not be better for Britain to give up her blockade, House answered that he thought not, unless Germany consented to wage more humane warfare.[83]

House had a long inconclusive discussion at luncheon at Grey's house with Asquith, Grey, and Balfour on February 11.[84] Grey was now discouraging. Britain, he said, could do nothing until one of her allies was ready to discuss peace. House again warned of the danger of too much delay. The United States could not intervene, he said, if it appeared that Germany was about to win a decisive victory.[85] Grey saw House alone three days later and tried to prepare him for an unhappy outcome. He personally believed, Grey said, that the time was ripe for the President to demand a peace conference. But other members of the Cabinet either did not share this view or else did not dare to express it. "Public opinion here would condemn any minister who would dare endorse such a proposal, and Grey believes they would even go so far as to smash his windows."[86]

What seemed to be the crucial discussion took place at a dinner at Lord Reading's on the evening of February 14 attended by Reading, House, Asquith, Grey, Balfour, and Lloyd George. They talked generally for two hours, and House made the correct prediction that the Germans would soon launch a massive assault against the French fortress of Verdun. The servants left at 10:30, and then conversation

---

[83] House Diary, February 10, 1916. House reported on this conversation in a letter to Wilson (Wilson Papers) on February 10, 1916. The *Allies*, he wrote, had agreed that Wilson should call a peace conference. They would reply affirmatively. If Germany did not follow suit, House continued, the United States would throw in all its weight in order to bring her to terms. "I am very happy to be able to write you this, and I hope to-morrow I may be able to confirm it by cable. If you can hold the situation at Washington clear of all complications, sending no notes, protests, etc., etc., to any of the belligerents, it looks as if something momentous may soon happen."

[84] By this time the French Ambassador, Paul Cambon, had read the text of a memorandum of House's conversation with Jules Cambon of February 2, 1916, to Lord Robert Cecil of the British Foreign Office and had also given Grey a copy of a dispatch from the French Foreign Ministry of February 9, 1916, summarizing what House told Briand and Jules Cambon on February 7.

[85] House Diary, February 11, 1916.

[86] *ibid.*, February 14, 1916.

turned to a possible peace conference. Wilson, House said, would be glad to come to The Hague and remain as long as he was needed. There was general discussion about Poland and division of Turkey. House then asked when the United States should demand an armistice and peace conference. Lloyd George would not suggest a date, but (so House believed) Grey was "evidently leaning toward an immediate venture in this direction." Asquith asked what House thought. He replied that the psychological moment would come once the Allies had made enough military progress to discourage the Germans. House thought that everyone agreed tentatively that this would be the right time. Then, at the end, came the really significant dialogue, as House recorded it and Lloyd George later remembered it:

"Asquith [House wrote] asked what we would do in the event Russia and France made separate peace with Germany before Great Britain could bring them into an agreement for the President to act. I replied that we would probably immediately set about building a large navy and army, and withdraw entirely from any interference with European affairs.

"Lloyd George was inclined to insist that we reach an agreement as to terms of peace before it was agreed that the President should intervene. I discouraged this view."[87]

"I was opposed [Lloyd George wrote] to the summoning of a conference without some preliminary understanding with the President as to the minimum terms which the Allies were to insist upon with his sanction and support. A conference without such an agreement would have been productive of the most serious consequences to the *morale* of the Allied Countries, in the event of its failure. . . .

"These terms were acceptable to the Prime Minister, Sir Edward Grey, Mr. Balfour, Lord Reading, and also to Colonel House. The latter, who knew President Wilson's mind better than any living man, was convinced that the terms would also meet the President's view of the justice of the case. . . . They included the restoration of the independence of Belgium and Serbia, and the surrender of Alsace and Lorraine to France, provided that the loss of territory thus incurred by Germany would be compensated by concessions to her in other places outside Europe. There were to be adjustments of the frontiers between Italy and Austria so as to liberate Italian communities still under the Austrian yoke. Russia was to be given an outlet to the sea. There were

[87] House Diary, February 14, 1916.

also to be guarantees against any future recurrence of such a catastrophe as this World War."[88]

"Asquith [House wrote] again asked what the President would do in the event he presided at the peace conference, and the Allies proposed a settlement which he considered unjust. I replied that he would probably withdraw from the conference and leave them to their own devices. On the other hand, he wished to know what the President would do in the event Germany proposed something totally unfair, and against the interest of civilization and humanity. In these circumstances, I thought the President would throw the weight of the United States on the side of the Allies. In other words, he would throw the weight of the United States on the side of those wanting a just settlement—a settlement which would make another such war impossible, and which would look to the advancement of civilization and the comity of nations."[89]

So there was House's plan for British statesmen to see starkly for the first time. There were now, apparently, no promises of American military intervention by a certain date, no reassuring words about seeing the Allies through to the end. There was only the promise that the United States would throw its "weight," whatever that might mean, to *either* side that would answer Wilson's call and follow his lead in a peace conference. And this would mean peace based on the *status quo ante bellum* for the most part, with only the possibility of the return of Alsace-Lorraine to France, if Germany was compensated and satisfied, and minor territorial changes. House had said many times before that the United States would insist upon restoration of Belgium and formation of a postwar league of nations. The conferees presumably assumed that these were the bedrock items of an American peace program. But it does not seem likely that House *guaranteed* the other items in the

[88] David Lloyd George, *War Memoirs of David Lloyd George* (2 vols.), I, 411-412; hereinafter cited as *War Memoirs*. There is an interesting restatement of the peace terms that the British thought that House had approved in a letter written not long afterward by a member of the Foreign Office in general comment on the House-Grey Memorandum. "Finally . . . ," he wrote, "a word about the *suggested* terms themselves. . . . Belgium is to be restored and the Balkans are to be restored to their prewar position. . . . France is to have Alsace-Lorraine. . . . Italy is to get what she wants and Russia is to get access to warm water at Constantinople. Poland is to be independent. . . . We are to be asked to give back German colonies. . . . Germany is to get Anatolia or compensation for the loss of Alsace-Lorraine." E. S. Montagu to H. H. Asquith, March 18, 1916, Asquith Papers; italics added.

[89] House Diary, February 14, 1916.

peace program that Lloyd George detailed. As Grey later put it: "President Wilson's object was to secure a peace which he considered would make a just end to the war, and be the beginning of enduring peace. He might invite the opinion of the Allies first, but he would explore the mind of Germany, too. His whole policy was founded on the assumption that the war was a stalemate, and that the most useful rôle of the United States was to promote an honourable end without a crushing victory. If either side, even Germany, were to agree with him in this, he would use the influence of the United States to bring the other side into line. His suggestion of mediation could not be confined to one side."[90]

Grey, if we may believe the account in House's diary,[91] talked on the day after this conference as if the decision for Wilson's mediation was as good as made. "He showed considerable emotion, walking up and down the room as he talked, making it clear, as far as he was concerned, that he thought immediate action should be asked for." He thought that the plan should be submitted to the entire Cabinet and promised to write a memorandum of his understanding with House.[92] Balfour and Reading, too, were encouraging,[93] and House sent the President a word of cheer on February 16.[94]

House saw the Foreign Secretary again the following morning. Grey had just received from Ambassador Cambon a full memorandum of House's conversation with Briand and Jules Cambon on February 7. House read it again and made the single reservation that "if the Allies put off calling for our assistance to a time when our intervention cannot serve them, then we will not make the attempt." Then Grey and House drafted a memorandum embodying what House had told the French and British. It is known as the House-Grey Memorandum and reads as follows:

"(*Confidential*)

"Colonel House told me that President Wilson was ready, on hearing from France and England that the moment was opportune, to propose that a Conference should be summoned to put an end to the war. Should the Allies accept this proposal, and should Germany refuse it, the United States would probably enter the war against Germany.

[90] Viscount Grey of Fallodon, *Twenty-Five Years, 1892-1916* (2 vols.), II, 133-134.
[91] It is apparently the only one that we will ever have. Grey later wrote in his memoirs that he kept no records of his conversations with House.
[92] House Diary, February 15, 1916.
[93] *ibid.*, February 16 and 17, 1916.
[94] E. M. House to W. W., February 16, 1916, Wilson Papers.

"Colonel House expressed the opinion that, if such a Conference met, it would secure peace on terms not unfavourable to the Allies; and, if it failed to secure peace, the United States would leave the Conference as a belligerent on the side of the Allies, if Germany was unreasonable. Colonel House expressed an opinion decidedly favourable to the restoration of Belgium, the transfer of Alsace and Lorraine to France, and the acquisition by Russia of an outlet to the sea, though he thought that the loss of territory incurred by Germany in one place would have to be compensated to her by concessions to her in other places outside Europe. If the Allies delayed accepting the offer of President Wilson, and if, later on, the course of the war was so unfavourable to them that the intervention of the United States would not be effective, the United States would probably disinterest themselves in Europe and look to their own protection in their own way.

"I said that I felt the statement, coming from the President of the United States, to be a matter of such importance that I must inform the Prime Minister and my colleagues; but that I could say nothing until it had received their consideration. The British Government could, under no circumstances, accept or make any proposal except in consultation and agreement with the Allies. I thought that the Cabinet would probably feel that the present situation would not justify them in approaching their Allies on this subject at the present moment; but, as Colonel House had had an intimate conversation with M. Briand and M. Jules Cambon in Paris, I should think it right to tell M. Briand privately, through the French Ambassador in London, what Colonel House had said to us; and I should, of course, whenever there was an opportunity, be ready to talk the matter over with M. Briand, if he desired it."[95]

House and Grey then talked about the future and agreed that Wilson's immediate mediation would bring greater benefits than those that might come from a costly Allied victory. "I called attention to the fact," House wrote in his diary, "that if the Allies were completely victorious, Russia, Italy and France would undoubtedly make demands and do things Great Britain would not approve, and which would not be in the interest of permanent peace. I drove in as hard as I could the gamble they were all taking by postponing action. One of the gambles Sir Edward had not thought of was the possible death of the President, either from natural causes or by assassination. I told him what would happen in the event [Vice President Thomas R.] Marshall became

[95] From the copy in the House Papers. Grey initialed this memorandum in the Foreign Office on February 22, 1916, and gave a copy to House on the following day.

President. All our plans would go up in smoke, and Europe would have to struggle along in the interminable fight without help from the United States. I called attention to the fact that the President only had another year of office, and of the uncertainty of his re-election. If the Republicans won, it might be very much the same as if Lord Curzon became Prime Minister here with a reactionary Cabinet. The United States might depart from peaceful paths and become jingoistic and imperialistic.

"Grey said with much feeling, 'history will lay a great charge against those of us who refuse to accept your proffered services at this time.' "[96]

Only final details remained to be arranged. House saw Grey again at his home on February 21. The latter had shown the French memorandum of the Paris conference of February 7 and the House-Grey Memorandum to Asquith, Balfour, and Lloyd George. He had, he added, also shown the Memorandum to Ambassador Cambon and assured him that the proposal was genuine. House asked Grey to remind Cambon that Wilson and House could not have any political advantage in mind, "for it was a well-known fact that adverse foreign comment was a political asset to any candidate running for President in the United States." House's account continues, "Grey smiled at this, but recognized its truth and said he would be certain to convey it to Cambon." House cautioned Grey against permitting a copy of "our *agreement*"[97] to get abroad. He might show it to different members of the Cabinet, but he should not give them copies. "In discussing the best time for the President's proposal, Grey thought it depended upon the opinion of the military leaders of the Allies. If they considered the situation warranted waiting a few months for military success, it would be necessary to yield to this opinion. He understands, however, that the President and I desire to act as soon as possible."[98]

Thus in House's mind a tentative understanding had already metamorphosed into an agreement, and Grey's seeming interest had changed into eagerness to proceed. There seemed to be no doubt that this was true after House's final conversations in London. Lord Chief Justice Reading told him on February 22 that Asquith had expressed his strong approval. The government, Reading went on, intended to launch a drive on the western front "so that the President's proposal may come

[96] House Diary, February 17, 1916.
[97] Italics mine.
[98] House Diary, February 21, 1916.

as soon as possible."[99] House made final arrangements with Grey on February 23,[100] boarded the *Rotterdam* at Falmouth, and sailed for New York on February 25. He advised Sir Horace Plunkett just before leaving London that the United States would be "in the thick of it" in the near future, perhaps within thirty days.[101]

There were interesting differences between reactions on both sides of the Atlantic.

House landed in New York on March 5 and went to Washington that same evening. He had lunch at the White House and a long automobile ride with the President and Mrs. Wilson on the next day and, as he put it, "outlined every important detail" of his mission. The Wilsons dropped him at the State Department where he talked to Lansing for an hour. House returned to the White House to read and discuss the Memorandum with Wilson. The President was enormously pleased. As we will see in the next chapter, he had already rather drastically changed one important aspect of his foreign policy, relating to armed merchantmen, in order to facilitate conclusion of the House-Grey Memorandum. What House told him now left no doubt in his mind that the English and French were actually eager for his mediation under House's plan. The great event to which he had looked forward since the outbreak of the war could not be far away, and he was prepared to take great risks in order to speed the coming of peace. He, like House, therefore took the Memorandum very seriously. As House rose to leave that evening Wilson put his hand on his shoulder and said, "It would be impossible to imagine a more difficult task than the one placed in your hands, but you have accomplished it in a way beyond my expectations." House replied that he would feel pride enough if only Wilson could have an opportunity to carry out the plan. "My dear friend," the President responded, "you should be proud of yourself and not of me, since you have done it all."[102]

House saw the British Ambassador, Spring Rice, on the following morning, March 7. The United States, House said, would finish by taking part in the war. The moment for intervention had not yet come, but it would come, he said, and the President's ideas on the subject were in process of formation. House also told the Ambassador that Great Britain would do well to tighten her blockade of Germany as much as

[99] *ibid.*, February 22, 1916.
[100] *ibid.*, February 23, 1916.
[101] Plunkett Diary, February 23, 1916.
[102] House Diary, March 6, 1916.

possible, since it was one of the most effective weapons that the Allies possessed.

Then House went to the White House to help Wilson prepare the cablegram to Grey. Wilson wrote it out in shorthand and then transcribed it on his own typewriter. It read as follows:

> I reported to the President the general conclusions of our conference of the 14th of February and in the light of those conclusions he authorizes me to say that, so far as he can speak for the future action of the United States, he agrees to the memorandum with which you furnished me with only this correction that the word "probably" be added after the word "would" and before the word "leave" in line number nine.
>
> Please acknowledge receipt of this cable.[103]

House informed Grey on March 10 that the President himself had written the cablegram.[104]

Meanwhile, Briand and Jules Cambon had already expressed their opinions quite clearly and honestly to House in Paris. They later received a copy of the House-Grey Memorandum, but they never mentioned it in correspondence with the British Foreign Office. Grey, according to Lord Bertie, also reported House's suggested terms ("France to be evacuated, ditto Belgium, France to have Alsace-Lorraine in return for some Colonies.") to the French government. Jules Cambon, the Ambassador wrote in his diary, "laughed it to scorn."[105] Briand's and Jules Cambon's position continued to be as they had explained it to House: They would of course welcome American military support, but they were not interested in a negotiated peace, and could not, on account of French public opinion, afford to be interested so long as there was any hope of an Allied military victory.

Ambassador Jusserand's advice also reinforced the natural reluctance of leaders in Paris to entrust the fate of France to the American President. Jusserand, commenting on House's conversations with Briand and Jules Cambon, advised the Foreign Ministry on about February 17 that the President's sympathies naturally lay with the Allies, but that he desired above all else to maintain peaceful neutrality for his country.

---

[103] E. M. House to E. Grey, March 8, 1916, House Papers. The sentence as amended read: "Colonel House expressed the opinion that, if such a Conference met, it would probably secure peace on terms not unfavourable to the Allies; and, if it failed to secure peace, the United States would probably leave the Conference as a belligerent on the side of the Allies, if Germany was unreasonable."

[104] E. M. House to E. Grey, March 10, 1916, *ibid.*

[105] Lady Algernon G. Lennox (ed.), *The Diary of Lord Bertie of Thame*, I, 311, entry dated February 26, 1916.

House's plan was not absolutely impossible, Jusserand continued, but it was so problematical that it would be very unwise to base policy upon it. House had taken pleasure for several months in tantalizing people in secret. It was an election year, and this fact was not without effect on Wilson's desire to play the role of grand peacemaker. Actually, Jusserand concluded, House's proposals were designed to help the President.

There was not much more discussion of the House-Grey Memorandum in London than in Paris. Grey gave a copy to Ambassador Paul Cambon on February 22, 1916. Cambon, after reading the Memorandum, observed that neither French nor British public opinion would tolerate such a proposal. Sir Edward agreed, adding that Wilson was looking for a role to play in order to silence attacks on his foreign policy. It was difficult, he went on, not to view Colonel House as a naive electoral broker come to Europe to try to put an end to the severe press attacks on Wilson, and to give himself, House, the appearance of a mediator with whom one chatted in all the capitals.[106] These remarks did not necessarily reflect Grey's true opinions, as he may have been trying to avoid arousing the suspicions of the French, whom he knew to be implacably opposed to the very suggestion of a negotiated peace.

Lloyd George says in his memoirs that Grey believed that Wilson's insertion of the word "probably" in the Memorandum "completely changed the character of the proposal," and that Grey therefore did not think it worthwhile to communicate the Memorandum to the Allies.[107] Lloyd George, like most writers of memoirs, was incorrect. As we have just seen, Grey gave a copy of the Memorandum to the French Ambassador almost as soon as it was drafted. The truth was that Grey took neither Wilson's verbal alteration nor the Memorandum itself really seriously. He circulated a copy among the inner group of the Cabinet known as the War Committee soon after House left. Then, once he had received House's cable of March 8, he informed the War Committee that President Wilson had substantially confirmed House's offer. "We

---

[106] Paul Cambon wrote soon afterward to his son: "Fundamentally, I think that this Colonel House has come simply to ask that the English and French press spare his President so as not to embarrass him when he is opening his campaign for the presidential election. Wilson, Puritan, professor, disinterested, detached from everything in appearance, is, in sum, only a candidate, and all his policy consists of running with the hare and hunting with the hounds in order not to lose a voice." P. Cambon "à son fils," February 13, 1916, Henri Cambon (ed.), *Paul Cambon, Correspondance, 1870-1924* (3 vols.), III, 99.

[107] D. Lloyd George, *War Memoirs*, I, 412.

ought," he went on, "to come to some decision as to whether President Wilson's suggestion should be discarded, or regarded as premature, or encouraged. This decision depends, I imagine, upon the opinion of military and naval authorities on the prospects of the War. I should therefore be glad of a meeting of the War Committee to consider the question."[108]

Grey's request stimulated some discussion before the meeting took place. The only evidence of it now available is the passionate denunciation of the House-Grey Memorandum written by E. S. Montagu of the Foreign Office to the Prime Minister after a conversation with him on the subject. He agreed with Asquith, Montagu wrote, that Wilson and House were first pro-American, next pro-Democrat, and, lastly, pro-Ally. "They believe the ascendancy of their party is essential to American wellbeing. In other words their chief motive is *electioneering*." But this, Montagu went on, was no reason to discard the Memorandum. There were more compelling reasons. First, the proposal was not honest or fair to Germany. In fact, one could not be sure that House had not made a similar proposal, *mutatis mutandis*, to the Germans. Second, there was no guarantee that Wilson would stand by the terms that House had outlined. Third, these terms, even if Wilson stood by them, could only be justified on the assumption that the Allies could not win the war. Indeed, they were such that Prussian militarists could claim that they had won the war. "I fear," he concluded, "if House could deliver the goods the goods are not good enough. It is not enough that we should secure a partial victory—it is not enough that Germany should be punished by her own self inflicted material damage. We must win a complete victory and that I think House cannot secure us."[109] It is quite possible that Montagu was reflecting Asquith's opinions in this letter.

The War Committee met on about March 20 and concluded that it was no time to suggest any kind of peace negotiations to the French, now engaged in a life and death struggle for Verdun. Grey and his colleagues decided for the time being to leave the initiative entirely to the French. As Grey explained to House:

"I propose therefore (1st) to let M. Briand know that since you left I have heard if France and England were willing, President Wilson would on his own initiative summon a conference to end the war on the terms and in the spirit indicated by you at Paris and London.

---

[108] E. Grey to members of the War Committee, March 15, 1916, Asquith Papers.
[109] E. S. Montagu to H. H. Asquith, March 18, 1916, *ibid.*

"I will say (2) that we could not put the matter before any of the other Allies unless after consultation with and in concert with the French Government and do not therefore propose to mention this subject at the Conference of Allies in Paris this week.

"(3) That if M. Briand has any views to express on the subject he will no doubt let me know them either himself or through M. Jules Cambon, while we are in Paris.

"The Prime Minister and I go there on Thursday evening [March 30]. Of course there is nothing in this to prevent your making any communication to the French that you think opportune."[110]

Grey informed the French Ambassador on the same day that he wrote the above letter that he had received reliable assurances that President Wilson had confirmed House's statements and was ready to call a conference with a view to concluding peace on a basis of terms indicated by his emissary, provided that France and Britain expressed a desire that he should do so. Sir Edward agreed when Paul Cambon remarked that the moment did not seem favorable for such a move. Briand and Jules Cambon did not mention the Memorandum at the Paris conference, and Grey did not, therefore, bring it up.[111]

It would have been the end of an interesting but not too serious episode if Grey had had his way. But great delusions die slowly. House had heard what he wanted to hear in Paris and London. He had deluded himself into believing that the British and French wanted American mediation for a negotiated peace. It did not matter that this was not true, or that British and French leaders had said nothing to indicate that it was either true or possible. House was out of touch with reality by the time of his conversations in Paris and his return to London. He consequently not only misinformed and misled President Wilson but also encouraged him to base fundamental foreign policy on the assumption that American mediation was possible in the immediate future.

Let us now see some of the consequences of this miscalculation.

[110] E. Grey to E. M. House, March 24, 1916, House Papers.
[111] E. Grey to E. M. House, April 7, 1916, *ibid.*

CHAPTER V

The Armed Ship Imbroglio

AMERICAN foreign policy went hurtling in opposite directions in January 1916. While House was attempting to promote intimate American cooperation with the Allies, Wilson and Lansing struck out on a course of their own that caused the British and French to wonder whether they were playing a double game. It was their campaign against armed merchant ships.

The President and Secretary of State had contemplated changing the rules governing treatment of armed merchantmen in the late summer of 1915 in the wake of the *Baralong* affair and arrival of an armed British steamer at the Port of Newport News.[1] Discussion abated as months passed and no new incident occurred. Then came reports of the suspected torpedoing of the armed British liner *Persia* in the Mediterranean on December 30, 1915. This alleged attack, coupled with a request from the Italian Ambassador for a copy of a State Department memorandum of September 19, 1914, concerning armed merchantmen, set Lansing to thinking about the larger aspects of the question once again. It was obvious, he wrote to the President on January 2, 1916, that the administration would have to act quickly to revise its rules since it was manifestly unfair to insist that a submarine should stop and warn an armed merchantman when the latter had the capacity to destroy its foe without ado. "The chief difficulty with the situation seems to me," Lansing went on, "to lie in this: If some merchant vessels carry arms and others do not, how can a submarine determine this fact without exposing itself to great risk of being sunk? Unless the Entente Allies positively agree not to arm any of their merchant vessels and notify the Central Powers to that effect, is there not strong reason why a submarine should not warn a vessel before launching an attack?" The safest and fairest solution, he suggested, would be to insist that merchantmen cease to carry guns large enough to sink a submarine, and to treat armed merchant ships as warships when they visited American ports.[2]

[1] For the background, see A. S. Link, *Wilson*, III, 668-671.
[2] R. Lansing to W. W., January 2, 1916, *The Lansing Papers*, I, 332-333. Armed mer-

Lansing received no word from the White House. Then the arrival of the new armed Italian liner, *Giuseppe Verdi*, at New York on January 6, 1916, prompted Lansing to set to work on a solution of the problem. Perhaps it would be possible, he wrote in a memorandum on January 7, to obtain a new *modus vivendi* to govern the entire conduct of submarine warfare, one that would not only avert the possibility of fresh incidents but also remove the issue from dispute for the balance of the war. Merchantmen armed with cannon, he went on, had the power to destroy submarines by a single shot. It was hardly fair to insist that the latter should follow the rules of cruiser warfare at such great risk to their own safety. It was reasonable, therefore, to demand that merchantmen should carry no armament *whatever*, and to deal with armed vessels as if they were ships of war.[3]

Lansing, in sending this memorandum to Wilson, explained that he had been trying to think of some way to mitigate the horrors of submarine warfare. If the policy announced by the memorandum was put into effect, the American government could ask the Central Powers for broad new guarantees in return. "I am sure," he went on, "the Teutonic Powers would agree to this, and I cannot see how the Entente Powers could reasonably object to such an arrangement. . . . This plan would be practically a *modus vivendi* and could be made reciprocal on account of the activities of British submarines in the Baltic. Would you advise my attempting to obtain such agreements?"[4]

---

chantmen could not have been used as cargo carriers if they had been defined as warships, for belligerent warships could stay only twenty-four hours in neutral ports and take on only enough fuel to reach their nearest home port.

[3] R. Lansing, "Memorandum by the Secretary of State . . . ," January 7, 1916, *ibid.*, pp. 334-335.

[4] R. Lansing to W. W., January 7, 1916, *ibid.*, p. 334. There is a memorandum in the Lansing Diary, dated January 9, 1916 (printed in R. Lansing, *War Memoirs*, pp. 102-104), purporting to reveal Lansing's real reasons for proposing such a *modus vivendi* at this time. The American people, Lansing wrote, were simply too divided and insufficiently aroused against "the barbarism of the Germans" to warrant risking a direct clash with Germany over the submarine issue. The American government could not contemplate going to war without the support of a united people. Thus for the time being the administration had to try to come to agreement with Germany until the American people realized that the German government was "the inveterate foe of all the ideals which we hold sacred and for which this Republic stands."

This memorandum, it must be said somewhat bluntly, has all the appearances of having been composed *ex post facto* in order to rationalize a move that most contemporaries soon regarded as a blunder of the first order. The idea of the *modus vivendi* did not suddenly occur to Lansing; he and Wilson had been thinking along its lines since September of 1915. More important, Lansing was willing, apparently even eager,

The records do not reveal whether Wilson thought much or little about this matter. We do know that he, like Lansing, did not attempt to discover through his naval advisers or the Allied Admiralties whether the Allies had embarked or were about to embark upon a general practice of arming merchantmen, or whether one or two small guns on the stern of a ship did in fact constitute offensive capacity *vis-à-vis* a submarine.[5] We do know that Wilson, like Lansing, had not failed to notice the signs, evidenced earlier in response to the *Hesperian* incident of September 1915 and only recently in reaction to the *Persia* incident, that public and, more particularly, congressional, opinion was extremely averse to making an issue with Germany over armed ships. The President obviously welcomed Lansing's proposal as a possible definitive settlement of the submarine question and a sure safeguard against war with Germany. Finally, he actually thought that Lansing's *modus vivendi* would be advantageous to the Allies. As he later explained to Colonel House: "Germany is seeking to find an excuse to throw off all restraints in under-sea warfare. If she is permitted to assume that English steamers are armed she will have found the excuse. If the English will disarm their merchant ships she will be without excuse and the English will have made a capital stroke against her. We are amazed the English do not see this opportunity to gain a great advantage without losing anything."[6] Thus he sent a brief but encouraging word to Lansing on January 10: "This [the proposed memorandum] seems to me reasonable, and thoroughly worth trying."[7]

Lansing first turned to the immediate problem posed by the arrival of the *Giuseppe Verdi*. He saw the Italian Ambassador, Count Macchi di Cellere, twice on January 10 and tried to persuade him to have the

to push the Germans to the point of ruptured relations and probable war in the *Lusitania* negotiations only two weeks *after* allegedly composing the memorandum in question.

[5] Wilson could not have found an answer to this latter question if he had asked it. German naval authorities argued at this time, as did Lansing, that *any* armament on a merchant ship was offensive and justified the submarine commander in sinking the merchantman without warning. This of course would have been the safest and easiest policy, but the argument itself was based largely on supposition. A number of submarines had had skirmishes with armed merchantmen, but the submarines seemed to have had no difficulty in protecting themselves or getting away. See Exhibit 4 of Ambassador Gerard to the Secretary of State, February 14, 1916, *Foreign Relations, 1916, Supplement*, pp. 189-190. The only armed ship that had yet *sunk* a submarine, the *Baralong*, was a British Q-boat, that is, a warship disguised as a merchantman.

[6] W. W. to E. M. House, February 16, 1916, Wilson Papers.

[7] W. W. to R. Lansing, January 10, 1916, *The Lansing Papers*, I, 335.

ship's guns removed. Lansing recalled the British Ambassador's earlier compliance with a similar request and remarked gravely on the *Ancona's* firing on a submarine after being duly warned.[8] The Ambassador communicated with his government, and Lansing, on January 13, accepted an Italian counteroffer that seemed to gain his objective. It was a promise in writing from di Cellere that the *Giuseppe Verdi* would use her guns only for defensive purposes and, moreover, would not fire on a submarine after being warned. The State Department, in announcing the agreement, emphasized that it constituted no precedent.[9]

Lansing next carefully redrafted his memorandum on armed ships in the form of a letter to the Allied envoys in Washington and sent it to the White House on January 17. He had decided not to send the letter to the German and Austro-Hungarian representatives in Washington, Lansing said, because the Central Powers would probably return a speedy acceptance, and Allied failure to concur would only intensify the rising anti-Entente sentiment in the United States.[10] "This draft," Wilson replied immediately, "has my entire approval. I hope that you will send it to the Governments you have indicated to me; and I most sincerely hope that they will feel that we are right in our argument and suggestion and will be willing to cooperate with us in attaining the object we have in view, an object which they must surely wish to accomplish as earnestly as we do, and which this seems in the circumstances the only feasible way of reaching."[11]

Lansing consequently sent copies to the British, French, and Russian Ambassadors and the Belgian Minister on January 18, the Italian Ambassador on the following day, and the Japanese Ambassador—as an afterthought—on January 24. He began by expressing the American government's fervent desire to end the dangers to human life that stemmed from use of submarines as destroyers of commerce. The American government, he went on, did not believe that a belligerent should be denied the right to use submarines against maritime commerce, since they had obviously proved their usefulness. Human life at sea could be protected only if warships carefully followed the rules of cruiser warfare in attacking merchantmen. The trouble was that submarines could not observe these rules while attacking armed mer-

---

[8] Based in part on the *New York Times*, January 11, 1916.

[9] *ibid.*, January 14, 1916; the Secretary of State to the Secretary of the Treasury, January 13, 1916, *Foreign Relations, 1916, Supplement*, p. 750.

[10] R. Lansing to W. W., January 17, 1916, *The Lansing Papers*, I, 336.

[11] W. W. to R. Lansing, January 17, 1916, *ibid.*

chantmen without running intolerable risks. Merchant ships had been permitted to arm in the past for defense against pirates and privateers, and armament that was once defensive in character had, on account of the emergence of the submarine, become in fact offensive. It did not seem "just or reasonable" to require submarines to expose themselves to risk of almost certain destruction by armed ships.

"It would therefore," Lansing continued, coming to the nub of the matter, "appear to be a reasonable and reciprocally just arrangement if it could be agreed by the opposing belligerents that submarines should be caused to adhere strictly to the rules of international law in the matter of stopping and searching merchant vessels, determining their belligerent nationality, and removing the crews and passengers to places of safety before sinking the vessels as prizes of war, and that merchant vessels of belligerent nationality should be prohibited and prevented from carrying any armament whatsoever." The American government would be pleased to approach the Central Powers with a view to their cooperation should the Allied governments approve the formula. "I should add," Lansing concluded threateningly, "that my Government is impressed with the reasonableness of the argument that a merchant vessel carrying an armament of any sort, in view of the character of submarine warfare and the defensive weakness of undersea craft, should be held to be an auxiliary cruiser and so treated by a neutral as well as by a belligerent government, and is seriously considering instructing its officials accordingly."[12]

Spring Rice cabled a paraphrase of the Secretary of State's "long and deplorable letter" to the British Foreign Office [in Telegram No. 223(R)] on January 21, 1916.[13] It arrived at a time when Sir Edward Grey and others at Whitehall were profoundly disturbed by unmistakable signs of rising Anglo-American tension. Resentment against the British maritime system, exacerbated by the State Department's stern note of October 21, was now obviously increasing. Spring Rice sent a long dispatch on November 21, for example, warning that the movement in the United States for reprisals against Great Britain could reach dangerous proportions, and urging authorities in London to expedite shipment of German goods in Holland to the United States and

[12] The Secretary of State to the British Ambassador, January 18, 1916, *Foreign Relations, 1916, Supplement*, pp. 146-148.

[13] C. Spring Rice to the Foreign Office, January 21, 1916, Telegram No. 223(R). copy in the Papers of Sir Horace Plunkett, Horace Plunkett Foundation, London; hereinafter cited as the Plunkett Papers.

come to terms with American meat packers. Former Senator Elihu Root talked privately with the British and French Ambassadors in Washington in late November and with a group of British officials in New York City soon afterward. He warned that a massive anti-British coalition was in process of being formed to apply pressure on Congress and said that it was unthinkable that the London government should not try to give relief to legitimate American commerce. "It is unnecessary to inform you," the unnamed person who reported on the New York meeting wrote to Grey in a telegram, "that Senator Root is foremost statesman in this country, and that his heart is wholly with the Allies." Grey was so impressed that he circulated this report in a Cabinet paper.[14]

Spring Rice's dispatches became increasingly apprehensive in late December and early January. He reported at the turn of the year, for example, that Congress might impose an arms embargo by nationalizing the manufacture of munitions and incorporate the provision into the army bill, thus making it impossible for the President to veto it.[15] "The spirit of Congress is somewhat menacing," the Ambassador warned again on January 13.[16] "The balance of opinion seems to be," he wrote on January 24, "that there is a growing feeling in Congress against England . . . & English sea power & that this may take the form of some embargo measure."[17]

Grey was even more disturbed by the knowledge that it would be extremely difficult, if not impossible, for the British government to make any important concessions to the United States. The Northcliffe press was at this very moment waging a fierce campaign against the Asquith government for allegedly failing to use British sea power effectively, and moderate editors were beginning to echo the accusation.[18] Officials in the Foreign Office had already drafted a reply to the American note of October 21, and it had been revised by Lord Curzon and Lord Lansdowne and sent to Paris for the approval of the French government. It attempted to prove that English maritime

[14] Cabinet paper captioned simply *Printed for the use of the Cabinet, November 1915*, Asquith Papers.

[15] See also C. Spring Rice to the Foreign Office, November 29, 1915, *ibid.* for another gloomy report.

[16] C. Spring Rice to E. Grey, January 13, 1916, S. Gwynn (ed.), *Letters of Spring Rice*, II, 308.

[17] C. Spring Rice to R. L. Borden, January 24, 1916, Borden Papers. This is cited as evidence of the general tenor of the Ambassador's dispatches to the Foreign Office.

[18] e.g., London *Westminster Gazette* and London *Pall Mall Gazette*, January 15, 1916.

measures had not in fact injured legitimate American trade with the European neutrals or, to a large degree, even with Germany.[19] This was more or less true,[20] but affirmation of the facts might not assuage American opinion, for the note made absolutely no concessions on the basic principles in dispute.[21]

It was all the more important to avoid any open provocation of American official and public opinion, Grey knew, because the Allies were now completely dependent upon American raw materials and munitions. There were, moreover, signs that they would soon become dependent upon American credit as well. The main problem was finding dollars to maintain the exchange rate and pay for the huge excess of imports over exports to the United States. The Anglo-French loan of 1915 had been an outright failure, if not a disaster. Anglo-French bonds had fallen to 94 by January 1916, in spite of large purchases by the British Treasury. Meanwhile the Treasury had resorted to shipment of gold and sale or hypothecation of British-owned American securities in order to obtain exchange. The total gold stock of the kingdom did not exceed £186,000,000, and any large inroad would drive the Treasury off the gold standard. The total value of United States dollar securities held in Great Britain was between £350,000,000 and £450,000,000. It was enough to see the Treasury through perhaps to the end of 1916, but disaster, "final collapse," threatened after that date. Any action meanwhile by the American government, no matter how seemingly trivial on the American side, impairing the flow of credit to the United Kingdom, or any change in American opinion that would affect the willingness of bankers to lend, could be fatal to the Allied cause.[22]

[19] Grey contrived to avoid sending the note until April 1916.

[20] Actually, the British blockade was still full of large holes, especially insofar as food was concerned. From January 1915 through November 1915 some 34,000 tons of butter, 11,000 tons of cocoa powder, 121,000 tons of coffee, 25,000 tons of eggs, 103,000 tons of herring, and vast quantities of other foodstuffs, some of which slipped through the British blockade, were exported from Holland to Germany. See Minister Richard von Kühlmann to J. von Kriege, January 14, 1916, German F. O. Archives. "The War Minister told me yesterday evening that he had not realized previously that imports from Denmark and Holland had the importance which he now, after he has gone into the matter deeply, realizes to be true. We would actually be without tea, coffee, or cigars if imports from these countries ceased." "Daily Report of Captain Mann," dated Pless, January 24, 1916, A. von Tirpitz, *Politische Dokumente*, ii, 469.

[21] *Printed for the use of the Cabinet, January 1916. CONFIDENTIAL January 24, 1916. Draft Reply to the United States Note of November 5, 1915*, Asquith Papers.

[22] The above paragraph is based upon the review of the military and financial situation at the beginning of 1916 printed in *Cabinet Committee on the Co-ordination of*

Uncle Samuels
"It pays to be neutral"
A British View of American Neutrality
Passing Show (London)

Finally, Grey was most upset by the strong suspicion, indeed, conviction, that Lansing's *modus vivendi* was part of a broad new understanding between Germany and the United States on the conduct of

Military and Financial Effort. SECRET. SYNOPSIS OF EVIDENCE, printed at the
Foreign Office, January 31, 1916, *ibid.*

submarine warfare. Reports that such would be the culmination of the *Lusitania* negotiations then in progress had poured into the British Foreign Office during early January. Spring Rice cabled on January 10 that it was generally believed in Washington that Germany would not consent to an agreement on the *Lusitania* until the United States had obtained concessions on the Allied blockade. He warned the Foreign Office to expect vigorous American action soon.[23] "The Germans are now praising the President, Lansing and Congress and presumably have received most satisfactory assurances," the Ambassador wrote on the following day.[24] During the next few days a remarkable series of articles by the American journalist, Frank H. Simonds, appeared in the New York *Tribune*. He reported that the administration, with an eye on the coming presidential campaign, had promised vigorous action against the Allied blockade in return for German concessions in the *Lusitania* controversy. Summaries of these articles were cabled to London, as well as to Paris. Spring Rice later informed House that Lansing had told the Italian Ambassador that "his purpose in proposing the disarming of Allied merchantmen was to please Germany and get a favorable settlement of the Lusitania controversy."[25] It is difficult to believe that Lansing could have been guilty of such a blunder, but Spring Rice undoubtedly cabled such a report to Grey. "It is," the Ambassador wrote to the Canadian Prime Minister about the proposed *modus vivendi*, "no doubt part of the proposed agreement with Germany on the Lusitania question. If Germany makes such an agreement our position here will be changed for the worse. And this we must regard as possible."[26]

This was the context of apprehension in which Grey read Spring Rice's Telegram No. 223(R) on about January 22. He was more upset by what the note seemed to impend for American relations *vis-à-vis* both Germany and England than alarmed about its immediate impact on the conduct of maritime warfare. The British had actually armed very few ships and recently none of those going to the United States, since the Germans had conducted virtually no submarine operations in British waters since September. "I have only once before seen Sir Edward so grave and disappointed," Page reported to the State Department after a conference at the Foreign Office on January 25, "and

---

[23] Ambassador Spring Rice to the Foreign Office, January 10, 1916, *ibid.*

[24] C. Spring Rice to H. Plunkett, January 11, 1916, Plunkett Papers.

[25] House Diary, March 7, 1916.

[26] C. Spring Rice to R. L. Borden, January 24, 1916, Borden Papers.

that was when he informed me that the British had sent the German Government an ultimatum. After he discovered that I had not been informed of the subject he seemed disposed to say little. He did say, however, that he indulged the hope that the Department had not foreseen the results of the proposal which was wholly in favor of the Germans theoretically and practically [and] wholly against the Allies. Then he asked me for House's address because, as I gathered, he had talked with him at my table so frankly and freely about the relations of our two Governments that he thought he ought to inform House that he [did not] then know that this proposal would come. He spoke as one speaks of a great calamity. He said that he would not mention the subject in his speech in the House of Commons to-morrow because the announcement that such a proposal had been made by the United States would cause a storm that would drive every other subject out of the mind of the House and of the country." Page then added his own maledictions against the *modus vivendi.*[27]

Perhaps it would be possible, Grey thought, to save the situation by persuading the American government to withdraw its proposal. Hence he dispatched the sternest note that he ever penned for the purview of the Washington administration. "I regard letter as described by you," he wrote in a cablegram to Spring Rice on January 25 (Telegram No. 179), "with most painful surprise: it had seemed to me incredible that upshot of controversy about German submarine warfare would be that United States Government would propose to justify and legalize wholesale sinking of merchant vessels by German submarines and to deprive British vessels of the chance of defence which the United States Government have hitherto recognised as legitimate." Merchant ships with guns on the stern were not in fact superior in armament to submarines. The United States was proposing that "sinking of merchant vessels shall be the rule and not the exception and that no chance of defence shall be allowed." Grey continued:

"Furthermore this is proposed by the United States when they have already presented in a note certain demands which if conceded would make it impossible for Great Britain and the Allies to prevent free export and import from or to Germany of all goods of any description whether contraband or not through neutral countries thus preventing us from applying to present conditions the principles applied by the United States Government itself in the Civil War. New methods

[27] Ambassador Page to the Secretary of State, January 25, 1916, *Foreign Relations, 1916, Supplement*, p. 151.

of warfare are to be conceded to Germany while the Allies are to be deprived of previously recognised means of pressure or even defence.

"I cannot adequately express the disappointment and dismay with which such an attitude on the part of the United States will be viewed here. . . ."[28]

Meanwhile, the British government would have to plan in concert with the French authorities to meet contingencies. Thus Grey dispatched a copy of Spring Rice's Telegram No. 223(R) to Paris on January 25 and gave a copy of his own Telegram No. 179 to Ambassador Paul Cambon.

Lord Bertie delivered Spring Rice's telegram to Briand on the same day. Sir Edward, Bertie added, had asked him to emphasize the extreme gravity of the situation and to request urgently that Briand give his reaction to a plan that had occurred to Grey. It was to ask the American government to send two representatives to Europe to discuss the general questions of the submarine war and the blockade with the French and British governments. Sir Edward, Bertie went on, could announce the plan in general terms in the House of Commons on the following day if Briand thought well of the idea. Briand thought very little of the suggestion. It was bound, he replied, to result in an outcome favorable to the Americans, and this in turn could only help the German cause. In other words, it was better to avoid a confrontation because the Americans were bound to win an argument on the legal issues.

Grey at this very time faced a massive effort by the Northcliffe press and other newspapers to force transfer of control over blockade measures from the Foreign Office to the Admiralty. It was focused in the House of Commons in a resolution offered by Arthur Shirley Benn, Unionist (Conservative) member for Plymouth, to the effect that all overseas traffic with Germany should be prevented by blockade.[29] Sir Edward beat off this attack by a masterful speech in Commons on January 26, 1916.[30] There was not much more that he could do but await the outcome of negotiations in Washington. Perhaps Lansing would withdraw the *modus vivendi*. If he carried out his threat to treat armed merchantmen as warships and demanded a direct

---

[28] E. Grey to C. Spring Rice, Telegram No. 179, January 25, 1916, copies in the Wilson and Plunkett Papers.

[29] *New York Times*, January 16, 1916; W. H. Page to W. W., January 22, 1916, Wilson Papers.

[30] *New York Times*, January 27, 1916.

British answer to the American note's indictment of British maritime practices, then it might be necessary to abandon the blockade altogether and to rest British practice squarely on international law. He would wait and see what had to be done.

Spring Rice called at the State Department in the morning of January 27 to deliver a copy of Grey's Telegram No. 179. Lansing read it carefully and then remarked that he had made his proposal in the conviction that the submarine, a new weapon, had to be recognized, and in order to prevent the cruel loss of innocent lives. He repeated the argument of the *modus* concerning the helplessness of a submarine before an armed merchant ship. What, Spring Rice asked, would the American government do if Germany continued to sink ships without warning after the Allies disarmed their ships? That, Lansing replied, would be an unfriendly act, a *casus belli*.

Spring Rice virtually sneered at this response. The American government, he said, would do in the future what it had done in the past—investigate, procrastinate, and then merely express displeasure. "If the agreement were accepted," he said, "the only difference in the situation would be that the ships attacked, like the 'Ancona,' would be treated as a helpless prey to be approached and destroyed with impunity by gun fire and torpedo." Lansing apparently held his temper and replied by reading from the British Admiralty's instructions to armed merchantmen (they proved, he said, that ships carried armament for the express purpose of destroying submarines) and citing the *Baralong* case. The American government, he warned, was considering treating armed merchantmen as cruisers, forbidding its citizens to travel on armed vessels, and taking drastic action against Allied ships that had been guilty of using the American flag for purposes of concealment (as the *Baralong* had done). Spring Rice, in a final taunt, intimated that he well understood that the *modus vivendi* "was part of a larger agreement which was being negotiated with Germany." Lansing "at once repudiated such a statement as wholly contrary to the fact."[31]

Lansing was plainly hurt and perhaps a little dazed by the ferociousness of the assaults by Grey, Page, and Spring Rice. He sent a copy

[31] C. Spring Rice to E. Grey, January 27, 1916, Wilson and Plunkett Papers. The British Embassy in Paris sent a paraphrase of this dispatch to the French Foreign Ministry, adding that Spring Rice had stated that his conversation with Lansing was of a friendly character!

of Grey's Telegram No. 179 and of Page's dispatch of January 25 to the President soon after Spring Rice left. "It seems to me," the Secretary of State wrote in a covering letter, "that the British Government expected us to denounce submarine warfare as inhuman and to deny the right to use submarines in attacking commercial vessels; and that these statements by Sir Edward Grey evidence his great disappointment that we have failed to be the instrument to save British commerce from attack by Germany." Page, he went on, obviously had absorbed too much British atmosphere. Nothing could be done about the *modus vivendi* until the Allies returned an official reply. If they refused to accept it, as seemed likely, then the American government should come to some conclusion about travel by Americans on merchantmen that were armed offensively. "I doubt," Lansing concluded, "whether we can insist that vessels so armed can be considered other than as auxiliary cruisers of the respective navies of the Allies."[32]

Wilson was in New York opening his preparedness tour on January 27 and did not see Lansing's letter until the following day. He did not answer it in writing but gave Lansing his reactions during a forty-five-minute conference in the Green Room of the White House just before dinner on January 28. No record of this conversation exists, but we can be fairly confident that Wilson said that he agreed entirely with Lansing and suggested that Lansing explain the situation to Colonel House and ask him to intercede in Paris and London. This, at any rate, is what Lansing did once he was sure that House was in the French capital.[33] The Secretary of State (or his secretary) also described the *modus vivendi* to reporters on the same day that he talked to the President, and newspapers reported the proposal in full and accurate detail on January 29.[34] This disclosure, it seems reasonable to conclude, was further evidence that the President and Secretary of State meant to persevere even to the point of adopting the preventive and punitive measures that Lansing had mentioned in his conversation with Spring Rice.

Lansing had in fact already given conclusive evidence of intention in a conversation with Baron Zwiedinek, Austro-Hungarian Chargé d'Affaires, on January 26, 1916. Zwiedinek had come to protest against the American government's action in permitting the armed Italian liner

[32] R. Lansing to W. W., January 27, 1916, *The Lansing Papers*, I, 338.
[33] R. Lansing to E. M. House, February 2, 1916, *ibid.*, p. 339.
[34] e. g., *New York Times*, January 29, 1916.

Verona to enter the Port of New York on January 24.[35] Lansing told him that the *Verona* would be granted clearance only because the Italian Ambassador had pledged that her guns would not be used offensively against a submarine. He knew that this was a grave question for the Central Powers, Lansing went on, and he had already proposed to the Allies that they abstain from arming merchantmen in return for German promises already given. Zwiedinek responded quickly to this momentous revelation. The German and Austro-Hungarian governments, he said, both held that submarines could not warn armed merchantmen and were contemplating issuing a declaration to this effect. The American government, Lansing replied, would "welcome it" if the Central Powers announced that submarines would deal with merchantmen with one or more guns as if they were auxiliary cruisers. It would however, he added, be advisable for them to wait a reasonable time, perhaps a month, in order to see whether the Allies would accept the *modus vivendi* that he had proposed. Zwiedinek immediately sent a report of this conversation by wireless to Vienna by way of Berlin.[36]

Zwiedinek's telegram brought the first good news that the German Chancellor and Foreign Office had received from Washington since the settlement of the second *Arabic* crisis.[37] Lansing's declaration could not have come at a more opportune time. The navy had long contended that submarines could not safely surface and warn armed merchantmen before sinking them. Commander Max Valentiner of the *U38* had captured a copy of the British Admiralty's instructions to captains of armed merchantmen aboard the armed steamer *Woodfield* on November 3, 1915. These instructions had confirmed German suspicions that armed British merchantmen were in fact obliged to hunt down, attack, and destroy submarines. Moreover, one Captain Kophamel, commander of the submarine flotilla at Pola, had sent a report to the German Admiralty on January 15 recommending that submarines be permitted to sink armed merchantmen in the Mediterranean without warning.[38] Most important, publication in German newspapers

[35] *ibid.*, January 27, 1916.

[36] Ambassador Bernstorff to the Foreign Office, January 20 [26], 1916, transmitting Chargé Zwiedinek to Baron Burián, German F. O. Archives; also printed in *The Lansing Papers*, I, 337.

[37] A news dispatch summarizing the reports about the *modus vivendi* that were published in the American press on January 29 also excited official German circles at the same time. See Karl von Treutler (Foreign Office representative at Supreme Headquarters) to the Foreign Office, January 29 and 31, 1916, German F. O. Archives.

[38] A. Spindler, *La Guerre Sous-Marine*, III, 114-115.

of the correspondence between the German and British Foreign Offices over the *Baralong* incident had just set off a storm of emotional comment and demands for severe reprisals.[39]

Holtzendorff did not miss the opportunity that these circumstances afforded to press hard for one form of intensified submarine warfare. He saw the Emperor on January 24, presented Kophamel's report, and urged unrestricted operations against armed merchantmen in all theaters immediately. The Emperor approved at once and instructed the head of the Admiralty to confer with the Chancellor so that the Foreign Office could make necessary diplomatic preparations.[40]

It would probably have been impossible for Bethmann to reverse this decision had he been disposed to try, and he must have read Zwiedinek's dispatch and news reports from America with unalloyed relief. If the American government would really welcome unlimited submarine operations against armed merchantmen, then, perhaps, he could find a way out of his intolerable impasse with Tirpitz, Holtzendorff, and Falkenhayn and an almost certain guarantee against a fatal break with the United States. Indeed, solid understanding with the United States on all aspects of the submarine war, to the great disadvantage of the Allies, would now be possible if he could only force the navy to accept the *modus vivendi* in its entirety. Bethmann was thus entirely responsive when he discussed policy toward armed merchantmen with Holtzendorff in the first days of February. The navy was entirely right, he said; the only question now was one of proper timing, so that the German government would appear to be granting Lansing's request for a breathing spell. Meanwhile, the Foreign Office would draft a declaration in cooperation with the Admiralty.[41]

Bethmann undertook the diplomatic preparations while work on the declaration of unlimited submarine warfare against armed ships went forward. "Germany and Austria Hungary," he informed Bernstorff in a personal wireless message on February 6, "will publish within few days declaration welcomed by Mr. Lansing that hereafter enemy merchant vessels armed with guns will be treated as auxiliary cruisers. All neutrals will be informed accordingly. Corresponding orders to naval commanders not to be put in force before end February. Please inform Mr. Lansing immediately."[42]

[39] *New York Times*, January 19, 1916.

[40] A. Spindler, *La Guerre Sous-Marine*, III, 115.

[41] *ibid.*, pp. 115-116; A. von Tirpitz, *Politische Dokumente*, II, 469-470.

[42] T. von Bethmann Hollweg to the German Embassy, Washington, Wireless Telegram No. 29, February 6, 1916, German F. O. Archives.

Zwiedinek, at Bernstorff's request, delivered this message to Lansing on February 9. The Secretary of State was disturbed only by Bethmann's assumption that he, Lansing, had said that he would "welcome" an all-out German campaign against armed merchantmen. He and Zwiedinek, he explained, had discussed the *modus vivendi* in their conference on January 26, and Zwiedinek had said that the Central Powers were contemplating a campaign against armed ships and asked when Lansing thought the campaign should begin. He had then replied, Lansing went on, "that the sooner it was done the better."[43] He had not used the word "welcome." He now realized that he had used unfortunate language, Lansing said, and he would be grateful if Zwiedinek informed his government of this conversation.[44] Bernstorff also talked to Lansing about Bethmann's message on February 10 or 11. Consequently the two following wireless telegrams went at once to Berlin:

[From Bernstorff] I have informed Mr. Lansing of contents of your wireless No. 29. He has not yet received answer from our enemies concerning his proposal to disarm merchant vessels. Mr. Lansing does not wish to give me copy of his note till he has received an answer which he expects will be refusal. Mr. Lansing reminded me of fact from beginning of controversy with us the American Government always spoke of unarmed merchant vessels (American note of May thirteenth nineteen hundred fifteen). [In other words, the United States had never made an issue of armed ships anyway.] Regarding objections of Mr. Lansing to the word "welcome" I refer to Baron Zwidineks [*sic*] wireless number 52.

[From Zwiedinek] I have informed Mr. Lansing of contents of your radiotelegram concerning armed enemy merchant vessels. On this occasion Mr. Lansing called my attention to a misunderstanding created by the

[43] Lansing, in a memorandum that he wrote immediately after reading a copy of Zwiedinek's dispatch of January 26, had reminded himself to tell Zwiedinek, when the opportunity arose, that he had not used the word "welcome" but had said that "if German and Austrian Govts. intended to issue such a declaration the sooner it was done the better." R. Lansing, "Memorandum by the Secretary of State," January 26, 1916, *The Lansing Papers*, I, 337. "(In making this latter statement," Lansing wrote in a memorandum immediately after his conversation with the Chargé on February 9, "I had in mind, though I could not tell Zwiedinek, the desirability of having a declaration of this sort before the final settlement of the *Lusitania* case, if such a policy was to be adopted, as it would materially affect the assurances which the German Government had given respecting merchant vessels, and I did not wish that the case after settlement should be reopened.)" R. Lansing, "Memorandum by the Secretary of State . . . , February 9, 1916," *ibid.*, p. 341. It is hardly necessary to point out that this is a curious explanation.

[44] *ibid.*, pp. 341-342.

use of the word "welcome." He did not wish to imply any initiative on his part and would not like this idea to prevail. Mr. Lansing however repeated that in his opinion there are certain reasons which might justify such a declaration on our part.

Please acknowledge receipt of wireless as Mr. Lansing wishes to know that his point of view is perfectly clear to my Government.[45]

These telegrams, arriving at the Foreign Office on February 11, brought Bethmann new assurance that the American government would acquiesce in all-out war against armed merchantmen. The Foreign Office had, in fact, on the preceding day given Gerard a copy of a declaration that Bethmann, Jagow, and Holtzendorff had all approved on February 8. It reviewed British practice in using armed merchantmen as submarine destroyers, repeated the arguments in Lansing's *modus vivendi*, and announced that German naval forces would soon receive instructions to treat armed merchantmen as warships. Accompanying the memorandum were a number of exhibits, including the text of the British Admiralty's instructions to armed ships.[46]

Bethmann gave the signal as soon as the telegrams from Washington arrived on February 11, and the Admiralty sent the following orders to the High Seas Fleet, the Navy Corps in Flanders, and the submarine flotilla at Pola:

Enemy merchantmen carrying guns should be regarded as warships and destroyed by all means.

Commanders should not, however, forget that errors which they might

---

[45] Both telegrams were sent in German Embassy to the Foreign Office, February 11, 1916, German F. O. Archives. Baron Burián acknowledged receipt of the message on February 20, whereupon Zwiedinek wrote a long wireless dispatch in reply on the same day recounting in detail his conversation with Lansing on January 26 and saying that Lansing actually had used the word "welcome." Baron Zwiedinek to Baron Burián, February 20, 1916, copy in *ibid.*

Of course the important point is that Lansing did give very positive encouragement to a submarine campaign against armed ships regardless of which word or phrase he used. This little dispute merits such attention only because Lansing later made so much of it in an effort to escape responsibility for his blunder. He left a memorandum in his diary ("Baron Erich Zwiedinek," dated November 1916) saying that Bernstorff had forced Zwiedinek against his will to send his dispatch of January 26, 1916, reporting that Lansing would "welcome" a submarine campaign against armed ships. Bernstorff had done this, Lansing wrote, in order to embarrass him and force his resignation. Lansing repeated this story in his *War Memoirs*, pp. 113-115. Both versions of this tale seem to have been almost entirely fabricated.

[46] Ambassador Gerard to the Secretary of State, February 10, 1916, 10 p.m., *Foreign Relations, 1916, Supplement*, pp. 163-166.

commit could lead to a rupture with neutral powers and that one should destroy a ship on account of its armament only if he is absolutely certain of the existence of this armament.

This order will go into force only on *February* 29 on account of the warnings sent to the neutrals by diplomatic routes.[47]

At the same time both the Vienna and Berlin governments announced that the campaign would begin on February 29.[48]

Lansing received a copy of the German memorandum[49] from the decoding room on Saturday, February 12, and took it home for study. He must have talked freely with reporters before leaving his office, for the correspondent for the New York *World* reported that "administration officials" were not disturbed by protests in the British press against the proposed *modus vivendi* and the new German submarine policy. A "high official," this reporter continued, said that the United States Government would have to make a formal response to the German memorandum before it went into effect, even though the Allies had not acted on the *modus vivendi*, because changes would have to be made in rules governing treatment of foreign merchantmen in American ports.[50] The *New York Times* correspondent added that there was a strong possibility that the American government would define armed merchantmen as warships and warn American citizens against traveling on them.[51] The same correspondent reported on February 14 that a careful canvass of official circles had failed to turn up any indication that the administration intended to make any protest against the new submarine campaign or was unsympathetic to the German point of view.[52]

This, it will be remembered, was the very time that House, back in

[47] A. Spindler, *La Guerre Sous-Marine*, III, 116-117.

[48] *New York Times*, February 11, 1916; New York *World*, February 12, 1916; Ambassador Gerard to the Secretary of State, February 10, 1916, 1 p.m., *Foreign Relations 1916, Supplement*, p. 163.

[49] Gerard telegraphed only the memorandum; he sent the enclosures by mail.

[50] New York *World*, February 13, 1916.

[51] *New York Times*, February 13, 1916.

[52] *ibid.*, February 15, 1916. These reports stimulated divided editorial comment. The New York *World*, February 15, 1916, New York *Nation*, CII (February 17, 1916), 183, and *Springfield* (Mass.) *Republican*, February 15, 1916, for example, defended the point of view that armed merchantmen were now in fact auxiliary cruisers, although the latter two questioned whether the American government was wise or right in changing the rules governing the treatment of armed merchantmen in American ports. The *New York Times*, February 14, 1916, and *New Republic*, VI (February 19, 1916), 57-59, on the other hand, declared that insistence upon adoption of the *modus vivendi* by the Allies would be a gravely prejudicial act.

London after his visit to Germany and France, was pressing toward his great goal of Anglo-American *entente*. More important, it was also the time when Wilson and Lansing seemed to be nearing agreement with Germany in the *Lusitania* negotiations. Receipt in London of press reports of the German armed ship memorandum and the American government's intention to acquiesce, even cooperate, in the new submarine campaign convinced Grey that the ugly rumors about a German-American understanding had been true.[53] He was disgusted and discouraged, and, on about February 14, he drafted a commentary to prepare the Cabinet for the Anglo-American crisis that impended. He first summarized the *modus vivendi* and then went on: "The substance of the United States plea and proposal appears to be that because the British Navy has driven German commerce from the seas, destroyed her cruisers and battleships that have left their ports, and blockaded the German navy in their home waters, free play should be given to the only hostile craft that keep the seas, a type of vessel which is physically incapable of complying with the undisputed laws of war as to capture, visit, and search, and the Allies should refrain from arming their merchant vessels, and quietly submit to capture and destruction. Moreover, the United States proposals are being made simultaneously with the issue of a German memorandum intimating that after the 1st March all enemy merchantmen carrying guns are not entitled to be regarded as peaceful merchantmen, and that they will be treated as belligerents."

Grey next reviewed legal authorities to prove that merchantmen had an undisputed right to arm defensively and defend themselves. The American government, he continued, would probably admit that this was a sound legal position and argue that development of the submarine had made it irrelevant. He then concluded with the following bitter accusations:

"The proposal of the United States is an attempt to re-adjust the balance of sea power in favour of our enemies by requesting the Allies to refrain from a practice which has been recognised from time immemorial down to the present day, and which has proved its effectiveness in the present war, in order that the Germans may not be deprived

---

[53] As they also convinced other European statesmen, notably in the French and Italian governments. The French Foreign Ministry, in commenting on the matter in a dispatch to the British Foreign Office on February 19, 1916, wrote that Lansing had obviously submitted his *modus vivendi* in accord with the German government. The Italian Foreign Minister told the American Ambassador in Rome that the German armed ship decree was the "first result of the American note." Ambassador T. N. Page to the Secretary of State, February 14, 1916, *Foreign Relations, 1916*, p. 169.

of the use of submarines in their interruption of enemy commerce, which they have only been able to render effective by disregarding not only the laws of nations but the elementary laws of humanity. . . .

"The presentation of these proposals by the United States simultaneously with the issue of the German memorandum has the appearance of producing a grave position of affairs in our relations with America. We have not yet received any official intimation of the terms of settlement of the 'Lusitania' dispute between Germany and the United States, but I cannot help feeling that the American proposals form part of a *transaction* between the two Powers. It is, if not unfriendly, at least unneutral of the United States to take this opportunity of reversing the whole of their previous attitude in regard to the freedom of neutrals to travel on belligerent merchant-vessels, armed or unarmed, if the reports in the newspapers rightly represent the United States view. Our conduct of naval warfare has endangered no single neutral or noncombatant belligerent life. . . . On the other hand, the result of the German submarine policy has been to bring death and destruction indiscriminately to their enemies and friends, and the price that the Allies are asked to pay for a German promise to refrain in the future from the commission of illegal and inhumane acts at sea is to give up a legitimate practice which has operated solely to the detriment of enemy combatants. The Allies are being asked to join in the paying for the loss of American lives on the 'Lusitania,' and their merchant-ships are threatened with exclusion from United States ports if they do not accept the American proposals."[54]

The Cabinet met in Washington in the morning of February 15 for the first full dress discussion of the armed ship question since the submission of the *modus vivendi*. Wilson, it is clear, had concluded that he would have to take a more active role and steer the ship of state in a new direction. Having encouraged Lansing to proceed without much thought about the consequences to Anglo-American relations, he must have been startled by Grey's reaction to the *modus vivendi* as expressed in Page's telegram of January 25 and Grey's own dispatch to Spring Rice of the same date, a copy of which was sent to the White House. Wilson had to admit that Grey was right in accusing the United States of threatening to change the rules during wartime to the great advantage of the Central Powers. The whole *démarche*, he

---

[54] *Printed for the use of the Cabinet. February 1916. CONFIDENTIAL*, copy in the Asquith Papers. Internal evidence shows that Grey wrote this memorandum no earlier than February 13 and no later than February 15, 1916.

probably thought, had been a mistake. Wilson and Colonel House discussed the affair after the latter returned from England in early March. "The President took occasion," House recorded in his diary, "to blame himself and Lansing for allowing this controversy to crop out. I thought it more Lansing's fault than his. Nevertheless, the President insisted upon taking the blame along with Lansing."[55]

The most important factor causing Wilson's shift in policy was surely knowledge that a decree implementing the *modus vivendi* unilaterally would wreck House's scheme for mediation. House himself had finally made this fact clear. Lansing informed him of the *modus vivendi* and British reactions on February 2,[56] and House replied directly to Wilson begging him not to take action "upon any of the pending questions between our government and that of the belligerents until I confer with you and the Secretary of State."[57] No one mentioned the *modus vivendi* in Paris, but House discovered British feeling on his return to London on February 9. Page was almost irrational on the subject, and Grey must have discussed it also, although the House diary is silent on this point, as on many others. House had his longest converations about armed ships with Sir Horace Plunkett on February 12, 13, and 14, and Plunkett appealed to him on the latter date "to cable the President strongly urging an abandonment of the proposal to the Allies, as bound to exasperate Anglo-American relations."[58] House sent an urgent message to Washington on that same afternoon, as follows: ". . . There are so many other issues involved in the controversy concerning armed merchantmen that I sincerely hope you will leave it in abeyance until I return. I cannot emphasize too strongly the importance of this."[59] It arrived at the State Department at 7.06 p.m., and Wilson and Lansing surely read it that same evening.

Wilson and Lansing conferred before the Cabinet meeting on the following day, February 15. We have no record of their conversation, but circumstantial evidence indicates strongly that they agreed that they had made a serious mistake in proposing the *modus vivendi* at this particular time, certainly in threatening to treat *all* armed ships as warships and intimating that they would warn Americans against

[55] House Diary, March 7, 1916.
[56] R. Lansing to E. M. House, February 2, 1916, *The Lansing Papers*, I, 339
[57] E. M. House to W. W., c. February 3, 1916, Wilson Papers.
[58] Plunkett Diary, February 12, 13, and 14, 1916. Plunkett repeated the arguments that he had used with House in H. Plunkett to W. W., February 23, 1916, Wilson Papers.
[59] E. M. House to R. Lansing, February 14, 1916, *The Lansing Papers*, I, 342.

traveling on them, and that they would have to jettison the *modus vivendi*. They also had to wrestle with the problem of finding some way to do this without making even more serious controversy with Germany inevitable once the armed ship decree was put into force.

Wilson and Lansing worked out an answer, perhaps in discussion during Cabinet meeting, and the Secretary of State called reporters to the State Department that same afternoon (February 15) to announce it to the world. The administration, he said, was still seriously impressed with the reasonableness of the argument that merchant ships should carry no armament whatever. But it would not insist upon changing the rules should the Allies reject the *modus vivendi*, and it would not classify defensively armed merchantmen as men of war. However, the American government might well insist that a merchant ship was armed offensively when its armament was superior to that of a submarine. Ordinarily, armed merchantmen did command superior force, but it was difficult to draw the line between offensive and defensive armament. The American government, Lansing continued, might permit the new German campaign to go into effect without taking any formal action one way or the other. The administration would not warn Americans against traveling on merchantmen armed solely for defense, and it would be a matter of serious concern[60] if Americans should lose their lives when submarines sank *defensively* armed vessels without warning. On the other hand, Lansing added, the American government did not assert that the impending German campaign was necessarily unlawful. It recognized that it would be extremely hazardous for a submarine to attempt to warn, visit, and search an armed ship. Mistakes were bound to occur. American action, in the event that Americans lost their lives when a submarine sank an armed ship without warning, would depend upon many things—whether the ship's armament was defensive or offensive, the circumstances of the attack, and so on.[61]

In other words, the American government would do its best to avoid controversy with either side. It would not change the rules governing treatment of armed merchant ships in American ports so

[60] Lansing used the words "breach of international law" in his statement summarizing this interview that he sent to American embassies and legations in Europe. See the Secretary of State to Diplomatic Officers in European Countries, February 16, 1916, *Foreign Relations, 1916, Supplement*, p. 170.

[61] *New York Times*, February 16, 1916; New York *World*, February 16, 1916. Lansing sent a summary of his statement to American diplomatic officers for transmission to the European governments. It is cited in the preceding footnote.

long as they were not offensively armed. But it would insist upon the right to determine for itself whether a merchant ship was armed defensively or offensively, and Americans would obviously travel at their own risk on ships armed for offense. German submarine commanders, on the other hand, would do well to remember their government's pledges concerning inoffensive merchantmen. Lansing reiterated this warning to the German Ambassador on February 17, when he told Bernstorff that he could not accept the latest German *Lusitania* note because of the uncertainty that now prevailed concerning future submarine policy.[62]

None of the major European belligerents seemed to be either irritated or surprised by Lansing's enunciation. The British were undoubtedly somewhat relieved because the direst American threat had been withdrawn. So also was Colonel House,[63] and Lansing's statement was perhaps helpful in the last stages of House's negotiations in London. There was a marked change in Grey's attitude toward the possibility of Wilson's mediation between February 14 and February 16, and it probably was no accident that Grey drafted the House-Grey Memorandum *after* news of Lansing's statement had come from Washington. Even so, the episode had surely convinced Grey that the American government was more interested in avoiding controversy with Germany than in diplomatic intervention for peace, *if intervention carried military risks*. This conclusion in turn was undoubtedly one factor in Grey's low estimate of the potentiality of the Memorandum.

The Allied leaders, particularly the French, did not like Lansing's intimation that the American government would impose its own definition of defensive and offensive armament, but they were not disposed to argue this point. They were more concerned to take advantage of the opportunity that Lansing's statement afforded to return a negative reply to his suggestion of a *modus vivendi*. The French Foreign Ministry prepared a draft note of rejection and sent it to the London Foreign Office on February 19, 1916. Grey decided for some reason to procrastinate and accepted the French note as the text of the British reply only on March 12. Then Ambassador Jusserand suggested

---

[62] "Memorandum of the Secretary of State . . . , February 17, 1916," *Foreign Relations, 1916, Supplement*, p. 172.

[63] E. M. House to W. W., February 16, 1916, Wilson Papers; the Diary of Chandler P. Anderson, February 16, 1916 (relating a conversation with House on that same day), Library of Congress; hereinafter cited as the Anderson Diary.

that it would be better for the Allied envoys to address the note to Lansing in the form of personal letters rather than as a joint note from the Foreign Offices, and this procedure was adopted.[64] Spring Rice, when he presented his reply, added his government's assurances that all armament on British merchant ships was intended solely for purposes of defense.[65]

Bernstorff and his superiors in Berlin were not displeased by Lansing's statement. In fact, it, along with news that the American government would not ratify the *Lusitania* settlement until German submarine policy had been clarified, spurred the Germans to unusually responsive action. The Secretary of State talked with Bernstorff about the armed ship question on February 16 and suggested that the German navy delay its new campaign for perhaps a month. The American government, he said, hoped that the belligerents would agree upon a *modus vivendi* that would prevent loss of life without denying the Germans effective use of the submarine. What worried him particularly, Lansing went on, was the danger that a submarine commander would make a mistake and sink an *unarmed* passenger vessel.[66] "I must respectfully repeat my opinion so often expressed," Bernstorff wrote two days later, "that, if a catastrophe similar to the *Lusitania* case occurs again, war with the United States can not be prevented by any art known to diplomacy."[67]

Receipt of these messages, along with news reports from Washington, found Bethmann and all high civilian leaders in the thick of the running battle with naval and army chieftains. The former, having won their modest objective—unrestricted operations against armed ships— were now pressing hard for their larger goal, a severely sharpened submarine campaign against *all* merchant shipping in the war zone on March 1, 1916. Bethmann was in the quandary of not knowing whether to risk defeat in opposing this demand by pressing for guarantees of safety for armed *passenger* ships. As he put it in a memorandum for

[64] See, e. g., Ambassador Spring Rice to the Secretary of State, March 23, 1916, *Foreign Relations, 1916, Supplement*, pp. 211-212.

[65] The Foreign Secretary to Ambassador Spring Rice, n.d., left at the State Department on March 23, 1916, *ibid.*, p. 212.

[66] Ambassador von Bernstorff to the Foreign Office, February 16, 1916, German F. O. Archives.

[67] Ambassador von Bernstorff to the Foreign Office, February 18, 1916, *Official German Documents*, II, 1287. Jagow had informed Bernstorff that no provision had been made to give immunity to armed passenger steamers. Foreign Secretary von Jagow to Ambassador von Bernstorff, February 15, 1916, German F. O. Archives.

the Foreign Office on February 19: "Concerning armed passenger steamers, the navy has made no special provision for them in its orders for the 29th of this month. As far as I know, only submarines in the Mediterranean have left with these orders, while no submarines are now in service off the English coast. The submarines assigned there will not leave until March 1, in the event that His Majesty should order the ruthless submarine war by that date. Before this time the matter will by no means be ripe for discussion. Must, therefore, an order be issued by the Admiralty to the effect that passenger liners, whether armed or not, must be protected, so long as the ruthless submarine campaign has not been commanded?"[68]

There was no choice, Bethmann decided, but to run the risk, and he saw the Emperor and his naval adviser, Admiral von Müller, in Berlin on February 22 and demanded that no new *Lusitania* incidents be permitted to occur on account of the destruction of an armed passenger ship. "He made a very desperate impression," von Müller commented in his diary on that same day. The Emperor repeated Bethmann's demand to Holtzendorff at Wilhelmshaven on the next day, adding that if he were a submarine commander, he would never torpedo a ship carrying women and children.[69] Holtzendorff consequently issued, on February 24, a supplement to the orders that had gone to fleet and flotilla commanders on February 11. The supplement read as follows:

1. The submarine campaign should be taken up again on the west coast of England. . . .

2. All enemy merchantmen must be destroyed unless the commander acquires the conviction that the ship encountered is not armed.

Until further orders, *liners*, whether armed or not, will *not* be attacked.

3. Ships will not, as a rule, be visited on account of the dangers which this practice carries.

4. After attacking submerged, the submarine will get away without revealing itself so that the nature of the attack (mine or torpedo) will remain not definitely known.

5. Commanders will be protected in case they commit mistakes.[70]

[68] T. von Bethmann Hollweg, memorandum for the Foreign Office, dated February 19 (?), 1916, *ibid.*
[69] W. Görlitz (ed.), *Regierte der Kaiser*, p. 158.
[70] A. Spindler, *La Guerre Sous-Marine*, III, 118. Spindler adds (*ibid.*, pp. 118-119): "The superior commander of submarines received complementary oral explanations, as follows: 'By the term "liners" one means large ships which serve exclusively in the transport of passengers but not mixed ships that carry freight and passengers. In case of doubt, one should permit the ship to pass. It is necessary in the present period of the submarine campaign to avoid all incidents that could lead to conflict.' "

W CHAPTER VI W

The Armed Ship Rebellion

LANSING's announcement of February 15, 1916, had in the meantime set off quick and violent agitation in Congress. Many representatives and senators did not understand the subtleties of the Secretary's explanation and thought that he had said that the American government would defend the right of its citizens to travel on all armed merchantmen. The first sign of such apprehension came on February 17, with the introduction by Representative Jeff: McLemore of Texas of a resolution requesting the President to warn all American citizens to refrain from traveling on armed merchant vessels.[1] Thomas Sterling, Republican from South Dakota, countered in the Senate on the following day with a resolution asserting that the American government should not acquiesce in the German armed ship decree. It set off a spirited debate in which Henry Cabot Lodge of Massachusetts and Charles S. Thomas, Democrat from Colorado, joined Sterling in denouncing the *modus vivendi*.[2] This prompted Thomas P. Gore, blind senator from Oklahoma, to begin to organize a movement to force the foreign relations committee to report the bills that he had introduced on January 5 at Bryan's request and with Representative Kitchin's approval. They prohibited issuance of passports to Americans traveling on any belligerent ship and American and neutral vessels from transporting American citizens as passengers while carrying contraband.[3]

There was much authentic confusion on Capitol Hill, and Senator Stone called on Wilson in the morning of February 21. He was, Stone said, in the dark. As chairman of the foreign relations committee, he was the President's spokesman on foreign policy in the Senate, and he had a right to know what the administration had in mind, particularly how it felt about the Gore resolutions. Wilson had been deeply troubled

[1] *Congressional Record*, 64th Cong., 1st sess., p. 2756.

[2] *ibid.*, pp. 2759-2769. The *Chicago Herald* had received the text of Lansing's note to the Allied governments of January 18, 1916, from a European correspondent and published it in full. Senator Lodge had it printed in the *Congressional Record*.

[3] *New York Times*, January 6 and February 23, 1916; J. L. Slayden to C. Kitchin, January 10, 1916, Kitchin Papers.

by the signs of a congressional outbreak.[4] He told Stone that he was eager to talk to congressional leaders and asked whether the Senator would be willing to return that same day with John W. Kern of Indiana, Senate majority leader, and Hal D. Flood of Virginia, chairman of the House committee on foreign affairs.

These three Democrats came to the White House that afternoon at five forty-five. Stone apparently opened the discussion by asking two searching questions: What would happen if a German submarine sank an armed ship carrying Americans as passengers or members of her crew? And what should be done if certain senators carried out their plan to introduce a resolution forbidding armed ships to leave American ports if they carried American passengers?

Wilson could not disclose to his callers what probably had been the chief reason for his and Lansing's shift in policy toward armed ships, namely, the hope that a return to a more neutral position would help to pave the way for his mediation under the House-Grey Memorandum. He did not, apparently, explain the nuances of meaning in Lansing's statement, or make clear that it did not necessarily portend dire conflict with Germany. He said that he would deeply regret the failure of the proposed *modus vivendi*, but that Great Britain and her allies would be within their rights if they rejected the proposal and insisted on arming their merchant ships. He was disposed to think that armed ships would have the right to use American ports. Then, according to one newspaper account, he "stopped speaking English and talked United States." The American government, he said, would go to almost any lengths to defend the right of Americans to travel on defensively armed merchant ships. He would consider it his duty to hold Germany to strict account if a German war vessel should torpedo without warning an armed merchant vessel carrying American passengers. Indeed, he would sever diplomatic relations if this occurred. Moreover, he would regard adoption of a resolution warning Americans against traveling on armed ships as a rank discourtesy.

Senator Stone, heretofore Wilson's most loyal and admiring supporter in the upper house, was not persuaded. It was futile, he said, to expect the Allies to adopt the *modus vivendi*. The American people did not want to go to war to vindicate the right of a few people to travel or work on armed vessels. There was nothing to do but warn Americans

[4] He called Postmaster General Burleson on the telephone at eleven o'clock in the evening of the day that the McLemore resolution was introduced and read the resolution to Burleson. A. S. Burleson to R. S. Baker, February 25, 1931, Baker Collection.

to stay off such ships. Growing excited, Stone banged his fist on the table and exclaimed, "Mr. President, would you draw a shutter over my eyes and my intellect? You have no right to ask me to follow such a course. It may mean war for my country. I must follow my conscience in this matter."[5]

Stone, Kern, and Flood repeated the substance of the conversation to dozens of representatives and senators that night and on the following day, February 22. Word also arrived in Washington on February 22 that the German Foreign Secretary had just said that submarines would attack without warning all belligerent armed merchant ships, whether carrying passengers or not.[6] The convergence of the reports from the White House and Berlin set off worried talk at both ends of the Capitol. Rumors grew each time they were repeated. Men were saying by the time that Congress met on February 23 that war with Germany was inevitable, even that Wilson wanted war. "The situation is so very grave that something must be done or we will go to war with Germany," one distraught Texas congressman wrote on that day. "Flood told me today that Stone & Kern (& he also) were afraid of an immediate break, & the two former thought the President was almost determined on war."[7]

Small groups of Democrats discussed the situation in offices and cloakrooms all through the morning and early afternoon. Then panic swept through the House of Representatives in the late afternoon. Veteran congressmen said that they had not seen anything so dramatic and sensational for many years, and none could recall any crisis that had developed so suddenly. Flood called Democratic members of the foreign affairs committee into secret session in the late afternoon, ostensibly to stem the tide. He only increased apprehension by telling members that the President would not yield and was, in fact, prepared to go to war to vindicate the right of Americans to travel on armed merchant ships. There was strong sentiment for reporting and voting on the McLemore resolution immediately. Every single Democratic

[5] The above account is based upon W. J. Stone to W. W., February 24, 1916, Wilson Papers, repeating the gist of Wilson's remarks, and reports in the New York *World*, February 23, 1916, and the *New York Times*, February 22, 23, and 24, 1916.

[6] New York *World*, February 23, 1916. This was a dispatch from Karl H. von Wiegand from Berlin of February 20, 1916, printed in the New York *World* and other newspapers on February 22, 1916. Actually, Jagow merely reiterated Germany's intention to treat armed merchantmen as warships; he did not specifically mention passenger ships.

[7] J. L. Slayden to O. G. Villard, February 23, 1916, Villard Papers. See also C. Kitchin to J. K. McGuire, February 23, 1916, Kitchin Papers.

member present signified that he favored the resolution. Flood succeeded in preventing action only by promising that he and other Democratic leaders would go to the White House on the following day and tell the President that the House would adopt a warning resolution unless he changed his policy toward armed merchantmen within forty-eight hours. Meanwhile, Senator Stone had been working with Speaker Clark and Majority Leader Kitchin to prevent an outbreak on the floor of the House, although all three strongly supported the McLemore resolution or its equivalent. They succeeded—the subject was not mentioned in the House on February 23—but a partial canvass at the end of the day indicated that a warning resolution would pass by a vote of four or three to one.[8]

Hysteria had given way to dogged determination to force the issue with the President by the time that Congress met on February 24. Speaker Clark called the White House by telephone at three-thirty in the afternoon and informed Tumulty that he, Kitchin, and Flood would like to call upon the President as soon as possible. Tumulty said that he would convey the message. The three congressmen sat in their offices until six-fifteen, waiting with mounting irritation. Clark, at least, went home in an angry mood, and a rumor ran through the House that the President had slighted the Speaker.[9]

The President spent the afternoon of February 24 secluded in his study. He talked to Lansing over the telephone,[10] and he probably suggested that the Secretary telephone Stone and Flood and tell them that the international situation had improved and urge them to prevent any discussion on the floors of the two houses. This, at any rate, is what Lansing did.[11] Wilson was also in touch with Tumulty and probably sent a word of encouragement to a small group of House Democrats led by Carter Glass of Virginia who were attempting to rally administration supporters. But the President refused to see any callers or to respond to Clark's message. He was not ready to receive the House leaders. This, he knew, was the gravest challenge to his leadership, and one of the gravest challenges to the President's conduct of foreign policy in American history. He had to plan his strategy carefully, for defeat through adoption of a warning resolution would wreck his

[8] *New York Times*, February 24, 1916.   [9] *ibid.*, February 25, 1916.
[10] The Desk Diary of Robert Lansing, February 24, 1916, Library of Congress; hereinafter cited as the Lansing Desk Diary.
[11] New York *World*, February 25, 1916.

standing with the Allied governments and also gravely impair his influence over German leaders. His standing at home and abroad, not the principle underlying a warning resolution, was the really important thing at stake. After all, he and Lansing had themselves been contemplating a warning resolution not so many days before. Somehow, some way, he had to take the initiative and strike hard before he confronted the House leaders.

A messenger delivered a long letter from Senator Stone while Wilson was thus engrossed. The Missourian began by repeating what he had said to congressmen about the White House conversation on February 21. He went on, as follows:

"Numerous Members of the Senate and House have called to discuss this subject with me. I have felt that the Members of the two Houses who are to deal with this grave question were entitled to know the situation we are confronting as I understand it to be. I think I should say to you that the Members of both Houses feel deeply concerned and disturbed by what they read and hear. . . . The situation in Congress is such as to excite a sense of deep concern in the minds of careful and thoughtful men. I have felt that it is due to you to say this much.

"I think you understand my personal attitude with respect to this subject. As much and as deeply as I would hate to radically disagree with you, I find it difficult from my sense of duty and responsibility to consent to plunge this nation into the vortex of this world war because of the unreasonable obstinacy of any of the Powers upon the one hand, or, on the other hand, of fool-hardiness, amounting to a sort of moral treason against the Republic, of our own people recklessly risking their lives on armed belligerent ships. I cannot escape the conviction that such a thing would be so monstrous as to be indefensible.

"I want to be with you and to stand by you, and I mean to do so up to the last limit; and I want to talk with you and Secretary Lansing with the utmost frankness—to confer with you and have your judgment and counsel—and I want to be kept advised as to the course of events, as it seems to me I am entitled to be. In the meantime I am striving to prevent anything being done by any Senator or Member calculated to embarrass your diplomatic negotiations. Up to the last you should be left free to act diplomatically as you think for the best to settle the questions involved. I need hardly say that my wish is to help, not to hinder you."[12]

[12] W. J. Stone to W. W., February 24, 1916, Wilson Papers.

Here, indeed, was a heaven-sent opportunity for a bold and ringing statement to the country and the world. He would answer Stone's letter and give both Stone's letter and his own to the newspapers for publication in the morning. Then, and then only, would he receive the delegation from the House of Representatives. Wilson began, probably in the late afternoon, to draft his reply in shorthand. He had completed a first draft when Tumulty brought a letter of his own suggesting that the President write an identical letter to Stone and Flood and listing some points to be emphasized.[13] Wilson then typed out his draft, incorporating parts of Tumulty's letter in his own text. The finished draft follows:

"I very warmly appreciate your kind and frank letter of today and feel that it calls for an equally frank reply.

"You are right in assuming that I shall do everything in my power to keep the United States out of war. I think the country will feel no uneasiness about my course in that respect. Through many anxious months I have striven for that object, amidst difficulties more manifold than can have been apparent upon the surface, and so far I have succeeded. I do not doubt that I shall continue to succeed. The course which the Central European Powers have announced their intention of following in the future with regard to undersea warfare seems for the moment to threaten insuperable obstacles, but its apparent meaning is so manifestly inconsistent with explicit assurances recently given up by those powers with regard to their treatment of merchant vessels on the high seas that I must believe that explanations will presently ensue which will put a different aspect upon it. We have had no reason to question their good faith or their fidelity to their promises in the past, and I for one feel confident that we shall have none in the future.

"But in any event our duty is clear. No nation, no group of nations, has the right while war is in progress to alter or disregard the principles which all nations have agreed upon in mitigation of the horrors and sufferings of war; and if the clear rights of American citizens should ever unhappily be abridged or denied by any such action we should, it seems to me, have in honor no choice as to what our own course should be.

"For my own part, I cannot consent to any abridgement of the rights of American citizens in any respect. The honor and self-respect of the nation is involved. We covet peace, and shall preserve it at any cost but the loss of honor. To forbid our people to exercise their rights for fear

---

[13] Tumulty apparently did not know about the letter from Stone.

we might be called upon to vindicate them would be a deep humiliation indeed. It would be an implicit, all but an explicit, acquiescence in the violation of the rights of mankind everywhere, and of whatever nation or allegiance. It would be a deliberate abdication of our hitherto proud position as spokesmen, even amidst the turmoil of war, for the law and the right. It would make everything this Government has attempted, and everything that it has achieved during this terrible struggle of nations meaningless and futile.

"It is important to reflect that if in this instance we allowed expediency to take the place of principle, the door would inevitably be opened to still further concessions. Once accept a single abatement of right, and many other humiliations would certainly follow, and the whole fine fabric of international law[14] might crumble under our hands piece by piece. What we are contending for in this matter is of the very essence of the things that have made America a sovereign nation. She cannot yield them without conceding her own impotency as a nation, and making virtual surrender of her independent position among the nations of the world.[15]

"I am speaking, my dear Senator, in deep solemnity, without heat, with a clear consciousness of the high responsibilities of my office, and as your sincere and devoted friend. If we should unhappily differ, we shall differ as friends; but where issues so momentous as these are involved we must, just because we are friends, speak our minds without reservation."[16]

This was President Wilson's single most important pronouncement on American neutral rights and duties. It has been reprinted hundreds of times and cited almost as many times to prove that he was doctrinaire, unrealistic, deceptive, mendacious, or bent upon war with Germany. The following, at least, should be said, by way of general explanation:

First. Wilson wrote the letter for the specific purpose of blunting a congressional challenge to his control over foreign policy. He was debating in public, appealing for public support, and he used the

---

[14] "The whole fabric of international law" was Tumulty's phrase.

[15] Compare the following passage in J. P. Tumulty to W. W., February 24, 1916, Wilson Papers: "What we are contending for in this matter is of the very essence of the things that have made America a sovereign nation. She cannot yield them without admitting and conceding her own impotency as a nation and the surrender of her independent position among the nations of the world."

[16] W. W. to W. J. Stone, February 24, 1916, as printed in the *New York Times*, February 25, 1916. The original of Wilson's typed letter is in the collection of Wilson materials gathered by Charles L. Swem, Princeton University Library; hereinafter cited as the Swem Collection.

debater's techniques of the bold attack, hyperbole, and overstatement.

Second. The letter was written hurriedly, under great pressure. It was not the product of careful thought and discussion. Wilson sent Lansing a copy and discussed it over the telephone with him before giving it to reporters,[17] but there was no time for any searching analysis and criticism.

Third. Much of the letter was historically inaccurate and gave an impression of a rigidity and dogmatism that had not hitherto characterized Wilson's policies toward the belligerents. Perhaps he had not "consented" to "abridgements of the rights of American citizens in any respect," but he had certainly acquiesced in many such abridgements.

Fourth. The letter did not, as it seemed, announce a general policy of unyielding defense of neutral rights to which Wilson would adhere in the future. He would acquiesce in many more abridgements of technical neutral rights before the year had ended. Nor did Wilson mean to take an adamant position against a German campaign against armed ships, even though his letter was so imprecise as to give this impression.

Fifth. The fact that Wilson used so many of the key phrases and sentences in Tumulty's letter is the best evidence we have of the stress under which the President was working. Tumulty, as Wilson well knew, was emotional, volatile, and certainly far from being a thoughtful person or an authority on international law.

What, then, did Wilson have in mind? The following are the author's deductions from circumstantial evidence:

First. Wilson's main purpose was to take an advanced position publicly before he had confronted congressional leaders, so that he could not be accused of yielding under threat or pressure.

Second. He knew that German leaders were contemplating a severely intensified submarine campaign. He had, for his part, resolved to make a firmer defense of American maritime rights *vis-à-vis* Germany in order to convince Allied leaders that they could proceed safely with a peace effort under his aegis. He was, consequently, issuing a broad warning to the Germans not to go too far, although he was careful not

[17] Lansing Desk Diary, February 24, 1916. There is the following curious entry in the House Diary, March 28, 1916: "It seems when the President wrote the letter to Senator Stone . . . the first Lansing knew of it was when he read it in the papers. I spoke to the President about this and asked him to be careful. He was not inclined to pay any attention to it, and said Lansing must understand that he, himself, was conducting foreign affairs, and he would do it in the way he thought best." Either House made this story up, or Lansing misinformed House, and Wilson, when House brought the matter up more than a month after it had occurred, forgot that he had read the letter to Lansing.

to define the safe boundaries of German submarine policy. It is significant that he did not specifically discuss the issue of *armed* merchantmen in his letter to Stone.

Third. He was also obviously trying to rally public support for his personal leadership and what might have to be a firmer defense of American neutral rights if the Germans should launch all-out or severely intensified submarine warfare. He hoped and believed that he could force the Germans to follow policies that would ensure maintenance of the German-American peace. But he could do this only if he had the support of a united people in taking the necessary risks. Without such backing he would be helpless in negotiation, and then the Germans would surely pursue policies that would drive the American people in blind fury into war.

Wilson had copies of his correspondence with Senator Stone mimeographed and given to the White House correspondents. Shortly afterward, at nine o'clock, he had Tumulty call Speaker Clark to say that the President would be pleased to receive a delegation from the House of Representatives at nine o'clock the following morning.

Clark, Flood, and Kitchin arrived at the White House at the appointed time on Friday, February 25, for what has come to be known in fact and fiction as the "Sunrise Conference."[18] The Speaker, colorful as always in his long coat and winged collar, said that the delegation had not come to argue but simply to inform the President about the formidable movement in the House for a resolution to warn Americans against traveling on armed ships. "We explained to the President," Clark told reporters immediately afterward, "how the House felt, in our judgment. I told the President that this warning resolution would carry two to one if they ever got a chance to vote. Some enthusiastic gentlemen, I said, thought it would carry three to one."

Wilson replied quietly but emphatically, saying that he intended to "see this thing through," and that he could not help it if Congress would not support him. Congress and the people would give him united support if they wanted to avoid war. Any yielding to Germany now, particularly adoption of a warning resolution, would only encourage both belligerent alliances further to transgress American rights, and the whole fabric of international law would fall to pieces. What would happen, one of Wilson's callers asked, if a German submarine sank an armed merchantman with Americans aboard? "I believe we should

[18] See A. S. Link, *Woodrow Wilson and the Progressive Era*, p. 213, for a review of the historiographical controversy over this conference.

sever diplomatic relations," Wilson replied. What would happen then? "Count von Bernstorff told Secretary Lansing," Wilson said, "that a break in diplomatic relations would be followed by a declaration of war by Germany." What would be the effect of American participation? It might, Wilson said, bring the war to an end much sooner than appeared possible at the present.

Clark, bridling at this remark, said that Wilson would have his support only so long as he, the Speaker, believed that the administration's policy would not lead to war. Indeed, he went on, he reserved the right to leave the chair and oppose the President's policy if it seemed to foreshadow hostilities.

Someone told Wilson that persons were saying that he wanted war with Germany. Why, Wilson replied, should anyone think that he wanted war? His course was the course of peace; adoption of a warning resolution could only lead to war. The American people would drive Congress to adopt a war resolution if Americans were killed on merchant ships. He had been jeered at, sneered at, and ridiculed for his efforts to maintain peace. "In God's name," he cried, "could anyone have done more than I to show a desire for peace?"

It was, as Clark told reporters, "very clear to all that the President stands on his letter to Senator Stone."[19]

The three congressmen returned to the Capitol at ten o'clock to find the rebels much subdued. Wilson's letter, published in the early morning newspapers, had already stunned advocates of a warning resolution, and the three Democrats' report of their conversation at the White House made it doubly certain that the President would not be intimidated. Kitchin, at least, was absolutely convinced that Wilson wanted war[20] and must have given gloomy tidings to his friends. Unnamed "responsible leaders" told reporters that a majority of House Democrats at heart still favored a warning resolution, but it was obvious that few of them had any stomach for a showdown fight. It was one thing to favor such a resolution, another to be willing to defy the President of the United States and leader of the Democratic Party.[21] At the

[19] The above is based upon reports in the *New York Times*, February 26 and March 3, 1916, and the *New York Evening Post*, cited in the *Springfield* (Mass.) *Republican*, March 4, 1916.

[20] See, é. g., C. Kitchin to M. L. Kelser, February 26, 1916; C. Kitchin to H. S. Lent, February 28, 1916; C. Kitchin to C. A. Snipes, February 28, 1916; C. Kitchin to C. H. Nash, February 29, 1916, all in the Kitchin Papers.

[21] *New York Times*, February 26, 1916. See also Timothy G. McDonald, "Southern

Goose-stepping
Kirby in the New York *World*

other end of the Capitol, Senator Gore introduced a resolution that same afternoon (February 25) calling on Americans to forbear from traveling on any armed ships and advising that Congress believed that no persons traveling on armed ships should be given passports.[22] But a careful poll of the Senate taken later in the day revealed that the Gore resolution would be defeated by a vote of seventy to twenty-five.[23]

Democratic Congressmen and the First World War," Ph.D. dissertation, University of Washington, 1961, pp. 137-138.

[22] *Congressional Record*, 64th Cong., 1st sess., p. 3120.

[23] New York *World*, February 26, 1916.

Wilson discussed the congressional situation with the Cabinet that morning from eleven to twelve forty-five. He talked with Burleson afterward, and the Postmaster General urged him to press for outright defeat of the McLemore resolution, and Secretary of the Treasury McAdoo and Attorney General Gregory concurred.[24] Wilson hesitated to risk battle so soon. Instead, he sought further to reassure congressional critics by having Secretary Lansing correct the impression of rigidity about armed ships that he, Wilson, had given in his letter to Stone. Lansing told reporters on February 26 that the administration would support the right of Americans to travel on armed merchantmen, but only if they were armed solely for defense. Moreover, Lansing continued, the Washington government was willing to discuss the proper definition of defensive armament with the Berlin authorities.[25]

This announcement virtually ended extreme congressional discontent, and Representative McLemore announced that he would not press for a vote on his resolution, at least not until the President had had ample time to conduct negotiations with Germany. Reports from Capitol Hill at the same time said that only twenty senators would now vote for the Gore resolution, and that two thirds of the Democrats and five sixths of the Republicans in the House would stand by the President if the McLemore resolution came up for consideration.[26] Perhaps it would be wise, Wilson must have concluded, to let the Gore and McLemore resolutions die in committee.

Meanwhile, receipt of Wilson's letter to Stone in Berlin on February 25[27] and its publication in the German press on the following day had set off either angry denunciations or expressions of doubt that the letter could be genuine.[28] It fell like a bolt in official circles, particularly the Foreign Office, where leaders feared that it meant war with America

[24] Lansing Desk Diary, February 25, 1916; A. S. Burleson to R. S. Baker, February 25, 1931, Baker Collection.

[25] *New York Times*, February 27, 1916.

[26] *ibid.*; New York *World*, February 27, 1916.

[27] It was sent by the usual news services and also by the State Department. See the Secretary of State to Ambassador Gerard, February 25, 1916, *Foreign Relations, 1916, Supplement*, pp. 177-178.

[28] K. H. von Wiegand, dispatch from Berlin, dated February 26, 1916, in the New York *World*, February 28, 1916; *Frankfurter Zeitung*, February 26, 1916, paraphrased in Ambassador Gerard to the Secretary of State, February 26, 1916, *Foreign Relations, 1916, Supplement*, pp. 179-180; Berlin *Taegliche Rundschau*, morning edn., February 27, 1916; Dietrich Schaefer in *ibid.*; Berlin *Kreuz-zeitung* and Berlin *Germania*, cited in the New York *World*, February 28, 1916.

The President and Mrs. Wilson soon after their wedding

The Great Commoner

Lindley M. Garrison

Claude Kitchin

James Hay

LEADERS IN THE PREPAREDNESS CONTROVERSY

The President and Mrs. Wilson in St. Louis on the preparedness tour

The President and Colonel House

Captain Franz von Papen

Captain Karl Boy-Ed

GERMAN AGENTS SENT HOME

Columbus, N. M., after Villa's Raid

General Pershing in Mexico

Louis D. Brandeis

was possible, if not inevitable. There was, consequently, much frantic activity in Wilhelmstrasse. Jagow wired to Bernstorff Exhibit 4 of the Foreign Office's note of February 10, listing instances when Allied armed ships had attacked submarines (Gerard had sent this by mail, and it had not yet arrived in Washington).[29] The Foreign Office on the same day (February 25) sent to Washington a summary of reports from the British press allegedly proving that British armed ships were specifically instructed to attack submarines.[30] A statement in the official *Norddeutsche Allgemeine Zeitung*, declaring that Wilson could not have understood the situation because the appendices to the German note of February 10 had not yet arrived in Washington, followed on the next day.[31] Finally, Jagow, on February 28, authorized Bernstorff to use something close to blackmail with Lansing if he and Baron Zwiedinek thought it wise to do so. They were authorized to tell Lansing that the Central Powers had instituted the campaign against armed ships in response to Lansing's own statements to Zwiedinek. The Berlin and Vienna governments would not mention these statements should no break with America occur. However, they would feel obliged to publish them should war occur, in order to make the enormous responsibility for such a catastrophe clear to the world.[32]

Bethmann was now between a murderous crossfire. Agitation for sharpened submarine warfare had been taken up by right-wing newspapers, university professors, businessmen, and the powerful Conservative Party. Worse still for the Imperial Chancellor, it was also becoming increasingly clear that the prime movers of this campaign, Tirpitz, Holtzendorff, and Falkenhayn, meant "unlimited" submarine warfare when they said "intensified" submarine warfare.[33] "We must have victory over England," Tirpitz wrote in a memorandum for the head

[29] Foreign Secretary von Jagow to Ambassador von Bernstorff, February 25, 1916, German F. O. Archives.

[30] Foreign Office to the German Embassy, Washington, February 25, 1916, *ibid.*; Ambassador von Bernstorff to the Secretary of State, February 29, 1916, *Foreign Relations, 1916, Supplement*, pp. 182-183.

[31] Foreign Secretary von Jagow to Ambassador von Bernstorff, February 26, 1916, German F. O. Archives.

[32] Foreign Secretary von Jagow to Ambassador von Bernstorff, February 28, 1916, *ibid.* Baron Zwiedinek, on February 20, had sent a long report to Baron Burián, commenting on Lansing's use of the word "welcome" in their conversation of January 26, 1916. Zwiedinek observed in the course of this dispatch that publication of the conversation would perhaps cause Lansing to lose his position, but that he and Bernstorff had agreed that it would not be wise to try to embarrass the Secretary of State. Baron Zwiedinek to Baron Burián, February 20, 1916, copy in *ibid.*

[33] As Karl Helfferich, *Der Weltkrieg* (2 vols.), II, 331, has said.

of the Army General Staff on February 10, for example, "and we will have it if we resume the submarine war unhesitatingly and *à outrance*. America will not be able to prevent us from winning, even if she takes up arms against us and puts no matter how many billions of dollars at the disposal of our enemies."[34] Von Falkenhayn agreed completely. "It boils down to the consideration," he wrote menacingly to the Imperial Chancellor on February 13, after reading Tirpitz's memorandum, "that the High Command does not have the right to renounce the submarine war. If this is the situation, then the political leaders must not have the right any longer to prevent the military High Command from using weapons which to it appear proper and necessary for victory."[35]

The desperate struggle in the inner circle came to a head in Germany just at the time that the armed ship controversy was developing in Washington. Holtzendorff, on February 19, sent Bethmann a copy of a memorandum on the possibilities of sharpened submarine warfare that the Admiralty staff had just completed. It was replete with graphs and tables on the English economy, particularly on English shipping, and it concluded that resumption of the submarine campaign under old limitations—safety for passenger vessels, respect for neutral shipping, and so on—would not (to quote Holtzendorff's own summary) "be sufficient to force England to peace and therefore would not offset the unavoidable danger of entanglement with neutrals." The destruction of English powers of resistance, Holtzendorff's summary continued, "is possible *only when all traffic to and from England is threatened with destruction on account of the submarine war, and all imports are suppressed to the utmost.*" (italics added) Should the new submarine campaign be waged without limitation, that is, should *all* ships in the war zone be destroyed, the memorandum concluded, then it was certain that England would be forced to make peace within at least six months. American participation would not matter, for the United States did not have enough new shipping to put at England's disposal to make any difference.[36]

---

[34] A. von Tirpitz to E. von Falkenhayn, February 10, 1916, A. von Tirpitz, *Politische Dokumente*, II, 472-473.

[35] E. von Falkenhayn to T. von Bethmann Hollweg, February 13, 1916, A. Spindler, *La Guerre Sous-Marine*, III, 125.

[36] H. von Holtzendorff to T. von Bethmann Hollweg, February 19, 1916, enclosing *Die Englische Wirtschaft und der U-Bootskrieg (The English Economy and the U-Boat War)*, memorandum dated February 12, 1916, German F. O. Archives. This memorandum had thirty-eight pages of text and a statistical supplement of sixty-six pages. The Admiralty circulated it widely among economic experts and business and banking

So there it was, finally out in the open, the demand for total war against all shipping, belligerent and neutral, accompanied by a guarantee of victory if only timid politicians had the nerve to try! Bethmann, Jagow, and Zimmermann sought some compromise with Holtzendorff at a conference at the Chancellor's Palace on February 22, but the Admiralty head was adamant, and the conferees agreed that the Emperor would have to decide. Holtzendorff refused a few days later even to give Bethmann information about the number of large submarines ready for service in English waters, saying that he was willing to take full responsibility for the accuracy of the memorandum's assumptions about the possibilities of an unlimited submarine campaign.[37]

The following, then, was the situation that confronted Bethmann on the eve of what well might be the most fateful Imperial Conference since the beginning of the war. The chief of the Army General Staff had declared that Germany faced almost certain defeat in a long war if she did not win in 1916. The chief of the naval General Staff, or Admiralty, had promised that submarine warfare without limit would surely bring the mistress of the seas to her knees within six months. How could the Emperor and his political spokesman refuse to yield when responsible military advisers concurred so emphatically? It was little wonder that Bethmann weakened momentarily, by asking Holtzendorff at their conference on February 22 to prepare a declaration announcing the beginning of unlimited submarine warfare.

However, receipt of Wilson's letter to Senator Stone in Berlin on February 25 hardened Bethmann's resolve to stand and fight. It emphasized the dangers of unlimited submarine operations against even armed ships, and it and news reports from Washington made it absolutely clear that all-out submarine warfare would lead quickly and decisively to war with America. Other messages were equally

---

leaders and obtained statements, mainly in approval, from them. They were enclosed in H. von Holtzendorff to G. von Jagow, February 27 and 29, 1916, and R. Koch to G. von Jagow, March 3 and 7, 1916, *ibid.*

[37] A. Spindler, *La Guerre Sous-Marine*, III, 126-127. Tirpitz, in reply to a direct inquiry from Bethmann, furnished the Chancellor with fairly detailed figures on the number of submarines available on March 1, 1916, and until the spring of 1917. T. von Bethmann Hollweg to A. von Tirpitz, March 5, 1916, and A. von Tirpitz to T. von Bethmann Hollweg, March 6 and 8, 1916, A. von Tirpitz, *Politische Dokumente*, II, 493-495. Actually, forty-four submarines were ready for service on March 1, 1916. But only twenty-nine of these were new long-range, diesel-powered submarines capable of operating off the western and southern coasts of Great Britain. Since only one third of the submarine fleet could be at stations at any given time, the Admiralty could not put more than ten large U-boats into the war zone at once.

disturbing. The Austrian Foreign Ministry sent word that it had consented to a campaign against *armed* ships only because it had thought that the United States would completely approve such action. It virtually begged the German government to take no steps that might lead to a break with the United States.[38] Richard von Kühlmann, German Minister at The Hague, wired on February 27 that there was no doubt that Holland would join the Entente Allies if America declared war on Germany.[39] The German Minister in Copenhagen warned on the following day that he could not guarantee Danish neutrality in the event of a German declaration of unrestricted submarine warfare and American entry into the conflict.[40] The Turkish government, through its representative at German Supreme Headquarters, made it known that it looked with extreme disfavor on an eventual break with America.[41]

There were certain things, Bethmann knew, that he could not do in these desperate circumstances. He could not stop the campaign against armed merchantmen and, in fact, did not want to. U-boat commanders already had their orders to sail for the English coast on February 29 and treat all armed ships as war vessels. But they also had instructions to spare armed passenger ships, and Bethmann hoped that he could avoid complications over the sinking of ordinary armed cargo carriers.[42] Nor could he completely oppose the navy's demand for an intensified submarine campaign. He would simply give the victory to his opponents if he appeared to be totally obstructive. His only hope of preventing a fatal all-out campaign was to find a compromise that would appease public opinion, satisfy the Emperor and moderate champions of U-boat warfare, and, at the same time, preserve peace with America.

Bethmann set down his thoughts and conclusions in a long memorandum that he signed on February 29, 1916. It was lucidly written, closely reasoned, and abundantly documented. It was also, as one authority has said, "without doubt one of the most significant documents dealing with German policy during the First World War."[43] The

[38] J. von Kriege, "Memorandum concerning Negotiations with Austria-Hungary over the Treatment of Armed Enemy Merchant Ships," dated February 25, 1916, German F. O. Archives.

[39] W. Görlitz (ed.), *Regierte der Kaiser*, p. 159, entry for February 27, 1916.

[40] Ulrich Brockdorff-Rantzau to the Foreign Office, February 28, 1916, German F. O. Archives.

[41] K. von Treutler to the Foreign Office, February 29, 1916, *ibid.*

[42] T. von Bethmann Hollweg to the Foreign Office, February 26, 1916, *ibid.*

[43] K. E. Birnbaum, *Peace Moves and U-Boat Warfare*, p. 58.

Imperial Chancellor, using a paper probably prepared by Dr. Johann von Kriege, legal expert of the Foreign Office, as a guide,[44] subjected the Admiralty's statistical claims to searching, almost harsh, analysis. Bethmann concluded, after citing copious statistical evidence of his own, that it was fatuous to believe that Germany's small number of submarines could really enforce a total blockade of the British Isles. No one doubted, he continued, that an all-out submarine campaign would bring America into the war. Wilson's stand on armed ships had made this perfectly clear. American intervention would embolden France and Russia, remove American pressure against the British blockade, demoralize Germany's allies, and cause a number of Germans to wonder whether the Reich could possibly win. Moreover, American participation would have important material consequences—an outpouring of American credit to the Allies, an end to the American provisioning of Belgium, and an increase in the American supply of war materials to the Allies, along with the dispatch of several hundred thousand volunteers to the western front. Rumania would probably jump on the Allied bandwagon. Holland and Denmark might enter the war against Germany. At best, under English pressure they would probably have to end all exports to Germany. "One, then, can ask himself whether our position is so desperate that we have to play our last card and risk our existence as a great power, indeed, our future as a nation, when the chances of winning—that is, the hope of defeating England before autumn—are so uncertain. One must certainly give a negative answer to this question."

The problem in view of the general military situation, Bethmann went on, was to find a way to carry on the U-boat war without courting a break with the United States. This could be done in four ways, as follows:

First. A campaign against maritime commerce on all the seas conducted according to the rules of cruiser warfare. This carried no risks whatever.

Second. Mine warfare around enemy coasts. This was legal and feasible.

Third. Unrestricted submarine operations against *armed* enemy ships on all the seas. Wilson's latest pronouncements indicated that the American government would not accept the German view on armed ships, but it seemed doubtful that America would go to war over them,

[44] "Considerations concerning the Admiralty's Memorandum, 'The English Economy and the U-Boat War,'" MS. dated February 25, 1916, *ibid.*

provided that the Germans could in every case prove that vessels destroyed had actually been armed. However, it was absolutely essential to avoid sinking armed passenger ships, since another *Lusitania* incident would surely cause a break with the United States.

Fourth. Unrestricted submarine warfare against unarmed *enemy* freighters in the war zone surrounding the British Isles. This might lead to complications with the United States because American sailors often took service on Allied ships. But the American government had never demanded any guarantees for the safety of ordinary freighters, and it seemed unlikely that it would make such a demand.

Such a broad-gauged campaign would have certain dangers, Bethmann concluded, and it would be necessary for submarine commanders to operate cautiously under strict orders. But it was worth trying, and all ensuing damage to English trade would be pure gain. The campaign against armed merchantmen might itself lead to a break with America, but Germany could not turn back because of President Wilson's caprice.[45]

Bethmann left soon afterward for Supreme Headquarters in the West at Charleville, in northern France, and gave the Emperor a copy of his memorandum as soon as he arrived on March 2. Bethmann also saw the Emperor after breakfast on the following morning and was delighted to hear His Majesty say that he agreed completely with his Chancellor and would not permit the folly of driving America into the war. Bethmann talked to Falkenhayn and Holtzendorff at five o'clock that afternoon. The chief of the Army General Staff still held his ground, but the naval chieftain admitted that it was necessary to avoid a break with America.

The long awaited Imperial Conference took place in the Emperor's headquarters at seven in the evening of March 4. William reviewed the situation, saying that as head of state he had to take very seriously a break with America and the alignment of other neutrals on the side of Germany's enemies. The crown and empire were at stake. On the other hand, everyone agreed that Germany had to win the war during 1916. Consequently, he intended to begin the unrestricted submarine campaign on about April 1—that was indispensable. He would not permit President Wilson to tell him how to use his submarines, and

---

[45] T. von Bethmann Hollweg, MS. memorandum dated February 29, 1916, in *ibid.*, printed in T. von Bethmann Hollweg, *Considérations sur la Guerre Mondiale* (2 vols.), II, 345-356; A. Spindler, *La Guerre Sous-Marine*, III, 128-140; and incompletely in *Official German Documents*, II, 1130-1139.

it was up to the diplomats to clear the way with the American people. Holtzendorff, responding to a question from the Emperor, gave a confused account of the number of submarines available and added hastily that an unlimited submarine campaign could force England to her knees within six to eight months. Falkenhayn observed that only a massive submarine attack could cause the English to think of peace. Then Bethmann repeated the arguments in his memorandum, emphasizing that American participation would mean Germany's defeat in a war of exhaustion. He was not, he said, willing to assume responsibility for such a catastrophe. He would gladly do what he could to prepare the way diplomatically for an all-out submarine campaign, but the time before April 1 was short, and he could in no way guarantee success.[46]

The conference adjourned without an Imperial directive. Holtzendorff left thinking that the Emperor had ordered inauguration of the unlimited submarine campaign on April 1. But the Supreme War Lord, bellicose among his chieftains, was notably pacific with Bethmann on the following day, March 5. He visited Bethmann in his garden after church to thank him for his help. "He stated without qualification that our U-boat forces were insufficient to overcome England; that as a matter of fact England could not be overcome; that if we were to challenge England to come out and fight us on the seas, in the face of a break with the United States, every Englishman would give up his last shirt before he would capitulate; that he was still banking on the commercial instinct of the British to finally make it clear to them that they have nothing to gain by continuing the war."[47] Bethmann, with Admiral von Müller's help, soon afterward drafted the following summary of the Emperor's decisions:

"1. The immediate announcement of an unlimited submarine campaign is rejected.

"2. During the month of March the ground with America and the European neutrals will be explored with the aim of making possible

[46] The above account is based upon T. von Bethmann Hollweg to G. von Jagow, March 5, 1916, *Official German Documents*, II, 1139-1142; Admiral von Holtzendorff's notes of the conference among Holtzendorff, Falkenhayn, and Bethmann of March 3, 1916, in A. von Tirpitz, *Politische Dokumente*, II, 502-503; Admiral von Holtzendorff's notes of the Imperial Conference of March 4, *ibid.*, pp. 503-505; Admiral von Müller's diary entry dated March 4, 1916, W. Görlitz (ed.), *Regierte der Kaiser*, pp. 161-162.

[47] T. von Bethmann Hollweg to G. von Jagow, March 5, 1916, *Official German Documents*, II, 1142.

the beginning of an unlimited submarine campaign on April 1, thus avoiding a break with America.

"3. His Majesty reserves to himself the decision whether and actually when all-out submarine warfare is to begin."[48]

During these same conferences the Emperor also approved Bethmann's suggestion of action that amounted to a severe reprimand of Tirpitz and led to the old sea dog's resignation as Naval Secretary on March 12, 1916.

It was, to be sure, a great victory for the Imperial Chancellor. He could now proceed with reasonable hope of preserving peace with the United States in spite of the unknown dangers of the campaign against armed ships. It was no less a victory for Woodrow Wilson. His bold defiance of Congress during the first days of the armed ship rebellion had been the principal factor in spurring Bethmann to risk his career in the desperate battle we have just related.

Perhaps the most striking irony of a story full of ironical situations was the fact that Wilson's actions in the aftermath of the armed ship rebellion in Congress were based upon misapprehension of German plans and purposes in the submarine campaign about to be launched.

Lansing, it will be recalled, had talked with Bernstorff on February 16, and the Ambassador's report of this conversation prompted the Foreign Office to send a long explanation of the German position on armed ships to Washington on February 18. The proposed campaign against armed ships, the dispatch said, did not violate any German pledges to the United States. Moreover, it had been decreed only after German authorities had seen the British Admiralty's secret orders to armed merchantmen. The Imperial government, in issuing new orders to its naval commanders, thought that it was acting in entire accord with the point of view that the American government had expressed in the proposed *modus vivendi*. Armed liners would be subject to attack without warning, but only if submarine commanders could prove that they carried armament aboard.[49]

[48] W. Görlitz (ed.), *Regierte der Kaiser*, pp. 162-163; the Imperial Chancellor to the Chief of the Naval Cabinet, March 9, 1916, A. von Tirpitz, *Politische Dokumente*, ii, 505.

[49] This was the Foreign Office to Ambassador von Bernstorff, Telegram No. 563, February 18, 1916, a copy of which does not seem to exist in the German Foreign Office Archives. Bethmann adverted to it in his memorandum for the Foreign Office of February 19, 1916, cited earlier; Secretary von Jagow, in his dispatch to Ambassador von Bernstorff, February 28, 1916, German F. O. Archives. For its text, see the German

Bernstorff received this dispatch only on February 27, on account of its length and the circuitous route that he and the Foreign Office had to use for telegraphing top secret communications in the German diplomatic code.[50] The Ambassador called reporters to the Embassy as soon as he had decoded the note and released a detailed summary of its contents. He added two points which he said were included in the telegram but apparently were his own contribution.[51] One was that Germany was willing to discuss the definition of offensive and defensive armament with the United States. The other was that the German government urged that Americans be warned not to travel on armed enemy merchantmen. Finally, the Ambassador gave the reporters a summary of Exhibit 4 of the German note of February 10 (citing instances when armed ships had attacked submarines), which he had just received by wireless.[52]

Bernstorff presented a copy of the Foreign Office's telegram, along with a copy of Exhibit 4, to Lansing on February 28, and the Secretary of State sent copies of both documents to the White House. There was not much that Wilson and Lansing could say officially in reply, for the full text of the German memorandum of February 10 and its various exhibits still had not arrived in Washington.[53] Wilson, on reading the memorandum just delivered by Bernstorff, could not have

---

Ambassador to the Secretary of State, handed to the Secretary of State, February 28, 1916, *Foreign Relations, 1916, Supplement*, pp. 181-182.

[50] Messages sent by this route went from Berlin to the German Ministry in Stockholm and from Stockholm over the Swedish diplomatic wire to Washington by way of Buenos Aires. Messages had to be re-sent from every point. Bernstorff and the Foreign Office could of course use the wireless and often did so for routine reports and information. But it was not a satisfactory channel for confidential communication, as all dispatches that Bernstorff sent or received were supposed to go or come through the American naval censor and the State Department. Actually, Bernstorff had access to a secret wireless apparatus and used it frequently to send messages in the German diplomatic code, as the collection of decoded messages given to Ambassador Page by some British authority and now to be found in the Page Papers reveals. (British Intelligence had captured copies of the German diplomatic code.) For long reports and dispatches, Bernstorff used the mails. Letters from Washington to Berlin usually took about three weeks for delivery.

[51] They were not included in the note that Bernstorff handed to Lansing on February 28, 1916.

[52] *New York Times*, February 28, 1916.

[53] The note finally arrived on March 6. There was a report in the *New York Times*, February 29, 1916, that the British had rifled the American diplomatic pouch aboard the *Nieuw Amsterdam* at Falmouth and seized the note. Lansing, without affirming the truth of the report, told the French Ambassador on March 1 that it would be a singularly grave matter if the report was true.

been greatly surprised by its announcement that the German government intended to proceed on schedule with the new campaign against armed merchantmen. What must have excited and alarmed him was its rather blatant threat against armed liners. It, along with the report in the newspapers on the same day that the German government had also suggested that Americans be warned against traveling on armed ships, raised the threat of all kinds of new perils. It was ironical that the Foreign Office had not informed Bernstorff and the President of the Admiralty's supplementary orders of February 24.[54]

Wilson pondered his response and probably discussed it with the Cabinet at its meeting on Tuesday morning, February 29. The German leaders, he concluded, still did not understand his intentions, or take them seriously if they understood, because they thought that Congress would not support a strong policy on armed ships and would probably continue to think this so long as the McLemore and Gore resolutions hung fire.[55] Consequently, he launched a new bolt in the afternoon of February 29—a letter addressed to E. W. Pou of North Carolina, acting chairman of the House rules committee. It read as follows:

"Inasmuch as I learn that Mr. Henry, the Chairman of the Committee on Rules, is absent in Texas, I take the liberty of calling your attention, as ranking member of the committee, to a matter of grave consequence to the country, which can, I believe, be handled under the rules of the House only by that committee.

"The report that there are divided counsels in Congress in regard to the foreign policy of the Government is being made industrious use of in foreign capitals. I believe that report to be false, but so long as it is anywhere credited it cannot fail to do the greatest harm and expose the country to the most serious risks.

[54] The only intimation of these orders came in a news dispatch from Berlin, printed in the Washington newspapers in the late afternoon of February 28. It said that submarine commanders would not violate instructions previously given to warn passenger liners. Bernstorff told reporters that he thought that this represented the German government's position. *New York Times*, February 29, 1916.

[55] *ibid.*, March 1, 1916. Wilson had no way of knowing about the impact of his letter to Senator Stone on Bethmann and the German Foreign Office, as Gerard's dispatches as usual shed no light on the titanic controversy that was coming to a head in the inner German circles. Gerard did report on February 26, 1916 (received February 27, *Foreign Relations, 1916, Supplement*, p. 179), that the German press had printed reports from London about the armed ship controversy in Congress to the effect that the House foreign affairs committee would not support the President's stand on armed ships. We may be sure that Wilson did not miss seeing this dispatch.

"I therefore feel justified in asking that your committee will permit me to urge an early vote upon the resolutions with regard to travel on armed merchantmen, which have recently been so much talked about, in order that there may be afforded an immediate opportunity for full public discussion and action upon them, and that all doubts and conjectures may be swept away and our foreign relations once more cleared of damaging misunderstandings.

"The matter is of so grave importance and lies so clearly within the field of executive initiative that I venture to hope that your committee will not think that I am taking unwarranted liberty in making this suggestion as to the business of the House, and I very earnestly commend it to their immediate consideration."[56]

It seemed like a bold challenge with "some of the old Andrew Jackson ring in it," as one Cabinet member said,[57] and it electrified the country.[58] Senators Stone and Kern and Representative Flood hurried to the White House at nine o'clock on the following morning, March 1, and Speaker Clark and Representatives Kitchin and Pou followed at ten. They all pleaded for delay and said that the foreign affairs committee, not the rules committee, was the proper body to report the McLemore resolution. Wilson replied that he had obviously erred in this respect, but he made it clear that he would accept nothing less than a clear-cut vote on an unamended McLemore resolution, without delay. He could not conduct foreign policy, he added, so long as the German government believed that Congress had repudiated his policies. The foreign affairs committee met for two hours that afternoon, but only four members were willing to report the McLemore resolution.[59]

Intensifying his pressure, Wilson sent his two chief dispensers of patronage, Burleson and McAdoo, to Capitol Hill on the following day, March 2, armed with a note in his own handwriting to show to Democrats. It read:

My dear Friends,

You have asked me just what I think necessary to clear up the existing situation and relieve the present embarrassment of the Administration in

[56] W. W. to E. W. Pou, February 29, 1916, *New York Times*, March 1, 1916.

[57] T. W. Gregory to R. L. Batts, March 1, 1916, the Papers of Thomas W. Gregory, Library of Congress.

[58] See, e. g., the surveys of press opinion in "Our Right to Travel on Armed Merchantmen," *Literary Digest*, LII (March 11, 1916), 625-627, and in *The Outlook*, CXII (March 8, 1916), 549-552.

[59] *New York Times*, March 2, 1916; New York *World*, March 2, 1916.

dealing with the foreign relations of the country. It seems to me absolutely essential that there should be a vote,—an early vote,—on the resolutions introduced by Mr. McLemore, of Texas. No other course would meet the necessities of the case.

Faithfully, Woodrow Wilson.[60]

Burleson and McAdoo turned the screws, particularly on members of the foreign affairs committee, and Democrats writhed under pressure from the White House and editors who were demanding that they stand by the President. "Whoever votes for these resolutions votes for German diplomacy against American diplomacy," the New York *World* declared in a typical blast.[61] Party discipline in the House had been shattered; not a single leader—that is, neither Clark, Kitchin, nor Flood—really stood with the President on the armed ship issue. Rumors were rife that these three Democrats were intriguing with Bryan in a cloakroom conspiracy to obtain adoption of the McLemore resolution and Clark's nomination for the presidency at the forthcoming national Democratic convention.[62] The fact that the three leaders suspected that one of Wilson's close advisers had planted the rumor[63] did not improve liaison between the White House and the Capitol.[64]

Congressional fears came out dramatically when Gore declared in a speech in the Senate on March 2 that he had it on good authority that the President had told congressional leaders that he expected war, and that American participation might end the struggle by midsummer and be a blessing to civilization. This evoked categorical denial by Senator Stone and Representative Flood that Wilson had ever said such a thing, and the following statement by Wilson: "When the attention of the White House was called to certain statements in Senator Gore's speech this afternoon, the President authorized an unqualified denial of any utterance to which any such meaning could be attached."[65] Wilson also wrote on the same day to a congressman: "I . . . am glad to have an opportunity of assuring you that the report that

[60] W. W. to A. S. Burleson and W. G. McAdoo, March 2, 1916, the Papers of Albert S. Burleson, Library of Congress; hereinafter cited as the Burleson Papers.

[61] New York *World*, March 3, 1916.

[62] See, e. g., J. C. O'Laughlin in the *Chicago Herald*, February 28, 1916.

[63] In fact, Tumulty was probably responsible. See J. P. Tumulty to W. W., February 24, 1916, Wilson Papers.

[64] Clark wrote a furious letter to Wilson on March 10, 1916, *ibid.*, demanding to know whether Wilson believed the rumor. Wilson either replied in conversation or in a letter of which he kept no copy.

[65] *New York Times*, March 3, 1916.

"When They Play 'America,' Stand Up!"
Donahey in the Cleveland *Plain Dealer*

you say was current that I was trying in some way to bring on war was too grotesquely false to deserve credence for a moment. If anybody ever strove harder to preserve peace than I have striven and am striving, I wonder who and what he could have been."[66]

Not all Democrats were convinced. "We are so near war that I feel that I ought to stay here—at least until tomorrow," Bryan, who had

[66] W. W. to W. Gordon, March 2, 1916, Wilson Papers.

rushed to Washington to hearten his followers, wrote to his wife the next day. "It is distressing to see so many men afraid to act. I am needed to give them courage & help to plan. Have already strengthened several & my statement given out tonight will I hope reach the country. . . . How little we know of the future. The President's action bears out my fears expressed when I resigned."[67]

The Senate, where sentiment behind the President was overwhelming, acted first by calling up the Gore resolution for vote on Friday, March 3. Just before the vote was taken Gore changed the preamble to read that destruction of American lives on armed merchantmen would constitute a cause of war between the United States and Germany. The resolution was tabled by a vote of sixty-eight to fourteen, but the parliamentary situation was so confused that many senators, particularly some in the minority, did not know what they were voting for.[68] Even so, the verdict could not have been much more emphatic. "The Senate," the New York *World* exulted, ". . . has declared in substance that the capital of the United States is still Washington and not Berlin; that the President of the United States is still Woodrow Wilson and not Wilhelm II, and that the foreign affairs of the United States are still in the hands of the President and not in the hands of the Kaiser."[69]

The House foreign affairs committee finally voted on Saturday, March 4, to report the McLemore resolution with a recommendation that it be tabled. Bryan redoubled his solicitations over the weekend,[70] and leaders of the National German-American Alliance intensified the lobbying campaign that they had been conducting in behalf of the McLemore resolution.[71]

The rules committee took the situation in hand on March 6 and scheduled a vote for the following day. The House of Representatives met at eleven in the morning of March 7, and debate and parliamentary maneuvering proceeded uninterrupted for seven hours. Administration supporters, led by Pou and Flood, easily beat down attempts to amend the McLemore resolution and defeat the rule governing debate. Then the House finally voted at about five-thirty on a resolution to table the McLemore resolution. It carried by a majority of 276 to

[67] W. J. Bryan to Mary B. Bryan, March 3, 1916, Bryan Papers, LC.

[68] *New York Times*, March 4, 1916.

[69] New York *World*, March 4, 1916.

[70] *New York Times*, March 5 and 6, 1916; *New York Evening Post*, March 6, 1916; *Chicago Evening Post*, March 6, 1916.

[71] See the documents published in the New York *World*, March 7, 1916.

142. One hundred eighty-two Democrats, ninety-three Republicans, and one Progressive voted to table; thirty-three Democrats, 102 Republicans, five Progressives, one independent, and one Socialist voted against tabling. Many Democrats probably voted to table because they did not wish either to embarrass their leader or jeopardize their claims to patronage. But few Republicans voted for partisan reasons. Most of the Republican majority against tabling came from the Middle West, where pacifist and German-American sentiment was strongest. The delegations from Iowa, Nebraska, Minnesota, and Wisconsin voted solidly against tabling. In contrast, New England congressmen, mainly Republican, voted twenty-nine to three in favor of tabling.[72]

The President followed the House's action all afternoon just as closely as if he were watching presidential election returns. He was elated by the outcome, as were editors who had given him decisive help all through the fight,[73] but he wisely decided not to issue a victory statement. Champions of a warning resolution were, for their part, not downcast. "Ninety per cent. of the members of the House, or more," McLemore wrote to a friend in Texas, "favored a simple warning resolution, but, as you say, they came under the whip."[74] Bryan added, "As the situation stood it did not make much difference which way they voted. . . . The real object had been accomplished by the discussion. The people of the United States are not willing to go to war to vindicate the right of Americans to take these risks; neither is Congress. The President knows it and we can now return to our work and await the results, confident that the jingoes can not drive us into war."[75]

There was much truth in Bryan's analysis. As Walter Lippmann pointed out, Wilson had smashed a rebellion and gained more freedom for negotiation.[76] But the significance of the outcome ran deeper than

---

[72] *Congressional Record*, 64th Cong., 1st sess., p. 3720; *New York Times*, March 8 and 9, 1916.

[73] e. g., *New York Times*, New York *World,* and *Springfield* (Mass.) *Republican*, all dated March 8, 1916.

[74] J. McLemore to H. E. Ellis, March 21, 1916, the Papers of Jeff: McLemore, University of Texas Library; hereinafter cited as the McLemore Papers.

[75] W. J. Bryan, "Distinction Without a Difference," *The Commoner*, xvi (March 1916), 2. "I am confident," McLemore wrote a friend, "that the resolution, although not adopted, served a splendid purpose for the time being and prevented this country from being drawn hastily into war simply to assist England at the request of Wall Street and the big dailies that are controlled by Wall Street influence." J. McLemore to J. G. Culbertson, March 31, 1916, McLemore Papers.

[76] W. Lippmann in the *New Republic*, vi (March 18, 1916), 181-182.

this. Bernstorff was not far from the mark in the following report to the Foreign Office:

"The fight between President Wilson and Congress has closed with a victory on the part of the former, or, to speak more accurately, with an apparent victory. . . . There is no doubt that the majority in both Houses is, even today, of the opinion that Americans should be kept off armed merchant ships. Wilson was able to win his Pyrrhic victory only by giving definite promises to the leaders of Congress that he would do all that he possibly could to avoid a war with Germany. It follows that we have gained the following remarkable advantage as the result of the past weeks, that the American people have expressed themselves through their chosen representatives against a war with Germany. Your Excellency is well aware that I have always prophesied that this would be the feeling of Congress, although Mr. Lansing, in his talks with me in the course of the negotiations concerning the *Lusitania*, always asserted the contrary."[77]

[77] Ambassador von Bernstorff to the Foreign Office, March 10, 1916, *Official German Documents*, II, 1289.

CHAPTER VII

The Columbus Raid and the Punitive Expedition

MEXICO seemed to be the one bright spot beyond American borders during the closing months of 1915. Wilson's recognition of the First Chief of the Constitutionalist Party, Venustiano Carranza, on October 19, 1915, accompanied by a lifting of the embargo on shipment of arms to *Carrancistas* and interdiction of shipment to Carranza's enemies,[1] seemed to Mexicans to signal the end of American interference and the beginning of really cordial relations between the two neighbors.

The American Special Agent in Carranza's camp had a long and cordial conversation with Jesús Acuña, Mexican Secretary of Foreign Relations, on October 22. Recognition, Acuña said, had paved the way for settlement of outstanding Mexican-American problems. "He further stated that General Carranza and his [Acuña's] office will want to deal on a perfectly frank basis with the Government of the United States in all future matters; that General Carranza, however, was cognizant of and appreciates all his rights. There are indications that recognition has brought a greater realization of responsibilities. This is not alone exhibited by remarks of the Foreign Secretary but by many of those close to Carranza. Many of them have frankly discussed this situation with me. They recognize the fact that many mistakes will be made but put forth the hope that excuses will be allowed, inasmuch as the officials of the new Government will be composed of men little versed in the art of constructive government."[2]

American officials gave many evidences of eagerness to be helpful in spite of many provocations and difficulties during the autumn of 1915. There was a particularly ugly situation in the Matamoros district, opposite Brownsville, Texas, where a bandit leader, Luis de la Rosa, constantly menaced life and property on the American side. He and his band wrecked a southbound train of the Gulf Coast Railroad near Tandy's Station, only five miles from the outskirts of Brownsville, on October 18, killing one American soldier and two

---

[1] W. W. to W. G. McAdoo, October 19, 1915, Wilson Papers; *New York Times*, October 21, 1915.

[2] J. W. Belt to the Secretary of State, October 22, 1915, the Papers of the Department of State, the National Archives; hereinafter cited as the State Department Papers.

civilians.[3] Loud demands came from leaders in Texas for punitive action,[4] but Wilson and Lansing were determined to give Carranza a chance to act first. This he did by dispatching troops to Reynosa in late November.[5] He also returned American good will by concluding an informal agreement with American military commanders in Browns-ville authorizing American and Mexican soldiers to pursue bandits on either side of the border for a distance of fifteen leagues.[6]

A more serious crisis could have developed if leaders in Washington had been disposed to permit one to develop. The troops of Carranza's arch rival, the defeated but unsubdued Francisco (Pancho) Villa, still occupied Ciudad Juárez, opposite El Paso, and many other towns along the border, and Villa was himself roaming through the States of Chihuahua and Sonora with a formidable force. He first learned that the United States had recognized Carranza from a newspaperman on October 31. He was also informed that the American government had permitted *Carrancista* authorities to transport troops across American territory for the defense of Agua Prieta, then menaced by *Villistas*. "He became very angry," the American correspondent reported, "and declared he was through with them all and that was how he was to be repaid for the protection he has given to Americans and other foreigners[;] that he would take Agua-Prieta if he had to fight the whole Carranza army and the United States combined."[7] Villa hit Agua Prieta with 13,000 men on November 1 and 2. He was repulsed with heavy losses and then withdrew into Chihuahua to menace and blackmail American ranchers and miners.[8]

[3] H. L. Yates *et al.* to the Secretary of State, October 19, 1915; General F. Funston to Adjutant General H. P. McCain, October 21, 1915, both in *ibid.*

[4] M. Sheppard to the Secretary of State, October 23, 1915; *ibid.*; Governor J. E. Ferguson to W. W., October 27, 1915, *ibid.*

[5] J. R. Silliman to the Secretary of State, November 22, 1915, *ibid.*

[6] Special Agent Belt reported that Acuña had said that "already arrangements had been made whereby American forces could pursue 'bandits' for a distance of fifteen leagues into Mexican territory; and that Mexican soldiers would have a like privilege when in pursuit of bandit bands causing trouble." J. W. Belt to the Secretary of State, November 9, 1915, *ibid.* This arrangement must have been made by the local military commanders with Carranza's consent. Lansing replied on November 11 that the State Department had no knowledge of the agreement. R. Lansing to J. W. Belt, November 11, 1915, *ibid.*

[7] General Funston to the Adjutant General, November 1, 1915, *ibid.*; G. C. Carothers to the Secretary of State, October 31, 1915, *Papers Relating to the Foreign Relations of the United States, 1915*, p. 775.

[8] G. C. Carothers to the Secretary of State, November 1, 3, 5, and 6, 1915, State Department Papers; General Funston to the Adjutant General, November 2, 1915, *ibid.*

Leaders in Washington continued to insist that Carranza should have an opportunity to take action in his own way. They did not have to wait long, for the First Chief sent his best general, Álvaro Obregón, with crack troops to the North in early November. They began a campaign that drove *Villistas* from all major port towns, including Juárez,[9] and from their major base in Chihuahua City, and decimated Villa's so-called army by the end of the year. "*De facto* government," Lansing could report on December 30, 1915, "is now in control of entire border territory, except for one or two unimportant sub-ports. Carranza troops from Chihuahua City are now policing Juarez. Several Villa generals have surrendered themselves and their commands. General Villa's whereabouts unknown, but supposed to be in Chihuahua mountains at the head of small following. Situation in Yaqui Valley appears to be improving and settlers have returned to Los Mochis. Mining companies are resuming operations in Chihuahua and Sonora."[10] The situation was so encouraging by early January that the Secretary of War asked for Lansing's views "as to the feasibility of withdrawing any or all of the troops now on the border from the duty on which they have been engaged and returning them to their permanent stations."[11] It seemed, indeed, that Mexico's long ordeal of revolution and civil strife was happily ended.

Administration leaders in Washington were of course heartened by the rapid return of peace, and they did not fail to see events in Mexico as vindication of their own much abused and criticized policies. Roman Catholic bishops and public spokesmen still bitterly resented recognition of the alleged despoiler of the Church in Mexico. Tumulty received a letter, for example, from a Roman Catholic layman in mid-November saying that there had been "such widespread criticism of the manner in which Catholic priests and sisters have been treated at the hands of Gen. Carranza in Mexico that many friends of the President are at a loss to understand why the Administration has been willing to recognize him."[12]

Here, Tumulty thought, was an opportunity to allay Catholic discontent and claim some credit for the administration at the same time. He pulled from the files a copy of a long letter defending administra-

[9] Actually, *Villistas* in Juárez surrendered the city without a fight on December 22, 1915.

[10] R. Lansing to Charles Parker, December 30, 1915, *ibid.*

[11] L. M. Garrison to R. Lansing, January 6, 1916, *ibid.*

[12] J. J. McGuire to J. P. Tumulty, November 14, 1915, New York *World*, November 29, 1915.

tion policies in Mexico that Leon J. Canova, head of the Mexican Affairs Division in the State Department, had recently drafted for him to send to another correspondent.[13] Tumulty, after making certain changes, had it retyped as a reply to McGuire. He gave it to Wilson soon afterward, saying that he would publish it if the President approved. "I have read this with a great deal of interest and appreciation," Wilson replied. "It seems to me to be the right thing and I am very glad indeed you are going to publish it."[14] What Tumulty did not say, and what Wilson did not comment on, was the obvious fact that Tumulty was the leading Roman Catholic member of the administration.

Tumulty began with a forthright defense of the Mexican Revolution as a great movement for liberty, no worse in its excesses than other great revolutions.[15] The Washington administration, he went on, had avoided military involvement, in spite of the agitation of self-interested Americans living in Mexico. As for the fate of Catholics in Mexico, there was no official record of a single outrage having been committed against nuns by Mexican soldiers. The American government had cooperated with Catholic countries in Latin America in recognizing Carranza. Tumulty concluded by quoting the assurances concerning religious freedom that the *de facto* government had given before its recognition.[16]

The letter, published in the newspapers on November 29, 1915, set off a new storm of denunciations from Catholic leaders and editors all over the country. "The present administration," a New York priest warned, "will wreck the Democratic party unless it changes its shameful methods of dealing with Catholics."[17] The editor of the *New World* of Chicago interpreted Tumulty's letter as an arraignment of

[13] It was J. P. Tumulty to Randolph W. Smith, November 11, 1915, Wilson Papers.

[14] W. W. to J. P. Tumulty, c. November 18, 1915, *ibid.*

[15] Wilson had made a similar observation a short time before. Frederic C. Howe had written to him on October 29, 1915 (*ibid.*), "The revolution through which Mexico is passing is not dissimilar to the French Revolution. It is primarily agrarian, economic and social. It is moved by the same kind of feudal abuses that prevailed in France under the old regime." Wilson replied on November 1, 1915 (*ibid.*): "I have several times noted the extraordinary similarity between the way things have been going in Mexico and the way they went in France a little over a hundred years ago, and I have noted with a great deal of interest your analysis of the matter."

[16] J. P. Tumulty to J. J. McGuire, November 27, 1915, New York *World*, November 29, 1915.

[17] The Rev. J. Mullany, Syracuse, N. Y., to J. P. Tumulty, December 2, 1915, Wilson Papers.

Roman Catholics.[18] Monsignor Francis C. Kelley, president of the Catholic Church Extension Society, and the Reverend R. H. Tierney, S.J., editor of *America*, issued public retorts, offering to furnish proof of the abuse of Mexican nuns and priests if any was needed.[19] "The truth of the matter," the leading Catholic newspaper in the lower South exclaimed, "is that Mr. Tumulty's letter is a political trick, written to disarm the 'widespread criticism' of his master. . . . Mr. Wilson has been 'watchfully waiting.' The Catholics of this country and all true citizens can also watchfully wait. The rights of Catholics may be disregarded, but they have votes, and at the polls in 1916 Mr. Wilson will receive their answer in the only way in which they can effectually give it."[20]

Wilson was both surprised and angered. What the Roman Catholic hierarchy wanted in Mexico, he had written a month before Tumulty's letter was published, was "something more than toleration."[21] He was discreet enough to refrain from direct reply to Catholic critics, but he included a ringing defense of his Mexican policies in his Annual Message to Congress on December 7, as follows:

"We have been put to the test in the case of Mexico, and we have stood the test. Whether we have benefited Mexico by the course we have pursued remains to be seen. Her fortunes are in her own hands. But we have at least proved that we will not take advantage of her in her distress and undertake to impose upon her an order and government of our own choosing. Liberty is often a fierce and untractable thing, to which no bounds can be set, and to which no bounds of a few men's choosing ought ever to be set. Every American who has drunk at the true fountains of principle and tradition must subscribe without reservation to the high doctrine of the Virginia Bill of Rights, which in the great days when our government was set up was everywhere amongst us accepted as the creed of free men. . . . We have unhesitatingly applied that heroic principle to the case of Mexico,

[18] The Rev. T. V. Shannon to R. Lansing, November 30, 1915, Lansing Papers.

[19] New York *World*, December 3, 1915.

[20] New Orleans *Morning Star*, December 4, 1915. For other hostile comment, see the *Baltimore Catholic Review*, December 11, 1915. For reports from worried Democratic leaders, see E. O. Wood (Democratic national committeeman from Michigan) to J. P. Tumulty, December 1, 1915, Wilson Papers, and Barry Murphy, Medina, N. Y., to J. P. Tumulty, December 14, 1915, *ibid.* For Catholic comment supporting Wilson, see the Rev. John A. Ryan to J. P. Tumulty, December 1, 1915, *ibid.*, and the Columbus (Ohio) *Catholic Columbian*, December 10, 1915.

[21] W. W. to R. Lansing, October 31, 1915, State Department Papers.

and now hopefully await the rebirth of the troubled Republic, which had so much of which to purge itself and so little sympathy from any outside quarter in the radical but necessary process. We will aid and befriend Mexico, but we will not coerce her; and our course with regard to her ought to be sufficient proof to all America that we seek no political suzerainty or selfish control."[22]

He was even more explicit about his determination in a private talk to members of the Democratic National Committee on December 8:

"Why, I have been in companies where it seemed as if I were the only man who really believed down in his heart that a people had the right to do anything with their government that they damned pleased to do, and that it was nobody else's business what they did with it. That is what I believe. If the Mexicans want to raise hell, let them raise hell. We have got nothing to do with it. It is their government, it is their hell. And after they have raised enough of it, it will sit so badly on their stomachs that they will want something else. They will get down to hard pan and make a government that will stay put, but unless you let them have it out, they won't have a government that will stay put."[23]

These were noble words, but at least one man knew when Wilson uttered them how difficult it would be for him to maintain such high resolve. He was Pancho Villa, scourge of northern Mexico. He had retired to the mountains of Chihuahua following severe defeats at Alomita, north of Hermosillo, on November 19 or 20, and at Nogales on November 26.[24] He seized some thirty Americans in Chihuahua soon afterward and threatened to kill them and many others if the American government did not cease its support of the *Carrancistas*.[25] He must have released his hostages—the records are silent about their fate—, for he sent one of his generals to the American Consul in Ciudad Juárez on December 17 with an offer to abandon resistance and retire to the United States if the American government would grant asylum.[26] "I am authorized by the President," Lansing replied on the following day, "to state that in case General Villa decides to take refuge in the United States immediately, this Government will grant refuge to him,

---

[22] *The New Democracy*, I, 408-409.

[23] From the transcript in the Swem Collection.

[24] G. C. Carothers to the Secretary of State, November 20, 1915, State Department Papers; F. Simpich to the Secretary of State, November 26, 1915, *ibid*.

[25] G. C. Carothers to the Secretary of State, December 16, 1915, Wilson Papers.

[26] Fidel Avila to W. W., December—, 1915, repeated in telegram from Consul T. D. Edwards to the Secretary of State, December 17, 1915, State Department Papers.

and will extend to him the full guarantees and immunity of a political refugee, provided he will, in turn, in his own behalf and that of such leaders as may remain on the other side of the border, extend full guarantees to all Americans in territory controlled by him, and provided Americans reported detained at Chihuahua be immediately released."[27]

Villa gave his answer in typically savage fashion on January 10, 1916, when a group of his soldiers, commanded by his chief lieutenant, Pablo López, stopped a Mexican-Northwestern train at the cattle station of Santa Ysabel fifty miles west of Chihuahua City. They removed eighteen American passengers, all connected with the American-owned La Cusi Mining Company of Cusihuriáchic, stripped and robbed them, and shot seventeen of them in cold blood, shouting "Viva Villa" while the butchery proceeded. One member of the party, Thomas B. Holmes, escaped miraculously.[28] It has been well established that Villa planned and ordered the robbery; there is some evidence, along with some doubt, that he was personally responsible for the murders.[29]

News of the massacre first came to Washington in dispatches from Zach L. Cobb, Collector of Customs at El Paso, on January 11. Reports in the newspapers confirmed the sad intelligence on the following day and set off violent agitation in Congress. Comment was particularly bitter in the upper house, where a resolution requesting the President to furnish certain information about events in Mexico, introduced by Albert B. Fall of New Mexico, had been approved only a few days before.[30] Senator Lawrence Y. Sherman of Illinois submitted a resolution calling for Pan-American occupation of Mexico if Carranza failed to protect foreign lives and property. William E. Borah of Idaho, Miles Poindexter of Washington, and Jacob H. Gallinger of New Hampshire said that the time had come to use force if Carranza could not honor his promises to protect foreigners. Even Senator Stone wavered in support of the President's policies. He had, he said, supported nonintervention against his own convictions. But he went on to plead that Wilson be given further opportunity to test

[27] R. Lansing to Consul T. D. Edwards, December 18, 1915, *ibid.*

[28] *New York Times*, January 12, 1916; Clarence C. Clendenen, *The United States and Pancho Villa*, pp. 225-226.

[29] *New York Times*, January 13, 1916; C. E. Clendenen, *The United States and Pancho Villa*, pp. 226-227.

[30] "Senate Resolution submitted by Mr. Fall," *Papers Relating to the Foreign Relations of the United States, 1916*, pp. 463-464; hereinafter cited as *Foreign Relations, 1916*.

the wisdom of his policies.[31] Excitement still ran high in Congress on the following day, January 13. Senator James Hamilton Lewis of Illinois, Democratic whip, introduced a resolution authorizing the President to use the armed forces to protect American life and property in Mexico, and a poll of the Senate revealed that more than a score of senators favored intervention of some kind. On the other side of the Capitol, Representative Hunter H. Moss, Jr., of West Virginia offered a resolution authorizing military operations in Mexico.[32]

There were loud echoes in the country at large, as wild anger and excitement greater than any since the sinking of the *Lusitania* surged through part of the American people. "This dreadful outrage," Theodore Roosevelt, who had an eye on the coming presidential campaign, exclaimed, "is merely an inevitable outcome of the policies that have been followed in Mexico for the last five years, and above all, the last three years."[33] Hearst's Los Angeles newspaper was violent in denunciation. "It is true at last," it said. "We ARE too proud to fight. . . . Why, even a little, despicable, contemptible bandit nation like Mexico murders our citizens, drags our flag in the dirt and spits at and defies this Nation of ours with truculent insolence."[34] Even the usually moderate *Independent* called for forceful action: "Unless within a very brief time Carranza shows himself able to comply with our demand to punish the murderers and to provide guarantees for the future, the President should send armed forces into Northern Mexico."[35]

Wilson had meanwhile moved serenely to calm the storm and bring the situation under control. Lansing dispatched a telegram to Carranza on January 12 urgently "requesting" him to apprehend and punish the Santa Ysabel murderers and send adequate forces to protect American mines in Chihuahua.[36] The President made it plain on the following day that he was not moved by the excitement on Capitol Hill. He told a number of senators who came to the White House to plead for action that he of course deeply deplored the crime at

---

[31] *New York Times*, January 13, 1916; *Congressional Record*, 64th Cong., 1st sess., pp. 942-948, 955-962.

[32] *New York Times*, January 14, 1916.

[33] *ibid.*

[34] *Los Angeles Examiner*, January 14, 1916.

[35] *The Independent*, LXXXV (January 24, 1916), 107-108. In the same vein, see *The New Republic*, v (January 22, 1916)*, 288, and *The Outlook*, CXII (January 26, 1916), 179. For a general survey of press comment, see "The Mexican Murders," *Literary Digest*, LII (January 22, 1916), 157-159.

[36] The Secretary of State to J. R. Silliman, January 12, 1916, *Foreign Relations, 1916*, p. 653.

Santa Ysabel and that the administration would do everything in its power to see that the murderers were punished. But, he added, the American government looked to Carranza for redress; he had no intention of yielding to the demand for armed intervention; and the murdered men had deliberately ignored the State Department's warning not to enter the part of Mexico in which they were killed.[37] Wilson repeated these statements to reporters on January 14, following a Cabinet meeting that morning. His declarations set off a new outburst by Senator Fall.[38]

The tide against warlike action had, in fact, already set in by the time that the Senator from New Mexico (the leading champion, along with Hearst, of war with Mexico) delivered his tirade. A considerable segment of public opinion had counseled restraint or condemned the very thought of armed intervention from the outset.[39] It was encouraged by Wilson's unequivocal refusal to countenance acts of war, and above all by Carranza's own vigorous efforts to apprehend and punish the murderers at Santa Ysabel. The First Chief rushed troops to Madera, whence the *Villistas* had fled; they killed two of Villa's "generals" and captured a number of his soldiers on January 13.[40] Carranza's reply to Lansing's telegram of January 12, published in American newspapers on January 17, gave further proof of his intentions. The First Chief said that he had already issued orders for the immediate pursuit, capture, and execution of the men responsible for the atrocity. Villa, he went on, had committed the outrage for the specific purpose of provoking American intervention. He would do his best to protect Americans in northern Mexico, but the American government should remember that protection was relative, and that disorders occurred even in the most stable societies.[41]

Public excitement had died entirely by now, and Wilson and Lansing arranged with Democratic leaders in Congress to bury the Mexican issue altogether. Lansing, in response to urgings from Senator Stone

[37] *New York Times*, January 14, 1916; New York *World*, January 14, 1916.

[38] *New York Times*, January 15, 1916; *Congressional Record*, 64th Cong., 1st sess., pp. 1062-1066.

[39] e. g., A. R. McCollum, editor of the *Waco Tribune*, to W. W., January 14, 1916, Wilson Papers; J. R. Dunlap to W. W., January 14, 1916, *ibid.*; Peace Committee of the California State Church Federation to W. W., January 15, 1916, *ibid.*; C. R. Crane to W. W., January 15, 1916, *ibid.*; New York *World*, January 15, 1916; *New York Times*, January 16, 1916; Chicago *Public*, xix (January 21, 1916), 49-50.

[40] *New York Times*, January 14, 1916.

[41] Special Agent Silliman to the Secretary of State, received January 16, 1916, *Foreign Relations, 1916*, pp. 659-660; *New York Times*, January 17, 1916.

(he, along with Lewis, had returned foursquare to the President's side on January 14), rushed completion of the State Department's response to the Fall resolution, and Wilson sent it to the Senate on February 17.[42] Meanwhile Stone, with the help of the now united Democratic members of the foreign relations committee, on January 19 had beaten down efforts by Senators Borah and Lodge to obtain a favorable vote on various resolutions authorizing the President to use the armed forces in Mexico.[43]

Wilson had what seemed to be the last word, in an address before the Motion Picture Board of Trade in New York City on January 27. "I found out what was going on in Mexico," he said, "in a very singular way,—by hearing a sufficiently large number of liars talk about it. . . . You know that the truth is consistent with itself; one piece matches another. Now no man is an inventive enough liar not to bring in large sections of truth in what he says, and after all the liars are done talking to you about the same subject it will come to your consciousness that long and large pieces of what they said matched; that in that respect they all said the same thing; that the variations are lies and the consistencies are the truth. They will not all tell you the same piece of the truth, so that if you hear enough of them, you may get the whole of the truth. And yet it is very tedious to hear men lie, particularly when you know they are lying."[44]

Was Wilson referring to Catholic leaders and spokesmen? One church periodical thought that he was. "In Catholic circles," it said, "the speech has caused a sensation. Leading Catholics here argue, that the President in shaping his policy regarding Mexico, did so after hearing a number of statements on the situation in that unhappy country. . . . By this process of elimination we find the liars to be Cardinal Gibbons, . . . Msgr. Francis Kelley, and Father Tierney, S.J. [among others]."[45] And one irate priest wrote to Tumulty a week later: "The sixteen millions of Catholic American citizens *do feel* profoundly outraged by President Wilson. . . . *You almost turned out a traitor to your own Catholic Church in order* to hold your office & please your *protestant* president. May God forgive you!!"[46]

[42] *ibid.*, January 15 and 16, and February 18, 1916. The President's message transmitting the report, along with the report itself, is printed in *Foreign Relations, 1916*, pp. 469-478.

[43] *New York Times*, January 20, 1916.

[44] *The New Democracy*, I, 447.

[45] Dubuque *Catholic Tribune*, February 10, 1916.

[46] The Rev. J. Gheldof to J. P. Tumulty, February 17, 1916, Wilson Papers.

Mexico dropped largely out of American sight during the following weeks. Villa was discreetly quiet, and his threatened attacks on Americans in Chihuahua did not materialize. There were rumors in early March that he intended to go to Washington to prove that he had not been responsible for the Santa Ysabel massacre. Actually, he was preparing for an attack on American soil, which he had contemplated as early as January 6, 1916.[47] Consequently, no one seemed disturbed when American border officials reported that he was moving with his band toward the border town of Columbus, New Mexico, some seventy-five miles due west of El Paso, even though the *Carrancista* commander in Juárez warned on March 6 that Pancho intended to commit some atrocity that would force the Washington government to send troops into Mexico. Brigadier General John J. Pershing, commander of Fort Bliss at El Paso, said that he had heard such reports too many times to take them seriously.[48] Colonel Herbert J. Slocum, commander of the 13th Cavalry at Columbus, learned on March 7 that Villa, with about 500 men, was not far south of the border, but reports on the following day indicated that he had turned southward. Thus Pancho Villa, thirsting for revenge and hoping to recover his standing as the hero of Mexico and provoke conflict between the Carranza regime and the Washington government, rode toward the most fateful atrocity of his brutal career, undetected and unharassed.

He struck Columbus with a force variously estimated at between 1,000 and 3,000 men at 4:15 in the morning of March 9. They rushed into the little town shouting "Viva Villa" and "Viva Mexico," firing indiscriminately, looting stores, and burning houses. Troops of the 13th Cavalry rallied quickly and drove the Mexicans into retreat within an hour. Then Major Frank Tompkins with a troop of thirty-two men, soon augmented to sixty in number, pursued the fleeing *Villistas* fifteen miles into Mexico for three hours. Total casualties, including those killed by Tompkins and his men, were about 67 Mexican dead and seven wounded and captured, seven American soldiers killed and five wounded, and eight American civilians killed and two wounded.[49]

[47] See F. Villa to E. Zapata, January 8, 1916, from San Geronimo Ranch, Chihuahua, State Department Papers. A copy of this letter was found in the saddle bags of one of Villa's officers later killed at Columbus, New Mexico. What was apparently another copy, dated January 6, 1916, was dropped by Villa at Columbus and printed in the *New York Times*, March 11, 1916.

[48] Frank Tompkins, *Chasing Villa*, p. 42.

[49] *New York Times*, March 10, 1916; Z. L. Cobb to the Secretary of State, March 9, 1916, State Department Papers; General F. Funston to the Adjutant General, March 10, 1916, Wilson Papers; report of H. J. Slocum, dated March 11, 1916, in "Weekly report

Subsequent deaths from wounds brought the American death toll to about nineteen.

There was no doubt that Villa had led the charge in person. "I was in Columbus," George C. Carothers, a Special Agent of the State Department wrote, "the afternoon of the day the attack took place, and examined the papers that were in the two wallets Villa lost on the battlefield during his retreat. The papers fully connect him with the Santa Isabel massacre, and also establish the fact that he decided to declare war on us last December. He is crazy, from what I could find out among the prisoners, goes about with his mouth open, and looks dazed. His obsession is to kill Americans, and he has undoubtedly what the Mexicans call 'Delirio de Grandesa' or Delirium of Greatness. He inspired his whole column with the conviction that they could conquer the United States, and that they would be in Washington within six months."[50]

Americans recoiled in unbelief and horror at news of the attack. "Nothing less than Villa's life can atone for the outrage at Columbus, N.M.," the New York *World* exclaimed in a typical editorial. ". . . Every drop of American blood shed at Columbus is on his hands. So far as it is possible for a bandit to be at war, Villa is now at war with both Mexico and the United States. The Mexican Government, in spite of the efforts of Carranza, has proved unable to cope with the situation, and so the duty of effective action devolves upon the United States."[51] Even Villa's old American friends and admirers were horrified. "It seems," his former agent in the United States wrote, "that in the last few months the varnish of civilization Villa acquired in four years disappeared again leaving him the primitive brute he was years ago."[52] "This is a different man than we knew," Carothers added. "All the brutality in his nature has come to the front, and he should be killed like a dog."[53]

News of the Columbus raid reached Washington late in the morning of March 9. Lansing probably informed the President by telephone—they apparently did not see each other that day—and the two leaders must have agreed then that they had no choice but to send an expedition

---

of general conditions along the Mexican border," No. 156, copy in the State Department Papers; F. Tompkins, *Chasing Villa*, pp. 48-64.

[50] G. C. Carothers to H. L. Scott, March 13, 1916, Scott Papers.

[51] New York *World*, March 10, 1916. For other press comment, see "Villa's Invasion," *Literary Digest*, LII (March 18, 1916), 700.

[52] F. A. Sommerfeld to H. L. Scott, March 10, 1916, Scott Papers.

[53] G. C. Carothers to H. L. Scott, March 13, 1916, *ibid.*

into Mexico to capture Villa and his band. In any event, the Washington correspondents reported that they made this decision, at least tentatively, on March 9. Lansing saw Eliseo Arredondo, Carranza's envoy in Washington, in the afternoon and apparently told him that the American government, determined to punish the perpetrators of the Columbus outrage, was contemplating taking action whether or not the *de facto* government approved.[54] A short time later, at four o'clock, the Secretary of State sent an urgent message to the First Chief, informing him of the Columbus raid and concluding ominously: "Convey foregoing to General Carranza for his information and advise him that this Government is suspending judgment until further facts can be learned, but you may say to him that this appears to be the most serious situation which has confronted this Government during the entire period of Mexican unrest and that it is expected that he will do everything in his power to pursue, capture, and exterminate this lawless element which is now proceeding westward from Columbus."[55]

Wilson discussed the Mexican situation with the Cabinet in the late morning of March 10. News had just arrived that Villa had killed four Americans before the Columbus raid and was now threatening to attack a colony of American Mormons at Casas Grandes, Chihuahua. General Frederick Funston, Commander of the Southern Department, had urged dispatch of an expedition to apprehend Villa and warned that Pancho would continue his depredations unless the United States struck quickly.[56] All Cabinet members agreed that Congress would adopt a resolution calling for armed intervention unless the government took vigorous action immediately. That, Wilson apparently said, was precisely what he was most eager to avoid. He was determined to avoid war with Mexico or participation in Mexican internal affairs. He realized that Villa had perpetrated the Columbus raid in order to force American military intervention. But it was clear that nothing short of the punishment of Villa and his followers would satisfy public sentiment. This, Wilson said, could probably be done quickly with a small force.

Much discussion of the wisdom of asking Carranza's permission for dispatch of a Punitive Expedition now followed. The administration, Wilson said, had no desire to appear to be invading Mexico against the

[54] *New York Times*, March 10, 1916.

[55] The Secretary of State to Special Agents Silliman and Belt, March 9, 1916, *Foreign Relations, 1916*, p. 481.

[56] F. Funston to the Adjutant General, March 10, 1916, *ibid.*, pp. 482-483.

wishes of the recognized central government. At the same time, there was danger that the First Chief would refuse to grant permission if it was requested, and the Punitive Expedition would have to be sent in spite of his refusal. The only solution, Cabinet members agreed, was to send the expedition and convey a broad intimation to Carranza that the American government would be grateful if he would kindly close his eyes to the requirements of diplomatic etiquette. "An adequate force," Wilson announced in a statement issued to reporters after the meeting, "will be sent at once in pursuit of Villa with the single object of capturing him and putting a stop to his forays. This can and will be done in entire friendly aid of the constituted authorities in Mexico and with scrupulous respect for the sovereignty of that republic."[57]

There was feverish activity in the War Department while the President and Mrs. Wilson entertained Ambassador and Mrs. Henry Morgenthau and Mr. and Mrs. Charles R. Crane at luncheon. Newton D. Baker, new Secretary of War, asked the Chief of Staff, General Hugh L. Scott, to prepare orders to be sent to General Funston at Fort Sam Houston in San Antonio, for assembly of a Punitive Expedition. They were completed by late afternoon, after a preliminary exchange between the War Department and Funston, and read as follows:

> You will promptly organize an adequate military force of troops from your department under the command of Brigadier General John J. Pershing and will direct him to proceed promptly across the border in pursuit of the Mexican band which attacked the town of Columbus, New Mexico[,] and the troops there on the morning of the ninth instant. These troops will be withdrawn to American territory as soon as the de facto government of Mexico is able to relieve them of this work. In any event the work of these troops will be regarded as finished as soon as Villa's band or bands are known to be broken up. In carrying out these instructions you are authorized to employ whatever guides and interpreters are necessary and you are given general authority to employ such transportation, including motor transportation, with necessary civilian personnel as may be required. The President desires his following instructions to be carefully adhered to and to be strictly confidential. You will instruct the commanders of your troops on the border opposite the state[s] of Chihuahua and Sonora, or, roughly, within the field of possible operations by Villa and not under the control of the force of the de facto government, that they are authorized to use the same tactics of defense and pursuit in the event of similar raids across the border and into the United States by a band or bands such as attacked Columbus, New Mexico, yesterday. You are instructed to make all

[57] *New York Times*, March 11, 1916.

practicable use of the aeroplanes at San Antonio, Texas, for observation. Telegraph for whatever reinforcements or material you need. Notify this office as to force selected and expedite movement.[58]

Baker took these orders to the White House for Wilson's approval at six-thirty in the evening. "There is no intention of entering Mexico in force," the Secretary of War explained immediately afterward in a statement that he and the President probably prepared during their conference. "A sufficient body of mobile troops will be sent in to locate and disperse or capture the band or bands that attacked Columbus. As soon as the forces of the de facto Government can take control of the situation any forces of the United States then remaining in Mexico will, of course, be withdrawn. The forces of the United States now on the border will be immediately recruited, but only for the purpose of safeguarding the territory of the United States from further raids."[59] The orders were sent that same night. "The President is sending a small force to break up that raiding body that attacked Columbus," the Chief of Staff explained on the following day. "He was told that this may spread thru all Mexico. He wants it for defensive purposes to break up that gang and come out without affecting the sovereignty of Mexico."[60]

Much if not everything, as it turned out, now depended upon Carranza. He had sent orders as soon as he received news of the Columbus raid to his commander in Chihuahua, General Luis Gutiérrez, to move quickly to apprehend and attack the *Villista* band.[61] The First Chief

[58] The Adjutant General to the Commanding General, Southern Department, March 10, 1916, copy in the State Department Papers.

[59] *New York Times*, March 11, 1916.

[60] H. L. Scott to L. Wood, March 11, 1916, Scott Papers.

[61] V. Carranza to L. Gutiérrez, March 10, 1916, Mexican Foreign Office, *Diplomatic Dealings of the Constitutionalist Revolution in Mexico*, p. 140; hereinafter cited as *Mexican White Paper*. This document, a translation of Mexican Foreign Office, *Labor internacional de la Revolución Constitucionalista de México*, is the basic source of information on the Mexican side for the Punitive Expedition and the controversy that it provoked. The only major Mexican secondary study is Alberto Salinas Carranza, *La Expedicion Punitiva*. Salinas Carranza leaned heavily on *Labor internacional, Foreign Relations, 1916*, and American memoirs, particularly Colonel Tompkins's *Chasing Villa*, but he apparently had access to some Mexican military archives and includes details about military operations that cannot be found elsewhere. Another significant feature of his book is a prologue by Luis Cabrera, whose retrospective analysis of the causes of Mexican-American discord in 1916-1917 makes interesting reading even if some of Cabrera's conclusions seem dubious at this date. Isidro Fabela, *Historia Diplomática de la Revolución Mexicana* (2 vols.), is a recent general work that covers, among other

was disturbed by receipt of Lansing's message of March 9 and of reports from Washington about the American government's plans. He had no intention of formally approving the entry of a large American force into Mexican territory. He would play for time in the hopes that his own men could catch Villa and an American expeditionary force would not go far or stay long if it was actually sent.

Hence Carranza, speaking through Foreign Secretary Acuña, replied somewhat obliquely to the Secretary of State on March 10. He had, the First Chief said, sent General Gutiérrez after Villa. And he asked permission for Mexican troops to enter the United States in pursuit of bandits "upon the understanding that, reciprocally, the forces of the United States may cross into Mexican territory, if the raid effected at Columbus should unfortunately be repeated at any other point on the border."[62] Receipt on March 11 of news that the American government meant to send a large expedition drew a second more somber warning from the First Chief. The Mexican government, he said, would regard dispatch of an expedition *without its permission* as an invasion of its national territory and an act of war, and the American government would alone be responsible for the tragic consequences.[63] Carranza at the same time sent orders to his commanders in Sonora and Veracruz to prepare to resist an American invasion by land and sea.[64] "I am secure . . . in assuming," he wrote on the next day to a friend at Veracruz, "that the Mexican people will worthily fulfill their duty, whatever may be the sacrifices they may have to assume to sustain their rights and their sovereignty."[65]

Arredondo read Carranza's message of March 11 to Lansing at four o'clock on Sunday afternoon, March 12. It, along with reports of feverish activity in Mexican garrisons along the border, caused Baker

---

things, events between the Santa Ysabel massacre and the withdrawal of the Punitive Expedition in 1917. Fabela leaned heavily on *Labor internacional* and Salinas Carranza and added nothing new by way of documentation. His work is chiefly useful for the understanding that it gives of the reactions of the Mexican ruling class to the Punitive Expedition and Mexican-American negotiations for its withdrawal.

[62] Special Agent Silliman to the Secretary of State, March 10, 1916, *Foreign Relations, 1916*, p. 485.

[63] First Chief Carranza to E. Arredondo, March 11, 1916, *ibid.*, p. 486.

[64] V. Carranza to M. M. Dieguez, March 11, 1916; V. Carranza to P. E. Calles, March 11, 1916; V. Carranza to A. Millán, March 11, 1916, all in *Mexican White Paper*, pp. 141-142.

[65] V. Carranza to H. Jara, March 12, 1916, printed in Veracruz *El Dictamen*, March 13, 1916.

to send an additional infantry regiment from Galveston to El Paso (four cavalry regiments had been sent during the preceding day).[66]

Wilson spent the weekend aboard the *Mayflower*. He returned to the White House on Monday morning, March 13, to find official Washington in an uproar over talk that Carranza would resist an American expedition and war with Mexico impended. The Chief of the War College Division of the Army General Staff recommended adoption of the War College's war plan, including its call for 400,000 volunteers "as soon as it is evident that Mexican troops will resist the progress of the expedition planned by the President in pursuit of Villa."[67] The Chief of Staff, General Scott, said that the least the government could do was to call out the National Guard and send a volunteer force of 150,000 men to defend the border.[68] Newspapermen were so excited by talk of hostilities that David Lawrence, head of the Associated Press Bureau, appealed to the President to ask reporters and editors throughout the country to avoid inflaming public sentiment.[69]

Wilson, reporters said, was infuriated. He discussed the Mexican situation with Speaker Clark, Representative Kitchin, Senator Stone, and Senator Willard Saulsbury of Delaware during the morning of March 13. Then Lansing came after lunch, and the two men went over Carranza's messages and discussed a reply. They obviously did not take the First Chief's war warning seriously, for Lansing had written in his desk diary immediately after Arredondo read the message to him on March 12 that it seemed to be for home consumption. Instead, they decided to accept Carranza's suggestion for an agreement permitting hot pursuit across both sides of the border, and to tell the *de facto* government that they understood that "the arrangement is now complete and in force and the reciprocal privileges thereunder may accordingly be exercised by either Government without further interchange of views." Lansing sent this message, adding profuse thanks for Carranza's willingness to cooperate, to the First Chief as soon as he had returned to the State Department.[70] Shortly afterward, Lansing

[66] *New York Times*, March 13, 1916.

[67] M. M. Macomb, memorandum for the Chief of Staff, March 13, 1916, Scott Papers.

[68] H. L. Scott, memorandum for the Secretary of War, March 13, 1916, *ibid*.

[69] D. Lawrence to W. W., March 13, 1916, the Papers of Frank L. Polk, Yale University Library; hereinafter cited as the Polk Papers. Frank L. Polk, Counselor of the State Department prepared a statement at Wilson's request, and it was given to reporters on March 21, 1916. See W. W. to F. L. Polk, March 13, 1916; F. L. Polk to W. W., March 17, 1916; and the statement, entitled "Handed to the Representatives of the Press, March 21, 1916," all in *ibid*.

[70] The Secretary of State to Special Agent Silliman, March 13, 1916, *Foreign Relations, 1916*, pp. 487-488.

gave to Arredondo and to reporters, for publication, a copy of a special announcement he had just received from the President (it was written on his own typewriter). It read:

> In order to remove any apprehensions that may exist either in the United States or in Mexico, the President has authorized me to give in his name the public assurance that the military operations now in contemplation by this Government will be scrupulously confined to the object already announced, and that in no circumstances will they be suffered to trench in any degree upon the sovereignty of Mexico or develop into intervention of any kind in the internal affairs of our sister Republic. On the contrary, what is now being done is deliberately intended to preclude the possibility of intervention.[71]

A message from John W. Belt, American Special Agent in Carranza's temporary capital, Querétaro, relaxed tension in Washington and allayed Wilson's fears when it arrived on March 14. This dispatch reported that the Foreign Secretary of the *de facto* regime had been greatly pleased by Lansing's note of March 13.[72] Wilson conveyed the good news to the Cabinet in the morning of March 14, remarking that it had relieved his apprehension.[73] However, a dispatch from General Pershing arrived in the evening with the report that the *Carrancista* commander at Palomas, just south of Columbus, had said that he would oppose the entry of the American expedition unless he received orders to permit the crossing. "It seems probable that Carranza troops are going to oppose U.S.," Pershing added. "This column is ready to move and other columns will be ready tomorrow. Small force moves across the border not later than noon the fifteenth unless otherwise ordered."[74]

Secretary Baker took this message to the White House at 11:15 that evening. Wilson said that if the report was correct he would not send

---

[71] From Wilson's typed draft in the State Department Papers. Wilson's covering letter (W. W. to R. Lansing, March 13, 1916, State Department Papers) read as follows: "Here is the statement I suggested during our conversation this afternoon. I would be very much obliged if you would issue it at your ealy [sic] convenience. . . . Will you not be kind enough to communicate this immediately to the Secretary of War." For the statement as published and sent to Mexico, see *New York Times*, March 14, 1916, and the Secretary of State to E. Arredondo, March 13, 1916, *Foreign Relations, 1916*, p. 489. Baker sent a paraphrase to General Funston on March 13. See the Adjutant General to General Funston, March 13, 1916, *ibid.*

[72] Special Agent Belt to the Secretary of State, March 13, 1916, *ibid.*, p. 488.

[73] *New York Times*, March 15, 1916.

[74] General Funston to the Adjutant General, March 14, 1916, transmitting the message from General Pershing, Polk Papers.

troops into Mexico because it would mean intervention and war.[75] Baker sent urgent new instructions to Pershing early the next morning, undoubtedly at Wilson's request. They directed him, in the event that the *Carrancista* commander refused to permit the Punitive Expedition to enter Mexico, to inform the War Department and await further orders.[76]

Tumulty talked with Wilson that same morning, March 15, arguing desperately that the Cabinet favored dispatch of the expedition and the President would not win a single electoral vote in the election in November if he hesitated for a moment. "Tumulty," Wilson replied, "you are Irish, and, therefore, full of fight. I know how deeply you feel about this Columbus affair. Of course, it is tragical and deeply regrettable from every standpoint, but in the last analysis I, and not the Cabinet or you, must bear the responsibility for every action that is to be taken. I have to sleep with my conscience in these matters and I shall be held responsible for every drop of blood that may be spent in the enterprise of intervention. I am seriously considering every phase of this difficult matter, and I can say frankly to you, and you may inform the Cabinet officers who discuss it with you, that *'there won't be any war with Mexico if I can prevent it,'* no matter how loud the gentlemen on the hill yell for it and demand it." Wilson went on:

"It is not a difficult thing for a president to declare war, especially against a weak and defenceless nation like Mexico. In a republic like ours, the man on horseback is always an idol, and were I considering the matter from the standpoint of my own political fortunes, I should at once grasp the opportunity and invade Mexico, for it would mean the triumph of my administration. But this has never been in my thoughts for a single moment. The thing that daunts me and holds me back is the aftermath of war, with all its tears and tragedies. I came from the South and I know what war is, for I have seen its wreckage and terrible ruin. It is easy for me as President to declare war. I do not have to fight, and neither do the gentlemen on the Hill who now clamour for it. It is some poor farmer's boy, or the son of some poor widow away off in some modest community, or perhaps the scion of a great family, who will have to do the fighting and the dying. I will not resort to war against Mexico until I have exhausted every means to keep out of this mess. I know they will call me a coward and a quitter, but that will not disturb me. Time, the great solvent, will, I am sure,

---

[75] House Diary, March 17, 1916.
[76] The Chief of Staff to the Adjutant General, March 15, 1916, Polk Papers.

vindicate this policy of humanity and forbearance. Men forget what is back of this struggle in Mexico. It is the age-long struggle of a people to come into their own, and while we look upon the incidents in the foreground, let us not forget the tragic reality in the background which towers above this whole sad picture. The gentlemen who criticize me speak as if America were afraid to fight Mexico. Poor Mexico, with its pitiful men, women, and children, fighting to gain a foothold in their own land! They speak of the valour of America. What is true valour? *I would be just as much ashamed to be rash as I would to be a coward. Valour is self-respecting. Valour is circumspect. Valour strikes only when it is right to strike. Valour withholds itself from all small implications and entanglements and waits for the great opportunity when the sword will flash as if it carried the light of heaven upon its blade."*[77]

It was in truth one of the great moments in Wilson's life. His eyes flashed, and his lips quivered as he spoke. He rose from his chair and walked to the window of his study. He would not permit war, moreover, he went on, because German agents had been hard at work to stir trouble between the United States and Mexico in order to free Germany from the threat of American retaliation if she launched unrestricted submarine warfare. It was beginning to look as if war with Germany was inevitable. If it came, America would need all her resources for the fight.

Tumulty was so moved that he made a record of Wilson's conversation,[78] but he was not persuaded. He rushed to Burleson's office and told him what the President had said. They called in Secretary of Agriculture Houston, and the three men drafted an impassioned letter saying that retreat at this point would be disastrous to the

[77] Tumulty apparently lifted the latter italicized sentences verbatim from Wilson's speech before the Gridiron Club on February 26, 1916 (for which, see *The New Democracy*, II, 127-128), and inserted them into his own text of Wilson's remarks. It is of course possible that Wilson said something very much like them to Tumulty.

[78] J. P. Tumulty, *Woodrow Wilson As I Know Him*, pp. 157-160. The present writer has concluded that the above record is authentic in spite of the facts that some of Tumulty's records of conversations with Wilson are highly fictionalized, Tumulty misdates the above conversation, and there is no memorandum of the conversation in the Tumulty Papers. There can be no doubt that Tumulty had a long conversation with Wilson in the morning of March 15, 1916, for Tumulty referred to it in a letter to Wilson later in the same day and told Colonel House about it on March 17, 1916. Tumulty's rendition of Wilson's conversation is, moreover, authentically Wilsonian in phrasing and content. It seems probable that Tumulty, realizing that he had just heard one of the great utterances of his life, went immediately to his office and put Wilson's words on paper, perhaps adding passages here and there as embellishments when he wrote his book. He did this on several occasions.

Democratic party, humiliating to the country, and destructive of American influence in the world at large.[79] It was mid-afternoon before Tumulty could sign the letter, and the President had gone to a matinée at Keith's Theater. Tumulty sent it to him there by a White House messenger.[80]

The decision to permit the Punitive Expedition to enter Mexico on schedule had, in fact, already been made by this time. Pershing had sent good news in the morning—that the *Carrancista* commander at Palomas had said not only that the American force might cross the border, but also that he and his men were eager to join in the chase. Hence no interdiction went from Washington, and Pershing entered Mexico at noon, local time, on March 15 with 4,000 men. A smaller force under Colonel George A. Dodd crossed the boundary at Hachita, New Mexico, at the same hour.

Except for two disquieting reports about Mexican unrest along the border, nothing but encouraging news came to Washington during the rest of the day. The Mexican Consul General in El Paso and *Carrancista* commander in Ciudad Juárez both said in the evening that General Obregón, the newly appointed Minister of War and Navy, had instructed all troops in their district to cooperate in every way with the American expeditionary force.[81] Another report arrived from Silliman in Querétaro later in the evening. He had, he said, conferred with Obregón and the new Secretary of Foreign Relations, Cándido Aguilar, in the afternoon. They had both affirmed that the Mexican government would approve and acquiesce in the American plan to send troops into Mexico to pursue and capture Villa, and General Obregón had added that his commanders would be instructed to cooperate with American officers.[82]

The auguries were, therefore, virtually all auspicious by the time that Secretary Baker conferred with the President at the White House at 9 p.m. on this same day, March 15. The single remaining task, they agreed, was dispatch of ironclad orders to prevent even the possibility of any aggressive action by American troops against forces of the *de facto* government. The following orders, drafted probably by the two men during their conference, were sent to Generals Funston and Pershing on the following day:

[79] J. P. Tumulty to W. W., March 15, 1916, Wilson Papers.
[80] House Diary, March 17, 1916.
[81] *New York Times*, March 16, 1916.
[82] Special Agent Silliman to the Secretary of State, March 15, 1916, *Foreign Relations, 1916*, p. 491.

In view of the great distance between the seat of Government and the forces in the field, the President regards it as of the utmost importance that General Funston and all officers in command of troops of the United States clearly understand the exact nature of the expedition of our forces into Mexico, and he therefore directs obedience in letter and in spirit to the following orders:

ONE. If any organized body of troops of the de facto Government of the Republic of Mexico are met, they are to be treated with courtesy and their cooperation welcomed, if they desire to cooperate in the objects of the expedition.

TWO. Upon no account or pretext, and neither by act, word or attitude of any American soldier, shall this expedition become or be given the appearance of being hostile to the integrity or dignity of the Republic of Mexico, by the courtesy of which this expedition is permitted to pursue an aggressor upon the peace of these neighboring Republics.

THREE. Should the attitude of any organized body of troops of the de facto Government of Mexico appear menacing, commanders of the forces of the United States are, of course, authorized to place themselves and their commands in proper situation of defense, *and if actually attacked they will of course defend themselves by all means at their command,* but in no event must they attack or become the aggressor with any such body of troops.

FOUR. Care is to be taken to have in a state of readiness at all times the means of rapid communication from the front to the headquarters of the General commanding the Department, and, through him, to the War Department in Washington; and any evidence of misunderstanding on the part of officials, military or civil, of the de facto Government of Mexico as to the objects, purposes, character or acts of the expedition of the United States, are to be reported to the Department with the utmost expedition, with a view to having them taken up directly with the Government of Mexico through the Department of State.[83]

Congress, with Wilson's knowledge and warm approval, on March 17 adopted a joint resolution offered by Senator Robert M. La Follette of Wisconsin. It approved use of the armed forces for the capture of Villa and his band and assured the Mexican government and people that the American government had no intention of violating Mexican sovereignty or interfering in Mexican domestic affairs.[84]

There was nothing else that Wilson could do now to make American intentions plain or to guard against unfortunate incidents. But two

[83] N. D. Baker to the Chief of Staff, March 16, 1916, Wilson Papers.
[84] New York *World*, March 18, 1916; *Congressional Record*, 64th Cong., 1st sess., p. 4274.

facts remained obscured by all the outward show of harmony and good feeling on both sides of the border. One was that Carranza still had not formally approved the entry of the Punitive Expedition into Mexico. The other was that Villa had no intention of being caught alive.

It was all good going if not altogether successful hunting for Pershing and his men during the first month of the chase. Moving rapidly, they reached the vicinity of Colonia Dublan, some eighty-five miles south of the border, on March 18. Villa retreated to the area of Namiquipa, where he found the passes through the Sierra Madre Mountains blocked by strong detachments of *Carrancista* cavalry under General Gutiérrez. *Carrancistas* attacked sharply at Namiquipa and El Toro on March 20 and 21, and Pershing sent Colonel Dodd and his 7th Cavalry to close the trap at the former town, with other columns bringing up the rear as fast as possible.[85] Villa broke through the widely dispersed Mexican forces with ease on about March 26 and retreated toward the Guerrero district of southern Chihuahua. He struck the *Carrancista* garrison at Guerrero on about March 28, killing or capturing all the 172 troops stationed there, and then moved northward to San Geronimo Ranch. Colonel Dodd surprised Villa's main force at Guerrero early in the morning of March 29 and drove his men into wild retreat toward the mountains. A large number of *Carrancista* prisoners being held for execution were liberated, and Villa's chief commander, General Eliseo Hernandez, was killed during the fight.[86] Colonel W. C. Brown and a squadron of the 10th Cavalry found 100 of the retreating *Villistas* near Bachiniva on April 1 and killed thirty of them. But Villa, even though wounded in the leg and transported in a litter, was far from being subdued. He was a master of guerrilla tactics operating in home country among more or less friendly people. He rallied his forces and made a successful retreat southward toward Parral.

The Punitive Expedition, now 6,675 men strong, had penetrated 350 miles into Mexico and was still no nearer to its objective than it had been on the day it entered Mexico. At least there had not yet been any unhappy incidents to menace Mexican-American relations. Local *Carrancista* commanders had refused to permit Pershing's men to enter

[85] Commanding General, Punitive Expedition, to Commanding General, Southern Department, "Preliminary Report of Punitive Expedition," March 27, 1916, State Department Papers.

[86] J. J. Pershing to F. Funston, March 30, 1916, *New York Times*, April 1, 1916.

towns, and Carranza's forces had proved to be either unwilling or unable to offer effective cooperation, although they had sent cordial messages and seemed to be friendly.[87]

However, tension between the American and *de facto* Mexican governments had been mounting the farther Pershing penetrated into northern Mexico. Carranza's policy in the beginning was to acquiesce under protest in the dispatch of the Punitive Expedition in the hope that it could do its work quickly and withdraw. He sent a note to Washington on March 17 objecting to the Punitive Expedition's entry into Mexico and saying that his earlier note proposing agreement for the mutual right of hot pursuit "should not and must not be understood as tolerating or permitting any expeditions into the national territory." It was not menacing in tone.[88] The Secretary of Foreign Relations, Aguilar, came back two days later, on March 19, proffering an agreement limiting the area of hot pursuit to sixty kilometers on either side of the border and the number of troops in any expedition to one thousand.[89]

Acting Secretary of State Polk took these two dispatches to the White House at 9:30 in the morning of March 20. Wilson and Polk were not disturbed, and they agreed to accept the Mexican proposal, subject to some modifications, insisting at the same time that it should not apply to the Punitive Expedition already in Mexico.[90] Thus one note went to the *de facto* government on that same day. It reiterated Wilson's assurances that the Punitive Expedition would be recalled as soon as it or the *de facto* government had accomplished the Expedition's objectives, said that the American government would approve the proposed agreement after certain modifications, and added: "General Carranza should be informed that in the present instance, however, this Government . . . accepted without any hesitation the proposal made by the Minister of Foreign Relations through Mr. Silliman on March 10."[91] A second note, dispatched through Arredondo on March 21, contained the American counterproposal for mutual right of hot pursuit that Wilson had read and approved. It imposed no limits on the distance or

[87] Commanding General, Punitive Expedition, to Commanding General, Southern Department, "Report on General Situation," April 14, 1916, copy in State Department Papers.

[88] Cándido Aguilar to E. Arredondo, March 17, 1916, *Foreign Relations, 1916*, p. 494.

[89] E. Arredondo to the Acting Secretary of State, March 19, 1916, *ibid.*, pp. 495-496.

[90] F. L. Polk to R. Lansing, March 21, 1916, Polk Papers.

[91] The Acting Secretary of State to Special Representative James L. Rodgers, March 20, 1916, *Foreign Relations, 1916*, pp. 499-500.

number of troops involved, saying only, "In no case will the pursuing forces establish themselves or remain in foreign territory for a time longer than is necessary."[92]

There was much discussion during the next two weeks about the agreement for hot pursuit. The Mexican Foreign Office came back on March 25 with virtually its original draft, but now amended to limit the stay on foreign territory of any expeditionary force to eight days.[93] "I have read these proposals with a great deal of interest, of course," Wilson wrote to Lansing after reading the new Mexican draft on March 30. ". . . Perhaps there are concessions in line with their suggestions which we could make, always assuming that it were agreed that they should not apply to the present expedition."[94] They conferred about the matter shortly afterward, and Lansing accepted the proposed Mexican draft almost *in toto* on April 4. "Since this protocol as redrafted could not be applied to the American forces now in Mexico," Lansing explained in a covering letter to Arredondo, "without their entire withdrawal from the pursuit of Villa and his band, in which they are engaged, and since it would be impracticable and unwise to withdraw the United States troops when the capture of these outlaws seems imminent, I have drafted a formal note (copy enclosed) excepting the present situation from the operation of the protocol, to which I trust your Government will be willing to assent at the same time as the protocol."[95]

Wilson was more upset during the last week in March and the first week in April by what were said to be a flood of false rumors from the border aimed at stirring war between the United States and Mexico than by any thought of trouble brewing with the *de facto* government. For example, there was a report, entirely false, on March 22 that General Luis Herrera, former military Governor of the State of Chihuahua, had deserted to Villa with 2,000 troops.[96] The Cabinet discussed the rumors on March 24. "I believe," Lansing said afterward, "a large part of these stories originate in the minds of interested persons

[92] E. Arredondo to C. Aguilar, March 21, 1916, *Mexican White Paper*, pp. 155-156.

[93] C. Aguilar to E. Arredondo, March 25, 1916, *ibid.*, pp. 159-162; "MEMORANDUM," accompanying E. Arredondo to the Secretary of State, March 27, 1916, State Department Papers. The "Draft of Agreement" printed in *Foreign Relations, 1916*, p. 502, is an incomplete translation.

[94] W. W. to R. Lansing, March 30, 1916, State Department Papers.

[95] The Secretary of State to E. Arredondo, April 4, 1916, *Foreign Relations, 1916*, pp. 507-508; E. Arredondo to C. Aguilar, April 5, 1916, *Mexican White Paper*, pp. 165-167, for the text of the American redraft of the protocol.

[96] *New York Times*, March 23 and 24, 1916.

who desire intervention." Another Cabinet member added that Americans owning property in northern Mexico were trying to agitate public opinion in both countries to bring on war. Senator Stone repeated these accusations in the Senate, adding that some Republicans were eager to capitalize on the Mexican situation.[97]

Wilson struck back hard in a public statement in the evening of March 25. The Punitive Expedition had been sent into Mexico, he began, for the single purpose of capturing the bandit, Villa, and was in no sense intended as an invasion of Mexico or an infringement of its sovereignty. He had already asked the various news agencies to use utmost care to avoid giving the impression that the Expedition was engaged in war operations and to refrain from publishing unverified rumors of unrest in Mexico. He went on as follows:

"It is my duty to warn the people of the United States that there are persons all along the border who are actively engaged in originating and giving as wide currency as they can to rumors of the most sensational and disturbing sort, which are wholly unjustified by the facts. The object of this traffic in falsehood is obvious. It is to create intolerable friction between the Government of the United States and the de facto Government of Mexico for the purpose of bringing about intervention in the interest of certain American owners of Mexican properties. This object can not be attained so long as sane and honorable men are in control of this Government, but very serious conditions may be created, unnecessary bloodshed may result, and the relations between the two republics may be very much embarrassed.

"The people of the United States should know the sinister and unscrupulous influences that are afoot, and should be on their guard against crediting any story coming from the border; and those who disseminate the news should make it a matter of patriotism and of conscience to test the source and authenticity of every report they receive from that quarter."[98]

Lansing immediately sounded out American Consuls in northern Mexico and reassured reporters on March 28 that the people and *de facto* authorities in that area were all cordially disposed toward the Punitive Expedition.[99] For his part, Wilson never named the "sinister and unscrupulous influences" allegedly at work. He undoubtedly had Senator Fall much in mind. Fall, for example, sent an alarming telegram

[97] *ibid.*, March 25, 1916; *Congressional Record*, 64th Cong., 1st sess., pp. 4741-4743.
[98] *New York Times*, March 26, 1916.
[99] *ibid.*, March 29, 1916.

from El Paso on March 28 to the Republican minority leader, Senator Jacob H. Gallinger of New Hampshire, and the Secretary of War, warning of an impending *Carrancista* attack on El Paso. "I would trust Senator Gallinger to try to tell the truth," Wilson wrote to Baker after reading the telegram, "but I do not think that Senator Fall even tries."[100] Senator Benjamin R. Tillman of South Carolina suggested that American oil operators were financing Villa. "The conclusions," Wilson replied, "seem as plain to me as they do to you. I think there is every evidence that the most sinister influences are at work and we shall have to expose them thoroughly before we can overcome them."[101] He did ask Tumulty to request the Departments of State and Justice to investigate alleged evil influences in El Paso on about April 12.[102] But the truth, insofar as one can tell from the records, was that Wilson did not know who the "sinister and unscrupulous influences" were because, apart from Senator Fall, they simply did not exist, or were not guilty of Wilson's accusations if they did exist.[103]

[100] W. W. to N. D. Baker, March 31, 1916, the Papers of Newton D. Baker, Library of Congress; hereinafter cited as the N. D. Baker Papers.

[101] B. R. Tillman to W. W., March 27, 1916; W. W. to B. R. Tillman, March 31, 1916, Wilson Papers.

[102] W. W. to J. P. Tumulty, n.d., with Tumulty's annotation, "Done 4/12/16," *ibid.*

[103] Administration officials cited only the false report about General Herrera's defection as evidence of a flood of malign rumors from the border. It is interesting to note that this report probably originated with George C. Carothers, a Special Agent of the State Department. In any event, Carothers reported Herrera's defection on March 22. G. C. Carothers to the Secretary of State, March 22, 1916, State Department Papers.

CHAPTER VIII

Brink of War: The *Sussex* Crisis

ARMED ships and submarines were the cause of as much trouble to President Wilson as Pancho and his men during March of 1916. The administration's most urgent task in the inconclusive aftermath of the congressional rebellion was to find a workable policy toward armed merchant ships. It had to be technically neutral and therefore defensible *vis-à-vis* the Allies and pro-Allied spokesmen in the United States. But it also had to avoid the likelihood of serious conflict with Germany in order to satisfy popular and congressional desire to avoid war over the issue of Americans traveling on armed merchantmen. And it could not avoid serious controversy with Germany if it did not provide some measure of safety for submarines operating against armed vessels.

The urgency—and extreme difficulty—of such an undertaking was intensified by certain revelations during the first two weeks of March 1916. For one thing, the British government, under pressure of German propaganda and accusations, on March 2 published the instructions that the Admiralty had sent to masters of armed merchant ships on October 20, 1915. They revealed that ordinary armed British merchantmen (as distinguished from troop transports and the like) carried strict orders against using neutral flags or any other form of disguise and were in fact instructed to use armament solely to prevent or resist hostile attack.[1] But they also made it clear, as the Berlin Foreign Office was quick to point out,[2] that the main burden of the German accusation was correct—that British armed vessels were under orders to fire upon submarines *after* they were warned and to resist search. Secondly, the full text of the German memorandum with its elaborate exhibits finally arrived in Washington on March 6. The evidence was so impressive that Lansing, a few days later, asked Ambassador Spring Rice for an official copy of the British Admiralty's instructions to armed merchant-

[1] *New York Times*, March 3, 1916.

[2] *ibid.*, March 6, 1916; Ambassador Gerard to the Secretary of State, March 7, 1916, *Foreign Relations, 1916, Supplement*, p. 201, enclosing the text of the semiofficial German comment on the British statement.

men.[3] The Secretary of State also gave a copy of the German memorandum and its exhibits to the newspapers for publication.[4]

Meanwhile, Wilson had himself been thinking seriously about the policy that the American government should adopt toward armed merchantmen. He had received a long and powerfully reasoned letter from Senator Paul Husting, Democrat of Wisconsin, on about February 27, suggesting that there was a reasonable and simple solution to the armed ship question. The United States should demand that the British guarantee that armed merchantmen would not fire on submarines while being warned and searched. If the British would not give such a pledge, Husting suggested, then the American government would be justified in treating armed ships as men of war.[5] "The suggestion made in your letter," Wilson replied on March 2, "interests me very much indeed and I am going to take the liberty of discussing it with the Secretary of State, who I am sure is as anxious as I am to do everything possible to bring justice out of chaos."[6] Wilson sent the letter to Lansing on the same day, saying that it seemed "worth serious discussion."[7] The two leaders must have conferred not long afterward, for the Secretary echoed Husting's suggestion in a memorandum that he prepared for the House foreign affairs committee on the next day, March 3. It might be possible, Lansing wrote, to distinguish between offensive and defensive armament. In any event, one could follow a simple rule of use and say that a merchantman was armed offensively, no matter how few guns it carried, when it fired on a submarine after being warned.[8]

Wilson gave some evidence of the direction of his thought immediately afterward. On March 3 Lansing drafted a reply to the note that Bernstorff had left at the State Department on February 28 and sent it to the White House for Wilson's perusal. Lansing's draft alleged that the Germans had admitted inaugurating a *new* submarine policy and accused them of breaking past pledges to the United States.[9] Wilson, obviously, was neither impressed by Lansing's argument nor eager to exacerbate opinion at home by debating the fundamental issues any

[3] *New York Times*, March 10, 1916.

[4] F. L. Polk to R. Lansing, March 16, 1916; R. Lansing to F. L. Polk, March 16, 1916, both in the Polk Papers; *New York Times*, March 18, 1916.

[5] P. Husting to W. W., February 26, 1916, Wilson Papers.

[6] W. W. to P. Husting, March 2, 1916, *ibid.*

[7] W. W. to R. Lansing, March 2, 1916, *ibid.*

[8] R. Lansing, "Memorandum on House Resolution 147," *The Lansing Papers*, I, 344-347, particularly 344.

[9] R. Lansing to W. W., March 3, 1916, Wilson Papers.

more than necessary with the German government. He did not reply in correspondence, and he must have instructed Lansing verbally not to send the note. In any event, it did not go to Berlin. Wilson gave further intimation of his position in conversations with Senator Stone and Colonel House on March 7. We have no record of the first conversation,[10] but it was significant that Stone canceled a speech on the armed ship question on the day following his conference at the White House.[11] To Colonel House, Wilson said that he "thought the best reply the Allies could make was a promise that they would strictly adhere to international law, and would not transgress it in any particular, and that their armament would be for defensive and not for offensive purposes."[12]

Lansing gathered all the materials he could find on armed ships and took them to Pinehurst, North Carolina, on March 13 for a brief vacation. He returned to Washington on March 23 with the draft of a memorandum detailing the American government's position. It affirmed the right of merchantmen to arm for defense and the duty of attacking warships to warn armed merchantmen and provide opportunity for evacuation of personnel before sinking them. But it also made it plain that the United States would regard armed merchantmen as auxiliary cruisers when it was known that they sailed under orders to hunt down and destroy submarines, or when they did in fact behave as if they were operating under such instructions.[13]

Lansing intended to discuss the memorandum with Wilson and then publish it soon after his return, but more urgent business intervened. To begin with, the Allied envoys in Washington, on March 23, finally responded for their governments to the Secretary of State's ill-fated letter of January 18, 1916, and Wilson and Lansing discussed the matter of a proper reply for more than a week. Lansing wanted to express the American government's strong displeasure over Allied rejection of the *modus vivendi*; Wilson insisted upon a more noncommittal reply.[14] Then the torpedoing of a French steamer, the *Sussex*, in the English Channel diverted attention from the armed ship question for another

[10] It was held in response to W. J. Stone to W. W., March 6, 1916, *ibid.*

[11] *New York Times*, March 9, 1916.

[12] House Diary, March 7, 1916.

[13] "Memorandum on the status of armed merchant vessels," March 25, 1916, *Foreign Relations, 1916, Supplement*, pp. 244-248.

[14] See the documents printed in *The Lansing Papers*, I, 349-351, and the Secretary of State to the British Ambassador, April 7, 1916, *Foreign Relations, 1916, Supplement*, pp. 223-224.

two weeks. Lansing sent his memorandum to Wilson on April 24.[15] They discussed it at a Cabinet meeting on the following day and agreed that it should be issued at once in order to prevent the German government from injecting the armed ship issue into negotiations then in progress over the *Sussex*. Lansing consequently gave the memorandum to the press on April 26 and telegraphed a summary to Ambassadors and Ministers in European countries and Japan on the following day.[16]

It was certainly clear enough now that the American government meant to follow a simple rule of use and take prompt action against merchantmen when they hunted submarines and resisted search. German officials were pleased. "All agreed," Gerard reported on May 3, "that the President's memorandum about armed merchantmen would seem to mean that he intended in cases where [the] English gave ships orders to fire immediately to either keep such ships out of American ports or warn Americans off."[17]

British leaders understood, too, and decided that it was wise to avoid controversy altogether. They consequently sent no armed merchantmen to the United States until the autumn of 1916, and not a large number then.[18] The French and Italians continued to arm ships sailing to American ports, but Lansing, in discussions with the French and Italian Ambassadors, never failed to make it clear that the Washington government was watching carefully and reserved the right to change its rules governing the treatment of armed ships in American ports. Moreover, no armed merchantman left an American harbor until its master and the French or Italian Ambassador had given a specific pledge that its armament would be used only for defense.[19]

[15] R. Lansing to W. W., April 24, 1916, *The Lansing Papers*, I, 351-352.

[16] *New York Times*, April 27, 1916; *Foreign Relations, 1916, Supplement*, pp. 244-248.

[17] Ambassador Gerard to the Secretary of State, May 3, 1916, *Foreign Relations, 1916, Supplement*, p. 253.

[18] The Permanent Undersecretary in the British Foreign Office, Lord Hardinge, told the French Ambassador in London on October 10, 1916, that his government, at the request of the United States, had disarmed all merchantmen sailing to American ports.

[19] The French Ambassador in Washington, Jusserand, followed the practice of his Italian colleague in giving a written pledge each time a French armed ship entered an American port until June 1916. Then he asked the State Department to permit French consuls to give the necessary assurance. Lansing approved this procedure. Jusserand, it is interesting to note, had great difficulty in persuading his government to give general assurances that French armed merchantmen would use their armament only for defense. Authorities in Paris agreed to ratify the pledge that Jusserand had already given only after making the reservation on April 25 that armed ships should have the right to resist search so long as the German threat to sink all armed ships on sight was still in force. The Italians made the same reservation on May 2, 1916.

Future events alone could reveal whether the compromise thus worked out by Wilson and Lansing provided the means of escaping controversy, particularly with the Central Powers. Much would depend upon whether the American leaders were really willing, when specific cases arose, to make an issue at all in view of the undercurrent in American public opinion against risking war over the alleged right of Americans to work and travel on armed merchantmen. Even more would depend upon German conduct of the larger submarine campaign, of which the *démarche* against armed ships was actually a minor part.

Work was going forward in Berlin in preparation for renewal of the undersea campaign at the very time that Wilson and Lansing were trying to achieve a workable solution of the armed ship issue. Bethmann, in his memorandum of February 29, had defined what he thought were the boundaries of safety. And he had promised at the Imperial Conference in Charleville on March 4 to do what he could to prepare the diplomatic ground for a possible unrestricted campaign against all commerce in British waters. On that same day he telegraphed to the Foreign Office in Berlin the text of a new memorandum that he and Holtzendorff had drafted.[20] It reviewed at length British alleged infractions of international law and ended by saying that the Imperial German Government was confident that the American people would "appreciate the German viewpoint as laid down above."[21]

The Foreign Office sent the memorandum to Bernstorff both by wireless and cable and gave a copy to Ambassador Gerard for good measure. Bernstorff handed the document to Lansing on March 8 and, with the Secretary's permission, also gave a copy to reporters on the same day.[22] Wilson was so irritated by the obvious effort to appeal directly to the American people and Congress that he suggested that Lansing ask Bernstorff why the memorandum was delivered to the State Department at all.[23] Lansing drafted a sharp reprimand on March 24, after his return from Pinehurst,[24] but Wilson apparently decided that it was too late to remonstrate. After all, Lansing had given Bernstorff permission to do what Wilson now condemned. The

[20] T. von Bethmann Hollweg to G. von Jagow, March 4, 1916, German F. O. Archives.
[21] The memorandum is printed in *Foreign Relations, 1916, Supplement*, pp. 198-200.
[22] *New York Times*, March 9, 1916.
[23] W. W. to R. Lansing, March 8, 1916, *The Lansing Papers*, I, 535-536.
[24] R. Lansing to W. W., March 24, 1916, enclosing a draft note to the German Ambassador, *ibid.*, pp. 536-537.

American people and their leaders might have taken the German statement seriously instead of ignoring it had they known what it portended. Admiral von Holtzendorff gave first evidence on March 13, by sending the following orders to the High Seas Fleet and the Navy Corps in Flanders:

1. Enemy merchant ships encountered in the war zone are to be sunk without warning.

2. Enemy merchantmen encountered outside the war zone are to be destroyed without warning only if they are *armed*.

3. Enemy liners must not be attacked by submerged submarines either within or without the war zone, whether they are armed or not. . . .[25]

These orders simply renewed the submarine campaign abandoned in October 1915, but with added protection for passenger ships. However, public pressure in Germany for an all-out campaign was mounting even while submarines were taking up stations off the British coasts. It found sharpest expression in resolutions introduced in the Reichstag by the National Liberal and Conservative parties on March 18.[26] There was pressure, too, from naval circles. Admiral von Holtzendorff, still believing that the Emperor meant to launch the unrestricted campaign on April 4, requested on March 31 that the Chancellor ask the Emperor for another Imperial Conference.[27] William was not pleased by the request, but he did instruct Bethmann to continue to try to clarify questions with America and to be prepared to report within a month.[28] Bethmann answered at once, warning that it was futile to expect any important change soon in the American point of view.[29] The Emperor replied that he agreed. But he added that the Chancellor could not postpone the decision *ad calendas graecas* and said that he would expect a definitive report by May or June as to whether or not the indispensable all-out submarine campaign could be launched without danger of complications with the neutrals. When Bethmann's spokesman said that an answer could be given now, and in the negative, William replied that diplomats would have to intensify their efforts.[30]

[25] A. Spindler, *La Guerre Sous-Marine*, III, 143.

[26] Ernest R. May, *The World War and American Isolation, 1914-1917*, pp. 259-270; see *Foreign Relations, 1916, Supplement*, p. 208, for the texts of the resolutions.

[27] T. von Bethmann Hollweg to K. G. von Treutler, March 31, 1916, German F. O. Archives.

[28] K. G. von Treutler to T. von Bethmann Hollweg, April 1, 1916, *ibid.*

[29] T. von Bethmann Hollweg to K. G. von Treutler, April 3, 1916, *ibid.*

[30] K. G. von Treutler to T. von Bethmann Hollweg, April 4, 1916, *ibid.*

This was the immediate background of what was soon to become the severest crisis in German-American relations between the outbreak of the war in 1914 and the rupture in relations between the two countries in 1917. A crisis was probably inevitable in view of the extraordinary discretion that the superior commander of submarines of the High Seas Fleet gave to commanders under the general orders issued on March 13. "As a general rule," this officer advised, "one should not approach merchant ships on the surface to visit them, examine their papers, etc. . . . Normal procedure will be to attack while submerged and invisible. . . . If the commander decides for some special reason to approach while surfaced, he must do so with the greatest care."[31] As we will see, commanders, restless from inaction since the early autumn, set to their task with enthusiasm, not to say abandon.

Ironically, the dire German-American crisis was touched off, not by a long range U-boat of the High Seas Fleet operating in British waters, but by one of the small UB submarines of the Navy Corps' Flanders Flotilla that sailed in the Hoofden, the English Channel, and off the eastern English coast as far north as Yarmouth. The UB29, Commander Pustkuchen, cruising in the English Channel in the fine afternoon of March 24, sighted a ship with two large masts approaching and submerged at 2:41 p.m. "The ship resembles a Channel packet vessel," Pustkuchen wrote in his log, "but it has only one stack and a bridge very much like that of a warship. As it does not follow the route prescribed by the British Admiralty for ships of commerce . . . it cannot be a liner. In view of its strange rear structure, I take it for a minelayer. It carries no flag and is painted black all over." Pustkuchen fired a torpedo at a distance of 1,300 meters at 2:55 western European time. "All the bow of the ship, including the bridge," he wrote in his log, "is in pieces. The bridge is covered with people. It is a transport. Sinking not observed. I make my getaway submerged."[32]

The victim was the *Sussex*, 1,353 tons, a Channel steamer owned by the London, Brighton, & South Coast Railway Company. She was sailing under the French flag on her regular voyage from Folkestone to Dieppe with some 325 passengers aboard, twenty-five of whom were American citizens. She did not sink and was towed to Boulogne. About eighty persons were killed or injured by the torpedo blast. Four Americans were injured, none killed.

[31] A. Spindler, *La Guerre Sous-Marine*, III, 146.
[32] *ibid.*, pp. 170-171.

First news of the incident came to Washington in brief press reports on March 24.[33] More complete accounts, including one from the French Naval Ministry saying that there was no doubt that the *Sussex* had been torpedoed, arrived on the following day.[34] They were accompanied by a dispatch from the American Consul at Bristol advising that the horse ship *Englishman* of the Dominion Line, with Americans among her crew, had been torpedoed in British waters.[35]

The dates March 25 and 26 fell on a weekend, and Wilson rather ostentatiously followed normal routine. He played golf on Saturday morning, March 25, and went for a long drive with Mrs. Wilson in the afternoon. He was in his pew at Central Presbyterian Church the next morning, spent most of the afternoon with Mrs. Wilson in the automobile, and had dinner at Mrs. Bolling's. He was also excited by news from Williamstown, Massachusetts, that his daughter, Jessie Sayre, had just been delivered of her second child.

However, tension was mounting in Washington by the time that governmental offices opened on Monday morning, March 27, and reporters noted that "high officials" did not attempt to conceal their fear that a graver crisis than the one that followed the sinking of the *Lusitania* might be in the making.[36] Lansing sent a note to London asking Page to ascertain whether the *Sussex* was armed, and another to Berlin requesting a prompt report from the German government.[37] Then, having heard no word from the White House, the Secretary of State dictated a letter that he hoped would awaken the President to the gravity of the situation. All reports, he wrote, indicated that the *Sussex* had been torpedoed; Wilson and he should determine the course they would follow in the event that the evidence pointed strongly to German guilt. "I do not see," he went on, "how we can avoid taking some decisive step. We can no longer temporize in the matter of submarine warfare when Americans are being killed, wounded, or endangered by the illegal and inhuman conduct of the Germans." The time for writing notes had passed; the American government should say in no uncertain terms that it would not tolerate the present method of

[33] *New York Times*, March 25, 1916.

[34] *ibid.*, March 26, 1916; Ambassador Page to the Secretary of State, March 25, 1916, *Foreign Relations, 1916, Supplement*, p. 214.

[35] New York *World*, March 26, 1916.

[36] *New York Times*, March 28, 1916.

[37] The Secretary of State to Ambassador Page, March 27, 1916, *Foreign Relations, 1916, Supplement*, p. 215; the Secretary of State to Ambassador Gerard, March 27, 1916, *ibid.*

submarine warfare. It should present an ultimatum to the German government and break relations if the Imperial authorities refused to admit unequivocally that the submarine campaign *in general* was illegal, pay indemnity for Americans killed and injured, and guarantee that the present method of warfare would cease.[38]

Wilson must have read this letter with mounting irritation at Lansing's obvious assumption that he, Wilson, had to be told what to do. He laid Lansing's letter aside. The trouble, he probably thought, was that no one really knew what the Germans were doing. Had they in fact begun the unlimited submarine campaign that Colonel House had predicted only a month before? He did not know because the Germans had chosen not to reveal the new orders to submarine commanders, indeed, had decided to say nothing about the new campaign beyond what information might be gleaned from the armed ship memorandum of February 10 and Bethmann's memorandum, which Bernstorff had delivered on March 8.

Wilson was determined in all events to avoid any show of haste or panic. Senator Stone telephoned on March 27 to ask Wilson to promise to talk about the *Sussex* case with him before he decided upon a course of action. Wilson replied that he would not put any drastic policy into effect until he had laid all the facts before both houses of Congress and obtained their sanction for the policy that he had decided upon.[39]

He discussed the crisis with the Cabinet at an unusually protracted meeting in the morning of March 28, and Lansing apparently reiterated what he had said in his letter.[40] The President played golf in the afternoon with Mrs. Wilson. Then Colonel House, who had rushed to Washington in the belief that only he could strengthen the President's backbone,[41] arrived at the White House just before dinner. "We . . . agreed to postpone more detailed discussion of affairs until to-morrow," House wrote in his diary. "We talked enough, however, for me to fathom what was in his mind; and from the way he looked at me, I am inclined to believe that he intends making excuses for not acting promptly in this new submarine crisis forced upon him by the sinking [*sic*] of the *Sussex*. He evidently does not wish to back up his former notes to Germany upon this subject. He does not seem

---

[38] R. Lansing to W. W., March 27, 1916, *The Lansing Papers*, I, 537-539.
[39] *New York Times*, March 28, 1916; House Diary, April 11, 1916.
[40] *New York Times*, March 29, 1916.
[41] House Diary, March 27, 1916.

to realize that one of the main points of criticism against him is that he talks boldly, buts acts weakly."[42] Wilson went off to dinner at the Raleigh Hotel. House remained at the White House to talk to Frank Polk, Counselor of the State Department. While they were talking news came that a submarine had sunk without warning another British ship, *Manchester Engineer*, with two Americans aboard as members of the crew.[43]

House saw Lansing at the State Department on the following day, March 29, after receipt of news of the torpedoing of yet another British steamer, *Eagle Point*, 130 miles south of Queenstown on March 28. No one at the State Department understood the new submarine campaign. Submarines had apparently sunk some ships without warning, others after warning. And none of the ships thus far destroyed had been armed. Lansing, House noted, was bellicose and believed that the United States had no recourse but an immediate rupture with Germany. The Secretary read the letter he had sent to the President, and House said that he certainly approved, provided that investigation justified a break. Both men agreed that Wilson would be extremely reluctant to back up his own threats.[44]

House saw the President again after lunch on March 30. It was a long conference, and House did most of the talking. He advised preparation for a break in diplomatic relations. Wilson replied that if that occurred the war would go on indefinitely because there would be no one to lead the way out. Could Wilson not turn misfortune into opportunity, House asked. As he recorded the conversation in his diary:

"I suggested that, when he sent von Bernstorff home, he should make a dispassionate statement of the cause of the war and what the Allies were fighting for. I suggested that he should say nothing unkind of the German people, but should strike at the system which had caused this world tragedy, and contend that when that was righted the quarrel with Germany, as far as we were concerned, would be ended. Then I thought at the right time—which would perhaps be by midsummer— I could go to Holland and, after a conference with the Allies and with their consent, I could open negotiations directly with Berlin, telling them upon what terms we were ready to end the war.

"I thought the same arrangement could then be carried out I had planned; that is, he should preside over the conference and we should

[42] House Diary, March 28, 1916.
[43] *New York Times*, March 29, 1916.
[44] House Diary, March 29, 1916.

take part. This would make our participation more effective than as a neutral, and we could do greater and better work in this way than we could in the way we planned."

House thought that Wilson was "visibly pleased" by this remarkable suggestion. What probably made a greater impression was House's warning that Wilson's failure to act soon would cost him the confidence of the Allies. Wilson concluded the conversation by asking House to see Bernstorff and tell him that the United States would surely enter the war unless there was some decisive change in submarine policy.[45]

House returned to New York not knowing what Wilson actually intended to do. It was Wilson's method to listen patiently and then to make up his own mind. He gave at least his tentative decision in a reply to Lansing's letter of March 27 that he typed on his Hammond portable probably immediately after House had left. It read as follows:

"I have your letter of the twenty-seventh in which you state your preliminary impressions about the *Sussex* case. My impressions are not quite the same. The proof that the disaster was caused by a torpedo seems to me by no means satisfactory or conclusive. And, if it was caused by a torpedo, there are many particulars to be considered about the course we should pursue as well as the principle of it. The steps we take and the way we take them will, it seems to me, be of the essence of the matter if we are to keep clearly and indisputably within the lines we have already set ourselves.

"But in this, as in other matters referred to in the papers I am now sending back to you, a personal conference is much the best means of reaching conclusions. We must have one very soon."[46]

It was doubtful, actually, whether Wilson wanted a personal conference with any importunate adviser, including House, at this particular time. There is no record of his talking to or corresponding with anyone about the submarine crisis on Friday, March 31, and he and Mrs. Wilson slipped away that evening for a weekend cruise on the *Mayflower*. They did not return to Washington until Monday morning, April 3. Intimates in the White House circle were distraught by fear that the President would do nothing. William Phillips, one of the Assistant Secretaries of State, rushed to New York on Sunday, April 2, to beg Colonel House to come back to Washington. He said that all the President's friends feared that he would permit Germany

---

[45] *ibid.*, March 30, 1916.
[46] W. W. to R. Lansing, March 30, 1916, *The Lansing Papers*, I, 539.

to do almost anything. Dr. Grayson followed Phillips. He, too, was worried. "Grayson thinks," House wrote in his diary afterward, "the President is a man of unusually narrow prejudices and is intolerant of advice. I did not argue the matter with him as I feel that while the President is not unwilling to accept advice from me, Grayson's general characterization of him is correct. Grayson says if one urges Wilson to do something contrary to his own conviction, he ceases to have any liking for that person. He does not like to meet people and isolates himself as much as anyone I have ever known. . . . His immediate entourage, from the Secretary of State down, are having an unhappy time just now. He is consulting none of them and they are as ignorant of his intentions as the man in the street."[47]

Bethmann, Jagow, and other leaders in Berlin had meanwhile been more worried by the still rising demand at home for all-out submarine warfare than by the prospect of dire crisis with the United States. For example, Ernst Bassermann, leader of the National Liberal Party, and Count Kuno von Westarp, Conservative spokesman, set off bitter debate in the Budget Committee of the Reichstag on March 28, 29, and 31 by demanding an unlimited undersea campaign. Bethmann reiterated the arguments of his memorandum of February 29, reviewed the general military situation, and maintained once again that Germany was in no position to risk war with the United States. "Our position," he said, "is no longer so favorable that we can endure many enemies, but it is not so bad that we are compelled to gamble, and, whatever happens, I will not join a gamble." One member of the Committee wrote in his diary, "The Chancellor was tense, tired, and nervous. He smoked one cigarette after another to quiet his nerves. To judge from the tempo at which he smoked during the committee proceedings, he must consume five or six dozen daily. His hair has become white, his face is lined with deep furrows. He seems the personification of despair."[48]

Gerard sent Lansing's inquiry about the *Sussex* to the Foreign Office on March 29. From there it was promptly relayed to the Admiralty for a report. Gerard on the following day addressed separate inquiries to Wilhelmstrasse about the *Englishman* and *Manchester Engineer*; he also sent inquiries on April 3 about the *Eagle Point* and the *Berwindvale*, another English ship torpedoed with Americans aboard.

[47] House Diary, April 2, 1916.
[48] H. P. Hanssen, *Diary of a Dying Empire*, pp. 135-141.

The first official news from Washington—a dispatch sent by Bernstorff on March 28 through Emil Klaessig of the Wolff News Bureau in New York City—arrived at the Foreign Office on April 2. It reported on the sentiment in favor of breaking relations with Germany in certain circumstances expressed at the Cabinet meeting of March 28. But it also added that Wilson and Lansing would take no hasty action until they had heard from Berlin, even though they were determined to have the submarine issue settled decisively without much delay. "Officials are inclined," Bernstorff concluded, "to make every allowance for Germany in conduct submarine warfare but attack on unarmed ferryboat they say is inexcusable and renders practically worthless all assurances previously given in protracted negotiations with Bernstorff."[49] Karl H. von Wiegand, the American correspondent in Berlin, told one Herr Roediger of the Foreign Office on April 3 that he had just learned through confidential sources that observers in Washington thought the administration viewed the *Sussex* and *Englishman* incidents very seriously.[50] The Foreign Office received another report on the following day, April 4, from the Washington correspondent of the *Kölnische Zeitung* telling of "wild rumors" to the effect that the American government would demand cessation of the submarine campaign altogether if the *Sussex* and *Eagle Point* had been torpedoed without warning.[51]

Such reports might ordinarily have caused extreme alarm. However, the Foreign Office received a long wireless dispatch from Bernstorff on about April 5 that brought happier news. "As soon as a new crisis arises Mr. Wilson will, as usual, at once bring it on with lightning speed and sweep us to the brink of war," the Ambassador wrote. "Whether we shall have such a crisis on account of the Sussex and whether the President will again shy away from war at the last moment, I can scarcely foretell, as this question, like all others at the present moment, will be settled only with reference to the approaching presidential election. Apart from the usual surprises common in this country, one might say that a balmy breeze is now blowing. This

[49] E. Klaessig, dispatch dated March 28, 1916, German F. O. Archives. Bernstorff, in early February 1916, had begun to send reports in English, and therefore not subject to much delay on account of censorship, through Klaessig. The Foreign Office knew that the message was the Ambassador's when it did not begin by naming the day of the week. Ambassador von Bernstorff to the Foreign Office, February 2, 1916, "Bernstorff Wireless Despatches—1916."

[50] Roediger to Count Max Montgelas, April 3, 1916, German F. O. Archives.

[51] Count M. Montgelas, memorandum dated April 4, 1916, *ibid.*

can be felt in the affection for peace shown by a population which will on no account be disturbed in making money and also in the development of the Mexican question." It looked, Bernstorff went on, as if Wilson had found a new loophole of escape from the submarine war in early peace action. That, too, would greatly enhance his chances for re-election.[52]

Still more reassuring news came from the Admiralty at the same time that Bernstorff's message arrived. The navy was certain up to now, the Admiralty's assistant head advised the Foreign Office on April 5, that a German submarine could not have attacked the *Sussex*. Moreover, the *Englishman* and *Berwindvale* had been sunk after warning and evacuation of their crews.[53] And Admiral von Holtzendorff sent word from Supreme Headquarters that the Foreign Office could tell the American government that reparation would be made if investigation subsequently proved that a German commander had, *contrary to orders*, torpedoed the *Sussex*. The commander of the Navy Corps in Flanders, Holtzendorff added, had said that it was impossible that a German submarine commander could have been responsible.[54]

Thus Bethmann could confidently reassure the Reichstag on April 5 that the submarine war would go forward. "No fair-minded neutral, no matter whether he favors us or not," he said, "can doubt our right to defend ourselves against this war of starvation, which is contrary to international law. No one can ask us to permit our arms of defense to be wrested from our hands. We use them, and must use them. We respect legitimate rights of neutral trade and commerce, but we have a right to expect that this will be appreciated, and that our right and duty be recognized—to use all means against this policy of starvation. . . . We fight for our existence and for our future."[55] The Reichstag confirmed this policy on the following day by adopting a resolution affirming the necessity for a submarine campaign, but with the reservation that it should be conducted with due regard to "the just interests of neutral nations."[56] It was, actually, a momentous victory

[52] Ambassador von Bernstorff to the Foreign Office, April 4, 1916, "Bernstorff Wireless Despatches—1916"; also printed in J. von Bernstorff, *My Three Years in America*, pp. 241-245. I have altered the translation slightly.

[53] Vice Admiral R. Koch to G. von Jagow, April 5, 1916, German F. O. Archives.

[54] K. G. von Treutler to the Foreign Office, April 5, 1916, *ibid.*

[55] *New York Times*, April 6, 1916.

[56] The President of the Reichstag to the Imperial Chancellor, April 6, 1916, A. von Tirpitz, *Politische Dokumente*, ii, 526; *Official German Documents*, ii, 1150-1151.

for Bethmann. The National Liberals and Conservatives, ardent champions of the submarine, had failed to win the crucial votes of the Centre Party for a resolution demanding an all-out campaign.

Meanwhile, events in Washington had been moving relentlessly to force the President's hand. Reports from British and French naval authorities, American eye witnesses aboard the *Sussex*, and investigators sent to Boulogne by Ambassador William G. Sharp in Paris had been pouring into the State Department since March 28. Wilson and Lansing knew beyond doubt by April 5 that the *Sussex* had not been armed or transporting troops. They knew, also, that a German torpedo, and not a mine, had struck the *Sussex* without any warning.[57]

The accumulation of incontrovertible evidence, and perhaps a letter from Colonel House on April 4,[58] convinced Wilson that there was no choice but to prepare for the worst, and he asked Lansing, on about April 5, to begin work on a note to Berlin. The Secretary of State completed his draft on the following day and handed it to the President at 2:30 in the afternoon. It cited recent submarine attacks upon the *Sussex* and other ships as proof that the Imperial German Government had "broken its solemn pledge to the Government of the United States," and it accused the Berlin authorities of adopting the "inhuman and illegal" practice of "wanton and indiscriminate slaughter of helpless men, women and children"—a "reversion to that barbarism which took no thought for human life and which caused the innocent and defenseless to suffer even more grievously than those who bore arms." The note had two concluding paragraphs. The first announced both that the American government would have no diplomatic intercourse with Germany so long as she continued her "lawless and inhuman method of warfare" *and* was in fact now severing diplomatic relations. The second merely warned that the American government would sever diplomatic relations unless the Imperial government unconditionally abandoned *all* submarine operations against *all* merchant vessels.[59]

On the same day, April 6, Lansing received a report from the American Minister in The Hague that a large Dutch passenger liner, *Tubantia*, and a Dutch freighter, *Palembang*, had been torpedoed and sunk without warning on March 16 and March 18, respectively.[60] The

[57] See the documents printed in *Foreign Relations, 1916, Supplement*, pp. 215-223.
[58] E. M. House to W. W., April 3, 1916, Wilson Papers.
[59] "Draft Instructions . . . ," *The Lansing Papers*, i, 540-542.
[60] Minister Henry Van Dyke to the Secretary of State, April 6, 1916, Wilson Papers.

Secretary of State sent this dispatch to the President on April 7 with the comment that it indicated the general policy now being pursued by German naval authorities.[61]

Colonel House had meanwhile returned to Washington in the late afternoon of April 5. Lansing came to the White House at six o'clock, and they read the note that the Secretary had just completed.[62] House saw the President on the following morning as he was going to his office for dictation. A break with Germany was inevitable, House said, and Wilson should begin now to prepare for it. The two men discussed the possibility of mediation under the House-Grey Memorandum, and Wilson typed out the following message to be sent to Sir Edward Grey:

> Since it now seems probable that this country must break with Germany on the submarine question unless the unexpected happens and since if this country should once become a belligerant [*sic*] the war would undoubtedly be prolonged I beg to suggest that if you had any thought of acting at an early date on the plan we agreed upon you might wish now to consult with your allies with a view to acting immediately.[63]

House then talked to Lansing and other Cabinet members in their offices. Secretary of Agriculture David F. Houston said that he knew nothing of what was going on. Secretary of the Interior Franklin K. Lane expressed the opinion that 80 per cent of the American people wanted peace at any price, and that it was doubtful whether Congress would sustain the President in breaking with Germany. "He said the Cabinet never knew anything except what they read in the newspapers, and that Lansing was considered merely a clerk."[64]

The Cabinet met at eleven in the morning on Friday, April 7, for what the correspondent for the *New York Evening Post* said was its most important meeting since the sinking of the *Lusitania*. Some members, according to this reporter, said that there was no need to wait longer before taking drastic action; others counseled waiting until official word about the *Sussex* incident had come from Berlin. But all apparently agreed that some kind of ultimatum should soon be sent. President Wilson left that evening with Mrs. Wilson for a cruise aboard the *Mayflower*, taking Lansing's draft note and other documents with him.[65]

---

[61] R. Lansing to W. W., April 7, 1916, *ibid.*

[62] House Diary, April 5, 1916.

[63] From the original in the House Papers.   [64] House Diary, April 6, 1916.

[65] *New York Evening Post*, April 7, 1916; also the *New York Times*, April 8, 1916.

Colonel House had returned to New York on the preceding day, April 6, and dispatched Wilson's cable to Sir Edward Grey. "The President and I framed this together when I was in Washington yesterday," House explained in a letter on April 7. "Our relations with Germany seem now to be going steadily to the breaking point and we are making all our preparations to that end. The instructions to Gerard to ask for his passports . . . is being prepared. The President and I both think if we are once in the war it will lengthen it indefinitely. . . . We thought you should know of the contemplated action so you might take counsel with your allies as to whether it would not be best for us to intervene now rather than to become a belligerent. We have another reason for this and that is we are not so sure of the support of the American people upon the submarine issue, while we are confident that they would respond to the higher and nobler issue of stopping the war."[66]

The mind's eye can see the wry smile on Grey's face as he read House's cablegram of April 6 suggesting that the Allies might prefer a dangerous American mediation to succoring American belligerency. He replied at once, before he received House's letter of April 7 and of course without consulting the French, saying that the time was not yet ripe to discuss the House-Grey Memorandum.[67]

House next had a somber conversation with Bernstorff in the morning of April 8, and the Ambassador was shocked by House's statement that the President would have to break relations with Germany if submarines were really sinking passenger ships without warning. Bernstorff, House went on, should tell the Berlin authorities that the President was completely discouraged, "that it had been only by the grace of God that American lives had not been lost upon ships torpedoed without warning; that it might happen to-day, to-morrow, or next week, but it would surely come unless they renounced their submarine policy and a break was inevitable." The unfortunate thing, the Colonel added, was that American participation would prolong the war,

[66] E. M. House to E. Grey, April 7, 1916, House Papers.

[67] E. Grey to E. M. House, April 8, 1916, *ibid*. House forwarded a copy of this cablegram to Wilson on the same day, April 8. Grey also wrote to House on April 7 saying that the Allies could not risk American mediation if the American government did not take a firm stand on the *Sussex* and other incidents. E. Grey to E. M. House, April 7, 1916, *ibid*. House received this letter on about April 19, when he sent a copy to Wilson. By this time the President had already made his decision in the *Sussex* affair.

whereas the President had intended to intervene to end it, perhaps in the mid-summer of 1916.[68]

Bernstorff rushed back to Washington to send the following message by the Washington-Buenos Aires-Stockholm-Berlin cable:

> House gave me a very gloomy view of the situation with regard to the *Sussex.* At the White House the situation is regarded as hopeless because the view is held that, in spite of Tirpitz's resignation, the German Government, with the best will in the world, cannot curb the submarine campaign. It has hitherto been merely due to good luck that no American has lost his life, and any moment might precipitate a crisis which would be bound to lead to a break. The American Government are convinced that the *Sussex* was torpedoed by a German submarine. A repetition of such mistakes would be bound to drive the United States of America into war with us, which Wilson would greatly regret, as he is anxious— as I have already reported—to lay the foundations of peace in a few months. If the United States were drawn into the war all hope of an early peace would be at an end.
>
> I request to be furnished with instructions which I can use to pacify the Government here, which now has doubt of our *bona fides.*[69]

It was a curious telegram, revealing that Bernstorff still did not comprehend the seriousness of the crisis then obviously burgeoning over the single case of the *Sussex.* It arrived at the Foreign Office only on April 11, too late to have much influence on German policy.

German naval authorities had been genuinely puzzled by reports that a submarine had attacked the *Sussex.* Commander Pustkuchen, to be sure, had reported torpedoing a minelayer on March 24 at the approximate spot where the *Sussex* was hit, and he had also drawn a sketch of the ship that he had attacked. Vice Admiral Reinhard Koch, assistant chief of the Admiralty, told Jagow on April 5 that the naval authorities were at a dead end in their investigation, and he suggested that the Foreign Office ask the American government to furnish information as to precisely where, when, and in what circumstances the attack on the *Sussex* had occurred.[70] Jagow sent the request to

[68] E. M. House to W. W., April 8, 1916, Wilson Papers. In his diary record of this conversation (House Diary, April 8, 1916) House noted that he told Bernstorff that he should warn the Berlin authorities that the situation was hopeless and a rupture inevitable on account of recent submarine depredations. This was a slight exaggeration, as Bernstorff's account of the conversation reveals.

[69] Ambassador von Bernstorff to the Foreign Office, April 8, 1916, German F. O. Archives.

[70] R. Koch to G. von Jagow, April 5, 1916, *ibid.*

Gerard at once, but he embodied it in a note the main burden of which was a declaration to the effect that the German government would not hesitate to make reparation should investigation reveal that a German submarine had actually attacked the *Sussex* contrary to assurances given the American government. The paragraph transmitting the request for specific details was so clumsily worded that Lansing apparently did not understand it to be an urgent request for information.[71] Or perhaps the Secretary of State understood this part of the message and ignored it for some reason. In any event, he did not reply.

Jagow heard a news report on April 9 that indicated strongly that the *Sussex* had been torpedoed at approximately the same time that Pustkuchen said he had fired on the minelayer.[72] It was apparently receipt of an alarming dispatch from Klaessig on April 9[73] that caused the Foreign Secretary to conclude that further delay might be fatal. Hence he did not renew his request to Washington for information or ask the Admiralty to resume its investigation. Instead, he handed to Gerard, on Monday night, April 10, a paraphrase of a memorandum about the *Englishman, Berwindvale, Manchester Engineer, Eagle Point*, and *Sussex* that Holtzendorff had sent to the Foreign Office two days before.[74]

The memorandum said that the *Berwindvale, Englishman*, and *Eagle Point* had been sunk after warning and evacuation of crews, and that the Admiralty was not able to determine whether a German submarine had attacked the *Manchester Engineer* and would be grateful for information about the incident from the American government.

---

[71] G. von Jagow to J. W. Gerard, April 5, 1916, in Ambassador Gerard to the Secretary of State, April 6, 1916, *Foreign Relations, 1916, Supplement*, p. 225.

[72] G. von Jagow to H. von Holtzendorff, April 9, 1916, German F. O. Archives.

[73] Klaessig reported on the Cabinet meeting of April 7, the administration's belief that a German submarine had attacked the *Sussex* in flagrant violation of German pledges to the United States, and the Washington government's intention to send an ultimatum threatening a break in relations unless the Berlin authorities abandoned illegal submarine warfare. E. Klaessig, radiotelegram, received at the Foreign Office, April 9, 1916, *ibid*. It is possible that Jagow interpreted this to be a message from Bernstorff, even though its text began by naming the day of the week upon which it was sent. If it was Bernstorff's message, then the Ambassador had suddenly come alive to the extreme seriousness of the developing crisis. Only the day before, on April 6, he had sent a laconic telegram suggesting that it would be well if the Foreign Office sent him a statement in the event that investigation proved that a German submarine had "sunk" the *Sussex* and concluding, "Under certain circumstances the situation here could become very critical." Ambassador von Bernstorff to the Foreign Office, April 6 (received April 8), 1916, *ibid*.

[74] For which, see H. von Holtzendorff to G. von Jagow, April 8, 1916, *ibid*.

It had been extraordinarily difficult to obtain precise information about the attack on the *Sussex*, the memorandum went on. A German commander had in fact torpedoed "a long black vessel without a flag, with a gray smokestack and a small gray superstructure," which he had taken to be a minelayer of the new English *Arabic* class, in the same locality where the *Sussex* was hit, and at approximately the same time. The German Admiralty, on April 6, had obtained pictures of the *Sussex* printed in the London *Daily Graphic* on March 27. They showed a vessel structurally very different from the ship that the commander had torpedoed.[75] (Copies of the photograph and Pustkuchen's sketch were enclosed.) From this evidence, the memorandum went on, the German government had to conclude that a German submarine had not torpedoed the *Sussex*. Perhaps she had struck a mine. The German government would be happy to receive any additional information that the Washington authorities might possess. It would also be glad to submit differences of opinion over the evidence to a mixed commission of inquiry.[76]

Jagow then sent Bernstorff two messages on the following day. The first, initialed by Bethmann, summarized the memorandum just delivered to Gerard and went on to try to clarify German intentions in the submarine campaign, as follows:

> Germany willing to conduct submarine warfare with due regard to neutral rights. We naturally stand by our assurances to America and have issued such precise instructions in this line that according human foresight errors are excluded. Should any mistakes happen contrary to expectation we are willing to remedy them in every way. Germany in face of daily increasing violations of International Law by England cannot give up submarine war altogether but regrets that England apparently succeeds to hire a few American citizens also for freightships in warzone which as you know are not immune by our promise, and thus tries to bring about break with America.
>
> Our bona fides cannot be doubted since Chancellor already second time announced before whole world Germany ready to conclude peace and pointed out only defensive aims. Our opponents however sneeringly refuse our outstretched hand and are still preaching Germany's lasting military and economic annihilation.[77]

[75] They did indeed. It later turned out that these photographs had been taken before the war, and that the *Sussex* had recently undergone alterations that made her look very much like a warship—and like the vessel that Pustkuchen depicted in his sketch.

[76] Ambassador Gerard to the Secretary of State, April 11, 1916, *Foreign Relations, 1916, Supplement*, pp. 227-229.

[77] G. von Jagow to Ambassador von Bernstorff, April 11, 1916, Telegram No. 130, in English, German F. O. Archives.

The second, written at Bethmann's request and approved by the Chancellor before transmission, was to be delivered confidentially to Colonel House. It follows:

> If President Wilson wishes peace this is in full agreement with Germany's wishes. Germany hopes that the formation of German-American relations will make possible cooperation to bring about peace.[78]

President Wilson had meanwhile been at work on his own draft of a *Sussex* note. He took Lansing's draft, it will be recalled, with him on the *Mayflower* on Friday night, April 7, and presumably began work on Saturday morning. For some reason he returned to Washington that afternoon. He spent Saturday evening and all of Sunday, April 9, closeted in his study. He canceled all appointments on Monday and worked alone all that morning.

Never before, not even during the *Lusitania* crisis, had such awful responsibility been his to carry alone. Lansing had been no help at all. His note was rude, insulting, and offensive to German self-respect, and its demand for total cessation of the submarine campaign was impossible. The note was nothing less than a declaration of war. Wilson decided at once that he would have to start all over. He knew and shared the deep aversion of the American people to the very thought of participation in the European conflict. He wanted to avoid belligerency for yet another reason—the hope, even expectation, that circumstances might soon permit his mediation. Yet he had to force the issue with the Germans. House was at least right about that. Otherwise the submarine campaign might degenerate into utter ruthlessness and drive Americans to war in blind fury, and he would lose all control of events if that should happen. And surely the Allies would not trust him enough to follow his leadership to peace if he did not show vigor and willingness to take the risk of war in this crisis.

The problem was to force the issue and yet leave the option for war or peace with the Germans. How excruciatingly difficult that was! We do not know when he found what he thought was the answer. Perhaps he knew it before he began. Perhaps it came in a blinding flash as he sat writing his shorthand draft or transcribing the hieroglyphic characters on his typewriter. He would not, he obviously decided at the outset, raise the issue of safety for armed ships. It was not worth risking failure of the negotiations and lack of united support from the American people. Moreover, he (along with Lansing) still had

[78] G. von Jagow to Ambassador von Bernstorff, April 11, 1916, *ibid.*

large doubts about the justice of a general demand that submarines follow rules of cruiser warfare in attacking armed merchantmen. That would depend upon whether armed ships themselves made this possible. On the other hand, he would not debate the *Sussex* case with the German government. There was nothing to debate; the evidence was conclusive. He would express his abhorrence of submarine warfare and present an ultimatum threatening a break in diplomatic relations. At the same time, he would make it possible for the Germans to accept *because acceptance would not mean yielding effective use of submarines as commerce destroyers.*

Wilson was so exhausted by Monday afternoon, April 10, that he spent two hours that afternoon driving in Virginia. He returned to the White House at 3:20 and went back to his study. He finished a typed draft late that night.

It began by summarizing the evidence in the possession of the American government describing the torpedoing of the *Sussex.* The American government believed that the German government failed to appreciate the gravity of the situation. Unhappily, the attack on the *Sussex* was not an isolated incident. It was, the American government had been forced to conclude, only additional proof that German naval authorities had decided to intensify their indiscriminate undersea destruction. The American government had protested earnestly against the submarine campaign when it was first launched. The Germans had promised to keep dangers to neutrals to a minimum and to take every possible precaution to safeguard the lives of noncombatants. The Imperial government had apparently found it impracticable to put the necessary restraints upon its submarine commanders. Again and again the Imperial government had given solemn assurances to the United States that at least passenger ships would not be sunk without warning, yet it had "often permitted its undersea commanders to disregard those assurances with entire impunity." The roll of Americans who had lost their lives as a result of submarine attacks had mounted into the hundreds. The American government had been patient. It had waited until the evidence of German intentions was overwhelming. The note concluded:

"It now owes it to a just regard for its own rights to say to the Imperial Government that that time has come. It has become painfully evident to it that the position which it took at the very outset is inevitable, namely that the use of submarines for the destruction of an enemy's commerce is of necessity, because of the very character of the vessels employed and the very methods of attack which their employment of course involves, utterly incompatible with the principles of humanity, the long established and incontrovertible rights of neutrals, and the sacred immunities of non-combatants.

"If it is still the purpose of the Imperial Government to prosecute relentless and indiscriminate warfare against vessels of commerce by the use of submarines without regard to what the Government of the United States must consider the sacred and indisputable rules of international law and the universally recognized dictates of humanity, the Government of the United States is at last forced to the conclusion that there is but one course it can pursue. Unless the Imperial Government should now declare its intention to abandon its present practices of submarine warfare and return to a scrupulous observance of the practices clearly prescribed by the law of nations, the Government of the United States can have no choice but to sever diplomatic relations with the German Empire altogether. It will await an early announcement of the future policy of the Imperial Government in the earnest hope that this unwelcome course will not be forced upon it."[79]

Colonel House, who had arrived at the White House at 7:10 in the morning of April 11, had breakfast with the President and Mrs. Wilson, and the three went to the President's study at nine o'clock. Wilson read the note to them, and House noted that his voice was faint and he did not seem well. House and Mrs. Wilson both said that the concluding paragraph was weak. Wilson, after declaring that submarines should never be used as commerce destroyers, had said in the next breath that he would break relations if the Germans did not conduct the right kind of submarine campaign! Why not be consistent and demand complete abandonment of the undersea weapon?

Wilson, House recorded in his diary, argued the matter patiently. "His contention was that if he did as we advised, it would mean a declaration of war, and he could not declare war without the consent of Congress. I thought if he left it as it was, it would place him in a bad position, for the reason it would give Germany a chance to come back with another note asserting she was willing to make the concessions he demanded, provided Great Britain obeyed the letter of the law as well. This seeming willingness of Germany to be fair would make a large part of the American public believe the German people were being treated unfairly, and that the President was unduly in-

[79] From Wilson's typed draft in the Wilson Papers.

sistent. He saw the danger of this, but contended that he was helpless.[80] I urged him to keep the note as he had written it and after eliminating the entire last clause [sentence], which he did, to say if Germany declined to agree immediately to cease her submarine warfare, that Ambassador Gerard was instructed to ask for his passports. This, I told the President, would come nearer preserving the peace than his plan, because the alternative of peace or war would be placed directly up to Germany in a single note, whereas, the other wording would still leave room for argument and in the end, war would probably follow anyway."

Wilson held his ground except to insert the word "immediately" before "declare" in the sentence beginning "Unless the Imperial Government should now declare," and to strike out the final sentence.

They discussed Wilson's promise to Senator Stone not to take action that might lead to a break in relations with Germany without first informing Congress and seeking the advice of its leaders. "The President spoke with much contrition for having foolishly made such a promise, but having made it, he was determined to live up to it, both in form and spirit." It was now nearly eleven o'clock, and Wilson had to go to a Cabinet meeting. "He was undecided whether to read the note to the Cabinet. He said he did not care for their opinion and was afraid to trust them with it; that the contents would be in the afternoon papers if he did so. He finally decided to read them the note almost in its entirety, but as an argument he had in mind against submarine warfare, and not as a note which he had prepared to present Germany."[81]

Wilson must have spoken severely to the Cabinet, for reporters noted that all members were remarkably reticent after the meeting![82]

All that remained for Wilson to do was to see the note through the final editing and wait a decent interval after the arrival of the German note of April 10, which he knew was on its way but had not yet been received at the State Department. Wilson handed Lansing his typed copy of the note after the Cabinet meeting and asked him to go through it for form, style, and accuracy. The text of the German note given to

---

[80] It is important to add that Wilson was here simply trying to avoid argument over the basic issue of war or peace. He obviously knew what he was doing in making a responsive German reply possible, and he was just as obviously doing this because he believed that it was right, not only because he did not want to take the power to declare war out of Congress's hands.

[81] House Diary, April 11, 1916.

[82] *New York Times*, April 12, 1916.

the press in Berlin arrived in Washington on the following day, April 12,[83] and Lansing went through Wilson's draft, making minor changes and rendering it directly responsive to the latest German communication. He also proposed to substitute a new conclusion that would have changed the meaning of the note in a very significant way. It read:

"It [the Government of the United States] can have no choice but to sever diplomatic relations with the German Empire until such time as the Imperial Government shall declare its purpose to abandon and shall abandon its present practices of submarine warfare, return to a scrupulous observance of the rules of naval warfare prescribed by the law of nations, and agree to make amends so far as is possible for the deaths and injuries suffered by citizens of the United States through the wanton attacks of German naval commanders on vessels of commerce.

"I have the honor to inform your Excellency that I am further instructed to request my passports and to depart from the German Empire as soon as possible, and to state that the Imperial German Ambassador at Washington will be requested to take his immediate departure for [from] the United States."[84]

It represented a slight retreat, for Lansing had earlier proposed demanding that the Germans give up the submarine weapon entirely. But the retreat might have been strategic. Perhaps Lansing was trying to lead Wilson to a break by suggesting that this was the best way to preserve peace while knowing that it was the surest route to belligerency. "It seems to me to say that we must sever relations *unless* Germany ceases her submarine practices weakens the communication very much," Lansing wrote in an accompanying letter, echoing House's advice. "The impression I get is this, that we say we will wait and see if you sink another vessel with Americans on board. If you do we will recall our Ambassador. Why should we postpone to the happening of another outrage action which I feel will do much to prevent such outrage? It impresses me we are actually endangering the lives of our citizens by such a course. I do not see that we gain anything strategically by postponing an action which I believe, and I think you agree with me, we will have to take in the end."[85]

---

[83] The official text did not come in over the State Department wire until the following morning.

[84] From the text printed in *The Lansing Papers*, 1, 546.

[85] R. Lansing to W. W., April 12, 1916, *ibid.*, pp. 546-547.

Chorus—"Majesty, We Never Sink Neutral Vessels!"
Kaiser—"Bless You, My Lambs!"

Carter in the New York *Evening Sun*

Lansing had a new copy of the note typed to show his omissions and additions and sent it to the President, along with this letter, on April 12.[86]

Nothing could have stopped the dispatch of the note now except (to speak hyperbolically) an announcement from Berlin that all submarines had been put in dry dock. Publication of the German note of April 10 set off great commotion in the newspapers, which had been

[86] It is now in the State Department Papers.

remarkably restrained up to this point. There were hoots and jeers at the allegedly clumsy German attempt to deceive the American government and people about the attack on the *Sussex*. "If the German Government," remarked the *Philadelphia Public Ledger*, "were deliberately showing its contempt for American intelligence it could hardly go about it better than by putting forth a statement so ludicrously incredible as this." Other editors referred to the "long black ship" of the German commander's report as the *Flying Dutchman*. Except for German-American commentators, virtually all editors found the German explanation completely unacceptable and demanded prompt and appropriate reply. The New York *World*, among others, even demanded immediate severance of relations on the ground that the German government had lied in denying that a submarine had torpedoed the *Sussex*.[87]

Wilson and Lansing did not comment on the German note, but they obviously were not persuaded by its seemingly ridiculous explanation of the *Sussex* affair or tempted by its offer to submit differences of opinion over the evidence to a commission of inquiry. Nor were they moved in any way by Jagow's Telegram No. 130 of April 11 to Bernstorff. It will be recalled that it had very clearly repeated German assurances regarding neutral shipping and said unequivocally that the Imperial government would make amends if one of its submarines had in fact attacked the *Sussex*. It might have been enough to stimulate some hope and discussion in Washington in ordinary circumstances. But circumstances were, obviously, far from ordinary. Men in Washington were determined (for varying reasons and with differing objectives in view) to use the *Sussex* incident to force the German government to a showdown on the major aspects of the submarine issue. Lansing received a copy of Jagow's telegram from the censor on April 14, and Bernstorff repeated its substance in a letter to House on the same day. Lansing put his copy in his private file and did not tell the President that he had received it.[88] House sent a copy of Bernstorff's letter to the White House on April 15, but with the denigrating comment, "I do not believe we can get anywhere through him, for he does not seem to know much more about what is in the mind of his Government than we do."[89]

[87] "Germany's 'Denial' in the Sussex Case," *Literary Digest*, LII (April 22, 1916), 1129-1131.

[88] It is printed in *The Lansing Papers*, I, 545-546.

[89] E. M. House to W. W., April 15, 1916, enclosing J. von Bernstorff to E. M. House, April 14, 1916, Wilson Papers. House also sent a copy of Bernstorff's letter to Lansing

Wilson was ready, and he waited now only for the final evidence to make an airtight case—affidavits of American survivors on the *Sussex* that had been sent on the American passenger steamer, *St. Paul.* During this interval he spoke to a throng of Democrats at a Jefferson Day Dinner in Washington on April 13. "God forbid," he exclaimed, "that we should ever become directly or indirectly embroiled in quarrels not of our own choosing, and that do not affect what we feel responsible to defend; but if we should ever be drawn in, are you ready to go in only where the interests of America are coincident with the interests of mankind . . . ? Are you ready for the test? Have you courage to go in? Have you the courage to come out according as the balance is disturbed or readjusted for the interest of humanity?"[90] It is doubtful that many persons understood the latter cryptic questions, but the audience responded with cheers and shouts of "Yes!"[91]

The affidavits arrived in Washington on April 15, and Wilson, foregoing his normal Saturday routine, worked all day in his study on the new copy of his note that Lansing had sent three days before, going over each sentence and making additional minor changes. He did not waste much time on the Secretary's extraordinary proposal for an immediate severance of diplomatic relations accompanied by an offer to resume them if the Germans satisfied American demands. Then, probably late in the morning, another letter from the Secretary of State arrived. Lansing wrote that he, too, had been going over the note, and that he was bothered by the formula in the ultimatum part reading as follows: "Unless the Imperial Government should now immediately declare its intention to abandon its present practices of submarine warfare and return to a scrupulous observance of the practices clearly prescribed by the law of nations, the Government of the United States can have no choice but to sever diplomatic relations. . . ." The trouble was, Lansing went on, that this would give the Germans an opportunity to ask for a definition of the clearly prescribed principles. Actually, these were not well defined except as to visit and search. Moreover, the Germans might raise questions about the differences between unarmed and armed merchantmen. As there was a decided difference of opinion about this matter, the Secretary concluded, why not, in order to avoid discussion, substitute the following

---

with the comment, "This has just come from B. and may interest you." *The Lansing Papers,* I, 547.

[90] *The New Democracy,* II, 145.

[91] *New York Times,* April 14, 1916.

simpler version: "Unless the Imperial Government immediately declares that it abandons its present method of submarine warfare against passenger and freight-carrying vessels, the Government of the United States can have no choice but to sever diplomatic relations with the German Empire"?[92] Wilson agreed, changing Lansing's wording to read: "Unless the Imperial Government should now immediately declare its purpose to abandon its present methods of submarine warfare against passenger and freight-carrying vessels, the Government of the United States can have no choice. . . ."

Wilson returned the final draft to the Secretary on April 17. "I have gone over it again and again," he wrote, "and believe now that it is sound at every point. I will see you to-morrow and agree with you as to the exact time at which it shall be sent. Will you not, in the meantime[,] have it put in code and made ready to send?" Wilson continued:

"May I not add this earnest caution? So soon as copies of your suggested revision of this paper were made at the State Department (or was it only a single copy,—the one I am now returning with my own final handling of it?) the newspapers became aware of its contents. Will you not use extraordinary precautions in having this final draft copied and make it *absolutely* safe against the newspaper men both in the transcription and in the coding? This seems to me of the essence of wisdom just at this juncture. I hope that you will make absolutely sure how it is handled and by whom, and hold each individual to the strictest responsibility, upon pain of immediate dismissal. The draft you sent me was undoubtedly given out from the Department (I mean the substance of it), for no one here saw it in the form in which I had written it or in your first redraft except myself."[93]

The promise he had made to Senator Stone, to "consult" congressional leaders before instituting any policy that carried risk of war, now lay heavily on Wilson's conscience. It had been prominently reported in the press, and there had been much speculation as to when the President would invite congressional leaders to the White House.[94] The trouble was that Wilson now had a very positive aversion to the very thought of any such discussion. Surely Stone, Kitchin, and Clark would not approve the note. What would he do then? Could he risk another congressional rebellion?

[92] R. Lansing to W. W., April 15, 1916, *The Lansing Papers*, I, 549-550.
[93] W. W. to R. Lansing, April 17, 1916, State Department Papers.
[94] e. g., *New York Times*, April 6, 15, and 16, 1916; New York *World*, April 16 and 18, 1916.

He discussed the matter with the Cabinet on April 18[95] and made his decision immediately afterward. He would put the note on the wire to Berlin and *then* tell congressional leaders what he had done. After this he would go before Congress and inform the whole body and the world. Such procedure honored neither the letter nor the spirit of his promise, but it would have to do. Hence he instructed Lansing following the Cabinet meeting to send the note to Berlin at six p.m. that day. Then he called Tumulty to his office and instructed him to go to the Capitol precisely at 4:30 p.m. and make arrangements for a joint session to meet at one o'clock on the next day. He was not to divulge the reason for the request. Meanwhile, Tumulty should ask the ranking members of the foreign affairs committees of the two houses to come to the White House at ten o'clock in the morning of April 19.

Bernstorff came to the State Department at four o'clock that afternoon (April 18) to make one final effort to halt dispatch of what he now knew was something like an ultimatum. He had a new note from Jagow, Telegram No. 140, sent by wireless on April 15 following receipt of dispatches from Klaessig and Bernstorff reporting American indignation over the German note of April 10 and the American government's general disquietude.[96] Jagow's new note was a full and frank avowal of instructions governing conduct of the submarine war. "We have modified submarine war to maintain friendly relations with America," it explained, "renouncing important military advantages and in contradiction with excited public opinion here." Then came a plaintive appeal: "We trust that American Government will appreciate this and not put forward new demands which might bring us into impossible situation."[97]

Bernstorff and Lansing had a very brief conversation. The Ambassador tried to draw Lansing into a discussion of specific American grievances, apart from the *Sussex* case. Lansing made sweeping accusations, but he had to admit under questioning that the American government had full and reliable evidence only on the *Sussex* incident, in other words (although Lansing did not admit this), that American charges of indiscriminate and wanton undersea attacks could not be

[95] One of them promptly leaked the discussion to reporters. *New York Times*, April 19, 1916.

[96] These were E. Klaessig, wireless dispatch received at the Foreign Office on April 12, and three wireless dispatches, one of which was from Bernstorff, received on April 15, 1916, German F. O. Archives.

[97] Secretary von Jagow to Ambassador von Bernstorff, Telegram No. 140, April 15, 1916, *ibid.*, also printed in a slightly different form in *The Lansing Papers*, I, 554-555.

substantiated. Bernstorff asked if there was anything he could do. Not for the present, Lansing replied. He would communicate something definite tomorrow.[98]

There was plenty of time to prevent dispatch of the note to Berlin, but Lansing, insofar as we know, did not inform Wilson of Jagow's Telegram No. 140 or of his conversation with Bernstorff. It probably would not have mattered if he had. The ship of state was running too firmly on its set course.

The note went forward on schedule, at 6 p.m., on April 18.[99] Wilson received Senator Stone, Representative Flood, and the ranking Republican members of the House and Senate foreign affairs committees at the White House at ten o'clock the next morning and summarized his note. Stone, at least, said nothing then, but he wrote to Wilson soon afterward, accusing him by implication of not playing fair and of violating their friendship.[100] Wilson, accompanied by Tumulty and two Secret Service men, arrived at the chamber of the House of Representatives at 12:59, shook hands with Speaker Clark and Vice President Marshall, and then began reading the speech that he had typed on his own machine. He read slowly in a low voice without any flourishes, and his speech was for the most part a paraphrase or repetition of the text of his note. "This decision [to send the ultimatum]," he concluded, "I have arrived at with the keenest regret; the possibility of the action contemplated I am sure all thoughtful Americans will look forward to with unaffected reluctance. But we cannot forget that we are in some sort and by the force of circumstances the responsible spokesmen of the rights of humanity, and that we cannot remain silent while those rights seem in process of being swept utterly away in the maelstrom of this terrible war. We owe it to a due regard for our own rights as a nation, to our sense of duty as a representative of the rights of neutrals the world over, and to a just conception of the rights of mankind to take this stand now with the utmost solemnity and firmness. I have taken it, and taken it in the confidence that it will meet with your approval and support. All sober-minded men must unite in hoping that the Imperial German Government, which has in other circumstances stood as the champion of all that we are now contending for in the

[98] "Memorandum by the Secretary of State . . . , April 18, 1916," *ibid.*, pp. 552-554.
[99] For its text, see the Secretary of State to Ambassador Gerard, April 18, 1916, *Foreign Relations, 1916, Supplement*, pp. 232-237.
[100] W. J. Stone to W. W., April 20, 1916, Wilson Papers.

interest of humanity, may recognize the justice of our demands and meet them in the spirit in which they are made."[101]

The delivery had taken just sixteen minutes, for the senators and representatives did not interrupt a single time. As one antiwar con-

Stop!

Kirby in the New York *World*

gressman said, "The president's message yesterday was received in absolute silence. A great seriousness is upon the great body of the membership of house and senate."[102] There was a burst of applause and one lone yell from the Democratic side when the President finished,

[101] *The New Democracy*, II, 153-159; the quotation is from pp. 158-159.
[102] W. W. Bailey to J. H. Waters, April 20, 1916, Bailey Papers.

and perhaps half the Republicans joined in the handclapping as they stood when Wilson left.[103] Most senators said afterward that they approved, but there was much bitter comment in the House of Representatives. The Republican minority leader, James R. Mann of Illinois, for example, observed that the President was unneutral, wanted war, and had sent his note in order to force a break.[104]

Bryan canceled a speaking engagement in New Orleans and rushed to Washington to encourage his followers in Congress to stand firm against war. He arrived on April 20 and left on the following day after concluding that there was nothing he could do to halt the progress toward hostilities.[105] The Socialist leaders, Allan Benson and Morris Hillquit, made caustic observations; a few Lutherans of German origin and two Milwaukee English-language newspapers condemned Wilson's alleged unneutrality; and Henry Ford called the President's speech "political bunk."[106] German-language newspapers were even more savage in criticism. It was unthinkable, one of them said, that the German government should yield to Wilson's demands so long as "British inhumanity against the civilian noncombatant population of Germany is continued."[107] Theodore Roosevelt issued a statement charging that the administration had only its earlier weakness to blame for the crisis.[108]

There was, actually, little open criticism, for chauvinism was the order of the day, and most persons who objected either did not want or dare to oppose their government in the midst of international crisis. Thus reaction in all parts of the country, particularly among the big city newspapers, seemed overwhelmingly favorable. "It is a grave act, but it is eternally right," the *New York Times* declared in a typical editorial. "Whatever may be the consequences, the need to do it was as imperative as the justification is complete. And action could no longer be deferred."[109] "The President is not seeking war," the New York *World* added. "There can be no war unless Germany commits an overt act of war, and if that is what Berlin is determined upon,

---

[103] *New York Times*, April 20, 1916.

[104] New York *Sun*, April 20, 1916.

[105] *New York Times*, April 20, 21, and 22, 1916; *Washington Post*, April 21, 1916.

[106] *New York Times*, April 21 and 24, 1916; *Milwaukee Sentinel*, April 20, 1916; *Milwaukee Free Press*, April 20, 1916; *New York Herald*, April 23, 1916.

[107] *New Yorker Staats-Zeitung*, April 20, 1916; also *New Yorker Herold*, April 20, 1916; Cincinnati *Freie Presse*, April 20, 1916; and St. Louis *Amerika*, April 20, 1916.

[108] *New York Times*, April 20, 1916.

[109] *ibid.*

nothing that the United States can do will prevent it, except at a price in shame and submission that no great nation will ever pay."[110]

Editors in Paris interpreted Wilson's address as almost certain evidence that the United States would soon be in the war. "Hail to you, American citizens," cried Georges Clemenceau, "who march back into the history of Europe under a great arch, on the front of which Washington, Jefferson, and so many others have carved the noblest claims of humanity."[111] And from London came grateful press recognition that, as the *Daily Graphic* put it, "the greatest neutral nation has taken a firm stand upon international law."[112] There also came official if private reassurance that the British government would of course welcome the United States as an ally.[113]

[110] New York *World*, April 20, 1916. See also the review of American press opinion in the *New York Times*, April 20, 1916, and in "Our Final Word to Germany," *Literary Digest,* LII (April 29, 1916), 1201-1204; also *New Republic*, VI (April 22, 1916), 301; *The Outlook*, CXII (April 26, 1916), 931-932; *Congregationalist and Christian World*, CI (April 27, 1916), 565; Chicago *Public*, XIX (April 28, 1916), 385-386; *The Independent*, LXXXVI (May 1, 1916), 159.

[111] Paris *L'Homme Libre*, April 22, 1916; also Stephen Pichon in Paris *Petit Journal*, Paris *Le Matin, Echo de Paris*, Paris *Journal des Debats*, Paris *Le Temps*, all dated April 21, 1916.

[112] Quoted in *Literary Digest*, LII (May 6, 1916), 1270.

[113] H. Plunkett to E. M. House, cablegram, April 20, 1916, Wilson Papers.

CHAPTER IX

The *Sussex* Pledge

AMBASSADOR Gerard handed the *Sussex* note to the German Foreign Secretary at 7:40 in the evening of April 20. Jagow, after remarking that a break seemed inevitable,[1] telegraphed a summary and sent a courier with a copy of the complete text to the Emperor and Imperial Chancellor at Supreme Headquarters in Charleville. Then Jagow gave it to the newspapers on April 22. They published it that afternoon and on the following day.

Virtually all German leaders were shocked and indignant, but the degree of public expression of outrage depended upon the spokesman's attitude toward the basic question: should war with America be avoided at the cost of limiting the submarine war? Frank comment had also been circumscribed by instructions from the Foreign Office. As Bethmann put it, "The words of the press must be firm and dignified but must avoid insults and provocations to America. It will be well if big name newspapers like B.[erliner] T.[ageblatt] and F.[rankfurter] Z.[eitung] do not lose their nerve."[2] Moderate spokesmen, ranging from *Vorwärts*, organ of the Social Democratic Party, to *Germania*, one of the voices of the Catholic Centre Party, called for cool heads and caution on both sides. As Theodor Wolff said in the *Berliner Tageblatt*, "The German nation and the vast majority of the German people desire no war with America. . . . But the German people will also endure this heaviest thing of all if the worst cannot be prevented. The German nation desires that its leaders should find the right road."[3] Spokesmen for the navy, Pan-Germans, and the Conservative Party, on the other hand, had difficulty restraining their anger and avoiding the wrath of the censor. Count Ernst von Reventlow, who echoed Tirpitz's views, was certain that the American leaders

[1] Ambassador Gerard to the Secretary of State, April 20, 1916, *Foreign Relations, 1916, Supplement*, p. 239; Ambassador G. Hohenloe-Schillingsfürst to S. Burián, April 21, 1916, quoted in K. E. Birnbaum, *Peace Moves and U-Boat Warfare*, pp. 75-76.

[2] T. von Bethmann Hollweg to G. von Jagow, April 21, 1916, German F. O. Archives.

[3] *Berliner Tageblatt*, evening edn., April 22, 1916; in this vein, see also Berlin *Vorwärts*, April 23, 1916; Berlin *Germania*, April 23, 1916; *Frankfurter Zeitung*, second morning edn., April 23, 1916; Berlin *Vossische Zeitung*, morning edn., April 25, 1916.

had decided to rescue the Allies from defeat.[4] "President Wilson's ultimatum," the *Taegliche Rundschau* agreed, "shows that America has decided that now is the time openly to go over to the ranks of Germany's enemies, and America's demands seek to prevent Germany from striking England, whose protector and ally America is, by depriving her of the submarine weapon."[5]

Meanwhile, receipt of the *Sussex* note at Supreme Headquarters had generated much gloom. Colonel von Treutler was "quite broken," while Admiral von Müller was in a deep depression intensified by bad news from Verdun. Bethmann was also downcast. He told von Müller that Germany could not yield and could only compose a moderate reply in the hope of encouraging antiwar sentiment in the American Congress.[6] The Emperor, who probably read the note in the morning of April 22, exploded both in English and German. His comments follow in part:

all in the name of *Humanity*.

"*Humanity*" in Wilson's head means unlimited possibilities for real or hypothetical citizens of U.S.A. to cruise about on hostile & armed merchantmen whenever they like in the zone of war. Should these partially paid protections to British ships by chance be killed or wounded by us it is "*inhuman*." But sending millions of shells & cartridges to England & her Allies to kill & maim 1000s of German soldiers is not "*inhuman*" but quite proper because very *lucrative*. To insult, hamper & illtreat all the small Neutrals, because they wish to *remain* "*neutral*" is perfectly right, as well as the trampling under foot of all international law & abrogating the London & Paris Declarations, which leaves the sea helpless open to British Piracy, that is quite admissible because done by England. The British threat of the *Hungerwar* against all *noncombattants*—women & children—in Central Europe, is absolutely *not* "*inhuman*" in Wilson's eyes & quite right. But that Germany should by *all means possible* parry this diabolical plan & the practices of England to put it into execution, even at the expense of some American passengers who have no right to get in its way—that is inadmissible & *very wrong* in the eyes of Wilson & most "*inhuman*." Either starve at England's bidding or war with America! That is, in name of Wilson's "Humanity."

William[7]

[4] Berlin *Deutsche Tageszeitung*, morning and afternoon edns., April 23, 1916; Berlin *Kreuz-zeitung*, April 23, 1916.

[5] Berlin *Taegliche Rundschau*, morning edn., April 23, 1916; in the same vein, see also *Berliner Lokal-Anzeiger*, morning edn., April 23, 1916; *Kölnische Zeitung*, second morning edn., April 23, 1916; *Kölnische Volkszeitung*, April 23, 1916.

[6] W. Görlitz (ed.), *Regierte der Kaiser*, p. 170, entries for April 21 and 22, 1916.

[7] The copy of the *Sussex* note with the Emperor's comments is in the German F. O. Archives.

A German Estimate of the President

"Look here, Mr. Lansing, what does it matter to us whether the Turks are committing atrocities on the Armenians or not, as long as we can't make them do it with American ammunition?"

Simplicissimus (Munich)

But William was calm when Bethmann saw him in the evening of April 22. He did not interrupt his game of skat, and he said only that Wilson had bridged the gap and given the Germans a pretext by demanding a different method against armed merchant ships.[8]

Bethmann rushed back to Berlin that same evening and spent a good part of April 23 and 24 at the Foreign Office. Jagow had already recovered from his shock and was now talking about the necessity of preventing a break with America.[9] A telegram from Bernstorff arrived soon after Bethmann returned to Berlin. It warned that Wilson was not bluffing and that Germany could avoid a rupture only by ceasing the submarine war against commerce while it negotiated with the United States about the proper methods of undersea operations.[10] A longer telegram from Bernstorff, repeating substantially the same advice, arrived on the following day, along with an appeal from Baron Burián urging the German Foreign Office to admit liability for the attack on the *Sussex* and do everything possible to maintain peace.[11]

By now Bethmann had apparently concluded that Germany had no choice but to yield, for he assured the Austro-Hungarian Ambassador on April 24 that he would "use all means to prevent a break with America."[12] This decision was reflected in what was apparently the first draft of the reply note to Washington, prepared by Doctor von Kriege along lines suggested, undoubtedly, by his superiors. It acknowledged full responsibility for the attack on the *Sussex*; announced that the guilty commander had been punished; declared that the German government, eager to preserve good relations with the United States, had decided to conduct its submarine operations only according to general rules of international law; and reserved the right to resort to sterner methods if the American government

[8] W. Görlitz (ed.), *Regierte der Kaiser*, pp. 170-171, entry for April 22, 1916. Von Müller added that he could not understand this remark. What the Emperor probably said was that Wilson had bridged the gap by *permitting* a different method of submarine warfare against armed merchantmen.

[9] As he had already said in G. von Jagow to T. von Bethmann Hollweg, April 22, 1916, German F. O. Archives.

[10] Ambassador von Bernstorff to the Foreign Office, Telegram No. 16, April—, 1916, received via the American Embassy in Berlin, April 23, 1916, *ibid.*

[11] Ambassador von Bernstorff to the Foreign Office, April 23, 1916, *ibid.*; Baron Burián to Ambassador Prince Hohenloe, enclosed in Ambassador Hohenloe to the German Foreign Office, April 24, 1916, *ibid.*

[12] See Bethmann's handwritten comments on the second document cited in the preceding footnote.

failed to compel the British to respect international law concerning neutral trade during wartime.[13]

There was, as Bethmann knew, a long distance between the drafting and dispatch of such a note, for the Emperor had not yet made a decision, and his final choice might well depend upon the advice of his chieftains. Holtzendorff had already made it plain that he thought that Wilson's main demand for an end to unrestricted warfare against Allied merchantmen *in the war zone* was "completely out of the question." He had also drafted a note of reply of his own. It declared that Germany would persevere in its present submarine campaign but would give it up altogether if England abandoned her attempts to starve the German people.[14]

Bethmann, consequently, dispatched a note to Bernstorff on April 23, as follows:

1. What does Wilson understand by giving up of the present methods?
2. By what answer can a break be avoided or at least delayed?
3. Would Wilson be moved to undertake steps against England regarding cessation of its illegal war?
4. How does Congress stand on the matter, will it also approve war?[15]

The Chancellor next summoned Karl Helfferich, Secretary of the Treasury, Admiral Eduard von Capelle, Tirpitz's successor in the Naval Ministry, von Jagow, von Holtzendorff, and others to the Imperial Chancellery on the following day, April 24. Von Capelle observed that conducting the submarine war according to rules of cruiser warfare would not lessen the effectiveness of submarines as commerce destroyers. Most submarines were now sinking merchantmen by cannon fire, anyway, he said.[16] Helfferich urged accompanying acceptance of Wilson's ultimatum with a request that he carry out his offer, made in his third *Lusitania* note of July 21, 1915, to join hands with Germany in a campaign for freedom of the seas even

---

[13] "Kriege's Draft," April—, 1916, *ibid*.

[14] Admiral von Holtzendorff to A. Zimmermann, April 22, 1916, enclosing "Thoughts for a Note of Reply," *ibid*.

[15] Secretary von Jagow to Ambassador von Bernstorff, Telegram No. 8, April 23, 1916, sent in code via the American Embassy, *ibid*.

[16] Von Capelle could have made an even stronger argument had he cited figures to prove the effectiveness of the submarine campaign since March 1, 1916, which had been conducted for the most part according to the rules of cruiser warfare. By British count, German submarines destroyed forty-two British, ten other Allied, and thirty neutral ships between March 1 and April 13, 1916. Consul General R. P. Skinner to the Secretary of State, April 13, 1916, *Foreign Relations, 1916, Supplement*, pp. 240-241.

during wartime. Only Holtzendorff refused to agree that concessions had to be made in order to prevent a fatal conflict with the
United States.[17] But the Admiralty head was not obstructive. He sent,
at Bethmann's request, the following orders to the High Seas Fleet
and the Navy Corps immediately after the conference: "Until further
orders, submarines are to carry out war against merchantmen only
according to prize orders [rules of cruiser warfare]."[18]

Bethmann now knew that there would at least be no new incidents
to break the precarious peace. He next called Gerard to the Chancellery on the following afternoon, April 25, to appeal for time. "He
said," Gerard reported, "that he personally was for peace with the
United States; that he regarded war between the two countries as the
greatest of calamities; that the decision lay with the Emperor who
had not yet come to a decision, but he hoped it would be for peace;
that he regretted that the American note had come in the form that
it had and had been widely published, instead of the demands in it
being made quietly and verbally with a chance for discussion; that this
open demand of the United States made it more difficult to deal with
public opinion which would require something of a strong nature
in return, especially as there were many people in Germany who were
bitter on this question. . . . The Chancellor said that he had twice
clearly expressed in the Reichstag a desire for peace; that he could
not of course state the terms before anyone was ready to confer, but
that the terms would be liberal; that he hoped that peace would be
made soon, as it would be a great disappointment at this time if instead
of peace America and Germany should go to war."[19]

There was nothing more that Bethmann could do in Berlin. Accompanied by von Holtzendorff, he took the night train for Charleville
and the final confrontation which was to be the supreme crisis in his
career to this time.

Events in Washington during the days immediately following dispatch of the *Sussex* note revealed that Wilson, Lansing, and House
were still grimly determined to force the submarine issue even at the
risk of war. Lansing sent detailed instructions to Gerard on April 21,

[17] K. Helfferich, *Der Weltkrieg*, ii, 341-342; Admiral von Holtzendorff's memorandum of April 27, 1916, summarized in K. E. Birnbaum, *Peace Moves and U-Boat Warfare*, pp. 78-79.

[18] A. von Tirpitz, *Politische Dokumente*, ii, 528.

[19] Ambassador Gerard to the Secretary of State, April 25, 1916, *Foreign Relations,
1916, Supplement*, pp. 243-244.

telling him what to do in the event that diplomatic relations were broken.[20] The Secretary of State also warned Bernstorff that discussion could not continue indefinitely and the German government, if it wished to avoid a break, should *announce* abandonment of its submarine campaign and then discuss methods of its renewal with the American government. "I do not think there is any other course," Lansing advised. "That certainly may be an impossible course for your Government to pursue, yet I see no other way."[21] Bernstorff then cabled to the Foreign Office, probably on the same day:

> Should Your Excellency wish to avoid a break, there appears, in view of the situation here, only one way out, that we declare our willingness to cease temporarily the submarine war against commerce [section missing] and meanwhile to negotiate with the United States concerning the methods of resuming the same so as to grant protection to neutrals. By such an arrangement England would naturally also be forced to return to international law.[22]

The German Ambassador saw Colonel House at his apartment in New York on the following morning, April 21.[23] "He was palpably nervous and showed signs of the crisis he feels is impending," House recorded in his diary. "He asked whether I thought it would be satisfactory if his Government agreed to suspend their submarine warfare temporarily in order to negotiate and see whether an agreement could be reached with us, which would enable them to continue upon a basis satisfactory to neutrals." Bernstorff thought that his superiors would yield a great deal if they thought that their concession might prompt Wilson to move for peace. "I convinced him, I think," House went on, "it was best for his Government to yield, and that it was best for our Government to make the demand we did. If we had not made it, the Allies would have lost confidence in us and we would have no influence with them in any effort we might make toward peace. They would consider us as innocuous as the South American Republics, and any demand we might make would be listened to with scant courtesy." Bernstorff promised to remain in New York in order to continue discussions.[24]

[20] R. Lansing to the American Embassy, Berlin, April 21, 1916, Polk Papers.

[21] "Memorandum by the Secretary of State . . . , April 20, 1916," *The Lansing Papers,* I, 555-559.

[22] Ambassador von Bernstorff to the Foreign Office, April —, 1916, received in Berlin, April 23, 1916, German F. O. Archives.

[23] Wilson had asked Lansing to request House to take up direct negotiations with Bernstorff.

[24] House Diary, April 21, 1916.

House reported on this conversation to Wilson by telephone that afternoon.[25] "I think it right," Wilson replied at once in a telegraphic message, "to discuss with the German Government any accommodation it may suggest provided their maritime warfare is entirely stopped during the discussion."[26] House called the Ambassador back to his apartment on the following morning, April 22, and read this part of the President's message to him. The Colonel also reiterated what he had said on the day before, that the Allies would follow Wilson's lead to peace only if he was firm with Germany.[27] Bernstorff returned to Washington to dispatch the following cablegram to Berlin:

At Wilson's request I am negotiating confidentially with House to avoid a break. As false as it may seem to us, the view nevertheless prevails here that we have not honored our guarantees either because we do not want to or cannot bridle our submarines. I have continually emphasized that a complete surrender of these is impossible simply because of our public opinion. Whether, on the other hand, it is possible, as I have suggested, to discontinue temporarily the submarine war against commerce in order to negotiate, I cannot judge from here. Even so, this suggestion would remove tension here. Wilson would accept the proposal and then be prepared to proceed against England as well as to make peace overtures. He believes that, supported by our concessions, a temporary period of quietude would be strong enough to force our enemies to enter into peace negotiations.

I see no other way to avoid a break. . . . The approaching anniversary of the sinking of the Lusitania will be used by the anti-German clique. They will say that nothing has been gained within the year from the Lusitania to the Sussex. That would be too much for Wilson as a presidential candidate. He will be driven into the war, and Congress will not hinder him, even though the country wants peace. We must excuse much which is for us incomprehensible on account of the heat of the election battle here. In any event, Wilson's main wish is not, as is often said, to help England, but rather to bring about peace and to be re-elected. At the moment he believes that the English would simply ridicule his suggestions of peace if he had won nothing from us with his notes.[28]

The only really important question at this stage was whether the Washington administration would relent to the degree of saying that

[25] E. M. House to W. W., April 21, 1916, Wilson Papers, repeating what House told Wilson over the telephone.
[26] W. W. to E. M. House, April 21, 1916, *ibid.*
[27] E. M. House to W. W., April 22, 1916, *ibid.*; House Diary, April 22, 1916.
[28] Ambassador von Bernstorff to the Foreign Office, April 23, 1916, received April 24, 1916, German F. O. Archives.

a pledge to conduct submarine operations according to the rules of cruiser warfare would preserve peace. No government that publicly announced abandonment of all use of submarines at the demand of the United States, or promised to conduct submarine operations according to rules imposed by the American government, could have survived in Berlin for more than an hour. Thus the decision for war or peace hung in part on the reply that the Washington government made to the Foreign Office's Telegram No. 8 of April 23 to Bernstorff, asking what Wilson meant by abandonment of "present methods" of undersea warfare.[29] The Ambassador took this cablegram to Colonel House in New York on April 25, and House still insisted that the Germans, if they wanted to avoid a break, had to "discontinue their submarine warfare entirely, and immediately, pending negotiations."[30] Bernstorff on the following day received a second message saying that the Imperial government might be prepared to give a pledge to conduct all submarine operations according to the rules of cruiser warfare, and asking whether such a promise would suffice.[31] Bernstorff repeated the question in a letter to House on April 26.[32]

The Ambassador, in a telegram on April 26, gave an answer to his superiors without waiting for a reply from House. He said that the American government would regard a cruiser type of U-boat war as legal. But, he went on, it would be much safer to discontinue the submarine campaign altogether during negotiations, and such action would surely spur Wilson to move for peace.[33]

House sent a copy of Bernstorff's letter of April 26, along with a copy of a memorandum summarizing the general rules of cruiser warfare, which Lansing had prepared, to Wilson on April 27. "If they will conduct their submarine warfare according to the rules laid down in the Memo. sent me by Lansing," House asked, "is it not all we can ask?"[34] That, indeed, was the crucial question, and Wilson had Lansing send a reply direct to Berlin on April 28. It repeated Lansing's memorandum as representing the American government's view of the rules that ought to govern a legal submarine campaign. And it ended with

[29] See above, fn. 15, p. 260.

[30] E. M. House to W. W., April 25, 1916, Wilson Papers.

[31] It was Secretary von Jagow to Ambassador von Bernstorff, Telegram No. 9, April 25, 1916, German F. O. Archives.

[32] J. von Bernstorff to E. M. House, April 26, 1916, House Papers.

[33] Ambassador von Bernstorff to the Foreign Office, Telegram No. 21, April 26, 1916, German F. O. Archives; also printed almost in full in *Official German Documents*, II, 1290-1291.

[34] E. M. House to W. W., April 27, 1916, Wilson Papers.

the ominous warning that the American government would soon break diplomatic relations unless the Imperial authorities announced abandonment of illegal methods. But it did make it plain that the United States would accept a "legal" submarine campaign, and it thus left one door of escape open to the German leaders.[35]

Events transpiring at this very moment at Supreme Headquarters in Charleville made it indisputably clear that American insistence upon a public German promise to abandon the submarine campaign entirely, even temporarily during negotiations, might well have been fatal to the German-American peace.

Bethmann arrived at Charleville on April 26 to find the Emperor's camp in some furor because General von Falkenhayn was arguing adamantly that Germany could not and should not yield effective use of its one sure means of defeating England simply to avert conflict with America.[36] Bethmann discussed the German reply to the *Sussex* note with Falkenhayn and Holtzendorff soon after his arrival. The Admiralty chieftain, admitting that a cruiser type of commerce war with submarines was a distinct possibility, said that he desired dispatch to America of guarantees that submarines would operate under prize orders. But the General still demanded all-out warfare against *all* ships in the war zone, aside from American ships in a specified safety zone. Bethmann was not alarmed. The Emperor had told him that he wanted in all circumstances to avoid a break with America, and Holtzendorff's surprising remarks indicated that the Admiral might yet become a firm ally.[37]

Then new developments turned the tide disastrously against the Imperial Chancellor. First, the commander of the High Seas Fleet, Admiral Reinhold Scheer, informed Holtzendorff on April 27 that he had called all submarines back from British waters since it was impossible to carry on a submarine campaign according to prize orders. "The commerce war with submarines against England," Scheer added, "ends herewith."[38] It was, Holtzendorff said, the predictable outcome of the order that he had sent at Bethmann's request on April 24.[39] It

[35] The Secretary of State to Ambassador Gerard, April 28, 1916, *Foreign Relations, 1916, Supplement*, p. 252.

[36] E. von Falkenhayn to T. von Bethmann Hollweg, April 25, 1916, German F. O. Archives.

[37] T. von Bethmann Hollweg to G. von Jagow, April 26 and 27, 1916, *ibid.*

[38] R. Scheer to H. von Holtzendorff, April 27, 1916, A. von Tirpitz, *Politische Dokumente*, II, 528.

[39] H. von Holtzendorff to G. A. von Müller, April 27, 1916, *ibid.*, p. 529.

was also probably blackmail, but it cut the ground from under the argument that an effective cruiser type of submarine campaign was possible. The wavering Holtzendorff, for example, at once swung back to advocacy of unrestricted warfare.[40]

A second blow fell on the same day. Admiral von Tirpitz informed the Emperor that he was sending a written statement "in this dark hour" and requested an audience before William made his decision on the *Sussex* note.[41] Although the Emperor refused to see Tirpitz,[42] he must have been profoundly moved by the old sea dog's memorandum. It declared that America desired Germany's defeat and would only increase its outrageous demands the more Germany conceded. Germany could not yield now without sacrificing its national honor. She could win if she only dared to try and gave free rein to eager submarine commanders. "It has been given to Your Majesty," Tirpitz concluded, "just as once it was given to Frederick the Great to fight the 'Kaunitz' coalition, to lead us through the trial by fire of world war to victory over England, the enemy of our emergence to world power. As an old and faithful servant, trusting in our victory and in the good weapon that will help us to win it, I implore Your Majesty to make the decision."[43]

Thirdly, Falkenhayn renewed his own efforts for unlimited warfare in the wake of Tirpitz's appeal. He now argued, as Bethmann put it:

"Return to cruiser war means the final surrender of the submarine war. The consequence would be abandonment of the hope of subduing England and the further result, a war of exhaustion. He would then be forced to give up the previous method of warfare, particularly against France. He must save men and munitions insofar as possible and limit himself to a passive defense. We would be defeated in such a war of exhaustion as we would run out of raw materials, munitions, and weapons even if we were to have sufficient foodstuffs.

"An agreement with America and at best the consequent return of England to the Declaration of London would perhaps bring us small quantities of foodstuffs, but they are not absolutely necessary. On the other hand, all imports of raw materials needed for production of

---

[40] H. von Holtzendorff to E. von Falkenhayn, April 27, 1916, *ibid.*
[41] A. von Tirpitz to William II, April 27, 1916, *ibid.*
[42] William II to A. von Tirpitz, April 28, 1916, *ibid.*
[43] A. von Tirpitz to William II, April 27, 1916, *ibid.*, pp. 529-534.

weapons and munitions would remain barred to us because they are in all circumstances contraband."[44]

Falkenhayn not only repeated these arguments to the Emperor but, worse still for Bethmann, also told William that he, Falkenhayn, would have to give up the attack against Verdun if the Emperor prevented the navy from using submarines effectively. The Verdun operation, he explained, had been planned on the assumption that France would collapse once Britain was severely weakened by the U-boat campaign.[45]

Bethmann appealed to the Foreign Office for data to use in parrying Falkenhayn's arguments, and he had these in hand, along with Bernstorff's Telegram No. 21 of April 26, when he saw the Emperor on April 30. "You have to choose between America and Verdun!" William exclaimed, adding that he was not at all inclined to yield the one weapon that promised victory against England merely in order to maintain peaceful relations with the United States.[46] The agony of decision was almost more than Bethmann could bear: "The thought of being that person in the affair on account of whose guilt hundreds of thousands of men might be sacrificed in vain before Verdun seemed to him as unbearable as the responsibility for the break with America."[47] The Emperor's words spelled the doom of all his policies and of the German Empire. He would resign and let Falkenhayn become Chancellor and take responsibility.[48]

Help from a most unexpected source came on the very day when all seemed lost. Admiral von Holtzendorff had just completed a memorandum to be used as a basis for an early audience with the Emperor. It surveyed the general military situation and outlook and then said that it was quite true that England could be struck mortally by an unlimited submarine assault, but only provided she did not receive new allies. Unlimited submarine warfare would, unhappily, plunge America into the conflict. The memorandum concluded:

"From the military point of view—at least from the naval point of

[44] T. von Bethmann Hollweg to G. von Jagow, April 28, 1916, German F. O. Archives.

[45] W. Görlitz (ed.), *Regierte der Kaiser*, p. 172, entry for April 30, 1916.

[46] K. Helfferich, *Der Weltkrieg*, II, 343; W. Görlitz (ed.), *Regierte der Kaiser*, p. 172, entry for April 30, 1916; T. von Bethmann Hollweg to the Foreign Office, April 30, 1916, summarized in K. E. Birnbaum, *Peace Moves and U-Boat Warfare*, pp. 82-83.

[47] K. Helfferich, *Der Weltkrieg*, II, 343.

[48] As he told Rudolf von Valentini, chief of the Civil Cabinet, on May 1. W. Görlitz (ed.), *Regierte der Kaiser*, p. 173, entry for May 1, 1916.

view—this risk could be accepted if need be, but from the economic point of view our situation would be considerably worsened. This rich and inaccessible country can carry on a war for ten years; it will bring to our staggering enemies considerable moral and material aid and will strengthen them and prolong their resistance—*and in particular England*. Our goal, which is to obtain an end of the war within a short time, will be frustrated, and Germany will be exposed to exhaustion.

"As the military situation does not at all compel us to play our last man now, it is necessary to protect our military advantage and to act *diplomatically* to prevent new enemies from assailing us, to look for and use new means of breaking the alliance of our enemies, and thus to open for us the possibility of a separate peace.

"If we are able to maintain peace with America, and if we, by concessions concerning the conduct of the submarine war, prompt America to exert pressure on England so that she will permit legal commerce between belligerents and neutrals, we will have obtained the economic succor which would put us in position to preserve our advantageous military situation for a long time and consequently to win the war.

"Rupture with America will, it is true, give the opportunity of trying our chances with the submarine war against England, but in circumstances which can bring no aid to us, no economic alleviation, if the war be prolonged. We will always have the recourse of accepting these conditions if our efforts to keep America out of the game miscarry. But in the post that I occupy I cannot accept the responsibility of renouncing these efforts at the destruction of some hundreds of thousands of tons which we could destroy in the enemy's commercial fleet during the several months that the negotiations must last."[49]

There was much discussion in the Imperial entourage after Holtzendorff gave his memorandum to Admiral von Müller, chief of the Naval Cabinet, in the afternoon of April 30. Holtzendorff, von Capelle, and von Müller all thought that Falkenhayn's position was outrageous, and von Müller, at Bethmann's request, agreed to present Holtzendorff's memorandum, as representing the navy's views, to the Emperor at once. He did so in company with Colonel von Treutler after dinner that evening, apparently with some fervor and obviously with much persuasiveness. "The Emperor," von Müller wrote in his diary, "immediately swung around, obviously relieved of a burden, for the thought of having America, too, on our neck was for him quite frightful. In

---

[49] A. Spindler, *La Guerre Sous-Marine*, III, 194-196.

spite of my counterargument he continued to maintain that the sharp submarine war had been a condition of the attack on Verdun, [but] he had confronted the Chancellor with the question only in order to produce clarity."[50]

There was an interruption on the following day, May 1, when the Emperor received Ambassador Gerard at luncheon in his chateau.[51] William was relaxed and almost friendly. "Do you come," he said, smiling, "like a Roman proconsul bringing peace in one hand and war (in the other)?" Gerard replied that he came hoping to adjust differences between two friendly peoples, and the Emperor then began what sounded to Gerard like a speech, and was in fact one carefully written in the Foreign Office.[52] There was some banter afterward, and some of William's wit was barbed. The Chancellor told Gerard in the evening that "he hoped the President would be great enough to take up peace, that Germany had won enough to be able to talk of peace without suspicion of weakness, and that this awful loss of life should cease. He said that he hoped Colonel House would take up the question and shall perhaps come here, under the President's direction."[53]

The decision was, therefore, already made when Bethmann talked to the Emperor in what had been scheduled as the decisive audience in the evening of that same day, May 1. The Chancellor again went over all ground thoroughly, arguing that the benefits from an unlimited submarine campaign could not possibly offset the fatal disadvantage of war with America. The decision on a *Sussex* note was, in the final analysis, a political one, and the Emperor should accept his Chancellor's advice, not Falkenhayn's. America would accept a cruiser type of submarine war; thus acceptance of Wilson's demands would not mean abandonment of the undersea weapon. Then Bethmann pre-

[50] W. Görlitz (ed.), *Regierte der Kaiser*, pp. 172-173.

[51] Gerard had come to Charleville on April 28 with the Counselor of the American Embassy in Berlin, Joseph C. Grew. See Walter Johnson (ed.), *Turbulent Era, A Diplomatic Record of Forty Years* (2 vols.), I, 221-241, for Grew's intimate and colorful record of this visit.

[52] It was G. von Jagow, "For His Majesty's Conversation with the American Ambassador," memorandum dated April 26, 1916, German F. O. Archives. It is important to point out that the Emperor did not follow the suggested wording in all respects. The memorandum suggested, among other things, that he tell Gerard that he had decided to instruct the Chancellor to prepare a note accepting Wilson's demands. The Emperor did not use this part of the memorandum.

[53] Ambassador Gerard to the Secretary of State, May 3, 1916, *Foreign Relations, 1916, Supplement*, pp. 253-255. For another account, see J. W. Gerard, *My Four Years in Germany*, pp. 324-344.

sented a draft of a note, based on von Kriege's original draft, on which he and the Foreign Secretary had agreed after much correspondence and many changes.[54]

Jagow and Bethmann had agreed, after reading Bernstorff's Telegram No. 21, that it would not be possible to promise even temporary cessation of the submarine campaign—the German public would interpret that as permanent surrender of the vaunted weapon.[55] Hence the note declared that the evidence sent by the American government seemed to indicate that a German submarine had torpedoed the *Sussex*. The German government would investigate further, and it would not hesitate to give full satisfaction if one of its submarines had been responsible. Then the note, after repudiating Wilson's charge that submarines had been sinking ships indiscriminately, announced that German naval authorities had been instructed to conduct submarine operations everywhere according to the general rules of international law concerning visit and search. This concession, the note warned at its conclusion, was made in the expectation that the United States would also compel the British to observe international law in the conduct of their maritime warfare, and the German government reserved complete liberty of decision should American efforts *vis-à-vis* the British fail. The note was deliberately silent on the status of armed ships, presumably because Wilson had not himself raised the issue.

The Emperor approved the draft without ado, saying that it was well phrased and dignified. Bethmann left as von Müller and von Valentini were arriving for dinner. William told them that the decision was made and he had decided not to hold an Imperial conference since he already knew the views of the army and navy.[56] He also talked after dinner on May 2 to Helfferich, who had just come to Charleville at Bethmann's request. "I had the impression," Helfferich

[54] There are at least eight different drafts of the *Sussex* note in the German Foreign Office Archives. See K. E. Birnbaum, *Peace Moves and U-Boat Warfare*, pp. 88-90, for an account of discussions over important points and analysis of changes, as well as the following relevant correspondence (all in the German F. O. Archives): G. von Jagow to T. von Bethmann Hollweg, April 27, 1916 (with reference to Telegram No. 311), April 27, 1916 (Telegram No. 56), April 28, 1916 (Telegram No. 65), April 28, 1916 (Telegram No. 68), April 29, 1916 (Telegram No. 78), and T. von Bethmann Hollweg to G. von Jagow, April 27, 1916 (Telegram No. 5), April 28, 1916 (Telegram No. 6), April 28, 1916 (Telegram No. 7), April 29, 1916 (Telegram No. 9), and April 29, 1916 (unnumbered telegram).

[55] G. von Jagow to T. von Bethmann Hollweg, April 29, 1916 (Telegram No. 73), *ibid*.

[56] W. Görlitz (ed.), *Regierte der Kaiser*, p. 173, entry for May 1, 1916.

wrote afterward, "that the decision had lifted a heavy weight from his heart. He talked wittily and cleverly about his conversation with Mr. Gerard. He said if one wants to play politics, one must know above all what the other person wants, because politics is first of all a two-way business. Gerard's remarks told him that Wilson was looking for a ladder to a new presidential term. For this reason he would prefer giving him the ladder of peace rather than the ladder of war, which would ultimately fall on our own heads."[57]

The only disgruntled person in the camp was von Falkenhayn. He was so angry that he requested permission to resign, saying that he had been much insulted by the Emperor's refusal to see him at the end. Von Müller thought that the General was merely preparing his defenses in the event that the attack on Verdun failed. Then he could say that the weak submarine policy had been responsible. Falkenhayn sulked for a day or two and then withdrew his request.[58]

The only remaining questions of any importance were the ones raised by Holtzendorff when he read a nearly final draft of the reply note on May 2. He suggested making it clear that the new orders did not apply to armed merchantmen, and he questioned the wisdom of characterizing the new orders to submarine commanders as being in conformity with international law (on the ground that such reference seemed to admit the illegality of previous methods).[59] But the arrival of Lansing's telegram to Gerard of April 28[60] left no doubt, as Jagow pointed out, that the American government expected nothing less than outright commitment to international law,[61] and the changes requested by the Admiralty chieftain were not made. Bethmann, accompanied by Holtzendorff and Helfferich, returned to Berlin on May 3. Jagow handed the note to Gerard in the evening of the same day. The Ambassador said that he did not know how his government would receive it but he personally found it very clever.[62]

The one remaining task in Berlin was to forewarn political leaders and editors. Jagow broke the news to the Budget Committee of the Reichstag on May 3, and Bethmann made further explanations on

---

[57] K. Helfferich, *Der Weltkrieg*, II, 344.

[58] W. Görlitz (ed.), *Regierte der Kaiser*, p. 174, entries for May 2 and 3, 1916.

[59] T. von Bethmann Hollweg to G. von Jagow, Telegram No. 9, May 2, 1916, German F. O. Archives.

[60] See above, pp. 264-265.

[61] G. von Jagow to T. von Bethmann Hollweg, Telegram No. 103, May 2, 1916, German F. O. Archives.

[62] G. von Jagow to K. von Grünau (representative of the Chancellor and Foreign Office at Supreme Headquarters), May 4, 1916, *ibid.*

May 5. The Conservative leader, Count von Westarp, was bitter in criticism, but the Committee approved the note on May 5.[63] Under-secretary Zimmermann called press representatives to the Foreign Office on May 5 and, after distributing copies of the German reply, explained why concessions had been necessary. He also emphasized that Germany retained full liberty of action in the event that Wilson could not bring England to observance of international law. Discussion of armed ships, he added, had been intentionally omitted.[64]

The note, published in the German press on May 5 and 6, drew virtually no hostile criticism, perhaps because Zimmermann had made it plain that the Chancellor would tolerate none. The *Taegliche Rund-schau* said, for example, that, while it believed that war with America was preferable to virtual surrender of the submarine weapon, it would support the government in the hope that its policy was the way to victory.[65] Most editors seemed genuinely relieved at the prospect of avoiding war with the mighty Republic of the West. As the semiofficial *Kölnische Zeitung* put it, "We really have enough enemies, and our enemies do not make it easy for us to beat them. We all know that Germany's back will be broken if we do not win this war. That is why all other thoughts ought to be brushed aside, and why only reasonable ones should be entertained. We must, therefore, avoid difficulties which might bring about war with America and leave responsibility for such a catastrophe to President Wilson, if he wants it. For this reason, we believe that the Emperor and his counselors had no alternative but to make the answer that they sent. It must have been hard for them, and we must swallow our justified wrath. We can do it, as our way does not lead to Canossa, but permits a peaceful outcome on the basis set forth by President Wilson."[66]

[63] K. von Westarp, *Konservative Politik*, II, 136-137; H. P. Hanssen, *Diary of a Dying Empire*, pp. 142-143.

[64] "Statements of His Excellency the Undersecretary of State Zimmermann on May 5, 1916, to representatives of the press," MS. memorandum in the German F. O. Archives.

[65] Berlin *Taegliche Rundschau*, evening edn., May 5, 1916.

[66] *Kölnische Zeitung*, evening edn., May 5, 1916, text slightly paraphrased; see also Berlin *Vossische Zeitung*, evening edn., May 5, 1916; *Frankfurter Zeitung*, evening edn., May 5, 1916; Berlin *Vorwärts*, May 6, 1916; *Berliner Tageblatt*, evening edn., May 5, 1916; Berlin *Boersen Zeitung* and Hamburg *Nachrichten*, quoted in the *New York Times*, May 7, 1916; and *Berliner Lokal-Anzeiger*, Berlin *Die Post*, Berlin *Germania*, Leipzig *Neuste Nachrichten*, and Hamburg *Fremdenblatt*, cited, among others, in Ambassador Gerard to the Secretary of State, May 6, 1916, *Foreign Relations, 1916, Supplement*, pp. 260-262.

Meanwhile, Wilson and his advisers had been following events in Germany mainly in the newspapers[67] and waiting with growing impatience for some reply from Berlin. "The Sword of Damocles of a rupture of German-American diplomatic relations still hangs over our heads," Bernstorff warned the Foreign Office on May 2. "... I am continually getting the impression in conversations with Colonel House and other Americans that the President will make himself absurd unless he gets some definite success in his diplomatic battle with Germany."[68] It was certainly true that Wilson was grimly determined to see the thing through. Colonel House talked to him at the White House in company with Lansing for an hour in the evening of May 3. "I find the President set in his determination to make Germany recede from her position regarding submarines," House wrote in his diary that evening. "He spoke with much feeling concerning Germany's responsibility for this world-wide calamity, and thought those guilty should have personal punishment."[69] Someone at the White House told reporters after this conversation that Wilson was not in a compromising mood, and that he was becoming restive over the delay in the German reply.[70]

Of course he did not have long to wait. A copy of the German reply, sent by wireless from Berlin on May 5, was rushed to the White House and delivered to the President in a Cabinet meeting at a few minutes after eleven o'clock. The official text, cabled by Gerard on May 4, arrived at the State Department in the evening of May 5.[71] A supplementary note about the *Sussex* incident, sent from Berlin on May 8, arrived in Washington in the evening of May 9. It accepted the American evidence and explained why German naval authorities had been misled into thinking that the submarine commander had attacked a mine layer. The commander had made an honest mistake, the note went on, but he had acted too hurriedly and thereby violated his strict instructions. The German government, the note concluded, "therefore expresses to the American Government its sincere regret regarding the

[67] The only dispatches from Gerard during the last week in April and the first days of May were the ones dated April 25 (received April 27) and May 3 (received May 4). They are cited in footnotes 19 and 53, this chapter.

[68] Ambassador von Bernstorff to the Foreign Office, May 2, 1916, "Bernstorff Wireless Despatches—1916."

[69] House Diary, May 3, 1916.

[70] *New York Times*, May 4, 1916.

[71] Ambassador Gerard to the Secretary of State, May 4, 1916, *Foreign Relations, 1916, Supplement*, pp. 257-260.

deplorable incident and declares its readiness to pay an adequate indemnity to the injured American citizens. It also disapproved of the conduct of the commander, who has been appropriately punished."[72]

Publication of the German note of May 4 evoked, insofar as one can judge from the documentary record, curiously little comment from public leaders, aside from editors. German Americans were of course overjoyed. The American Embargo Conference and American Truth Society had recently arranged for the sending of some 200,000 telegrams and letters to congressmen and senators begging them to stand firm for peace.[73] Now German-American newspapers, unanimously agreeing that the Berlin authorities had met Wilson's demands fully, gratefully hailed the end of the crisis.[74]

Most editors of English-language newspapers analyzed the note carefully, and many of them added the most searching commentaries on German-American relations that had appeared in print since the *Lusitania* crisis, if not since the outbreak of the war. Perhaps half of them thought that the note satisfied American demands. Another quarter thought that it was rude, insulting, and only barely satisfactory. The remaining quarter, including the New York *World, Atlanta Journal*, and *Boston Evening Transcript*, either said that the reply justified a break in relations or else called on Wilson to sever relations at once. As the *World* put it: "The German reply to the United States is arrogant, insolent and insulting. . . . The American people can accept the German answer as it stands if they like. . . . The World prefers to face the facts."[75]

---

[72] Ambassador Gerard to the Secretary of State, May 8, 1916, *ibid.*, pp. 265-266.

[73] *New York Times*, April 26 and 27, 1916; Chicago *Standard*, LXIII (May 6, 1916), 1123. "During the present serious crisis," Bernstorff reported to Bethmann on May 3, "I thought it my duty to leave no means untried in strengthening the peace party by influencing Congress and public opinion and, *in case of emergency, mobilizing everything against the government*. To this end an urgent report on the deliberations of Congress on the armed ship question by the well-known journalist, Bayard Hale, has been published, and 30,000 copies have been distributed throughout the country. As a result, some 200,000 telegrams and letters, mainly from the Middle West but also from other parts of the country, were sent to Congress last week as the crisis boiled up. . . . The considerable funds which the above-mentioned action . . . required will appear in the voucher. I considered myself justified in using these funds because it was a question of war or peace." J. von Bernstorff to T. von Bethmann Hollweg, May 3, 1916, as quoted in K. E. Birnbaum, *Peace Moves and U-Boat Warfare*, pp. 348-349. My translation.

[74] See the review of German-American editorial opinion cited in the New York *World*, May 6, 1916.

[75] *ibid.* For detailed reviews of press opinion, see *ibid.*; *New York Times*, May 6, 1916; and "How Germany's Reply Is Received," *Literary Digest*, LII (May 13, 1916),

"The more I study the reply the less I like it," Lansing wrote to Wilson in the morning of May 6. "It has all the elements of the 'gold brick' swindle with a decidedly insolent tone. . . . The first impression is bad; the second, good; and the third unsatisfactory. At least that is the way my mind has been impressed thus far. But my final judgment I am not ready to give, without further study."[76] He enclosed a copy of the note along with a memorandum that he had written the day before after reading a copy of the text sent by wireless. It compared the old orders under which submarine commanders had operated with the new ones (which the German note described in some detail) and raised grave doubt as to whether the new instructions constituted "a declaration of abandonment of the present methods of warfare."[77]

The ultimate decision was of course Wilson's alone to make. He read the wireless text of the German note in the afternoon of May 5 and then sent a telegram to Colonel House soliciting his advice. Next he went to the golf course with Mrs. Wilson for the rest of the afternoon. House was now as eager to maintain the German-American peace as he had earlier been to break it. He replied at once that the Germans had made very large concessions indeed, that there were no grounds now for severing relations, and that he felt strongly that no formal reply should be returned.[78]

Wilson must have been pleased by this counsel of peace, but he made his own decision, uninfluenced by House, Lansing, or the newspapers. It was to accept the German reply as affording complete satisfaction, but to make it plain that the American government would continue to insist upon German respect for American rights on the seas regardless of what the British did. Foregoing church attendance, Wilson spent all morning and early afternoon in his study on Sunday, May 7, at work on a reply. He typed out the following note on his Hammond and gave it to Lansing for his scrutiny:

"The Government of the United States notes with satisfaction that the Imperial German Government 'is prepared to do its utmost to confine the operations of the war for the rest of its duration to the fighting forces of the belligerants' [*sic*] and that it is determined to

1351-1353. For other significant comment, see the New York *Nation*, cii (May 11, 1916), 509, and *The New Republic*, vii (May 13, 1916), 25, 26-27, 28-29.
[76] R. Lansing to W. W., May 6, 1916, *The Lansing Papers*, i, 563-564.
[77] "Memorandum on the New Orders to Submarines as Contained in the German Note of May 4, 1916," *ibid.*, pp. 564-565.
[78] E. M. House to W. W., May 6, 1916, Wilson Papers.

impose upon all its commanders at sea the limitations of recognized international law upon which the Government of the United States has felt it to be its duty to insist; and it is very gratifying to the Government of the United States that the Imperial German Government has been prompted to take this action not only by its recognition of the binding force of the principles of international law involved but also by its desire to perpetuate the friendship which has so long subsisted between the two nations and by its reluctance to do anything that might bring on 'the great doom' which would seem to 'threaten the entire civilized world should this cruel and sanguinary war be extended and prolonged.' Throughout the trying months which have elapsed since the German note of February, 1915, the Government of the United States has been guided and restrained by the same motives in its patient and persistent efforts to bring the critical questions which have since then arisen between the two Governments to an amicable settlement. The Government of the United States will confidently rely upon a scrupulous execution henceforth of the now altered policy of the German Government and the prevention thereby of further danger of an interruption of the friendly relations of the two Governments.

"The Government of the United States feels it necessary to add that it takes it for granted that the Imperial German Government does not intend to make the maintenance of the policy which it now announces contingent upon the course or result of diplomatic negotiations between the Government of the United States and any other government now involved in the existing war, notwithstanding the fact that the language used in the note of the Imperial German Government of the fourth of May might seem in certain passages to be susceptible of that construction. The Government of the United States cannot for a moment entertain the suggestion that the rights of its citizens upon the high seas as affected by the acts of German naval commanders should in any way or in any degree be made contingent upon the attitude or action of any other government with regard to the rights of neutrals and noncombatants. Responsibility in such matters is single, not joint or conditional, absolute, not relative."[79]

Lansing discussed this draft with the President at the White House during the evening and took it home for further study. He was, as he wrote to Wilson on the following morning, more and more convinced

[79] From Wilson's typed note in the State Department Papers.

that Wilson had been too effusive, and he sent for the President's consideration a shortened draft that omitted references to gratification.[80] "You are," Wilson replied at once, "probably right about cutting out all 'satisfaction,' and I am quite content to have the note go as you have amended it."[81] Lansing put it on the wire to Berlin at 4:15 that afternoon.[82] At the same time he gave reporters a brief explanatory statement, which Wilson had earlier approved.[83]

The President's retort, published in the American press on May 9, evoked almost universal approval. As the *New York Times* expressed it: "The people of the United States hear their own voice and read their own thought in the note that went from Washington to Berlin yesterday. It commands admiration as the just and perfect answer to Germany's word that came to us in such a questionable shape. . . . We accept no conditions. Limiting mental reservations, if there were any, we cast out. We are the dupe of no ambiguity or adroitness of phrasing."[84]

Gerard delivered Wilson's rejoinder to Jagow in the early afternoon on May 10. Bernstorff, after talking with Colonel House on May 5, had sent the good news that the Washington administration had received the German note of May 4 favorably and would make no formal reply.[85] Receipt of the new American note cast a momentary pall over the Emperor's entourage, then at Bad Homburg. Bethmann told Admiral von Müller that he was discouraged, although he calmly "accepted the impertinence of Wilson's reply, proceeding from the principle: There must be no more sentimentality in our policy."[86] William read the text without agitation. "He stated spontaneously that the tone, to be sure, was abrupt, but that it was a rear guard action of one in the right who

---

[80] R. Lansing to W. W., May 8, 1916, *The Lansing Papers*, I, 565-566.

[81] W. W. to R. Lansing, May 8, 1916, *ibid.*, p. 566.

[82] The Secretary of State to Ambassador Gerard, May 8, 1916, *Foreign Relations, 1916, Supplement*, p. 263.

[83] *New York Times*, May 9, 1916; W. W. to R. Lansing, May 8, 1916, *The Lansing Papers*, I, 567.

[84] *New York Times*, May 9, 1916.

[85] Ambassador von Bernstorff to the Foreign Office, May 6, 1916 (received May 8, 1916), German F. O. Archives. "Immediately after boarding the train [for Bad Homburg]," Admiral von Müller wrote in his diary on May 9, 1916, "the Emperor called for the Cabinet chiefs and informed us of a telegram from Count Bernstorff (our Ambassador in Washington) according to which Wilson had accepted the German note but will not answer it. His Majesty very satisfied, sees in this a fine success for Bethmann Hollweg." W. Görlitz (ed.), *Regierte der Kaiser*, p. 175.

[86] *ibid.*, pp. 175-176, entry dated May 10, 1916.

still wished to trump something. As a matter of fact, the conflict is to be considered as settled."[87] That, too, was the opinion of relieved editors and businessmen in Berlin. Stocks rose in price in heavy trading on the Berlin Bourse after publication of Wilson's note on May 10,[88] while many editors openly rejoiced at the lifting of the dark cloud.[89]

It was remarkable that so much praise in editorial pages and letters of congratulation did not turn Wilson's head. He had demonstrated the mighty power of the pen, negotiated skillfully, with enough but not too much pressure, defended established principles of international law, and bent the proud Imperial German Government to his will. He had asserted and vindicated neutral rights fully and triumphantly against a belligerent power for the first time since the outbreak of the war. He was now, also for the first time, a principal actor in the tragedy being played out in Europe, and he would inevitably have a larger role to play the longer the drama continued.

That role, he well knew, would not be easy. For one thing, now that he had forced the Germans to terms he would have to move as relentlessly to persuade or force the Allies to consent to the grand culmination of his plans—a peace *démarche* under the House-Grey Memorandum. And if that effort failed he would have to force the Allies to show some semblance of respect for international law in the conduct of their maritime warfare. His reply to Germany of May 8 notwithstanding, he could not deny the inexorable logic of the German note. America could not coerce one alliance and let the other go without running certain risks. Bethmann made this plain in a personal message to the President on May 11. "Chancellor," Gerard reported, "sent for me this afternoon and I had talk with him for about three quarters of an hour. He says that the general situation on account of his difficulties at home is very dangerous still. He begged me to say that he did not intend to make the least trace of a threat, but hoped that I could make the situation clear to you. He fears that if in four or six weeks nothing is done by us to enforce international law against England, that the press here, a majority of the Reichstag, and public opinion generally, will clamor for a resumption of the former style of

---

[87] K. von Grünau to the Foreign Office, May 11, 1916, German F. O. Archives.

[88] *New York Times*, May 11, 1916.

[89] e. g., *Berliner Lokal-Anzeiger*, morning edn., May 10, 1916; Berlin *Zeitung am Mittag*, May 10, 1916; *Kölnische Zeitung*, noon edn., May 10, 1916; *Frankfurter Zeitung*, evening edn., May 10, 1916; The Berlin *Deutsche Tageszeitung*, evening edn., May 10, 1916, doubted that the submarine controversy had really been settled.

submarine warfare and that his position unless he consents will become untenable."[90]

Only the future could reveal whether Wilson could steer a middle course sternly. Meanwhile, relations with Mexico had taken a bad turn at the inception of the *Sussex* crisis, and war clouds were forming on the southern horizon. Let us now see how and why this happened, and what the outcome was.

[90] Ambassador Gerard to the Secretary of State, May 11, 1916, *Foreign Relations, 1916, Supplement*, p. 267.

CHAPTER X

Careening toward War with Mexico

EVENTS by early April 1916 were conspiring to force both Wilson and Carranza to make fundamental new decisions about the Punitive Expedition. Pershing's failure to capture Villa, and Pancho's retreat to the Parral district and perhaps into northern Durango State during the first days of April, created a host of difficulties and necessities. For one thing, Pershing's supply situation was now nearly impossible. As General Funston explained in a dispatch to the War Department on April 10:

"Villa's continued retreat . . . makes our present line of communication and supply preposterous both on account of its length and because of conditions of roads. Only our advance cavalry which has probably reached Parral or is farther south can have any effect on chase. All the remainder of the thousands of troops are keeping up a line of communication that is unable to get supplies to the extreme front. In other words the line of communication is so long that the troops in rear guarding it consume nearly everything that can be brought up along it. A glance at the map will illustrate the point."[1]

Pershing's overextension would require, as Funston pointed out in the same message, new lines of communication through the State of Chihuahua. They in turn would mean sending reinforcements and a further occupation of Mexican territory.

But to what purpose, and with what consequences? It was obvious now that Villa would not be easily caught, and that the American government faced the alternative of recalling the Punitive Expedition or undertaking a long campaign and occupying part of northern Mexico. As Pershing advised on April 14:

"It is very probable that the real object of our mission to Mexico can only be attained after an arduous campaign of considerable length. It is possible that the truth of this statement may not be fully appreciated. But it should be realized that the country through which our cavalry is now operating is unfamiliar to every member of the command; very few white men of any class know it in the interior; it is sparsely settled

[1] F. Funston to the Adjutant General, April 10, 1916, State Department Papers.

by ignorant people usually unreliable, and almost wholly terrorized by roving bands of robbers and bandits. . . . Under such conditions, our various forces have had to rely for their guidance upon the inaccurate knowledge of untried American employees, or else upon the uncertain information of frightened or unwilling natives. Thus have well laid plans often miscarried and the goal has moved further and further into the future. . . . Almost the exact contrary is true as to Villa and his men. Villa is entirely familiar with every foot of Chihuahua, and the Mexican people, through friendship or fear, have always kept him advised of our every movement. He carries little food, lives off the country, rides his mounts hard and replaces them with fresh stock taken wherever found. Thus he has had the advantage since the end of the first twenty-four hours after the Columbus raid occurred. . . .

"Success then will depend upon (a) our continuing occupation of as many distinct localities as possible in the territory to be covered; (b) the establishment of intimate relations with a sufficient number of reliable inhabitants in each locality to assure their assistance in obtaining trustworthy information; (c) a very full and accurate knowledge of the country through which we may operate, to be obtained by careful study and reconnaissance; (d) the maintenance of ample and regular lines of supply, especially through the large extent of unproductive or mountainous territory; and a sufficient number of men and animals to occupy localities and keep fresh columns constantly at work. . . . The execution of the general plan has already been begun and will be pushed to completion as fast as possible."[2]

But such plans as Funston and Pershing were already beginning to put into operation could only lead to serious trouble, perhaps war, with the *de facto* government. Carranza had tolerated the Punitive Expedition's entry under protest in part because Obregón had obviously counseled cooperation, and in part because Wilson's statements had led the First Chief to believe that Pershing would not stay long. Unrest and bitterness against the American violation of national dignity were spreading through Mexico by early April 1916. Public opinion would have compelled Carranza to try to force American withdrawal in any event. But the First Chief needed no prodding, for he was a proud nationalist who regarded himself as the protector of Mexican sovereignty and independence.

This critical moment coincided with the most intense period of the

[2] General Pershing to the Commanding General, Southern Department, "Report on General Situation," April 14, 1916, *ibid.*

Sussex crisis. Wilson's mind was completely concerned with relations with Germany, and there is little evidence that he discussed or thought about the Punitive Expedition at this time—the one time he might have ordered withdrawal without seeming to be yielding to Mexican pressure. There was, we know, some serious talk in Washington about withdrawal at this very time. Lansing discussed the matter with Baker on April 5; Tumulty telephoned about withdrawing the troops three days later.[3] "I do not know," General Scott wrote on April 8, "how long this thing is going to continue. It seems to me that Pershing has accomplished about all he was sent for. . . . It does not seem dignified for all the United States to be hunting for one man in a foreign country. . . . If the thing were reversed, we would not allow any foreign army to be sloshing around in our country 300 miles from the border, no matter who they were."[4] Lansing had several conferences about the Punitive Expedition on April 10, but none, insofar as we know, with the President. The Secretary of State apparently made the decision against withdrawal after a conference with the Attorney General on that day.[5] Perhaps he thought that Carranza would continue to acquiesce, even though Funston opened new lines of communication and sent additional troops to Mexico. This, at any rate, was Funston's own opinion and advice: "If we simply go ahead and do it there will probably be no opposition."[6]

Some kind of incident was bound to occur with so many American troops so deep in Mexico. It happened on April 12 at Parral, near the border between Chihuahua and Durango, when Major Frank Tompkins and about one hundred troops of the 13th Cavalry entered the town to buy food and forage. A mob of civilians gathered in the square and began to shout "Viva Villa," "Viva Mexico," and verbal abuses. The mayor urged Tompkins to leave quickly, and Tompkins and his men

---

[3] Lansing Desk Diary, April 5 and 8, 1916.

[4] H. L. Scott to J. T. Dickman, April 8, 1916, Scott Papers.

[5] Lansing Desk Diary, April 10, 1916. It is certainly possible that Lansing was subconsciously motivated by his own deeply rooted dislike of Carranza, which he had manifested on several occasions during the summer of 1915, and also by suspicion of the economic objectives of the Mexican Revolution, which came out almost virulently after adoption of the new Mexican Constitution of 1917. Leon J. Canova, head of the Mexican Affairs Division in the State Department, was still hard at work in his intrigues against the First Chief, and it seems most probable that Lansing was also affected by Canova's advice hostile to the *de facto* government. See, e. g., L. J. Canova to the Secretary of State, February 8, 1916, Polk Papers, and L. J. Canova, "*Confidential Memorandum* for use at the conference with the Secretary and the Counselor," dated February 14, 1916, State Department Papers.

[6] F. Funston to the Adjutant General, April 10, 1916, *ibid.*

began to withdraw. The mob followed the Americans to the outskirts of the town, pelting them there with stones and bullets. Some three hundred soldiers from the local garrison joined the fray, and Tompkins had to fight all along his road of escape to Santa Cruz, eight miles from Parral. Two Americans were killed and six, including Tompkins himself, were wounded in the fighting; from forty to one hundred Mexicans were killed.[7]

Word of the outbreak spread like wildfire through Mexico. There was much unrest but no incident along the border, but American-owned mines in the vicinity of Parral were apparently sacked and burned.[8] General Obregón sent orders to General Ismael Lozano, commander in the Parral district, to halt the violence against American personnel; and Carranza dispatched a telegram to Washington, admitting that Mexicans had been guilty in the affair. He also pleaded for prompt withdrawal of the Punitive Expedition on the ground that more serious incidents were bound to occur if Pershing's forces remained any longer on Mexican soil.[9]

News of the Parral affair came to Querétaro just as leaders of the *de facto* government were putting finishing touches on a reply to the American note of April 4 accepting the proposed Mexican protocol for the mutual right of hot pursuit across the border. The Mexican note reviewed negotiations with the Washington government since the Columbus raid and asserted that the *de facto* government had never formally approved dispatch of the Punitive Expedition to Mexico. Then it withdrew altogether the suggestion of an agreement for hot pursuit, on the grounds that Villa's band had been dispersed and the *de facto* government was itself taking measures to complete the extermination of the *Villistas.* "The First Chief of the Constitutionalist Army, invested with the executive power of the Union," the note concluded, "considers that it is now time to treat with the Government of the United States upon the subject of the withdrawal of its forces from our territory."[10] The "delicate international question between the Governments of Mexico and the United States . . . ," Carranza's organ

[7] General Pershing to the Commanding General, Southern Department, April 15, 1916, *Foreign Relations, 1916,* p. 520; C. Aguilar to E. Arredondo, April 12, 1916, *Mexican White Paper,* p. 173; *New York Times,* April 17, 1916; account of José de la Luz Herrera, Mayor of Parral, in *ibid.,* April 30, 1916; A. Salinas Carranza, *La Expedición Punitiva,* pp. 153-171; F. Tompkins, *Chasing Villa,* pp. 137-142.

[8] G. C. Carothers to the Secretary of State, April 14, 1916, State Department Papers.

[9] V. Carranza to E. Arredondo, April 12, 1916, *Foreign Relations, 1916,* p. 514.

[10] C. Aguilar to the Secretary of State, April 12, 1916, *ibid.,* pp. 515-517.

in Mexico City announced on the following day, as it published this note, "is on the way to settlement without impairing the national honor which the First Chief is known to defend so patriotically."[11]

Wilson discussed Carranza's note and the entire Mexican situation with the Cabinet on April 14, and there was general agreement that Pershing should not be recalled until the *de facto* government had demonstrated either ability or willingness to cooperate in the pursuit of Villa.[12] Consequently, Lansing, that same afternoon, returned a brief answer to Mexico City, whence Carranza and his government had recently moved. It was to be delivered in the form of a verbal communication and, after reiterating American objectives, called on the *de facto* government to join the American government in an effective campaign. It also intimated that the Punitive Expedition would not be recalled so long as Villa wielded influence and power in northern Mexico.[13] Carranza replied somewhat testily a few days later, saying that he desired a formal written answer, and intimating that his government would not discuss the question of withdrawal until it had received a proper reply.[14]

The worst danger to the Mexican-American peace in the wake of Parral was not Carranza's grim and mounting determination to force American withdrawal. He was not quite prepared to force a showdown. The direst peril was the possibility that Pershing, who was then at Satevo, about eighty miles north of Parral, might take rash action on his own initiative. He was infuriated by the attack on his troops and sent a stern demand through the American Consul at Chihuahua City to General Gutiérrez, military Governor of the State of Chihuahua, for the prompt arrest and punishment of the persons guilty of the Parral outrage.[15] Lansing instructed the Consul to hold the demand until ordered to deliver it.[16] Pershing also called for the urgent dispatch of an additional infantry regiment and cavalry regiment—they were sent to Columbus on April 18—and retreated to Namiquipa, some 180 miles north of Parral, leaving Colonel Brown and his 10th Cavalry Regiment at Satevo on advanced guard.

---

[11] Mexico City *El Democrata*, April 13, 1916.

[12] *New York Times*, April 15 and 16, 1916.

[13] The Secretary of State to Special Representative J. L. Rodgers, April 14, 1916, *Foreign Relations, 1916*, pp. 518-519.

[14] Special Representative Rodgers to the Secretary of State, received April 17, 1916, *ibid.*, p. 522.

[15] J. J. Pershing to L. Gutiérrez, April 14, 1916, State Department Papers; Consul Marion Letcher to the Secretary of State, April 15, 1916, *ibid.*

[16] R. Lansing to Consul Letcher, April 16, 1916, *ibid.*

Pershing penned an angry dispatch to General Funston from Nami-quipa on April 17. *Carrancista* forces, he said, had occasionally been helpful, but they had usually done everything possible to obstruct his progress, and the local population had been treacherous and openly hostile. The attack at Parral had certainly been premeditated. The *de facto* government was utterly unable to control either its own troops or the civilian population; in fact, anarchy prevailed in all sections in which the Punitive Expedition had operated. "In order to prosecute our mission with any promise of success," he concluded, "it is therefore absolutely necessary for us to assume complete possession for time being of country through which we must operate; and establish control of railroads as means of supplying forces required. Therefore recommend immediate capture by this command of City and State of Chihuahua, also the seizure of all railroads therein."[17] Pershing then called in the reporters attached to his headquarters on the following day, April 18, and repeated his indictment of the *de facto* forces. He also permitted the correspondents to embody it in a story to American newspapers, along with the General's announcement that he had ended pursuit of Villa in view of the peril from *Carrancistas*.[18]

Receipt of Pershing's telegram of April 17 so shocked Wilson and Secretary Baker—adoption of the General's recommendations would have meant nothing less than all-out war with Mexico—that they sent the wise and cautious General Scott in haste to confer with General Funston at his headquarters at Fort Sam Houston. They recommended giving up the chase of Villa without, however, withdrawing completely. As Scott explained in a telegram on April 22:

> It is evident Carranza troops concentrating to oppose our southward advance. There are three courses open, one to drive our way through by force after recuperation and seizure of railroad to supply large reinforcements that would be necessary for this purpose. It is believed that this will not result in capture of Villa who can go clear to Yucatan. Second course open is for Pershing to concentrate forces some where near Colonia Dublan where water rations to include May fifteenth and considerable forage are now on hand. At this point road from Columbus strikes Mexican Northwestern railroad and protection can be given Mormon colonists [at Casas Grandes]. These troops can be maintained here indefinitely as an incentive

[17] J. J. Pershing to F. Funston, April 17, 1916, No. 115, *Foreign Relations, 1916*, pp. 521-522. J. J. Pershing to F. Funston, April 17, 1916, No. 117, State Department Papers, is a continuation of the preceding telegram.

[18] e. g., the dispatch from Namiquipa, dated April 18, 1916, printed in the *New York Times*, April 21, 1916.

to Carranza forces to kill or capture Villa if we have use of Mexican Northwestern Railroad. Only other course open [is] to remove our troops from Mexico as it is felt that longer they stay south of Casas Grandes more acute will be present situation. With Villa in hiding very small chance exists of finding him in a population friendly to him and daily becoming more hostile to us. Realizing that first course cannot be considered General Funston and I recommend second course. Approach of rainy season which will make Columbus road impassable will make it necessary for us to have use of Mexican Northwestern Railroad from Juarez to Casas Grandes.[19]

This message reached the War Department in Washington at a few hours before daylight on Saturday, April 22, and Baker took it to the White House soon after breakfast, before the President had gone to his office. Wilson approved Funston's and Scott's recommendation at once. It seemed to be the only course open. It would avoid the political embarrassment and diplomatic humiliation of withdrawal at the same time that it minimized the risk of further conflict with Mexican troops. Thus Baker told reporters that the President had approved the recommendation from San Antonio and authorized Funston and Scott to put it into effect at once. He or someone in the War Department also intimated that American troops would stay on police duty in northern Mexico until the *de facto* government had captured and crushed Villa and his band.[20]

Receipt of two friendly messages from Obregón and Carranza on April 18 and April 21[21] prompted Wilson and Lansing to suggest to the First Chief on April 22—the same day that new plans for the Punitive Expedition were approved—that it might be well if Generals Scott and Funston went on to El Paso and conferred there with General Obregón or some other high Mexican army leader about possible military cooperation between the two governments.[22] Carranza, encouraged by Pershing's retrenchment and eager for an opportunity to negotiate to speed the Punitive Expedition's progress northward, replied approvingly.[23]

[19] H. L. Scott to the Secretary of War, April 22, 1916, Scott Papers.

[20] *New York Times*, April 23, 1916.

[21] E. Arredondo to the Secretary of State, April 18, 1916, *Foreign Relations, 1916*, p. 523; J. L. Rodgers to the Secretary of State, April 21, 1916, *ibid.*, p. 527.

[22] The Secretary of State to Special Representative Rodgers, April 22, 1916, *ibid.*, pp. 527-528. Wilson and Lansing made this decision at a conference at the White House that began at 6 p.m. on April 22, 1916.

[23] J. L. Rodgers to the Secretary of State, April 24, 1916, *ibid.*, pp. 528-529.

President Wilson, in the instructions that he undoubtedly wrote on his own typewriter and were sent to Scott and Funston on April 26, unveiled the new plans concerning the Punitive Expedition and hopes for relations with the Mexican government that had been forming in his mind during the past four days. The American government, he said, wanted to avoid even the appearance of interference in Mexican domestic affairs, but there was always the danger that American public opinion would compel general intervention if Villa should repeat his Columbus raid. The American government also realized that Mexican public opinion had to be taken into account. Scott and Funston should suggest to Obregón that American troops were in Mexico for one reason only, to capture Villa, and that this objective could be best achieved if American and Mexican forces worked together. Pershing might well remain in northern Chihuahua and join the campaign only when *de facto* troops had driven Villa close to American lines. "The Government of the United States," Wilson added, "has no pride involved in who makes the capture, and its only interest is that it should be done expeditiously so that American troops can be withdrawn and the peace of its borders secured." Scott and Funston should say that any "peremptory command" for withdrawal of the Punitive Expedition was a diplomatic question to be settled by the two governments, but they might explain that withdrawal would only increase the danger of conflict and would "in any event be very difficult."[24]

Obregón arrived in Ciudad Juárez in the morning of April 28 and greeted Scott and Funston in the Mexican customs house in that city at five o'clock in the afternoon of April 29.[25] Discussions the following morning soon revealed that, as Scott put it, "Obregon came up here for one thing to be discussed and we for another."[26] The two Americans, after repeating the gist of their instructions, appealed for Mexican cooperation, at least permission for the American army to use the Mexican railways. Obregón was outwardly friendly, but to each request he replied that he could discuss only the immediate recall of the Punitive Expedition.[27] Baker took Scott's and Funston's telegram reporting this conversation to the White House at 12:30 p.m. that day— Sunday, April 30—and a reply went to El Paso framed as Wilson had

[24] The Adjutant General to Generals Scott and Funston, April 26, 1916, *ibid.*, pp. 530-532.

[25] *New York Times*, April 30, 1916.

[26] H. L. Scott to Mrs. Mary M. Scott, April 30, 1916, Scott Papers.

[27] Generals Scott and Funston to the Secretary of War, April 30, 1916, *Foreign Relations, 1916*, pp. 533-534.

suggested. It said that the Washington government recognized the reasonableness of Obregón's suggestions and was eager to comply. However, the message continued, the American government was bound to protect its citizens against hostile attack. It would withdraw its forces to a place nearer the border than present, *to be approved by General Obregón*. From there the Punitive Expedition could cooperate effectively with forces of the *de facto* government. "If General Obregon," the dispatch concluded, "will agree to the selection of such a place and assure us railroad facilities for supply . . . [it] will show that the *de facto* Government understands temporary character of our presence and approves it as furthering the common object of the two Governments."[28] Baker, a short time later, advised his envoys to play for time if a break seemed imminent.[29]

Carranza had in fact already decided to run the risk of war to force withdrawal of the Punitive Expedition; giving open approval of the presence of American troops anywhere on Mexican soil was the very thing that he was most determined to avoid. He sent a moving personal appeal to Wilson and Lansing on May 1, saying that it was inconceivable to him that the American government would insist on maintaining troops in Mexico, and that Wilson would certainly recall them unless he had decided "to wage an unjustifiable war against us."[30] Scott and Funston, in a telegram on the same day, agreed that there was no hope that the Mexicans would yield on the essential point. "We expect a flat ultimatum to get out of Mexico at once or take the consequences," they continued. "If acceded to this will be a complete victory for Mexicans over the United States in the eyes of the Mexican people already arrogant and encourage further aggressions." They would not, therefore, see Obregón again until they had received instructions from Washington. It was common belief, they concluded, that Carranza and Obregón had broken.[31]

Wilson sent his reply after a conference with Baker in the morning of May 1. It read:

> Your telegram fully considered. This Government cannot withdraw troops from Mexico until it is satisfied that danger to our people on the border is removed. Ask for further conference with General Obregon, urge

[28] The Adjutant General to General Scott, April 30, 1916, 7:50 p.m., *ibid.*, pp. 534-535.
[29] The Adjutant General to General Scott, April 30, 1916, 11:59 p.m., *ibid.*, p. 535.
[30] E. Arredondo to R. Lansing, May 1, 1916, original in the Wilson Papers.
[31] Generals Scott and Funston to the Secretary of War, May 1, 1916, *Foreign Relations, 1916*, pp. 535-536.

again considerations in previous telegram of Secretary of War, and urge that they be submitted to General Carranza, as matters of so great gravity should be determined by the respective Governments. This will show whether General Obregon is acting independently. If General Obregon declines to consider any other course than that already announced by him and a break in your conference therefore becomes necessary, announce to him that you feel obliged to say to him quite frankly that the United States will, in your opinion, retire its troops to a place suitable for the protection of the borders of our own country and maintain them there until we are satisfied that the danger is past; that while there, they will of course in every way scrupulously respect the dignity of the people and of the De Facto Government of Mexico and do nothing to give offense, but that if our troops, so disposed, are attacked or their operations for the protection of the people of the United States are obstructed, the consequences, however grave, will rest upon General Obregon. Safeguard your own persons in retiring from the interview; and if it terminates in such a break as above outlined, concentrate the American troops in position thoroughly prepared for defense. On no account give excuse for attack. If attacked, take all necessary steps to make answer decisive and speedy.[32]

General Scott had already concluded by the time he received this message that there was no point in continuing formal talks. Thus he met Obregón privately in the Hotel Paso del Norte in the company of a mutual friend, A. J. McQuatters, president of the Alvarado Mining Company of Parral, at noon on May 2. "I could never have accomplished anything in open conference with all sorts of hostile elements as a gallery to which Obregon must play to—," Scott confided to his wife, "so I sent a No. of mutual friends to Obregon entirely unknown to each other & apparently independent of me—to work in Obregon's mind as to the hopelessness of a conflict with the U.S., of the sincerity of the President's feelings toward Mexico."[33]

The conference lasted from noon on May 2 to 12:30 a.m. on May 3. "An agreement was reached this morning," Scott reported to Washington on May 3, "after a continuous struggle of twelve hours duration which was not equaled by any similar struggle with the wildest and most exasperated Indian heretofore encountered."[34] It stipulated simply

[32] The Adjutant General to General Scott, n.d., but May 1, 1916, Wilson Papers, also State Department Papers.

[33] H. L. Scott to Mrs. Mary M. Scott, May 4, 1916, Scott Papers.

[34] Generals Scott and Funston to the Secretary of War, May 3, 1916, *Foreign Relations, 1916*, pp. 537-538. See also H. L. Scott, *Some Memories of a Soldier*, pp. 525-528, for another colorful account, presumably accurate in spite of General Scott's carelessness in matters of detail in this autobiography.

that the American government had decided—since the Punitive Expedition had already largely accomplished its objective and the *de facto* government had declared its intention to maintain the pursuit of Villa and protect the border—to withdraw the Punitive Expedition from Mexico, commencing the movement immediately. "The decision of the American Government to continue the gradual withdrawal . . . ," the memorandum embodying the agreement concluded, "was inspired by the belief that the Mexican Government is now in a position and will omit no effort to prevent the recurrences of invasion of American territory and the completion of the withdrawal of American troops will only be prevented by occurrences arising in Mexico tending to prove that such belief was wrongly founded."[35] "If the result is not satisfactory," Scott added to his wife, "let them send some one else to arrange it."

Wilson was delighted. "I have examined, with the Secretary of War," he said in a statement given to reporters at 10 p.m. on May 4, "the report made by General Hugh L. Scott. . . . The full text of the proposed agreement will be given out immediately upon its acceptance by both Governments. In general, I may say that it provides a basis of co-operation which promises to prevent misunderstanding and strengthens the cordial relations of the two republics."[36] Baker prepared a statement on the following day, May 5, signaling American approval, to be issued in Wilson's name as soon as Carranza had added his endorsement.[37] As edited by Wilson, it said that there were no large bodies of *Villistas* within 400 miles of the border, and *de facto* forces were perfectly competent to cope with the dispersed remnants. "The ratification of this agreement by the two governments," the statement concluded, "removes all controversy from their relations, and I have therefore decided officially to receive Mr. Arredondo, Ambassador-designate of Mexico, and shall direct Mr. [Henry P.] Fletcher presently to proceed to Mexico City as the representative of the United States to that Republic."[38]

[35] "Memorandum of conference . . . ," May 2 [3], 1916, *Foreign Relations, 1916*, pp. 538-539.

[36] *New York Times*, May 5, 1916.

[37] N. D. Baker to W. W., May 5, 1916, Wilson Papers.

[38] "Statement by the President," MS. dated May 5, 1916, *ibid*. Wilson, Lansing or Baker also made not too subtle efforts to encourage Obregón to break away from Carranza's control. General Scott, in response to a telegram from the War Department, visited Obregón on May 4 and asked if Eliseo Arredondo and Henry P. Fletcher would be acceptable to him as Mexican Ambassador to the United States and American Ambassador to Mexico, respectively. Obregón replied that he was sure that they were

It was well that Carranza delayed decision and Wilson did not issue this pronouncement when it was written. On that same day and the next, May 5 and 6, a band of some two hundred alleged *Villistas*—it later turned out that they were simply irregulars with no connection with Pancho—forded the Rio Grande River in the isolated Big Bend district and raided the little settlements of Glen Springs and Boquillas, Texas, killing three and wounding two American soldiers, killing a boy nine years old, and carrying off two civilians, who were later found alive.[39] News of the incident did not reach the outside world until May 7. Carranza at once claimed that the raid was the work of bandits on the American side,[40] but General Funston, with Secretary Baker's approval, moved troops into the Big Bend district and sent Colonel Frederick W. Sibley and troopers from the 8th and 14th Cavalry regiments in hot pursuit on May 7. They returned to Boquillas two weeks later after killing a few bandits and penetrating more than 180 miles into Mexico.[41] Meanwhile, a wave of excitement swept through Congress,[42] the Governor of Texas called for occupation of all of Mexico,[43] and Wilson, on the same day (May 9), mobilized the 4,500 troops of the National Guards of Texas, Arizona, and New Mexico for border patrol duty and directed Baker to send an additional 4,000 regulars to the border.[44]

Wilson kept his head in the aftermath of the Glen Springs-Boquillas raid; his strengthening of the border forces was nothing more than what his military advisers, especially General Funston, said were minimum precautions. The President revealed his still strong determination to avoid hostilities in a conversation with the correspondent, Ray Stannard Baker, on May 11, as follows:

---

both gentlemen, but that such matters were beyond his competence to discuss. Obregón received other American visitors on May 5—a commission of bankers representing Thomas D. Ryan & Company of New York. They came with news that President Wilson had agreed that their company might lend large sums of money at low interest to the *de facto* government, provided only that Obregón, the strong man of Mexico, approved the loan contract. Obregón replied that he would be glad to refer the bankers to the proper Mexican authorities, but that Carranza, not he, exercised executive authority in Mexico. Á. Obregón to V. Carranza, final report dated June 27, 1916, *Mexican White Paper*, pp. 200-202.

[39] *New York Times*, May 8, 1916; Vice Consul W. P. Blocker to the Secretary of State, May 7 and 8, 1916, *Foreign Relations, 1916*, pp. 540, 544-546.

[40] Mexican Foreign Office to E. Arredondo, two dispatches, May 8, 1916, State Department Papers; V. Carranza to E. Arredondo, May 8, 1916, *ibid.*

[41] *New York Times*, May 9, 18, and 23, 1916.

[42] *ibid.*, May 8, 1916.   [43] *Dallas Morning News*, May 10, 1916.

[44] *New York Times*, May 10, 1916.

"He said his Mexican policy was based upon two of the most deeply seated convictions of his life. First, his shame as an American over the first Mexican war, and his resolution that there should never be another such predatory enterprise. Second, upon his belief in the principle laid down in the Virginia Bill of Rights, that a people has the right 'to do what they damn please with their own affairs.' (He used the word 'damn.') He wanted to give the Mexicans a chance to try. . . . 'It may prove,' he said, 'that we shall have to go in finally and make peace.' He . . . said that the greatest trouble was not with Mexico, but with people here in America who wanted the oil and metals in Mexico, and were seeking intervention in order to get them. He referred to the Mexican boundary as one of the longest in the world, and declared with shut jaw that he would not be forced into war with Mexico if it could possibly be avoided. He does not want one hand tied behind him at the very moment that the nation may need all of its forces to meet the European situation. He emphasized the enormous undertaking it would be to pacify Mexico: 'Five hundred thousand men at least.' "[45]

The aftermath of the Glen Springs-Boquillas raid, particularly the dispatch of the Sibley expedition, had its most dangerous impact on Carranza, indeed, on all articulate Mexicans. The First Chief instructed Obregón on May 6 to continue to negotiate for prompt withdrawal of the Punitive Expedition without conditions.[46] Obregón saw Scott and Funston on the following day and asked whether the raid in the Big Bend district would prevent American approval of the agreement that they had signed on May 3. The Americans replied that it would not, even though it would certainly have afforded a good excuse if the American government had wanted to disrupt negotiations and delay the withdrawal. Obregón, much shaken by recent events, begged Carranza to approve the agreement and then work for evacuation of all American forces, including the new expedition just sent into Mexico. It was the only way to prevent war, Obregón concluded; life or death for Mexico would depend upon Carranza's reply.[47]

It was probably receipt of news that the Sibley expedition had entered or soon would enter Mexico that tipped the balance in Mexico City. In any event, the First Chief replied on May 7, reiterating that

[45] From Baker's notes of this conversation, printed in R. S. Baker, *Woodrow Wilson,* VI, 74-75.

[46] V. Carranza to Á. Obregón, May 6, 1916, *Mexican White Paper*, pp. 176-178.

[47] Á. Obregón to V. Carranza, May 7, 1916, *ibid.,* pp. 178-181.

the Glen Springs-Boquillas raid was the work of trouble makers on the American side and instructing Obregón to tell General Scott that he, Carranza, did not approve the memorandum and would resist further American expeditions as invaders.[48] Carranza, a short time later, instructed Obregón to order Generals Plutarcho E. Calles and Jacinto B. Treviño, both of whom were in Juárez, to return to their headquarters in view of the delicate situation.[49] It was, Obregón knew, a decision for war, or at least to run the risk of war. He consequently informed Scott and Funston on May 8 that his government could not accept the memorandum because it did not specify a date for withdrawal of Pershing's forces. Scott reminded him that he had himself signed the agreement. That fact, Obregón replied, proved that Carranza had more sense than he.

Obregón also made one last desperate effort at the same conference to avert hostilities, proposing a simple verbal understanding for the immediate withdrawal of the Punitive Expedition, dispatch of large numbers of Mexican troops to Chihuahua for defense of the border, and effective Mexican-American cooperation in the future.[50] Carranza was not entirely pleased and suggested a new text for the protocol;[51] Scott and Funston quite mistakenly thought that Obregón's proposal was a cover for full-scale Mexican mobilization in Chihuahua for action against Pershing's command.[52] They submitted a counterproposal at the next meeting, on May 9, providing for gradual retirement of the Punitive Expedition to Namiquipa and further withdrawal northward once the President was convinced that the Mexican government was able and willing to protect the border.[53] Scott warned Obregón two days later, on May 11, that the American government would not only not withdraw its troops from Mexico, but would send many more men to the border if the *de facto* government did not approve his new proposal. Obregón replied hotly that he would not tolerate any threats,

[48] V. Carranza to Á. Obregón, May 7, 1916, *ibid.*, pp. 181-182.

[49] V. Carranza to Á. Obregón, May 7, 1916, *ibid.*, pp. 183-184.

[50] Generals Scott and Funston to the Secretary of War, May 8, 1916, *Foreign Relations, 1916*, pp. 543-544; Á. Obregón to V. Carranza, two dispatches, May 8, 1916, *Mexican White Paper*, pp. 185-187.

[51] V. Carranza to Á. Obregón, May 9, 1916, *ibid.*, p. 189.

[52] Generals Scott and Funston to the Secretary of War, May 8, 1916, *Foreign Relations, 1916*, pp. 543-544. It was this dispatch that advised and prompted the calling of the National Guards of Texas, Arizona, and New Mexico into federal service and the dispatch of additional regular troops to the border. For proof of Obregón's sincerity, see Á. Obregón to V. Carranza, May 10, 1916, *Mexican White Paper*, pp. 190-193.

[53] Generals Scott and Funston to the Secretary of War, May 9, 1916, Polk Papers.

and the conferees agreed to meet again later in the afternoon. They returned only to conclude that further talks were useless and to leave each other, they said, as friends.[54] "The ending of these conferences," they declared in a public statement, "does not mean, in any way, the rupture of the good relations of friendship between the conferees nor between the respective Governments."[55]

Wilson and his advisers were not at all disturbed by the disruption. There seemed to be abundant grounds for optimism. Pershing reported on May 11 that there was no evidence that *de facto* forces had any hostile intentions.[56] Even more encouraging was the long telegraphic report that Scott sent from El Paso in the morning of May 12. The situation, he advised, was no longer acute, for the Mexicans would do their best to carry their share of the burden of defense, and Obregón would have greater strength with his people to cooperate than if an agreement had actually been ratified. Moreover, Scott went on, Doctor Juan N. Amador, legal adviser in the Mexican Foreign Office who had been with Obregón since May 3, had just dictated the following statement: "That [in] all of these talks General Obregon, in my opinion, has had the conviction of the good faith in which General Scott, on the part of the American government, has been acting; but the simple promise to control the situation not being sufficient, he is now going to show evidently to the government of the United States that he is able to handle the situation in Mexico, with full control of his troops, which he is going to distribute in the zone of Parral and on the Mexican side of the Rio Grande frontier in sufficient numbers as to guarantee safety for that region and try to avoid future trouble. That by that way, it being the intention of the U.S. to withdraw, as it has been repeatedly stated by General Scott, the withdrawal of the troops will have to occur because of the demonstration of the fact of the Government of Mexico being powerful enough to control the situation."[57]

This was good news, indeed, and Wilson read these telegrams to the Cabinet in the morning of May 12, and an administration spokesman, probably Newton D. Baker, gave reporters a detailed explana-

[54] Á. Obregón to V. Carranza, final report, dated June 27, 1916, *Mexican White Paper*, pp. 204-206.

[55] *New York Times*, May 12, 1916.

[56] J. J. Pershing to General Funston, May 11, 1916, quoted in General Funston to the Adjutant General, May 12, 1916, Wilson Papers.

[57] H. L. Scott to the Secretary of War, May 12, 1916, *ibid.*

tion of the government's plans in the wake of new developments. The Mexican and American foreign ministries could discuss the future of the Punitive Expedition, he said, and the American government would meanwhile maintain the *status quo* in the belief that Carranza would make diplomatic "noises" over Pershing's presence in Mexico but was not prepared to risk a break with the United States.

This spokesman (or some other) also intimated that Obregón and Scott had concluded a secret oral agreement for military cooperation along the border. The *de facto* government was sending large new forces to Coahuila and Chihuahua. Hence the Punitive Expedition had already entrenched in the long rectangular area comprised, roughly, by lines running from El Paso south to San Antonio, Mexico (southwest of Chihuahua City), from San Antonio west to Guerrero, from Guerrero north to Columbus, and from Columbus east to El Paso. Pershing's men would patrol this part of the State of Chihuahua, giving special protection to American colonists at Casas Grandes, Colonia Dublan, Madera, Pearson, Barbicora, and Cusihuiriáchic. Pershing would remain in Mexico until the American government was convinced that the border and American colonists in Chihuahua were absolutely safe.[58]

General Scott returned to Washington on May 15 to reiterate orally what he had said in writing and to add that General Obregón had agreed to send 10,000 picked troops into the Big Bend and Parral districts, ordered General Treviño to head off the bandits who had raided Glen Springs and Boquillas, and promised that *Carrancista* troops in Sonora (west of Chihuahua) would not menace Pershing in any way. The border situation, Scott went on, was better than at any time since Pershing entered Mexico. Wilson and members of the Cabinet were much gratified when Baker repeated this intelligence to them on May 16.[59]

There would have been less complacency in Washington if leaders there had not made the mistake of continuing to believe—because they wanted to—that Obregón, not Carranza, was the real power in Mexico, and of refusing to take Carranza's warnings seriously. The proud First Chief, under heavy pressure from opinion at home, was determined to compel Pershing's withdrawal from every square inch of Mexican soil. To him, as to a large segment of articulate Mexican

[58] *New York Times*, May 13, 1916.
[59] *ibid.*, May 17, 1916.

opinion, the failure of the Obregón-Scott-Funston negotiations, and particularly the entry of the Sibley expedition, had portentous significance: The American government would not yield voluntarily; ordinary diplomatic processes offered no hope of relief; the *de facto* government now had to force a showdown at the risk of war.

Carranza had already sent war warnings to all Mexican commanders in northern Mexico on May 8.[60] In reaction against Sibley's entry he ordered his forces at Matamoros and Nuevo Laredo on May 18 to fight any American troops that crossed the border along any part of the line under their command.[61] Orders went at the same time to all Mexican governors and commanders to prepare for war,[62] while large reinforcements were rushed to the States of Coahuila and Chihuahua. General Treviño, for example, left Saltillo for the border area with 15,000 men in twenty-six trains on about May 20.[63] The official organ, *El Pueblo* of Mexico City, opened a heavy propaganda attack, accusing the United States of wanting to turn back the Revolution and restore the rule of *científicos* and bishops, and concluding: "In refusing to be the base puppet of Yankee felony, we not only defend the national life, the honor, the dignity, and the independence of a people, but also those of a race,—from the common mother who gave us her blood and her language."[64]

It was perfectly obvious what the Mexicans intended to do, and optimism in Washington and American military circles ebbed rapidly. "There are heavy movements of [Mexican] troops north for ostensible purpose of suppressing bandits but numbers suspiciously large for needs," Funston warned Pershing on May 19. "I consider it likely that considerable force of Mexicans will occupy country on your front and then ask you to retire claiming they are able to maintain order in region. In such event you will decline to accede and if they attempt to approach your command in too large force or place themselves in position to endanger your line of communications you will protest and immediately inform me of facts. If any part of your force is

[60] See Carranza's telegrams to various generals on this date, *Mexican White Paper*, pp. 184-185.

[61] V. Carranza to General A. Ricaut and General R. Garza, May 18, 1916, *ibid.*, p. 207.

[62] e. g., Consul C. I. Dawson, from Tampico, to the Secretary of State, May 13, 1916, and Consul T. D. Bowman, from Frontera, to the Secretary of State, May 16, 1916, *Foreign Relations, 1916*, pp. 547-548.

[63] J. R. Silliman, from Saltillo, to the Secretary of State, May 22, 1916, State Department Papers.

[64] Mexico City *El Pueblo*, May 24, 1916.

attacked by an undoubted organized body of de facto government troops you will attempt to destroy all of their forces within reach taking care not to become too deeply involved or expose your lines of communications. For a time we shall not be able to support you. In case of such an attack on you rush information to me without waiting to give details as it is essential that we learn of it before Mexican commander on the border. Danger from Moral, Coahuila[,] greatly increased as troops have left Bavispe Valley and are concentrated along railway south of Agua Prieta[,] Sonora."[65]

Carranza and officials in the Mexican Foreign Office had meanwhile been at work on a note intended to compel a showdown. It was completed on May 22, published in the Mexico City press on May 31, and delivered to the State Department on the same day, in spite of an advance categorical warning from Washington that the American government could not yield because of the domestic political situation.[66]

The note, 12,000 words in length, reviewed the earlier negotiations over an agreement for hot pursuit and the futile Obregón-Scott-Funston parleys. The Mexican government, it said, had appealed in vain for evacuation of the Punitive Expedition. Now it had to insist upon its withdrawal in the full knowledge that it would have no recourse but to defend its territory by arms if the American government refused, although it, the Mexican government, would resort to every pacific method to solve the conflict. The Mexican government also felt compelled to appeal to the President, Secretary of State, Senate, and American people for a frank avowal of the intentions of the United States toward Mexico. President Wilson had promised to recall the Punitive Expedition once its work was done. The American government had agreed that the *Villistas* were dispersed, yet Wilson still refused to withdraw Pershing's forces. This and other developments clearly indicated that the American government was maintaining troops in Mexico sheerly for reasons of domestic politics. The Punitive Expedition's entry constituted an invasion of Mexican territory. Its large infantry and artillery contingents were meant for use against Mexican troops. The Mexican government had been eager to cooperate with American military forces in defense of the border, but the American government had tried to prevent the *de facto* government from establishing its con-

[65] General Funston to the Adjutant General, May 19, 1916, repeating General Funston to General Pershing, May 19, 1916, State Department Papers.

[66] This was Charles A. Douglas (Carranza's legal agent in Washington) to Luis Cabrera (Finance Minister in the *de facto* government), telegram, May 27, 1916, copy in the Polk Papers, reporting on a conversation with Secretary Lansing.

trol in northern Mexico. The Washington government was mainly interested in protecting American interests in that region. It had earlier supported Villa and prolonged the civil war in Mexico for the same reason, permitted Mexican rebels to organize conspiracies against Mexico on American soil, and impeded the export of arms and ammunition to the *de facto* authorities. The Mexican people and government were absolutely sure that the American people did not want war with Mexico, but they needed proof that the American government and military authorities were of the same disposition. The best evidence of friendly intentions would be prompt withdrawal of all American troops from Mexican territory.[67]

Polk, after receiving the note from Arredondo, sent copies to Lansing and Wilson as soon as it was translated. "The tone, as you will notice," the Counselor wrote to the President, "is decidedly unsatisfactory and, in some places, impertinent."[68] Lansing read the document with mounting fury, penning such remarks as "Insulting," "Makes out the U S a liar," and "Again a liar" on the margins.[69] It was probably he who suggested to the President that "it might be well to consider the advisability of returning the Note on account of its offensive tone."[70] Wilson, for his part, made a point of canceling a Cabinet meeting scheduled for June 2, in order to emphasize that he did not expect an immediate crisis, and he or some administration spokesman told reporters on June 1 that the American government would withdraw the Punitive Expedition in its own way and time. The note, reporters said, caused scarcely a ripple in administration circles.[71] It did not cause much furor, either, when newspapers published it on May 31 and June 1. Most editors thought that it had been written mainly for home consumption.[72]

Mexicans waited for events that would plunge them into war while officials in the State Department began the draft of a reply and the American army commenced construction of a first-class military highway from Columbus to Namiquipa.[73] Arredondo, in a talk on June 2

[67] C. Aguilar to the Secretary of State, May 22, 1916, *Foreign Relations, 1916*, pp. 552-563.

[68] F. L. Polk to W. W., May 31, 1916, Wilson Papers.

[69] Lansing's comments may be found on the copy in the State Department Archives.

[70] F. L. Polk to W. W., June 1, 1916, Wilson Papers.

[71] *New York Times*, June 2, 1916.

[72] See the brief review of American press reaction in "Carranza Mentions the Door," *Literary Digest*, LII (June 10, 1916), 1689-1690.

[73] *New York Times*, June 1, 1916.

with his friend, David Lawrence, said that he feared that war would come. "He said Carranza was being called a 'traitor' on every side since he was consenting to the occupation of Mexican territory by foreign troops. He added that the desire for war with the United States was growing, that Carranza was not writing his notes for 'home consumption' since he had suppressed the first series of exchanges. . . . He said that many officials of the Mexican government were beginning to feel that it would be better for Mexico to die, better for it to be strangled while fighting than to submit in humiliation to what would in the end be the same thing."[74] It was true, and Mexican officials restrained the anti-American sentiment then surging through northern Mexico only with great difficulty.[75]

President Wilson and Secretary Baker warned Funston of the dangerous possibilities, asking whether Pershing was not too far south in Mexico for safety.[76] They also dispatched an additional 1,600 regular troops to the border on June 12.[77] It seemed a few days later that general hostilities were inevitable even before the American note of reply could be completed. Some sixty Mexican irregulars crossed the Rio Grande at San Ignacio, forty miles south of Laredo, Texas, and attacked an American border patrol on June 15, killing three and wounding seven soldiers, one of whom died soon afterward.[78] The War Department immediately ordered prompt pursuit of the bandits. General Alfredo Ricaut, *Carrancista* chieftain at nearby Matamoros, warned the American commander at Brownsville, General Parker, that he was under orders to resist any Americans who crossed into Mexico.[79] An American cavalry force of four hundred men crossed the Rio Grande on June 17, returning to American territory on the following day after a brief skirmish with unidentified Mexicans.[80] There was no serious

[74] D. Lawrence to W. W., June 2, 1916, Wilson Papers.

[75] G. C. Carothers to the Secretary of State, June 7, 1916, State Department Papers, reporting on an anti-American riot in Chihuahua City on the night of June 6, 1916; J. R. Silliman to the Secretary of State, June 8 and 10, 1916, *ibid.*, reporting on an attempted anti-American demonstration in Saltillo; W. P. Blocker to the Secretary of State, June 10 and 11, 1916, *ibid.*, reporting on an attempted demonstration in Piedras Negras; also the general review of unrest in northern Mexico in the *New York Times*, June 10, 1916.

[76] For Funston's reply, see F. Funston to the Adjutant General, June 12, 1916, Wilson Papers.

[77] *New York Times*, June 13, 1916.

[78] Consul J. H. Johnson to the Secretary of State, June 15, 1916, *Foreign Relations, 1916*, p. 575; *New York Times*, June 16, 1916.

[79] *ibid.*

[80] *ibid.*, June 18 and 19, 1916.

fighting only because General Ricaut failed to make contact with the fast-moving Americans.[81]

This was the incident that set war machinery in motion on both sides. General Treviño, military commander in Chihuahua, sent the following telegram, at Carranza's personal instruction, to Pershing at Casas Grandes on June 16:

> I have orders from my Government to prevent, by the use of arms, new invasions of my country by American forces and also to prevent the American forces that are in this State from moving to the south, east or west of the places they now occupy. I communicate this to you for your knowledge for the reason that your forces will be attacked by the Mexican forces if these instructions are not heeded.

Pershing replied at once, without consulting his superiors:

> I am in receipt of your telegram. . . . In reply you are informed that my Government has placed no such restrictions upon the movements of the American forces. I shall therefore use my own judgment as to when and in what direction I shall move my forces in pursuit of bandits or in seeking information regarding bandits. If under these circumstances the Mexican forces attack any of my columns the responsibility for the consequences will lie with the Mexican Government.[82]

The War Department received news of this exchange on June 16. General Scott on that same day instructed the Chief of the War College Division to prepare plans, to be completed within a week, for an invasion of Mexico on the lines of the various railways from the north. "There should be a plan," Scott added, "for the protection of the border, and an invasion on each of the lines of railway; a plan for taking over the railways as we go along, with personnel to manage them, repair gangs, bridge builders, etc.; the establishment of lines of communications; and the protection of American property in Mexico near the border that can be reached promptly. . . ."[83] Mexican authorities on that same day and immediately afterward called all male residents in Ciudad Juárez to the colors, issued guns to citizens in Nuevo Laredo, and dismantled all Mexican war vessels in Veracruz harbor and shipped official archives to Mexico City.[84]

[81] A. Ricaut to V. Carranza, June 18, 1916, *Mexican White Paper*, pp. 221-222.

[82] These telegrams are printed in *Foreign Relations, 1916*, p. 577.

[83] H. L. Scott, "Memorandum for Chief, War College Division," June 16, 1916, Scott Papers.

[84] *New York Times*, June 17, 1916; Consul A. B. Garrett to the Secretary of State, June 17, 1916, State Department Papers; Consul W. W. Canada to the Secretary of State, June 18, 1916, *ibid.*

The President and Secretary Baker pored over these reports at a long conference at the White House on Saturday evening, June 17. Nothing was left, they agreed, but to call out the entire National Guard (aside from the already mobilized National Guard units of Texas, Arizona, and New Mexico), totaling between 100,000 and 125,000 men, for service on the border in order to free the approximately 30,000 regulars in the area for operations in Mexico in the event of war. Baker sent the call on June 18.[85] Secretary Daniels, on that same day, ordered additional gunboats on both the east and west coasts to join the small American naval forces already in Mexican waters.[86] Also on that same day, uniformed *de facto* troops fired on a landing party from the gunboat *U.S.S. Annapolis* in Mazatlán harbor on the western coast, killing one and wounding several sailors.[87] Lansing, on the following day, June 19, instructed the State Department's representative in Mexico City, James Linn Rodgers, to assist Americans who desired to leave the country and to ask the British Chargé to take responsibility for American interests in the event of a break in relations.[88] "It looks to me as if the war will be on in a few days," General Scott wrote on June 20.[89]

This was the situation as Lansing completed a draft of the reply to the Mexican note of May 22. He sent a revised copy to Wilson on June 15, after a conference with the President in the morning.[90] "I have gone very carefully through this note and think it adequate and excellent," Wilson replied on June 18. "I have here and there altered the wording, but nowhere the meaning of it. I showed it to Baker last evening, and he makes, after taking it away for careful perusal, the enclosed suggestion,[91] which I think an excellent one. They might as

---

[85] *New York Times*, June 18 and 19, 1916.

[86] The following warships were stationed in Mexican waters at this time: battleship *Nebraska* at Veracruz, gunboats *Machias* and *Marietta* at Tampico, gunboat *Wheeling* at El Carmen, cruiser *Cleveland* at Guaymas, supply ship *Glacier* and cruiser *Albany* at Manzanillo, and gunboat *Annapolis* and transport *Buffalo* at Mazatlán. *ibid.*, June 19, 1916.

[87] *ibid.*, June 20, 1916; *U.S.S. San Diego* to the Secretary of the Navy, June 21, 1916, State Department Papers, transmitting report from Commander A. G. Kavanaugh of the *U.S.S. Annapolis*; Á. Obregón, telegraphic announcement dated June 18, 1916, copy in *ibid.*, repeating the report of the military commander of the Port of Mazatlán, General Manuel Mezta.

[88] R. Lansing to J. L. Rodgers, June 19, 1916, *ibid.*

[89] H. L. Scott to W. L. Brown, June 20, 1916, Scott Papers.

[90] R. Lansing to W. W., June 15, 1916, *The Lansing Papers*, II, 557.

[91] This was N. D. Baker to W. W., June 18, 1916, *ibid.*, pp. 557-558, suggesting that Lansing make it clear that the United States would not permit export of arms and munitions to Mexico so long as Mexican commanders menaced American troops.

well know at once *all* that they will be up against if they continue their present attitude."[92] Lansing made the changes that Baker suggested and then handed the document to Arredondo on June 20.

It began by expressing the American government's surprise and regret over the "discourteous tone and temper" of the *de facto* government's note of May 22. The American government, it went on, had viewed the progress of the revolution in Mexico with deep concern and increasing disappointment. Mexico had been torn asunder by war and banditry; numerous American citizens had been barbarously murdered; the safety of the United States itself had been constantly threatened during the past nine months. The bandit Villa had murdered Americans at Santa Ysabel and plundered Columbus, New Mexico, with entire impunity from punishment on the Mexican side. It was technically true that the *de facto* government had not formally consented to the entry of the Punitive Expedition, but subsequent events had proved that Carranza never would have endorsed any agreement for effective military cooperation. The American government had shown good faith by promising, in the Scott-Obregón memorandum, gradually to withdraw its forces from Mexico—but only on condition that the *de facto* government was willing and able to preserve order in northern Mexico and prevent depredations against American territory. General Scott had rejected Obregón's plan for Mexican-American defense of the frontier *only* because it was coupled with a demand for immediate withdrawal of Pershing's troops.

Lansing then turned to the charge that the State Department and private American citizens had prolonged the civil war in Mexico in various ways. Discreetly ignoring a large part of the historical record, he cited events since Carranza's recognition to prove that the accusation was unjust. He then emphatically repudiated the *de facto* government's insinuation that the United States had territorial ambitions in Mexico. The American government, the note went on, had been extraordinarily patient in face of the *de facto* government's failure to protect either American lives and property in Mexico or the security of the border. The American government had been forced to conclude that the *de facto* authorities were unable to afford such protection. The duty of protecting its own citizens fell, therefore, upon the American government. It would be happy if the Mexican government fulfilled this international obligation. "If, on the contrary," the note warned in conclusion, "the *de facto* Government is pleased to ignore this obliga-

[92] W. W. to R. Lansing, June 18, 1916, *ibid.*, p. 557.

tion and to believe that 'in case of a refusal to retire these troops there is no further recourse than to defend its territory by an appeal to arms,' the Government of the United States would surely be lacking in sincerity and friendship if it did not frankly impress upon the *de facto* Government that the execution of this threat will lead to the gravest consequences. While this Government would deeply regret such a result, it cannot recede from its settled determination to maintain its national rights and to perform its full duty in preventing further invasions of the territory of the United States."[93]

Lansing gave a copy of the note to all Latin American envoys in Washington on June 21. With Wilson's approval[94] he accompanied the note with assurances that the United States had no thought of interfering in Mexican domestic affairs if war should unhappily occur. "Hostilities," he added, "in short, would be simply a state of international war without purpose on the part of the United States other than to end the conditions which menace our national peace and the safety of our citizens."[95]

"As I read this," Wilson wrote to Lansing in the afternoon of June 21, in reply to his suggestion for a special note to Latin American envoys, "'extras' of the evening papers are being cried on the Avenue which, if true, mean that hostilities *have* begun." The President was referring, without knowing it, to the Carrizal incident which seemed to signal the outbreak of war. It happened in the following way.

General Pershing, informed that a large body of *de facto* troops were being concentrated at Villa Ahumada, on the Mexican Central Railroad about ninety miles east of his headquarters near Colonia Dublan, sent Captain Charles T. Boyd with Troop C of the 10th Cavalry on June 17 to investigate. Pershing gave Boyd strict instructions to avoid a fight, informed him of General Treviño's order, and especially warned him not to enter any place garrisoned by Carrancista troops.[96] Pershing telegraphed orders on the same day to the commanding officer at the

[93] The Secretary of State to Secretary Aguilar, June 20, 1916, *Foreign Relations, 1916*, pp. 581-592.

[94] R. Lansing to W. W., June 21, 1916; W. W. to R. Lansing, June 21, 1916, *The Lansing Papers*, II, 558-559.

[95] The Secretary of State to the Argentine Ambassador *et al.*, June 21, 1916, *Foreign Relations, 1916*, p. 592.

[96] E. A. Garlington, Inspector General, "Fourth Indorsement on the Report of investigation of the encounter between American and Mexican forces at Carrizal, Chihuahua, June 21, 1916," memorandum dated October 2, 1916, Wilson Papers; hereinafter cited as "Fourth Indorsement."

American base at Ojo Federico to send another troop from the 10th Cavalry toward Villa Ahumada. "It is reported a large force Mexican troops is assembling at Ahumada," these orders read, "and it is desired to get information as to their numbers and movements. This is a reconnaissance and not for the purpose of bringing on a fight. It is understood General Trevino has given orders to all his troops to fire on our detachments moving out from our lines of communication. . . . The troops should take every precaution against surprise. If any large force is seen, prompt report should be made of it."[97] Consequently, Captain Lewis S. Morey set out with Troop K for Villa Ahumada on that same day.

The two troops, comprising together seventy-six soldiers and a Mormon guide, converged at the Santo Domingo Ranch, twelve miles west of the pueblo of Carrizal, in the evening of June 20. Boyd, the senior officer, assumed command. They set out for Villa Ahumada early the next morning. The direct road ran through Carrizal, nine miles southwest of Villa Ahumada, but there were two other routes. Morey suggested taking one of the latter; Boyd seemed determined to go through Carrizal and finally decided to do so. He sent a messenger into Carrizal to the *jefe político* at seven o'clock to say that he was on a peaceful mission and requested permission to pass through Carrizal. The local Mexican commander, General Felix Gomez, sent Lieutenant Colonel Genovevo Rivas Guillén out to talk. Boyd said that he had heard of a robbery in Santo Domingo and wanted to apprehend the bandits and a deserter in Carrizal. Rivas replied that there were no bandits in the pueblo and that Boyd would have to pass over dead Mexicans if he went through the town. General Gomez came out a short time later. He had orders from General Treviño, he said, to attack Americans moving in any direction but northward. Surely Boyd knew about these orders. Boyd admitted that he was aware of them but said that he had his own orders to go to Villa Ahumada and had to obey them. Gomez said that he would have to fire if the Americans attempted to go through Carrizal. Would not Boyd be willing to wait four hours, the Mexican asked, until he could telegraph to Juárez to request permission for the Americans to enter the town? Boyd refused, and each chieftain returned to his troops.

"Captain Boyd," the Inspector General of the United States Army

[97] De R. C. Campbell to Commanding Officer, Ojo Federico, June 17, 1916, repeated in General Pershing to General Funston, June 26, 1916, quoted in General Funston to the Adjutant General, June 27, 1916, *ibid.*

wrote after a thorough investigation, "felt that audacity was necessary; that a bold front would secure him from an attack by the Mexican forces; that even though he were mistaken in the opinion that no fighting would result, any resistance which might be offered by the Mexicans would be perfunctory and could readily be brushed aside. There is also evidence which tends to show that Captain Boyd believed that if his command were attacked by the Mexican forces such a crisis would ensue as would immediately bring into action all available United States forces. In short Captain Boyd's attitude immediately before the fight at Carrizal was over-confident; it appears that he was not greatly impressed with the Commanding General's instructions to avoid a 'clash with the Mexican troops.' " The Mormon scout, Lemuel Spillsbury, also said that Boyd was imbued with the idea that a skirmish would bring him quick promotion and told him that the Mexicans were bluffing and would not fight.

The Mexican troops, between 120 and 200 in number, had meanwhile taken a position in full view behind an irrigation ditch west and south of Carrizal. Boyd ordered his men to advance toward their line. The Americans dismounted about two hundred yards from the Mexicans, and firing began. The Mexicans, to quote Captain Morey's laconic report, "did not run." On the contrary, they fought bravely for an hour and did murderous work with a single machine gun. Then they drove off the Americans' horses and hit the American right flank. The American troopers now rapidly disintegrated as a unified fighting force—their officers were now dead or out of action—and the battle was over within another hour. General Gomez and Captain Boyd were dead, and Captain Morey was wounded. The Mexicans lost thirty dead and forty-three wounded. Fourteen Americans were killed; twenty-five, including the Mormon scout, were captured and sent as prisoners to Chihuahua City, and an unknown number escaped and were wounded.[98]

[98] This account is based upon the following statements and reports: E. A. Garlington, "Fourth Indorsement," Wilson Papers; G. Rivas Guillén to General F. Gomez, c. June 21, 1916, printed in Mexico City *El Pueblo*, July 1, 1916; Captain L. S. Morey, report written at 9:15 a.m., June 21, 1916, printed in the *New York Times*, June 26, 1916; L. S. Morey, report written at Colonia Dublan and dated June 25, 1916, transmitted in General Pershing to General Funston, June 26, 1916, retransmitted in General Funston to the Adjutant General, June 27, 1916, Wilson Papers; L. Spillsbury, statement enclosed in J. B. Treviño to J. J. Pershing, June 24, 1916, transmitted in General Funston to the Adjutant General, June 25, 1916, State Department Papers, also printed in the *New York Times*, June 30, 1916; L. Spillsbury, statement printed in *ibid.*, June 25, 1916; Colonel F. L. Treviño to R. V. Pesquiera, June 26, 1916,

Colonel Rivas telegraphed news of the engagement to General Francisco Gonzáles, *Carrancista* border commander in Ciudad Juárez, and the Mexican Consul in that city telephoned the report to Zach L. Cobb, American Collector of Customs in El Paso, in the late afternoon. Cobb wired the brief report to the State Department at 6 p.m.[99] Press reports reached Washington before Cobb's dispatch, and Wilson first learned of the affair when he heard newsboys shouting on Pennsylvania Avenue and sent an aide to buy a copy of the extra.

Pershing received his first word from General George Bell, Jr., in El Paso in the evening of June 21 and thought that it signaled the beginning of a general Mexican attack against his command. "Under circumstances," he wired to Funston late that night, "recommend execution of plan to seize Mexican Central railroad and Chihuahua, moving troops in two columns, one to Ahumada other to Gallego. Northern column to cooperate with General Bell's forces from El Paso. . . . Ready to start east upon receipt of approval."[100]

Wilson and Baker discussed this telegram, along with a covering message from Funston, at the White House at 9:30 a.m. on June 22. "Clearly General Pershing," Baker wired to Funston that morning, "has not had any direct report from commanding officers of troops involved in Carrizal fight. The Secretary of War approves your suggestion that no direction should be given to General Pershing to make the moves which he recommends until official report is received and transmitted here and action authorized from here."[101] Funston replied that afternoon, saying that in view of the absence of official information from Pershing he thought that the conditions which the War Department had stipulated as setting the stage for actual war had not yet materialized. Even so, he went on, he was sure that the Mexicans planned to blow up international bridges and bombard one or more American port towns. General Bell, he went on, had reported that Mexican troops from Juárez were going to Villa Ahumada in order to

---

printed in *ibid.*, June 28, 1916; J. B. Treviño to the Assistant Secretary of War and Navy, June 29, 1916, *Mexican White Paper*, pp. 261-264; and the accounts by Daniel González, G. Rivas Guillén, and W. P. McCabe, in A. Salinas Carranza, *La Expedición Punitiva*, pp. 276-300.

99 Z. L. Cobb to the Secretary of State, June 21, 1916, State Department Papers.

100 J. J. Pershing to Major Farnsworth at Columbus, New Mex., Telegram No. 278, for transmission to General Funston, June 21, 1916, 11 p.m., the Papers of the Punitive Expedition, National Archives; hereinafter cited as the Punitive Expedition Papers.

101 Adjutant General to General Funston, June 22, 1916, in N. D. Baker, "Memorandum for the Chief of Staff," June 22, 1916, Wilson Papers.

attack Pershing, probably that night. Would the War Department, Funston concluded, rush an answer as to whether he should take initiative to secure the bridges? The job would have to be finished before nightfall if it was to succeed.[102] Baker must have telephoned this dispatch to Wilson. "The Secretary of War," Baker replied at once, "desires you to act promptly to meet any emergency . . . with a view to preventing attack on American towns, supporting American forces, etc., but before undertaking execution of any general plans, send all information as to situation in Mexico to the Department, so that the question as to the actual existence of a state of war can be decided here."[103]

Wilson was holding the reins on his generals even while he feared that the Mexicans had themselves begun general hostilities. "The break seems to have come in Mexico; and all my patience seems to have gone for nothing," he wrote to Colonel House that same day. "I am infinitely sad about it. I fear I should have drawn Pershing and his command northward just after it became evident that Villa had slipped through his fingers; but except for that error of judgment (if it was an error) I cannot, in looking back, see where I could have done differently, holding sacred the convictions I hold in this matter. Right or wrong, however, the extremest consequences seem upon us. But INTERVENTION (that is the rearrangement and control of Mexico's domestic affairs by the U.S.) there shall not be either now or at any other time if I can prevent it! We as yet know nothing from our own officers about the affair at Carrizal. We shall no doubt have heard from them before this reaches you."[104]

The first substantial report from Pershing arrived at the War Department at 4:17 a.m. on June 23. It said that one of five enlisted men who had returned from Boyd's troop had reported a treacherous Mexican ambush. "In view of positive warning given by me to Boyd himself regarding just such an occurrence," Pershing went on, "his action inexplicable, but final judgment should be *reserved* until further reports are received." He had given orders, Pershing advised, for dispatch of a strong force to Villa Ahumada, leaving cavalry to cut the Mexican Central Railroad at Gallego. He would also attack Pearson, Chihuahua, that night and take possession of the Mexican Northwestern Railroad. Funston, in transmitting this portentous intelligence to the War

[102] F. Funston to the Adjutant General, received June 22, 1916, 4:44 p.m., Papers of the Office of the Adjutant General, Document File, National Archives.

[103] N. D. Baker, "Memorandum for the Chief of Staff," June 22, 1916, *ibid*.

[104] W. W. to E. M. House, June 22, 1916, House Papers.

Department, said that he had repeated the Department's message of June 22 to Pershing, but that it would apparently reach him too late to halt his movement.[105]

Baker took this message to the White House at 9:15 in the morning of June 23, and he and Wilson waited all day for news that Pershing had begun offensive operations. The Cabinet discussed the Mexican situation in the morning, and Baker soon afterward ordered all National Guard units sent to the border as fast as they could be made ready for service. The rest of the day brought only receipt of a message from Carranza to the Speaker of the House of Representatives of the Cuban Congress, saying that Mexico had no recourse but to repel the American invaders.[106] Two messages from Pershing arrived at the War Department late that night or early the next morning. The first, obviously written before the General had received Baker's message of June 22, gave some details of the Carrizal incident and said that the Mexicans had surrounded Boyd's column during the conference between Gomez and Boyd and had fired first. But something, which he did not explain, had caused Pershing to defer his offensive plans. "In view of all circumstances," he wrote, "shall await your approval before carrying out my intention expressed in last sentence my number two eighty. All other preparations under way."[107] The second dispatch acknowledged receipt of Baker's instructions, sent a fairly full and accurate report of the Carrizal affair, indicating that Boyd had been the aggressor, and said that Pershing had done no more than send a squadron to Santo Domingo Ranch to rescue survivors.[108]

Wilson conferred with Lansing and Baker for an hour at the White House on the next morning, Saturday, June 24. They probably discussed these reports, and they apparently agreed to postpone decision on general action until more complete information was in hand.[109] There was tremendous agitation at the White House some time later in the day, when a messenger brought a note that Arredondo had just delivered to the State Department. It read as follows:

[105] General Funston to the Adjutant General, June 22, 1916, State Department Papers, transmitting J. J. Pershing to Major Farnsworth, Telegram No. 280, June 22, 1916, Punitive Expedition Papers.

[106] V. Carranza to O. Ferrara, June 23, 1916, *New York Times*, June 24, 1916.

[107] J. J. Pershing to Major Farnsworth, Telegram No. 281, for transmission to General Funston, June 22, 1916, Punitive Expedition Papers.

[108] General Funston to the Secretary of War, June 23, 1916, *Foreign Relations, 1916*, p. 594, transmitting J. J. Pershing to Major Farnsworth, June 23, 1916, Punitive Expedition Papers.

[109] *New York Times*, June 25, 1916.

"I am directed by my Government to inform your excellency, with reference to the Carrizal incident, that the Chief Executive, through the Mexican War Department, gave orders to General Jacinto B. Treviño not to permit American forces from General Pershing's column to advance further south, nor to move either east or west from the points where they are located, and to oppose new incursions of American soldiers into Mexican territory. These orders were brought by General Treviño to the attention of General Pershing, who acknowledged the receipt of the communication relative thereto. On the 22d [*sic*] instant, as your excellency knows, an American force moved eastward quite far from its base, notwithstanding the above orders, and was engaged by Mexican troops at Carrizal. As a result of the encounter, several men on both sides were killed and wounded and 17 [*sic*] American soldiers were made prisoners."[110]

Tumulty nearly exploded with anger. He telephoned to the Secretary of State, demanding immediate action. "I may be an excitable person but sometimes my judgments in the past have been verified," he wrote immediately after the conversation. "I think I know how the American people feel on this matter. If I were President this moment or acting as Secretary of State, my message to Carranza would be the following: 'Release those American soldiers or take the consequences.' This would ring around the world. In the name of God, why do we hesitate longer?"[111] At about the same time a news report came from Chihuahua saying that General Treviño had ordered his troops to attack American columns that had been seen advancing from Colonia Dublan in the direction of San Antonio and Ojo Caliente, if the Americans did not retreat. It also included the first statement of the Mormon scout, Spillsbury, affirming that the Americans had been aggressors at Carrizal.[112] Wilson waited during the balance of the day, following his ordinary Saturday afternoon routine by taking a long drive with Mrs. Wilson. He received Baker at the White House at eleven that evening. The two men presumably discussed a third message from Pershing giving additional details of the Carrizal battle.[113]

[110] E. Arredondo to the Secretary of State, June 24, 1916, *Foreign Relations, 1916*, p. 595.

[111] J. P. Tumulty to R. Lansing, June 24, 1916, Lansing Papers; in the same vein, J. P. Tumulty to W. W., June 24, 1916, Tumulty Papers.

[112] *New York Times*, June 25, 1916.

[113] It was General Funston to the Secretary of War, June 24, 1916, *Foreign Relations, 1916*, p. 594.

The President thought that he saw the situation clearly by Sunday morning, June 25. The Mexicans had either made war deliberately at Carrizal or else would open general hostilities within a few hours or days. Carranza's repetition of his orders to Treviño and his matter of fact, almost (as it must have seemed to Wilson) insolent announcement of the "engagement" at Carrizal left no doubt about that. The details of the Carrizal affair were not particularly important. What mattered was Carranza's announced implacable determination to refuse to permit American forces to perform their sacred duty to protect American citizens against attacks from Mexican soil. Retreat under the First Chief's threats was unthinkable and impossible. He had to accept the decision for war if Carranza made it. Moreover, he had to force Carranza to return the prisoners even at the risk of having to begin hostilities himself. American public opinion would tolerate no other course.[114] Hence Wilson called Lansing to the White House at ten o'clock in the morning and gave him the following message to be sent at once to Rodgers in Mexico City:

"The Government of the United States can put no other construction upon the communication handed to the Secretary of State of the United States on the twenty fourth of June, by Mr. Arredondo, under instruction of your Government, than that it is intended as a formal avowal of deliberately hostile action against the forces of the United States now in Mexico, and of the purpose to attack them without provocation whenever they move from their present position in pursuance of the objects for which they were sent there, notwithstanding the fact that those objects not only involved no unfriendly intention towards the Government and people of Mexico, but are on the contrary, intended only to assist that Government in protecting itself and the territory and people of the United States against irresponsible and insurgent bands of rebel marauders.

"I am instructed, therefore, by my Government to demand the immediate release of the prisoners taken in the encounter at Carrizal, together with any property of the United States taken with them, and to inform you that the Government of the United States expects an early statement from your Government as to the course of action it wishes the Government of the United States to understand it has determined upon, and that it also expects that this statement be made through the usual diplomatic channels, and not through subordinate military commanders.

[114] As the *New York Times*, June 26, 1916, summarized Wilson's views.

"*CONFIDENTIAL.* If you are asked, or opportunity offers, you may state that the expectation of an early statement means that the Government of the United States will not wait many hours for a reply."[115]

This ultimatum went to Mexico City at 1 p.m. Wilson sent word to Senators Stone and Lodge and Representative Flood that he would be pleased to receive them at the White House at 8 p.m. that evening. He then spent the afternoon with Mrs. Wilson in the country. The congressional leaders on foreign policy came to the White House at the appointed time. Wilson read Arredondo's note of June 24 and his own reply. The situation, Wilson said, was obviously extremely critical. He wanted congressional leaders to be informed; he also wanted them to know that he desired to appear before Congress within a few days to make a statement of the situation and request authority to take appropriate action. He would wait a reasonable period for a reply from the *de facto* government and General Pershing's official report on the Carrizal affair before taking the final step.[116]

There was some discussion in administration circles on the following day, June 26, of Pan-American mediation, first suggested unofficially on June 24 by Ignacio Calderon, Bolivian Minister in Washington, and accepted "in principle" by Arredondo on June 25.[117] Lansing told reporters in the afternoon that the offer would not be accepted if it was made. Carranza could avert war, he said, only by releasing the prisoners and making a clear avowal of friendly intentions toward the Punitive Expedition.[118] The Secretary of State further explained his position in a private memorandum, which he read to Wilson over the telephone, and which the President undoubtedly approved. The Carrizal incident, Lansing said, was not a fit subject for mediation since Mexican forces had attacked American troops under direct orders of the *de facto* government. Therefore, that government was "wholly responsible for the lives lost and for the capture and imprisonment of American soldiers." The Washington government had made its demand, and "a demand, of which the justice is beyond controversy, is not a proper subject for mediation." In any event, it was doubtful that the *de facto* government was sincere in saying that it was ready to accept mediation.[119]

---

[115] The Secretary of State to Special Representative Rodgers, June 25, 1916, State Department Papers.

[116] *New York Times*, June 26, 1916.

[117] *ibid.*, June 25 and 26, 1916.   [118] *ibid.*, June 27, 1916.

[119] R. Lansing, "ATTITUDE ON MEDIATION IN MEXICAN CONTROVERSY," memorandum dated June 26, 1916, State Department Papers.

It is interesting that the President and Secretary of State made this decision, which might have been a choice for war, after reading the first complete and accurate account of the Carrizal engagement—the report that Captain Morey had written immediately after the battle, proving beyond doubt that Boyd had attacked after being refused permission to go through Carrizal. It was sent to Washington on June 25[120] and published in the morning newspapers on the following day, hours before Wilson and Lansing decided to refuse mediation. It is only fair to add that Pershing sent an additional report on June 26 saying that papers found on Boyd's body strongly indicated that General Gomez had planned an ambush and tried to draw Boyd into a trap.[121]

Wilson, according to White House correspondents, was convinced that Carranza would both reject his demand and be unable to restrain his forces in northern Mexico, even if he decided to yield.[122] The President, consequently, set to work at some time during June 26—it was undoubtedly during the evening—on his message to Congress. He had discussed this with Baker and had before him a draft that Baker had prepared at his request.[123] Wilson began by saying that relations between the United States and the *de facto* Mexican government were critical, and that some sort of action was necessary. He then reviewed the Columbus affair, dispatch of the Punitive Expedition, and negotiations with the *de facto* authorities for Pershing's recall. Carranza, Wilson went on, had instructed his forces to attack any part of the Punitive Expedition moving in any direction but northward. General Gomez obeyed these orders at Carrizal on June 21 by attacking American troops on an ordinary scouting mission, notwithstanding the fact that Captain Boyd had informed Gomez of his errand in the most friendly spirit and courteously sought permission to pass through Carrizal. Wilson here followed Pershing's reports in characterizing Boyd's demeanor and approach. They were not exactly accurate. "It has become evident," Wilson continued, "that the *de facto* government will neither use its own forces in any effectual way to protect the people of Texas, New Mexico, and Arizona nor permit us to take the steps absolutely necessary to protect them." There was, therefore, no alternative but to clear northern Mexico of armed forces of every kind.

[120] In General Funston to the Secretary of War, June 25, 1916, *Foreign Relations, 1916*, p. 596.

[121] General Funston to the Adjutant General, June 26, 1916, Wilson Papers.

[122] *New York Times*, June 27, 1916.

[123] N. D. Baker to W. W., June 26, 1916, Wilson Papers.

"An end must be put to an intolerable situation, and we are left to put an end to it alone."

It would, Wilson continued, be his duty to ask for a declaration of war if he was dealing with a fully constituted government. There had been no such government in Mexico since President Francisco Madero's assassination in 1913. In other words, the United States no longer recognized the *de facto* government headed by Venustiano Carranza as being a properly constituted authority. Americans understood and had deep compassion for the tragic plight of the Mexican people. War against them would be heartless and unrighteous. Americans must help, not harm, the people of Mexico. In this spirit, Wilson continued, he was asking for authority to use the armed forces in any way that might be necessary to protect the frontier and, if necessary, enter Mexican territory and require suspension of all military activity until a constitutional Mexican government had been established and was willing to assume the task of preserving order.

Such action, Wilson concluded, was not and would not be intervention in the affairs of the Mexican people. "It does not lie with the American people to dictate to another people what their government shall be or what use shall be made of their resources, what laws or rulers they shall have or what persons they shall encourage and favour. I have been bred in an old school of American principle and practice: I know what American history means and what spirit in affairs the American people have most passionately and habitually preferred. I know that they desire no one who professes to speak for them to interfere with the liberties of any people and that I am speaking their deepest principle of action when I say that we wish not a single foot of Mexican territory, not a single hour of political control in Mexico."[124]

Wilson had completed this draft at least by the late morning of June 28. Baker came to lunch on that day, and the two men undoubtedly went over the document then. Wilson spent the balance of the afternoon on the golf course with Mrs. Wilson. After dinner, at 8:15, he drove to Lansing's home and left a copy of the message for his perusal. The only evidence of Lansing's reactions were the words "? Haiti S Domingo Nicaragua Panama" that he wrote on the margin at the point at which Wilson said "It does not lie with the American people to dictate to another people what their government shall be. . . ."

Meanwhile, other developments between June 26 and June 28 gave

[124] "TO THE CONGRESS. JUNE, 1916," MS. in *ibid.*

additional cause to believe that war would break out at any moment. Fifteen thousand heavily armed *de facto* troops arrived at a Mexican base opposite Naco, Arizona, on June 26. They seemed to be poised for an invasion of American territory.[125] Pershing at the same time awaited orders to drive to Gallego or Villa Ahumada, where he would meet forces under General Bell coming down from El Paso.[126] In the State Department, Canova was preparing a memorandum suggesting that the American government announce that it regarded the First Chief and his colleagues as being no better than bandits and outlaws and intended to strip the *de facto* government of all authority.[127]

News reports from Juárez and El Paso that General Treviño had ordered the release of American prisoners and made provision for their transportation to the border arrived in Washington late Wednesday night, June 28, probably while Lansing was going over President Wilson's message. Official confirmation, along with news that Mexican officials had intimated that the orders to General Treviño to attack Pershing's command in certain circumstances might have been changed, came a short time later in a telegram from Rodgers in Mexico City.[128]

Tension in Washington had relaxed visibly by the following morning, even though the State Department received a second message from Rodgers, advising that Carranza had instructed the Foreign Office to inform the American government that the orders to Treviño were still in force.[129] But Wilson was freed of the necessity of having to take immediate violent action to obtain release of the prisoners, and he now began to do some serious second thinking about the possibility of war with Mexico. The great question at this moment—the morning of June 29—was whether he would continue to press the demand for assurances that *de facto* troops would not attack American forces in Mexico in any circumstances, thus perhaps forcing the issue to the point of war, or whether he would in fact, if tacitly, accept Carranza's implied stipulation that the Punitive Expedition might remain for a while provided that it did not move outside a severely circumscribed area.

[125] *New York Times*, June 27, 1916.

[126] General Funston to the Adjutant General, June 27, 1916, Wilson Papers.

[127] L. J. Canova to the Secretary of State, June 28, 1916, State Department Papers.

[128] Special Representative Rodgers to the Secretary of State, June 28, 1916, 10 p.m., *Foreign Relations, 1916*, p. 597.

[129] Special Representative Rodgers to the Secretary of State, June 29, 1916, State Department Papers.

We do not know all his thoughts at this time, but we can be certain that the catalyst prompting him to consider a new course was an extraordinary eruption in public opinion that had just occurred. Aside from the Hearst press and a few jingoes who wanted war, there had been little belligerent sentiment during the first stages of high tension with Mexico.[130] Not even news of the Carrizal incident had set off any general agitation for hostilities; on the contrary, it prompted fervent appeals for peaceful settlement.[131] They swelled in number during the following week, mainly in response to the propaganda campaign waged by the American Union Against Militarism, a pacifist group. It published advertisements in leading newspapers on June 26 reprinting Captain Morey's report and asserting that the Mexicans could not be blamed for demanding that American troops on Mexican soil march no further into Mexican territory.[132] This advertisement prompted widespread echoes in the press[133] and a new flood of telegrams to the White House. They ran ten to one against any form of war with Mexico.[134] Additional telegrams poured into the White House following announcement of the release of the prisoners in Chihuahua on June 28.[135] There were even more on the next morning. "Hundreds of telegrams were delivered to the White House this morning urging the President to take all possible steps for peace with Mexico," one correspondent reported. "Many of the telegrams suggested that the United

[130] See "Let Us Try to Keep the Peace," *Congregationalist and Christian World*, CI (July 6, 1916), 8, for a thoughtful analysis of and comment on the restraining influence of moderate editorial opinion during the crisis.

[131] e. g., Massachusetts Branch, Woman's Peace Party, to W. W., June 21, 1916, Wilson Papers; Twelfth Street Meeting, Philadelphia, Society of Friends to W. W., June 21, 1916, *ibid.*; O. G. Villard, A. Pinchot, *et al.* to W. W., June 21, 1916, *ibid.*; B. C. Marsh to W. W., June 22, 1916, *ibid.*; F. Lynch to W. W., June 22, 1916, *ibid.*; W. J. Bryan to J. Daniels, June 24, 1916, Daniels Papers; Queen Anne Congregational Church, Seattle, to W. W., June 22, 1916, Wilson Papers; Yellowstone County Trades and Labor Assembly, Billings, Mont., to W. W., June 23, 1916, *ibid.*; J. A. Marquis, D. D., Moderator, Presbyterian Church in the United States of America, to W. W., June 24, 1916, *ibid.*; citizens' mass meeting, Nashville, Tenn., to W. W., June 25, 1916, *ibid.*

[132] e. g., New York *World*, June 27, 1916. For a review of this campaign, see *The Survey*, XXXVI (July 8, 1916), 379-380.

[133] See the survey of press opinion in "The 'Necessity' of War with Mexico," *Literary Digest*, LIII (July 8, 1916), 51-53.

[134] e. g., Executive Board, Woman's Peace Party, to W. W., June 27, 1916, Wilson Papers; H. A. Overstreet *et al.* to W. W., June 27, 1916, *ibid.*; and other telegrams in Series II of the Wilson Papers.

[135] F. C. Howe to W. W., June 28, 1916, *ibid.*; A. Pinchot to W. W., June 28, 1916, *ibid.*; J. H. Ralston to W. W., June 28, 1916, *ibid.*; C. W. Eliot to W. W., June 28, 1916, *ibid.*

States ought to be willing to arbitrate the questions in dispute. White House officials seemed to regard the great bulk of telegrams as a pretty marked indication of the feeling of the country."[136]

Wilson's replies suggest that he had been profoundly moved and also shaken. "My heart is for peace," he wrote to Jane Addams and other members of the Executive Board of the Woman's Peace Party, "and I wish that we were dealing with those who would not make it impossible for us."[137] He discussed his proposed message to Congress with Lansing between 11:30 a.m. and 12:10 p.m. on June 29.[138] Then, having received news that the prisoners had been delivered at El Paso, he suddenly decided to accept an invitation to speak to the Associated Advertising Clubs in Philadelphia. "I believe," he said in his impromptu address that same afternoon, ". . . that America . . . should be ready in every point of policy and of action to vindicate at whatever cost the principles of liberty, of justice, and of humanity to which we have been devoted from the first. [Cheers.] You cheer the sentiment, but do you realize what it means? It means that you have not only got to be just to your fellow men, but as a nation you have got to be just to other nations. It comes high. It is not an easy thing to do."[139]

Tension in Washington revived somewhat on June 30 after receipt of a news summary of a memorandum that the Mexican Foreign Office issued to accompany publication of the American note of June 20 in the Mexican press.[140] But Wilson had made his decision. It was to break the bonds that events had fastened upon him and strike boldly for peace, thereby gaining the control that he had momentarily lost. He used an address to the New York Press Club in the evening of June 30 to speak to the American people, Mexico, indeed, the entire world. Part of his charismatic outpouring follows:

"Of course it is the duty of the Government, which it will never overlook, to defend the territory and people of this country. It goes without saying that it is the duty of the administration to have constantly in mind with the utmost sensitiveness every point of national honor.

[136] New York *Evening Sun*, June 29, 1916, quoted in *The Survey*, xxxvi (July 8, 1916), 379.

[137] W. W. to Jane Addams *et al.*, June 28, 1916, Wilson Papers. See also W. W. to A. Pinchot, June 30, 1916, *ibid.*, and W. W. to C. W. Eliot, June 30, 1916, *ibid.*, for significant expressions.

[138] Lansing Desk Diary, June 29, 1916.

[139] *The New Democracy*, ii, 213-214.

[140] *New York Times*, July 1, 1916.

"But, gentlemen, after you have said and accepted these obvious things your program of action is still to be formed. When will you act and how will you act?

"The easiest thing is to strike. The brutal thing is the impulsive thing. No man has to think before he takes aggressive action; but before a man really conserves the honor by realizing the ideals of the Nation he has to think exactly what he will do and how he will do it.

"Do you think the glory of America would be enhanced by a war of conquest in Mexico? Do you think that any act of violence by a powerful nation like this against a weak and distracted[141] neighbor would reflect distinction upon the annals of the United States?

"Do you think it is our duty to carry self-defense to a point of dictation into the affairs of another people? The ideals of America are written plain upon every page of American history.

"And I want you to know how fully I realize whose servant I am. I do not own the Government of the United States, even for the time being. I have no right in the use of it to express my own passions. . . .

"And I have constantly to remind myself that I am not the servant of those who wish to enhance the value of their Mexican investments, that I am the servant of the rank and file of the people of the United States."

The applause was so deafening by now that Wilson had to stop frequently until it had subsided. He went on:

"I get a great many letters, my fellow citizens, from important and influential men in this country, but I get a great many other letters. I get letters from unknown men, from humble women, from people whose names have never been heard and never will be recorded, and there is but one prayer in all of these letters: 'Mr. President, do not allow anybody to persuade you that the people of this country want war with anybody.'

"I got off the train yesterday and as I was bidding good-by to the engineer he said, in an undertone, 'Mr. President, keep out of Mexico.' And if one man has said that to me a thousand have said it to me as I have moved about the country. . . .

"I am for the time being the spokesman of such people, gentlemen."[142]

---

[141] The text in *The New Democracy*, ii, 218, which renders this word as "destructive," is inaccurate.

[142] New York *World*, July 1, 1916; *The New Democracy*, ii, 218-219.

The President's remarks provoked an outpouring of letters and telegrams such as the White House staff had not seen since the *Lusitania* crisis. "My eyes are filled with tears of gratitude," wrote a woman from Detroit.[143] "You appealed to the true America as only Lincoln did before you," a great labor leader added.[144] "If war with Mexico is essential to success at the polls and the avoidance of the same means defeat, let's go down under the flag of right, justice and humanity," an Alabama Democrat urged.[145] "You have . . . sensed the feeling of the country concerning Mexico," Colonel House wrote, truly, after reading the address. "The people do not want war with Mexico. They do not want war with anybody, but least of all a country like that."[146]

As the next volume will show, this was the turning point. Peace with Mexico was now at least possible.

[143] Elizabeth S. Hitchcock to W. W., July 1, 1916, Wilson Papers.

[144] A. Furuseth to W. W., July 1, 1916, *ibid.*

[145] J. C. Anderson to W. W., July 2, 1916, *ibid.*

[146] E. M. House to W. W., July 1, 1916, *ibid.* In the same vein, see, e. g., W. W. Bailey to W. W., July 1, 1916, Bailey Papers; Mary E. Woolley to W. W., July 1, 1916, Wilson Papers; Texas Mexican Inter-denominational Sunday School Convention to W. W., July 2, 1916, *ibid.*; S. Axson to J. P. Tumulty, July 2, 1916, *ibid.*; W. J. Bryan to C. Kitchin, July 2, 1916, Kitchin Papers.

CHAPTER XI

A Variety of Domestic Concerns

Nor since the Republican party came apart at the seams in 1910 had the American political scene seemed so confused as during the early months of 1916. Republicans were slowly recovering from their great rupture. Theodore Roosevelt was now back in the G.O.P. in all but name. But no one could predict whether the men who had followed him into the Progressive party in 1912 would also return with him to the Republican fold in 1916. Nor could anyone foretell what policies Republicans might unite upon, for they were, if anything, more divided than their opponents on the great issues of the day.

The conservative eastern wing of that party, led, among others, by former President Taft, former Secretary of State Elihu Root of New York, and Senator Henry Cabot Lodge of Massachusetts, favored strong preparedness, an end to Wilsonian reform, and repeal, at least, of the Underwood-Simmons Tariff Act of 1913. They spoke, frankly and proudly, for great business and industrial interests, and they looked forward to the campaign of 1916 as an opportunity to lead voters back to "sound" American principles of political economy. Except for Taft, they favored a strong posture toward Mexico, even military intervention if that was necessary to protect American interests, and policies favorable toward the Allies. Root, in a speech in New York City on February 15, 1916, and Lodge, at Lynn, Massachusetts, on March 16, signaled the beginning of the conservative Republican assault against the President's leadership. It was and had been, they said, weak and cowardly. Wilson had abandoned moral leadership by refusing to condemn Germany's violation of Belgian neutrality. He had written eloquent notes without doing anything to protect American rights against Mexican and German aggressions. As Lodge summarized the indictment, "since the foundation of the Government, with the exception of the Administration of Buchanan, there has been no Administration in power which has been so injurious to the United States, both at home and abroad, as that now in control at Washington."[1]

[1] See the New York Times, February 16, 1916, for the text of Root's speech, the Boston Evening Transcript, March 17, 1916, for the text of Lodge's address.

The Issue

Carter in the New York *Evening Sun*

It was an indication of the uncertainty and division in high Republican circles that some leaders and spokesmen even of the eastern conservative wing feared that a Republican campaign based mainly upon this indictment could lead only to disaster.[2] It was obvious, particularly after the vote on the Gore and McLemore resolutions, that Republican leaders and rank and file in the Middle West, one of the

[2] e. g., *New York Evening Post*, February 16 and March 18, 1916; W. H. Taft to G. J. Karger, February 20, 1916, Taft Papers.

main centers of the party's strength, wanted desperately to avoid entanglement in the European war and would be highly receptive to any candidate who promised to maintain peace if possible. As one editor observed, Republicans had set out to prove that Democrats were divided on foreign policy and had ended, in the vote on the McLemore Resolution, by exhibiting "themselves to the country as far more torn apart and still less ready to stand up for American rights unabridged."[3] Moreover, midwestern Republicans, particularly in rural areas and small towns, were, in contrast to many Easterners, cool toward substantial preparedness and still very much interested in reform, particularly measures that would benefit farmers.

Democrats were also rent by conflict. As we have seen, Wilson's preparedness program had disaffected large numbers of progressives and rural Democrats. Bryan, angered by the President's stand on preparedness and armed ships, was on the verge of open rebellion. Wilson's preparedness program seemed in a shambles at the time of Garrison's resignation, and consensus was apparently nowhere in sight in Congress. Worse still, Democratic congressional leaders seemed unable to make any progress on the balance of the modest domestic program that Wilson had set for them in conferences on January 24, 25, and 26—a new revenue bill to provide increased funds for the armed forces, measures to establish a tariff commission and a federally owned and operated merchant marine, and a bill extending autonomy or independence to the Philippines.

There was much comment in the public press on the alleged lack of presidential leadership and incapacity of Democrats to provide effective national government.[4] Wilson, even though diverted and distracted by unending foreign complications, had neither abandoned leadership nor plans for far-reaching new measures to complete his reform program. We have no evidence of his systematic analysis of the general political situation in early 1916 and what he thought the Democrats would have to do before going to the country in the forthcoming campaign. But all later evidence confirms the assumption that he, like many other political observers, concluded:

First, that in spite of apparent confusion there was a strong public and congressional consensus on preparedness, and that it favored only moderate increases in the armed forces.

---

[3] *New York Evening Post*, March 8, 1916; in the same vein, *Collier's*, LVI (March 25, 1916), 14.

[4] See above, pp. 42-45.

Second, that the only hope for Democratic victory in 1916 lay in attracting the large independent progressive element who usually voted Republican, a sizable minority of Progressives who had followed Theodore Roosevelt in 1912, and a larger portion of the midwestern farm vote than usually went to the Democratic party. This was the most obvious fact of American political life in 1916. Wilson had polled only about 42 per cent of the popular vote four years before. A reversion to normal voting patterns in 1916, as had, indeed, seemed to be taking place since 1914, could only mean Republican victory as usual.

Certainly Wilson could read the political signs as well as other contemporary observers. It was, actually, clear by the time of Garrison's resignation that it would not be impossible to obtain a compromise preparedness program that would satisfy majority opinion. It was also as clear as daylight that Democrats could win enough ordinarily Republican votes to stay in power only if they gave convincing proof that they were an effective instrument of the kind of reform that Progressives, independents, and agrarians wanted. Roughly speaking, they demanded the kind of program that Roosevelt had advanced in 1912 and called the New Nationalism—among other things, *national* measures to stimulate business and protect underprivileged or disadvantaged groups like workers and farmers. The great Wilsonian New Freedom program—the Underwood-Simmons Tariff Act, with its provision for an income tax, the Federal Reserve Act, the Federal Trade Commission Act, and other measures—had to some degree satisfied Progressive demands. But Wilson and a majority of Democrats in Congress had drawn the line sternly against national legislation to give special advantages to classes and groups. For example, they had refused to grant immunity to labor unions from prosecution for violating the antitrust laws and to establish a federally operated system of rural credits, on the ground that such measures were discriminatory class legislation. They had also refused to support national legislation, most particularly a child labor bill, that seemed to invade the police power of the states. And yet it was obvious that they would have to reverse themselves and enact these and other measures if they were to persuade independents, Progressives, and midwestern farmers that they led a great national party that had struck the shackles of state rights and *laissez-faire* dogma.

It seemed to be a cruel exigency that demanded that Wilson and his party abandon old principles and embrace new ones as the price of retaining power. Such appearances were, as they usually are in

American political life, deceptive, indeed, unreal. To begin with, general progressive thought and objectives on the national level had been in ferment and flux since 1912, and the change had all led in the direction of the New Nationalism. Even southern Democrats, who were wedded more than their northern and western colleagues to state rights and *laissez faire*, had shown surprising willingness to adopt nationalistic solutions. Wilson, too, had moved with what seemed to be the inexorable tide. He had accepted far greater national control of the money supply and banking system in the Federal Reserve Act than he had originally envisaged. He had also accepted a quasi-Rooseveltian solution of the problem of regulation of business in the Federal Trade Commission Act. He was deeply committed to certain political principles, but not to particular details and methods. He was, quite simply, at a point of metamorphosis in his thinking about legislative policy, and the political exigencies only hastened the change. He was, finally, eager to build a great national party with strength in all sections, and he had obviously concluded that commitment to an advanced progressive program was a necessary first step.

All of this has been said to provide the background and show the political context of one of the most startling political developments in American history. It saw Wilson become almost a new political creature and the Democratic party under his leadership and goad become at least momentarily transformed into an agency of advanced nationalistic reform. But we are getting far ahead of our story. The transformation did not occur totally in the early months of 1916. On the contrary, it went forward so gradually that many political observers were startled once they realized what had transpired.

The first sign of what might be crudely called the new orientation came with Wilson's nomination of Louis D. Brandeis, the "people's lawyer" of Boston, to fill the vacancy on the Supreme Court caused by the death of Associate Justice Joseph R. Lamar on January 2, 1916. The idea of choosing Brandeis, who was easily the leading progressive lawyer and most effective critic of big business and finance in the United States,[5] occurred to several men,[6] but it was apparently the Attorney General, Thomas W. Gregory, who first made the sugges-

[5] See Alpheus T. Mason, *Brandeis, A Free Man's Life*, for a superb biography.
[6] See N. Hapgood to R. S. Baker, October 26, 1931, and May 10, 1932, Baker Collection, on the part that Hapgood and Cary T. Grayson played; also A. Pinchot to W. W., January 27, 1916, Wilson Papers, and W. Kent to W. W., January 27, 1916, *ibid.*, both urging Wilson to appoint Brandeis.

tion to the President. Gregory went to the White House soon after Lamar's death and asked Wilson if he had thought about a successor. Wilson replied that he had been waiting to hear from Gregory. "I am going to make a suggestion," Gregory said, "and I am going to ask you not to respond to it for a week. I am going to recommend Louis Brandeis for the Supreme Court. My reason is that he is one of the most progressive men in the United States, and equal to the best in learning and ability."[7]

Wilson, most assuredly, needed little if any prompting. He had wanted Brandeis in his Cabinet in 1913 and failed to appoint him only for what seemed to be good political reasons and because Colonel House was strongly opposed. Since 1913 the Bostonian had been the one man whose advice on domestic legislation Wilson respected most. On two occasions—during discussions over the Federal Reserve bill and antitrust legislation—Brandeis's counsel had been decisive with the President. We can be sure that Wilson eagerly seized the opportunity to honor his friend and enliven the Court. Wilson must have had Brandeis very much in mind when he spoke as follows to the Gridiron Club in Washington some months later:

"The day of cold thinking, of fine-spun constitutional argument, is gone, thank God. We do not now discuss so much what the Constitution of the United States is as what the constitution of human nature is, what the essential constitution of human society is, and we know in our hearts that if we ever find a place or a time where the Constitution of the United States is contrary to the constitution of human nature and human society, we have got to change the Constitution of the United States. The Constitution, like the Sabbath, was made for man and not man for the Constitution. I have known of some judges who did not perceive that. I have known of some judges who seemed to think that the Constitution was a strait jacket into which the life of the nation must be forced, whether it could be with a true regard to the laws of life or not. But judges of that sort have now gently to be led to a back seat and, with all respect for their years and their lack of information, taken care of until they pass unnoticed from the stage. And men must be put forward whose whole comprehension is that law is subservient to life and not life to law."[8]

Wilson sent Brandeis's name to the Senate on January 28, without

[7] R. S. Baker, interview with T. W. Gregory, March 14-15, 1927, MS. in the Baker Collection.

[8] Address to the Gridiron Club, December 9, 1916, Swem Collection.

going through the futile form of asking Senators Lodge and John W. Weeks of Massachusetts whether the nomination was acceptable to them. It was nothing less than an act of defiance, not merely of conservative senators, but, more importantly, of all the powers of organized wealth in the country. "If Mr. Wilson has a sense of humor left," a Washington correspondent chortled, "it must be working overtime today. When Brandeis's nomination came in yesterday, the Senate simply gasped. . . . There wasn't any more excitement at the Capitol when Congress passed the Spanish War Resolution."[9]

Boston politicians, conservatives, defenders of the *status quo*, and men who liked to think of themselves as devotees of constitutional government were stunned and furious. Colonel House, then in London, said that he was appalled by the news.[10] "The fact that a slimy fellow of this kind by his smoothness and intrigue, together with his Jewish instinct, can almost land in the Cabinet, and probably on the bench of the Supreme Court of the United States," a Boston Democratic politician lamented, "should teach an object lesson to men who believe that for the future generations manhood should be the test."[11] Former President Taft almost went into trauma when he heard the news. "It is," he wrote, "one of the deepest wounds that I have had as an American and a lover of the Constitution and a believer in progressive conservatism, that such a man as Brandeis could be put in the Court, as I believe he is likely to be. He is a muckraker, an emotionalist for his own purposes, a socialist, prompted by jealousy, a hypocrite, a man who has certain high ideals in his imagination, but who is utterly unscrupulous, in method in reaching them, a man of infinite cunning, . . . of great tenacity of purpose, and, in my judgment, of much power for evil."[12] The *New York Times* had a ponderous word: "It need never be said, and cannot rightly be said that the court needs among its members some advocate of 'social justice.'"[13]

Progressives and leaders in various social justice causes were of course overjoyed. "It took courage & sense to make this appointment," Amos Pinchot wrote in a letter rejoicing, "& I take off my chapeau to the President."[14] Senator La Follette agreed, writing, "In appointing Mr. Brandeis to the Supreme Bench President Wilson has rendered a great

[9] G. J. Karger to W. H. Taft, January 29, 1916, Taft Papers.
[10] Anderson Diary, February 10, 1916.
[11] W. F. Fitzgerald to T. J. Walsh, January 29, 1916, Walsh Papers.
[12] W. H. Taft to G. J. Karger, January 31, 1916, Taft Papers.
[13] *New York Times*, January 29, 1916.
[14] A. Pinchot to N. Hapgood, c. January 29, 1916, Wilson Papers.

The Blow That Almost Killed Father
Kirby in the New York *World*

public service. . . . To take him after these years of identification with the struggle for social justice, knowing the powerful forces arrayed against him is proof indisputable that when the President sees the light he is not afraid to follow it."[15] The appointment, the single tax organ said, tended to restore faith in President Wilson.[16] It was, a Progressive spokesman affirmed, a momentous act, a landmark in the history of modern democracy.[17] Jews were pleased, for Brandeis was

[15] R. M. La Follette, "Brandeis," *La Follette's Magazine*, VII (February 1916), 2.
[16] *The Public*, XIX (February 4, 1916), 97.
[17] *Collier's*, LVI (February 26, 1916), 14.

a leading Zionist and the first Jew nominated to the Supreme Court in American history.[18] The most extravagant praise came from bodies of organized labor throughout the United States.[19] Brandeis had been one of their most effective tribunes.

A much longer and harder fight than Wilson had anticipated lay ahead in the Senate. But that, as it turned out, was many weeks in the future, and Wilson, meanwhile, had many other things to do.

The quarrel between Garrison and the House military affairs committee, to say nothing of the armed ship controversy, was so diverting that the President was unable to give much new thought to a domestic program for the first session of the Sixty-fourth Congress until the first days of March. Burleson, at Wilson's request, prepared revised legislative agenda on March 4. They included, in addition to the bills upon which Wilson and Democratic congressional leaders had agreed in late January, conservation legislation, a measure to speed construction of levies on the Mississippi River, and a corrupt practices bill. Wilson added a bill to extend the self-government of Puerto Rico.[20] He discussed the enlarged program with Speaker Clark and Representative Kitchin on March 13,[21] and the House Democratic caucus approved the agenda on March 24.[22]

Preparedness legislation remained the most perplexing and potentially the most divisive issue; it also consumed most congressional energy and the time that Wilson could give to domestic problems during the late winter and spring of 1916. Garrison's resignation had cleared the air between the Capitol and White House and seemingly marked the final demise of the Continental Army. The main question now was whether the plan for strengthening the reserve forces through enlargement and thoroughgoing federalization of the National

[18] e. g., Israel H. Levinthal, on behalf of Temple Petach Tikvah, Brooklyn, to W. W., January 29, 1916, Wilson Papers; Rabbi Israel Efros, Lynn, Mass., to W. W., February 9, 1916, *ibid.* President Millard Fillmore had offered a Supreme Court appointment to Judah P. Benjamin, who declined.

[19] e. g., E. Bohm, secretary, Central Federated Union of Greater New York, to W. W., January 29, 1916; International Ladies' Garment Workers Union to W. W., January 29, 1916; W. Green, for the United Mine Workers of America in annual convention, January 29, 1916; San Francisco Labor Council, resolution adopted January 28, 1916; Houston Labor Council to W. W., February 16, 1916, all in *ibid.*

[20] A. S. Burleson to W. W., March 4, 1916, *ibid.*, with Wilson's emendations.

[21] New York *World*, March 14, 1916; W. W. to C. Clark, March 15, 1916, Wilson Papers, commenting on their discussions.

[22] *New York Times*, March 25, 1916.

Guard, upon which the House military affairs committee insisted adamantly, was feasible, indeed, constitutional. This question was quickly settled, at Representative Hay's suggestion, by the Attorney General in a long memorandum to the President on February 25, 1916. It completely vindicated Hay's argument by affirming that the power of the United States Congress over the National Guard was to all intents and purposes unlimited, and that there were no constitutional barriers to effective federal control.[23] Wilson was convinced. He carefully scrutinized the bill that the military affairs committee had already drafted, giving special care to the provisions to federalize the National Guard. He wrote these comments to Burleson probably near the end of February:

"The following seem to me serious omissions from this bill and I would be very much obliged to you if you would kindly call Mr. Hay's attention to them:

"1. There is no specific provision that the President shall have authority to call the Militia 'into the service of the United States' for purposes of manoeuvre and camp drill, or for training in association with units of the federal army. Such a provision, if constitutional, seems to me of the utmost importance. If it is constitutionally impossible, the system seems to me clearly inadequate.

"2. So far as I can see, there is no provision by which any authority but that of an individual State can initiate discipline by court martial for failure to comply with the federal regulations or to carry out the prescribed discipline. This, too, is a very serious omission.

"3. The oath and terms of enlistment prescribed do not include any obligation to serve in reserve after service with the colours. Or is this obligation contained in some law to which reference is made in the references to the Revised Statutes?

"You will see that all these are points which go to the essence, namely, that the federal government should have the directly controlling hand in peace times as well as when war comes over this auxiliary force."[24]

They were important points, indeed. Hay's committee accepted the suggestions cheerfully, and Wilson urged Hay to report the revised bill as soon as possible.[25]

The committee unanimously reported what was called the Hay bill

[23] T. W. Gregory to W. W., February 25, 1916, Wilson Papers.
[24] W. W. to A. S. Burleson, n. d. but c. February 25, 1916, Burleson Papers.
[25] J. Hay, "Woodrow Wilson and Preparedness," MS. in the Baker Collection.

on March 6. "I am authorized to state by the President of the United States," Hay said as he began debate on March 18, "that this bill meets his approval. In other words, it is his bill."[26] It increased the Regular Army from about 100,000 to 140,000 officers and men and brought the National Guard at its then strength of about 129,000 men under strict control of the War Department. The House struck out a provision for a federally operated nitrate plant and added an amendment offered by Representative Augustus P. Gardner of Massachusetts to permit short-term enlistments in the Regular Army, to be followed by service in an inactive reserve for six years. Thus amended, it was approved by a vote of 403 to two after brief debate on March 23.[27]

Everyone, except champions of the Continental Army and all-out preparedness, seemed pleased. "I cannot let the occasion of the passage of the Army bill through the House by so significant a majority pass," Wilson wrote to Hay, "without sending you my warm congratulations. The action both of the Committee and of the House must be a source of real gratification to the country as the first step towards adequate preparation for national defense."[28] "I think, myself," Kitchin also wrote, "that we have scored a victory in the Military bill as it passed the House."[29] The Majority Leader was of course right. The victory, to this point, at any rate, belonged almost entirely to the antipreparedness group.

However, preparedness had more ardent friends in the Senate, particularly in the military affairs committee and its volatile chairman, George E. Chamberlain of Oregon. That committee had reported its military reorganization bill on March 4, long before the House approved the Hay bill. It authorized the War Department to raise and train a national volunteer force, not to exceed 250,000 men in number—in other words, the Continental Army, without that incendiary name and smaller in size than Garrison had recommended. Moreover, it increased the Regular Army to about 178,000 men within five years, provided for service in the inactive reserve for men who had completed their enlistment in the Regular Army, and federalized the National Guard.[30]

Debate began and proceeded in the Senate while tension with Ger-

[26] *Congressional Record*, 64th Cong., 1st sess., p. 4396; *New York Times*, March 19, 1916.

[27] *ibid.*, March 24, 1916; *Congressional Record*, 64th Cong., 1st sess., p. 4731.

[28] W. W. to J. Hay, March 24, 1916, Wilson Papers.

[29] C. Kitchin to J. K. McGuire, March 31, 1916, Kitchin Papers.

[30] *New York Times*, March 5, 1916.

many mounted in the *Sussex* crisis. Chamberlain, on April 6, narrowly beat down an effort by Southerners, who feared formation of Negro volunteer units, to defeat the provision for a national reserve force.[31] Numerous amendments, all introduced to increase the size and strength of the army, were adopted during the next two weeks. Then the Senate, in high excitement, approved the measure by a voice vote on April 18, a few hours after Lansing had dispatched the *Sussex* ultimatum to Berlin. The Chamberlain bill as adopted increased the Regular Army to 250,000 men, retained provision for a national reserve army of 261,000 men, and federalized the National Guard while increasing its authorized strength to 280,000. It also included entirely new provisions for federal construction of a plant to manufacture synthetic nitrates, a high school and college reserve training program, which Wilson had recently enthusiastically endorsed,[32] and a National Guard section in the Army General Staff.[33]

The two houses were obviously far apart, and the conference committee appointed to reconcile the bills wrangled without coming in sight of agreement when it met on April 27, 28, and 29. Provisions concerning the size of the Regular Army, the national volunteer reserve army, and a federally operated nitrate plant were the main bones of contention. The impasse was so deep, indeed, that members intimated that they could not reach accord.[34] It was at this point, apparently, that Hay appealed to the President to mediate. The House leader sent the President a memorandum clarifying the major differences between the House and Senate bills. Wilson indicated in marginal comments that he preferred the House provisions for federalizing the National Guard, because they provided for more effective federal control; he also seemed to indicate approval of the Senate's provision for a national reserve force by putting a check mark by the paragraph analyzing it. He then explained his point of view on the question of numbers:

"I think Mr. Hay will agree with me that the situation of the country in regard to its foreign relations has changed so much since the House bill was passed as to make it admissible to reconsider the question of the numerical strength of the army.

[31] *ibid.*, April 7, 1916; *Congressional Record*, 64th Cong., 1st sess., p. 5587.
[32] W. W. to H. S. Vail, April 3, 1916, Wilson Papers.
[33] *New York Times*, April 19, 1916; *Congressional Record*, 64th Cong., 1st sess., p. 6376.
[34] *New York Times*, April 30, 1916.

"The *peace* strength provided for in the Senate Bill seems to me much too large; but I am not sure that it would not be wise to come somewhere very near its figures in the number of units it creates. (Mr. Hay will remember that I have all along been keen on this point of the number of units, and have desired, in particular, as many officers as I could get authorization for.) The number of engineering units seems to me especially important, and the number of units of field artillery more important than the number of units of infantry.

"What I hope is, that the measure can be so framed as to give us an ample skeleton and unmistakable authority to fill it out at any time that the public safety may be deemed to require it."[35]

This advice broke the impasse, at least momentarily, on the issue of the strength of the Regular Army. The House members of the conference committee agreed on May 1 to retain the number of units provided by the Senate bill, while the Senate members tentatively agreed to reduce the peacetime strength of the Regular Army to 180,000 men, with the stipulation, however, that the President could increase that strength by Executive Order at any time to about 218,000 men.[36] The conferees further agreed on May 3 to increase the authorized strength of the National Guard to approximately 400,000 men.[37] However, the Senate conferees revived their demand for a Regular Army of 250,000 men on the following day and said that they would not yield the provision for the nitrate plant. Hay and his colleagues replied that they would have to go back to the House for new instructions.[38]

Wilson called Hay to his office on May 4, as soon as he received word of this impasse. They must have talked about all major issues in dispute, but we know definitely only that Wilson urged approval of the Senate's provision for a federal nitrate plant.[39] The House yielded on this point on May 8; however, it refused, by votes of 221 to 142 and 251 to 109, to accept the Senate's demands concerning the strength of the Regular Army and the modified Continental Army.[40] The result, when the conference committee met again, was a compromise that gave the President almost everything that he had asked: increase in the strength of the Regular Army to 206,169 men, but with pro-

[35] W. W., memorandum for J. Hay, undated MS., but c. April 30, 1916, Baker Collection.
[36] *New York Times*, May 2, 1916.
[37] *ibid.*, May 4, 1916.
[38] *ibid.*, May 6, 1916.
[39] *ibid.*, May 5, 1916.
[40] *ibid.*, May 9, 1916.

vision for further expansion by presidential order to 254,000 men; a large increase in the number of units in the Regular Army, particularly of engineer and field artillery regiments; expansion of the authorized strength of the National Guard (federalized under the terms of the House bill) to 425,000 men, thus compensating for abandonment of the Continental Army scheme; provision for construction of a nitrate plant to cost not more than $20,000,000; and authority to draft men into service during wartime in order to bring the Regular Army to authorized strength.[41] The Senate approved the conference report on May 17, the House, on May 20, and the President signed the Hay-Chamberlain, or Army Reorganization, bill on June 3.

Army spokesmen and leaders of the preparedness movement were sick at heart, particularly over abandonment of the Continental Army and the bill's reliance on the National Guard as the first line of defense. "The measure," General Leonard Wood warned Colonel House, "is a menace to public safety in that it purports to provide a military force of value. . . . It will be solid and effective in only one line, and that will be in a raid on the federal treasury. . . . The thing is dangerous to a degree exceeding anything ever attempted in legislation in this country. . . . It has not the support of the members of the General Staff of the Army or of the Army as a whole. It would be far better to have no Army legislation than to have this measure put through."[42] The Hay-Chamberlain bill, General Scott and a member of the Army War College agreed, was a "gold brick."[43] Roosevelt later called it "one of the most iniquitous bits of legislation ever placed on the statute books"—a "foolish and unpatriotic . . . bit of flintlock legislation."[44] Representative Gardner, a leader in the defense movement, exclaimed that it was a fake preparedness bill that every pacifist in the House could support;[45] and the executive committee of the National Security League, a leading preparedness organization, begged Wilson to veto the measure.[46]

Such fulminations only caused antipreparedness leaders to contemplate with greater pleasure what they said was *their* victory. "The mil-

[41] *ibid.*, May 14, 1916.

[42] L. Wood, "Memorandum with respect to legislation affecting Militia," MS. sent to E. M. House on April 17, 1916, original in the Wilson Papers.

[43] W. H. Johnston to H. L. Scott, May 26, 1916, Scott Papers.

[44] T. Roosevelt to A. C. Wiprud, December 21, 1916, Roosevelt Papers; T. Roosevelt to S. Menken, December 23, 1916, *ibid.*

[45] *New York Times*, May 21, 1916.

[46] Robert Bacon to W. W., May 26, 1916, Wilson Papers.

Mother Hubbard—"Help Yourself."

Starrett in the New York *Tribune*

itary bill as it stands," Warren Worth Bailey's newspaper rejoiced,
"now provides for reasonable preparedness."[47] Oswald Garrison Villard's newspaper had some sober words for extremists: "If those mil-
itaristically inclined citizens and editors who are denouncing Congress because it has not given them precisely the number of soldiers
they wished, or introduced compulsory service, were to take the trouble
to read the bill . . . they would, we believe, be amazed at its compre-
hensiveness and its far-reaching character."[48]

[47] *Johnstown Democrat*, May 25, 1916.
[48] *New York Evening Post*, May 23, 1916.

This was Wilson's own view. He had never wanted a measure to put the country more or less on a war footing. All along he had demanded only reasonable military preparedness, that is, a moderate expansion of the Regular Army and substantial strengthening of the defensive reserve forces. He knew the risks of war with Germany, but he simply was not willing to pay the political and social costs of effective preparation for a war that might not, after all, occur. More important, perhaps, he knew far better than his critics that he had obtained the most possible in the circumstances. As he explained to a frantic critic, "I think no one not on the ground can appreciate the difficulties of working out a complicated piece of legislation, and if you were viewing the thing a little nearer at hand, I think that you would feel a little less vexation about the Army bill."[49] The truth was, as Wilson pointed out in the same letter, that the Hay-Chamberlain bill reflected what was by now the settled consensus of the country. It was a happy and not entirely fortuitous fact that it also reflected Wilson's own estimate of the best solution.

The House and Senate naval affairs committees had been quietly at work, biding their time all through the weeks while controversy over the army bill was coming to its climax. There was virtually no disagreement either in Congress or the country at large over the need for some kind of naval expansion. Doctrinaire pacifists opposed it in principle; but they spent most of their energy fighting the big army men, for they never feared navalism as the same dire threat to American institutions as militarism. And to numerous and widely different groups of Americans—for example, southern and western producers of raw materials who resented the British blockade, men who hoped for war with Germany or feared Japan, and old-fashioned nationalists— the thought of a great navy flaunting American power and might had an irresistible appeal. The only question in the spring of 1916, then, was how far to go.

The House naval affairs committee gave the first answer by approving a naval appropriations bill on May 18, 1916, that rejected Secretary Daniels's request for endorsement of a five-year building program and immediate construction, among other vessels, of two dreadnoughts. It provided, instead, for five battle cruisers, twenty submarines, four cruisers, ten destroyers, and lesser craft. The bill, although it provided more tonnage than Daniels had requested for the first year, was actu-

[49] W. W. to C. A. Munn, May 12, 1916, Wilson Papers.

ally a minor triumph for the small navy Democrats led by Walter L. Hensley of Missouri. It also included a rider offered by Hensley promising American participation in a postwar conference to discuss disarmament and establish machinery for the arbitration of international disputes.[50] "The greatest problem of the hour," the *New York Times* said indignantly, "has been bungled by men who have proved themselves unfit for their task."[51]

Antipreparedness leaders were delighted that the committee had done no more. Kitchin expressed their reaction to Oswald Garrison Villard as follows: "I am gratified to know that you are pleased with the report of the Naval Affairs Committee. The bill as reported carries entirely too much appropriation by many millions, but it is infinitely better than the program first proposed. Striking out the five-year feature I consider a great victory for us, as well as striking out the dreadnaughts [*sic*]. Of course, the Henseley [*sic*] amendment . . . is a great moral step for peace, and strengthens the bill wonderfully, in my judgment."[52]

There was controversy almost from the first moment when Representative Lemuel P. Padgett of Tennessee, chairman of the naval affairs committee, introduced the bill on May 24. Republican members, continuing the fight that they had begun in committee, pressed unsuccessfully for amendments for two dreadnoughts or six battle cruisers. All that the Democrats would concede was an increase in the number of submarines from twenty to fifty (but forty-seven of them were to be small coastal defensive boats) and in the appropriation for naval aviation from $2,000,000 to $3,500,000. The Democrats themselves added as a rider a bill already approved by the Senate for construction of a governmental armor plate factory.[53]

[50] *New York Times*, May 19, 1916.

[51] *ibid.*

[52] C. Kitchin to O. G. Villard, May 24, 1916, Kitchin Papers.

[53] *New York Times*, May 31 and June 1, 1916. Approval of the armor plate bill was a personal triumph for Senator "Pitchfork" Benjamin R. Tillman of South Carolina, who had been feuding with armor plate manufacturers since the Spanish-American War. Tillman introduced his bill to establish a governmental armor plate facility on December 9, 1916, and soon won Wilson's strong support for the measure. See B. R. Tillman to W. W., January 5 and 8, 1916, and W. W. to B. R. Tillman, January 6 and March 31, 1916, all in the Wilson Papers. Armor plate manufacturers at once offered to reduce their prices if the Senate rejected the Tillman bill. Tillman refused, and the manufacturers then threatened to raise the price of armor plate $200 a ton if the measure passed. *New York Times*, February 2 and 9, 1916. This blunder caused a great public outcry and assured adoption of the bill. See, e. g., the New York *World*, February 10, 1916, and *The Independent*, LXXXV (February 21, 1916), 253.

Thus amended, the naval appropriations measure passed the House on June 2 after a Republican substitute for a vastly larger program had been narrowly defeated by a vote of 189 to 183.[54] "When this preparedness hysteria is over," Kitchin wrote to the Democratic members of the naval affairs committee to congratulate them on their victory, "the country is going to feel indebted to you, as many of us now are, for the great work you have done and the hundreds of millions of dollars you have been largely instrumental in saving by the modification of the original [administration] program."[55] Wilson also had grateful words for Representative Padgett: "I want to express to you my warm admiration of the way in which you have handled a difficult matter in framing and putting through the naval bill."[56]

It was, Wilson knew, only the beginning. He had not interfered with proceedings in the House, most probably because he knew that strong navy men dominated the Senate and would compel considerable changes. They did not disappoint him. The naval affairs committee on June 30 reported a breathtaking bipartisan measure to get the entire original administration program under way within three years instead of five. It called for construction to begin during the next fiscal year on four dreadnoughts, four battle cruisers, four cruisers, twenty destroyers, thirty submarines, and lesser craft. General debate began in the upper house on July 13, with the progressive Republicans, George W. Norris of Nebraska, John D. Works of California, and Moses E. Clapp of Minnesota, offering the only significant opposition. The Senate approved the bill—including a provision appropriating funds for the armor plate factory and a rider repeating the Hensley peace declaration—by a vote of seventy-one to eight on July 21, 1916.[57]

Democrats, with the help of progressive Republicans, pushed the bill through the Senate on March 21, 1916. *New York Times*, March 22, 1916. The armor plate manufacturers, particularly Bethlehem Steel Company, now applied heavy pressure on the lower house once the Tillman bill went before the naval affairs committee. New York *World*, March 27 and 31, April 1, 1916. "There is every evidence," Wilson wrote, "that the most sinister influences are at work and we shall have to expose them thoroughly before we overcome them." W. W. to B. R. Tillman, March 31, 1916, Wilson Papers. The naval affairs committee reported the Tillman bill favorably to the House on April 5. It was incorporated into the naval appropriations bill on May 31 in order to hasten its passage.

[54] *New York Times*, June 3, 1916; *Congressional Record*, 64th Cong., 1st sess., pp. 9189-9190.

[55] C. Kitchin to O. Callaway, June 3, 1916, Kitchin Papers.

[56] W. W. to L. P. Padgett, June 8, 1916, Wilson Papers.

[57] *New York Times*, July 1, 1916; *Congressional Record*, 64th Cong., 1st sess., p. 11384.

The President intervened decisively once the naval bills had been sent to the conference committee. He invited the House committee members to the White House on July 27 and pleaded for the Senate bill.[58] Wilson nowhere set down all the reasons for his action, but they are not hard to find. As we will see in the next volume, he had already committed the United States to membership in a postwar international security organization. The nation would therefore need, as he had also already said in the Democratic platform, a navy "fully equal to the international tasks which this Nation hopes and expects to take part in performing." In addition, Wilson undoubtedly shared the general American fear that Japan would emerge from the war expansionistic and aggressive, perhaps as an ally of Germany.[59] A more immediate cause of the President's action was the tension between the United States and Great Britain then coming to a head, and Wilson's fear that Anglo-American relations might be imperiled in the future if reactionaries gained control of the British government. "Let us build a navy bigger than hers and do what we please," he told Colonel House on September 24.[60]

The House conferees resisted for a while, but Wilson maintained heavy pressure. Representative Padgett, spokesman for the small navy Democrats, caved in completely after the President told him in a second conference on August 8 that approval of the Senate bill was "imperative."[61] Indeed, Padgett himself moved acceptance of the main features of the Senate measure in the House on August 15. His motion carried by a vote of 283 to fifty-one, with only thirty-five Democrats, (mostly antipreparedness Southerners), fifteen Republicans, and one Socialist holding out to the end against the presidential pressure. "Approval of this building program," Kitchin shouted, "means that the United States today becomes the most militaristic naval nation on earth."[62] The bill, he wrote a few days later, "condemns our provisions for National arbitration and world peace as hypocrisy and mockery."[63]

Approval by the conference committee and the two houses followed rapidly, and Wilson signed the naval appropriations bill, along with a measure recently adopted to provide funds for army expansion, in a

[58] *New York Times*, July 28, 1916.
[59] On this point, see Outten J. Clinard, *Japan's Influence on American Naval Power, 1897-1917*, pp. 145-172.
[60] House Diary, September 24, 1916.
[61] *New York Times*, August 9, 1916.
[62] *ibid.*, August 16, 1916; *Congressional Record*, 64th Cong., 1st sess., p. 12700.
[63] C. Kitchin to Mrs. J. Malcolm Forbes, August 19, 1916, Kitchin Papers.

gala ceremony at the White House on August 29. "I think that the whole country will feel," he said to an audience of congressional leaders and officers from both services, "that this Congress has accomplished a very remarkable part of the program of national defense. This bill that I have signed for the army is merely the Appropriation bill; it is not the bill by which we reorganized the army, of course you understand, but it does carry with it a very much needed revision of the articles of war[64] and it does mean that the finances of the nation are to stand behind the reorganization of the army and its use for adequate national defense.

"The navy bill is a very remarkable measure. Never before by one single act of legislation has so much been done for the creation of an adequate navy. Our navy has steadily grown. I think the development of that arm of force has always had the enthusiastic support of the nation. It is a matter of unusual gratification, therefore, that we should have been able at this time to do so much, to do it so well as I believe it to be done in this bill, and to do it with such unanimity of support and opinion."[65]

Two final measures rounded out Wilson's preparedness program in the spring and summer of 1916. One was a bill, suggested and drafted by Newton D. Baker, to create a civilian agency to study the nation's economic and human resources, in order, as Baker put it, to "make the calling out and mobilizing of the industrial resources of the nation as automatic as the mobilization of its army."[66] Wilson approved enthusiastically, and Representative Hay introduced the measure on May 23, saying that it was the President's own bill.[67] House leaders later incorporated it in the army appropriation bill in a provision creating a Council of Executive Information for the Coordination of Industries and Resources for the National Security and Welfare, composed of the Secretaries of War, the Navy, Commerce, Agriculture, Labor, and the Interior.[68] The Senate fortunately changed the name of the new body to the Council of National Defense. Wilson, on

[64] Wilson had vetoed this bill on August 18 because he objected to one provision in the revised articles of war exempting retired army officers from trial and punishment by courts martial. Congress adopted the measure again, revised to meet the President's objection, on August 25, 1916. *New York Times*, August 19 and 26, 1916.

[65] *ibid.*, August 30, 1916.

[66] N. D. Baker to W. W., April 7, 1916, Wilson Papers.

[67] *New York Times*, May 24, 1916.

[68] *ibid.*, June 17, 1916.

October 11, 1916, named seven distinguished leaders in various walks of life to an Advisory Commission.[69] This beginning of the agency that would later take responsibility for American economic mobilization in the First World War went virtually unnoticed both in Congress and the press.

The second measure was the shipping bill, the cause of the most violent congressional controversy during the preceding session. Wilson, in a speech before the Pan-American Financial Conference in Washington on May 24, 1915, had given notice of intention to persevere;[70] and McAdoo, as we have seen,[71] had worked hard to stimulate public support during the late summer and autumn of 1915. The Secretary of the Treasury completed a new draft of the bill on about December 10, 1915, and Wilson then set to work to avoid a repetition of the debacle that had seen the Ship Purchase bill defeated in the Senate in early 1915 by defecting Democrats.[72] The President wooed most assiduously Senator James P. Clarke of Arkansas, who had almost single-handedly wrecked the Ship Purchase bill,[73] but he did not neglect Representative Kitchin and Representative Joshua W. Alexander of Missouri, chairman of the House committee on the merchant marine, whose support was also essential. They, at least, promised to close ranks behind the shipping bill that Alexander introduced on January 31, 1916.

It was a more ambitious and far-reaching measure than the Ship Purchase bill of 1915. It established a United States Shipping Board of five members and authorized this agency to spend up to $50,000,000 to purchase, construct, or charter vessels and operate them through a subsidiary shipping corporation in regular service if it could not lease them to private firms on terms to protect the public interest. This was

[69] *ibid.*, October 12, 1916.

[70] *ibid.*, May 25, 1915.

[71] Above, p. 36, n. 68.

[72] He took this precaution perhaps in response to W. G. McAdoo to W. W., December 11, 1915, the Papers of William Gibbs McAdoo, Library of Congress; hereinafter cited as the McAdoo Papers.

[73] W. W. to J. P. Clarke, January 13, 1916, Wilson Papers. Clarke went through McAdoo's bill and returned it, probably on January 15, indicating that he objected only to the provision empowering the proposed shipping board to purchase or charter vessels. "This is what Senator Clarke thinks can be put through," Tumulty wrote for Wilson on the copy of the bill. "The Senator would like to have you look it over. Then arrange a conference with him." Wilson, not long afterward, appeared unannounced at Senator Clarke's hotel and conferred with the Arkansan for half an hour in a corner of the hotel parlor. Wilson must have persuaded Clarke to withdraw his objection to the provision for purchase and charter. *New York Times*, January 27, 1916, saying that this incident occurred "one evening last week."

the main feature, somewhat revised, of the Ship Purchase bill. What was new in the legislation of 1916 was a provision giving the Shipping Board sweeping authority—comparable to that exercised by the Interstate Commerce Commission over railroads—over rates and services of all common carriers engaged in transportation of passengers and freight between American ports and between American and foreign ports. The new bill did not forbid the Shipping Board to purchase merchant ships of belligerent nationality.[74] Fear of serious controversy with the Allies if the Board purchased German vessels lying in American harbors had been one of the principal causes of controversy over the Ship Purchase bill in early 1915.

American shipping companies were, as before, violently opposed to "this socialistic scheme,"[75] but Alexander's committee made steady progress in hearings. It had completed a revision by late April. "The necessity for action in this matter," Wilson wrote to Alexander on May 1, while returning a copy of the committee's draft, "grows daily more evident and more pressing."[76] He did not have long to wait. Alexander reported the bill, changed to provide that lines operated by the Shipping Board should go out of business within five years after the end of the European war, on May 9, and the House of Representatives approved it by a vote of 209 to 161 on May 20.[77] There was little active opposition but much apathy among Democrats in the Senate,[78] accompanied by a fear of purchase of German vessels. But administration leaders finally persuaded Democratic senators to caucus on the Alexander bill on July 8. They amended it by forbidding the Shipping Board to purchase any ship of belligerent nationality, and they then agreed to win adoption even if it took all summer.[79] The presidential campaign was now under way, and debate was desultory and fitful until the Senate approved the measure in a strict party vote on August 18. The President signed the bill on September 7.[80]

It is curious that contemporaries should have been so blind to the long-range significance of the Shipping Act of 1916. It went through

[74] *ibid.*, January 31, 1916.
[75] T. G. Gordon, secretary, United States Merchant Marine Association, form letter to C. Kitchin, January 31, 1916, Kitchin Papers.
[76] W. W. to J. W. Alexander, May 1, 1916, Wilson Papers.
[77] *New York Times*, May 21, 1916; *Congressional Record*, 64th Cong., 1st sess., p. 8374.
[78] As the majority leader, Senator Kern, made plain in J. W. Kern to W. G. McAdoo, July 5, 1916, Wilson Papers.
[79] *New York Times*, July 9, 1916.
[80] *ibid.*, August 19 and September 8, 1916.

an indifferent Congress only because the President insisted. It provoked no controversy or comment in the public press. Yet it was one of the most important and constructive measures of the Wilson era. What had been hastily conceived in the autumn of 1914 as a means of relieving a temporary scarcity of bottoms had metamorphosed into a measure launching the federal government into comprehensive regulation of ocean rates and services by a new independent commission. Subsequent legislation and practice would also transform this agency into the promoter and sustainer of the first nearly adequate American merchant marine to sail the seas since the Civil War. Contemporaries did not know it, but the Shipping Act of 1916 marked the rebirth of the American merchant marine.

Certain aspects of the preparedness program, notably the regulatory features of the Shipping Act and the bill establishing the Council of National Defense, gave some evidence of Wilson's determination, signaled by the Brandeis nomination, to build support for a broad new coalition of Democrats, independents, and former Progressives. Much more obviously indicative of a new orientation were three measures designed to woo important elements in a potential new coalition.

The first was a bill to create a Federal Tariff Commission. The idea of a nonpartisan, independent agency to advise on tariff policy went back at least to the 1890's. President Taft had found authority in a minor provision of the Payne-Aldrich Tariff Act of 1909 to establish a Tariff Board, but it fell victim to the intense partisan struggles of 1910-1912, and Congress abolished it in the latter year.[81] Then Theodore Roosevelt's Progressive party, in its platform in 1912, called for a "non-partisan scientific Tariff Commission ... [with] plenary power to elicit information, and for this purpose to prescribe a uniform system of accounting for the great protected industries." It was a thoroughly progressive alternative to the Republican practice of indiscriminate protection and Democratic legislation based on doctrinaire adherence to the principle of tariffs for revenue only. But a "scientific" tariff could be another name for a protective tariff if the commission was so minded, and businessmen and manufacturers rallied again to the plan in large numbers. The Chamber of Commerce of the United States approved it overwhelmingly in April 1913, and a Tariff Commission League (suc-

[81] Joseph F. Kenkel, "The Tariff Commission Movement: The Search for a Nonpartisan Solution of the Tariff Question," unpublished Ph.D. dissertation, University of Maryland, 1962, pp. 1-97.

cessor to an earlier National Tariff Commission Association) was organized in Chicago in August 1915 to press a nationwide propaganda campaign.[82] As Wilson's friend and supporter in Boston, Edward A. Filene, warned soon afterward, business sentiment was so strongly united behind the commission plan that Democratic victory in 1916 might well depend upon its satisfaction.[83]

Wilson had almost savagely condemned Roosevelt's proposal for a tariff commission in 1912, ridiculing the notion that experts could give useful advice on tariff rates, or any other subject, for that matter.[84] As late as August 1915 he was still promising to "explode the nonsense that the Republican speakers are uttering [about the need for a tariff commission] very thoroughly."[85] But such warnings as the one from Filene could not be disregarded, particularly when Robert L. Owen of Oklahoma, chairman of the banking committee in the Senate, whom Wilson greatly respected, wrote enticingly in early January 1916: "As a matter of Party expediency, . . . a tariff commission would conciliate two millions or three millions of progressive men who would be glad to support the Democratic Party except for their obsession on the protective tariff principle."[86] In other words, adoption of a tariff commission bill was the obvious way to neutralize the impending Republican campaign on the tariff issue, insofar as former Progressives were concerned.

The thing was no sooner said than done,[87] and the President signified his change of mind in a long letter to the House majority leader and chairman of the ways and means committee, Representative Kitchin, on January 24, 1916. "The more I have thought about the matter," Wilson wrote, "the plainer it has become to me that we ought to have some such instrumentality as would be supplied by a tariff board." It

---

[82] *The Outlook*, cx (August 25, 1915), 943-944.

[83] E. A. Filene to W. W., September 9, 1915, Wilson Papers.

[84] John Wells Davidson (ed.), *A Crossroads of Freedom, the 1912 Campaign Speeches of Woodrow Wilson*, pp. 113, 160-161.

[85] W. W. to J. M. Cox, August 27, 1915, Wilson Papers.

[86] R. L. Owen to W. W., January 5, 1916, *ibid*.

[87] This, actually, is a mild exaggeration. There were many discussions in the administration in December 1915 and January 1916, particularly among the President, Secretary Houston, and Secretary Lane, who were strong proponents of the tariff commission plan, and Secretary of Commerce William C. Redfield, who was very much opposed. See J. F. Kenkel, "The Tariff Commission Movement," pp. 108-113. Wilson was undoubtedly much influenced by a memorandum by Professor Frank W. Taussig of Harvard University, the pre-eminent tariff economist in the United States, endorsing the commission plan with certain reservations. It was F. W. Taussig to D. F. Houston, December 17, 1915, Wilson Papers.

could gather evidence, advise the administrative agencies and Congress, and be particularly helpful in obtaining information about the unfair "dumping" of foreign products upon the American market. He was, Wilson concluded, writing this letter in the hope that the ways and means committee would be willing to act promptly.[88]

Kitchin talked with the President on the following day, January 25, and left the White House intimating that he would support a tariff commission bill, albeit unenthusiastically.[89] But he must have indicated some displeasure in the conversation, for Wilson wrote again at Tumulty's suggestion, on January 26, to explain why he had altered his views. "I have changed my mind," he said, "because all the circumstances of the world have changed and it seems to me that in view of the extraordinary and far-reaching changes which the European war has brought about it is absolutely necessary that we should have a competent instrument of inquiry along the whole line of the many questions which affect our foreign commerce." The broader question of tariff policy, he said, was not involved.[90]

Democratic leaders throughout the North and industrial areas of the Middle West thought that it was a capital stroke. "There is no one thing that you can do that will strengthen our Party in the North more than to create a non-partisiam [sic] tariff commission," the "only active participent [sic] in Democratic Politic [sic] and manufacturer of Fur Felt Hats in 'captivity' " wrote from Danbury, Connecticut, to Kitchin. " . . . The manufacturers and business men of New England will hail this movement with great pleasure, and it will go a long ways to dis-arm 'The Tariff Fakers' of this section."[91] The president of the National Association of Manufacturers said in a press release that it found "vindication of its efforts to remove from party politics forever an issue destructive of national development."[92]

A Tariff Commission bill, drafted by McAdoo or experts in the

[88] W. W. to C. Kitchin, January 24, 1916, Kitchin Papers, published in the *New York Times*, January 27, 1916.

[89] *New York Times*, January 26, 1916.

[90] J. P. Tumulty to W. W., January 25, 1916, Tumulty Papers; W. W. to C. Kitchin, January 26, 1916, Kitchin Papers, published in the *New York Times*, January 27, 1916.

[91] M. T. Cuff to C. Kitchin, January 25, 1916, Kitchin Papers. In the same vein, see also Representative W. E. Cox of Indiana to W. W., January 26, 1916, Wilson Papers, and E. O. Wood, Democratic national committeeman from Michigan, to W. W., January 31, 1916, *ibid.*

[92] "President Pleases N. A. M.," undated press statement by George Pope, MS. in *ibid.*

Treasury Department at Kitchin's request,[93] was introduced in the House of Representatives on February 1 by Henry T. Rainey of Illinois, next to Kitchin in seniority on the ways and means committee, because Kitchin had finally concluded that he could not support the measure with much enthusiasm.[94] It created a nonpartisan (or bipartisan)Tariff Commission of six members, to serve staggered twelve-year terms at the then high salary of $12,000 a year. The Commission, given sweeping investigatory powers and authority to put witnesses under oath, was specifically instructed to report from time to time to the President, the ways and means committee, and the finance committee of the Senate, and to make special investigations and reports when so requested by these authorities.[95]

The measure was virtually lost in the rush of the spectacular controversies and events of the next three months, and Wilson had to write to Rainey in early May to remind him of his deep interest in the bill. "I am exceedingly anxious," Wilson added, "that nothing should happen which would prejudice its passing even in the way of delay."[96] Democrats in the ways and means committee had not forgotten; they had simply agreed to incorporate the Tariff Commission bill as a provision in the new revenue bill upon which they were then working. It went through under this aegis on September 7, amended to extend the scope of the Commission's purview and reduce the salaries of commissioners to $7,500 a year.[97] Wilson named the members on March 21, 1917.

The chief significance of the Tariff Commission provision was what it symbolized. The proposal had been sponsored and pressed by virtually the entire nonfinancial business community and opposed by low tariff Democrats like Kitchin, Oscar W. Underwood, and—to a certain point—Woodrow Wilson. Approval of the measure was, therefore, a victory for protectionists and a defeat for champions of a low tariff. It was also vindication of the argument that the data upon which tariff rates were to be based was better collected by so-called experts than politicians.

The supreme significance of the Tariff Commission provision was

[93] See W. G. McAdoo to C. Kitchin, February 1, 1916, Kitchin Papers.

[94] Kitchin expressed his frank opinion of the Tariff Commission idea in a letter to B. R. Bowker, April 15, 1916, *ibid*.

[95] *New York Times*, February 2, 1916.

[96] W. W. to H. T. Rainey, May 10, 1916, Wilson Papers.

[97] *New York Times*, September 8, 1916; J. F. Kenkel, "The Tariff Commission Movement," pp. 119-121.

the evidence that it gave of a movement in Wilson's thought and Democratic policies toward protectionism in particular circumstances and the idea that tariff policies should be used to encourage national economic development. Another provision of the Revenue Act of 1916 shed additional light. It afforded large protection to the American chemical industry against the German Farben Trust by imposing ad valorem duties of 30 per cent on dye-stuffs, medicines, and synthetics.[98] They were to be reduced by 20 per cent each year for five years, to be sure, but this concession to Democratic low tariff sentiment could easily be repealed in the future. As Wilson, who was primarily responsible for the new chemical rates,[99] said in a letter to the president of the Illinois Manufacturers' Association, "It ought to be possible . . . to make the question of duties merely a question of progress and development, a question of adapting means to ends, of facilitating and helping business and employing to the utmost the resources of the country in a vast development of our business and enterprise."[100] This, as Kitchin admitted when the letter was read in the House of Representatives, sounded very much like protectionist talk.

The third measure designed to satisfy an important interest group was the rural credits bill, now the principal objective of organized farmers, particularly in the Middle West. There had not been, at least since about 1912, much disagreement among responsible public leaders and economists about the need for machinery to channel long-term credit to farmers more efficiently and cheaply. But there had been

[98] *New York Times*, September 8, 1916.

[99] Wilson had discussed the possibility of giving protection to chemicals with Secretary Redfield and Secretary McAdoo in January 1916. W. C. Redfield to W. W., January 4, 1916, Wilson Papers; W. W. to W. G. McAdoo, January 19, 1916, *ibid.* Other discussions followed, and Wilson conferred with Kitchin in March and won his approval of a special chemicals bill. See W. W. to W. C. Redfield, February 28, 1916, *ibid.*; W. W. to Representative E. J. Hill (author of the special bill to impose new chemical rates), March 27, 1916, *ibid.*; W. W. to W. C. Redfield, April 4, 1916, *ibid.*; and especially A. C. Imbrie, "Memorandum of talk with President Wilson March 8th, 1916," copy in the Baker Collection.

[100] W. W. to S. M. Hastings, July 28, 1916, Wilson Papers, also printed in *Congressional Record*, 64th Cong., 1st sess., p. 12380. Wilson made his new position on the tariff clear in an authorized interview with a Washington correspondent a short time later. He still believed firmly in a competitive tariff policy, he said, but he was prepared to act on the facts and even give protection in order to build up industries necessary to the United States. It would be possible, Wilson went on, to formulate a tariff policy that would command the overwhelming support of the American people regardless of party affiliation. It would, he added, be the height of folly to reduce tariff rates drastically. L. Ames Brown, "Preparedness for Peace, an Authorized Statement of President Wilson's Plans," *Collier's*, LVIII (September 16, 1916), 12-13.

insurmountable differences over proper method. Farm leaders and their spokesmen in Congress wanted a system organized, underwritten, and administered by the federal government. Secretary of Agriculture Houston and conservatives proposed a cooperative system, modeled after German land banks, organized and financed entirely by private interests. Wilson had been in the thick of this fight since it first came to a head in Congress in the spring of 1914. He had then blocked a rural credits bill providing a large measure of federal participation by threatening a veto, asserting that it was "unwise and unjustifiable to extend the credits of the Government to a single class of the community." His deep convictions against special class legislation, which he said came out of the fire of conscience, had not changed by the late winter of 1915, when he again opposed a measure for a federal rural credits system.[101]

Wilson gave no clue to his position in his third Annual Message of December 7, 1915. He merely said then that Congress "should put into early operation some provisions for rural credits," and leaders of the cause on Capitol Hill, Senator Henry F. Hollis of New Hampshire and Representative A. F. Lever of South Carolina, had to proceed not knowing whether they would again run on the presidential reef. They and other members of a joint congressional committee on rural credits hammered out a new bill during December 1915 and January 1916 with the help of Leonard G. Robinson, director of the Jewish Agricultural Industrial Aid Society.[102]

The measure, completed in mid-January, created a Federal Farm Loan Board of five members to organize and supervise at least twelve Federal Land Banks. The Land Banks in turn would lend money, obtained by sale of tax-exempt bonds, at a maximum interest rate of 5 per cent to farmers organized in credit cooperatives called "national farm loan associations" on long terms against the security of their land. The most vital—and potentially controversial—provisions were the ones for underwriting the system. They stipulated, first, that each Land Bank should begin with a capital of $500,000, and that the federal government should purchase any stock not subscribed by individuals or

[101] See A. S. Link, *Wilson*, II, 261-264, for the background and development of this controversy.

[102] For the background and analyses of the joint committee's measure, known as the Hollis bill, see Leonard G. Robinson, "Congress Has Bill to Aid Nation's Farmers," *New York Times Magazine*, February 6, 1916, pp. 9-10; *New York Journal of Commerce*, February 18, 1916; and Herbert Quick, "The Rural-Credit Firing Squad," *Saturday Evening Post*, CLXXXVIII (April 15, 1916), 29-31, 101-102.

private firms within ninety days after the stock had been offered for sale; second, that the federal Treasury should supply up to $6,000,000 a year at 2 per cent interest to the system if the sale of Land Bank bonds did not raise sufficient money. It was an ingenious compromise between conflicting points of view. Progressives were pleased by the bill's provision for federal organization and control and its guarantee of federal money for adequate capitalization and operation. Conservatives approved the measure's encouragement to farmers' cooperatives and its provision for private purchase of the stock and bonds of Land Banks. As Carter Glass of Virginia, conservative chairman of the House banking committee, wrote, "There is an element of considerable government aid in the bill, but the objection to this is met with the statement that ultimately the government subscription to the capital stock of the land banks will be repaid."[103]

Everything depended now on the President. Circumstantial evidence makes it clear that he had already decided to yield on the controverted point of federal underwriting and control. He knew that congressional leaders would accept nothing less, and that there would be no rural credits legislation unless he gave in. It was equally clear that midwestern farmers with an attentive eye on Capitol Hill might well decide the outcome of the forthcoming election. "If the Democratic Party fails to give suitable legislation on the subject," Frank G. Odell of Omaha, secretary of the American Rural Credits Association, warned on January 9, 1916, "it will hurt itself greatly with the farmers, especially in the Middle West. The support of farmers, which would be engaged by rural credit legislation, is necessary to the Democratic Party in the Middle West to offset the pro-German vote which will be solidly Republican."[104] Wilson was perhaps also influenced by the annual report that the Comptroller of the Currency, John Skelton Williams, sent to Congress on January 10. It revealed that interest rates for farmers were still usurious in some areas.[105]

Hollis and Lever went to the White House at ten o'clock in the morning on January 28, 1916, for what was to be the decisive conference with the President and Secretary Houston. "I had fully intended coming with Senator Hollis and Mr. Lever . . . ," Senator Owen had written to Wilson two days before, "but find that I shall be compelled

---

[103] C. Glass to E. S. Johnson, January 22, 1916, the Papers of Carter Glass, University of Virginia Library; hereinafter cited as the Glass Papers.

[104] *New York Times*, January 10, 1916.

[105] *Annual Report of the Comptroller of the Currency, . . . December 6, 1915* (2 vols.), I, 22-23, 149-161.

to be out of the city at that time. I am in sympathy with the point of view presented by Senator Hollis, and I hope that you may see your way clear to acquiesce in his proposal, for which I believe he will give you sound reasons."[106] Hollis explained the joint committee's bill, and the conferees then apparently discussed only the provision for federal underwriting of the new system. Houston repeated objections that he had voiced forcefully several times before. Perhaps, Lever suggested, the President would accept the compromise figure of $3,000,000, instead of $6,000,000, as the amount that the federal government should promise to provide annually if necessary. "I have only one criticism of Lever's proposition," Wilson allegedly replied, "and that is that he is too modest in the amount." Hollis and Lever were somewhat stunned, but Lever managed to reply, "Mr. President, we will make it $6,000,000 and I believe with this we can bring in line a lot of the radicals and pass the Bill."[107]

The Hollis bill was an administration measure from that day forward. It was criticized by some farm leaders because its machinery for mobilizing credit was too limited,[108] by spokesmen of tenant farmers and single taxers because it offered no benefits whatever to the landless,[109] and most of all by conservatives because it put the government directly into the business of supplying credit to one class. "A use of Government cash and Government credit," exclaimed former Governor Myron T. Herrick of Ohio, a leader in the fight for a private system of rural credits, "is contemplated for private purposes on a scale never attempted in any other country. . . . The programme of the present Democratic Administration embraces enterprises of a private nature to be done by the United States Government. . . . The Hollis bill points the way."[110] The *New York Times* agreed, saying: "There is developing in this country a notion that the people, especially agricultural people, are born with a right of access to unlimited amounts of cheap capital.

---

[106] R. L. Owen to W. W., January 26, 1916, Wilson Papers.

[107] Based on A. F. Lever to R. S. Baker, March 22, 1927, Baker Collection, which is the only record of this conference.

[108] L. Woodard, California Division, Farmers' Union, to C. Glass, February 26, 1916, Glass Papers.

[109] G. W. Maddox to Representative T. M. Bell, February 2, 1916, copy in *ibid.*; J. G. Maguire to W. W. Bailey, May 9, 1916, Bailey Papers; W. W. Bailey to J. G. Maguire, May 19, 1916, *ibid.*; *The Public*, xix (May 12, 1916), 462; Lincoln *Nebraska Farmer*, May 3, 1916, quoted in *ibid.*, p. 448; Topeka *Capper's Weekly*, October 28, 1916, quoted in *ibid.*, November 3, 1916, p. 1050.

[110] M. T. Herrick, "Rural Credits," New York *Sun*, April 24, 1916; see also M. T. Herrick, "Some Objections to the Federal Farm Loan Act," *North American Review*, cciv (December 1916), 837-849.

The cheaper it is the better. . . . The farmer wants to be subsidized."[111]

Such objections had no weight either with progressives who held other views about the proper functions of government or with the great majority on Capitol Hill who were more concerned with the farm vote than with doctrinal disputation. The Senate, after two weeks of sluggish debate, approved the Hollis bill by a vote of fifty-eight to five on May 4. The measure, slightly changed in some of its details by Glass's committee, passed the House by a vote of 295 to ten on May 15.[112] The conference committee quickly ironed out the differences, accepting the House's provisions for capitalizing Federal Land Banks at $750,000 instead of $500,000 each and permitting loans against improvements as well as land. Wilson signed the bill on July 17 at a White House ceremony attended by congressional leaders and representatives of all major farm organizations. The presidential campaign had begun, and Wilson did not fail to make as much political capital as he could in his little speech, which follows:

"On occasions of this sort there are so many things to say that one would despair of saying them briefly and adequately, but I cannot go through the simple ceremony of signing this bill without expressing the feeling that I have in signing. It is a feeling of profound satisfaction not only, but of real gratitude that we have completed this piece of legislation, which I hope will be immensely beneficial to the farmers of the country.

"The farmers, it seems to me, have occupied hitherto a singular position of disadvantage. They have not had the same freedom to get credit on their real estate that others have had who were in manufacturing and commercial enterprises, and while they have sustained our life, they did not in the same degree with some others share in the benefits of that life. . . .

"I look forward to the benefits of this bill, not with extravagant expectations, but with confident expectation that it will be of very wide-reaching benefit, and incidentally it will be of advantage to the investing community, for I can imagine no more satisfactory and solid investments than this system will afford those who have money to use.

"I sign the bill, therefore, with real emotion, and am very glad to be honored by your presence, and supported by your feelings. I have no doubt in what I have said regarding it."[113]

[111] *New York Times*, May 8, 1916; also *ibid.*, May 17 and 22, 1916.
[112] *ibid.*, May 5 and 16, 1916.
[113] *ibid.*, July 18, 1916.

The President appointed the members of the Federal Farm Loan Board only ten days later, and the new rural credits system was in operation well before election day. Wilson had meanwhile signed two other measures of special benefit to farmers. One was the Good Roads Act, approved on July 11, aimed in part at getting farmers out of the mud. It established a Bureau of Roads in the Department of Agriculture with funds to assist the states in building highways according to federal standards. The other was the Warehouse Act, approved on August 11, which Wilson and Secretary Houston had been recommending to Congress since 1914. It permitted bonded warehouses to issue receipts against certain agricultural commodities, these receipts to be good collateral for loans from national banks.

Wilson and Democratic congressional leaders had meanwhile worked through controversy to partial fulfillment of an objective dear to the hearts of anti-imperialists and pacifistic progressives—independence or autonomy for the Philippine Islands. Debate and controversy over Philippine policy had begun even before the United States annexed the islands, and Democrats under Bryan had stood firmly for early independence and given such a pledge in their platform in 1912. Wilson had earlier approved annexation of the Philippines,[114] and he had grave doubts in 1912 about the wisdom of the Democratic platform's promise. But the matter was not momentous enough to justify obstruction of an obviously strong determination among party leaders; and Wilson, on December 28, 1912, approved a bill sponsored by Representative William A. Jones of Virginia, chairman of the House committee on insular affairs, to confer independence within eight years after establishment and operation of a new all-Filipino government.[115] Subsequent pressures and events, notably opposition from the Roman Catholic hierarchy, Secretary Garrison, and the Bureau of Insular Affairs in the War Department (the agency directly responsible for administration of Philippine affairs),[116] caused Wilson to draw back from a promise of independence at a specified time. He announced his policy on sending former Representative Francis Burton

[114] A. S. Link, *Wilson: The Road to the White House*, pp. 27-28.

[115] *Richmond Times-Dispatch*, December 28, 1912.

[116] For evidence on Roman Catholic activity, see the *Boston Herald*, January 4, 1913; James Cardinal Gibbons, article in the *Boston Evening Transcript*, February 19, 1913; and W. H. Taft to O. M. Reid, April 7, 1913, Taft Papers. For Garrison's early position, see L. M. Garrison to W. W., April 24, 1913, Wilson Papers.

Harrison of New York to Manila as Governor General in October 1913. "We regard ourselves as trustees," he said, "acting not for the advantage of the United States, but for the benefit of the people of the Philippine Islands. Every step we take will be taken with a view to the ultimate independence of the islands and as a preparation for that independence, and we hope to move toward that end as rapidly as the safety and the permanent interests of the islands will permit. After each step taken experience will guide us to the next." He would take the first at once, he went on—appointment of a majority of Filipinos in the upper house of the Philippine legislature, thus giving Filipinos control of both houses.[117]

This marked the beginning of a long and earnest effort to speed the progress of Philippine democracy and administration.[118] Wilson and Garrison worked with Representative Jones intermittently during the spring of 1914 on a new organic act.[119] It first reaffirmed American intentions to withdraw entirely from the islands as soon as a stable native government was established and next created a bicameral Philippine legislature composed of a vast majority elected by the Christian tribes and a small minority appointed by the Governor General to represent non-Christian provinces. The legislature would have virtual autonomy in internal affairs, subject to the veto of the Governor General (who would still be appointed by the President of the United States) and the general review of the American Congress.[120] "We have done," Secretary Garrison said, "that which we think was wise and conservative and thoughtful to take the next step in laying the groundwork for this hoped-for eventful condition [of readiness for 'successful, self-controlled government']."[121]

The House of Representatives approved the Jones bill, as the new

[117] *New York Times*, October 7, 1913.

[118] Well detailed in Julius W. Pratt, *America's Colonial Experiment*, pp. 205-206, and Francis B. Harrison, *The Corner-Stone of Philippine Independence: A Narrative of Seven Years*.

[119] W. W. to L. M. Garrison, June 4, 1914, Wilson Papers; W. W. to W. A. Jones, June 11, 1914, *ibid.*; *New York Times*, June 4, 1914.

[120] *New York Times*, June 12, 1914. For a severe criticism of the measure as representing an attempt to impose an American frame of government on a people with different political experience and institutions, see H. J. Ford to W. W., January 4, 1915, Wilson Papers.

[121] "Memorandum dictated by the Secretary of War, for the use of General McIntyre," MS. dated July 30, 1914, the Papers of Lindley M. Garrison, Princeton University Library. General Frank E. McIntyre was head of the Bureau of Insular Affairs in the War Department.

measure was called, by a vote of 212 to sixty on October 14, 1914,[122] but Republicans easily blocked approval by the Senate during the hectic, crowded lame-duck session of 1914-1915.[123] Harrison warned from Manila that Filipino expectations were so great that disaster would ensue if the measure failed to pass.[124] Wilson had no intention of giving up the fight. "I think I have every reason to be confident that the Jones Bill will pass substantially in its present form at the approaching session of Congress," he replied. "Certainly I will put my full weight behind it and seek to secure its enactment at as early a date as possible."[125]

He was as good as his word, issuing a clear call for approval of the measure, along with a comparable bill for Puerto Rico, in his Annual Message of December 7, 1915. "I do recommend them to your early adoption," he said, "with the sincere conviction that there are few measures you could adopt which would more serviceably clear the way for the great policies by which we wish to make good, now and always, our right to lead in enterprises of peace and good will and economic and political freedom."[126]

Democratic leaders in both houses were as determined as Wilson to dispose of the matter. The only possible obstacle was an amendment that Senator Clarke of Arkansas intended to offer when the Jones bill was reintroduced. It instructed the President to arrange for entire American withdrawal from the Philippines and to proclaim Philippine independence within from two to four years after the meeting of the legislature created by the measure. The President should also attempt to negotiate a treaty with other powers guaranteeing Philippine independence for five years after American retirement. Failing this, the United States would give such guarantee unilaterally.[127]

[122] *New York Times,* October 15, 1914; *Congressional Record,* 63rd Cong., 2d sess., p. 16629.

[123] Taft and Root, the great architects of American administration in the Philippines, were the two men principally responsible for rallying Republicans in the Senate. See W. H. Taft to H. C. Lodge, December 5, 1914, Taft Papers; W. H. Taft, testimony before the Senate committee on the Philippines, January 2, 1915, *New York Times,* January 3, 1915; W. H. Taft to H. F. Lippitt, February 7, 1915, Taft Papers; W. H. Taft to J. H. Gallinger, February 19, 1915, *ibid.;* H. C. Lodge to W. H. Taft, February 20, 1915, *ibid.;* E. Root to W. H. Taft, February 20, 1915, *ibid.*

[124] F. B. Harrison to C. Kitchin, August 31, 1915, Kitchin Papers; F. B. Harrison to J. P. Tumulty, August 31, 1915, Wilson Papers.

[125] W. W. to F. B. Harrison, October 11, 1915, *ibid.*

[126] *The New Democracy,* I, 418-419.

[127] G. M. Hitchcock to J. P. Tumulty, January 11, 1916, Wilson Papers; *New York Times,* January 18, 1916.

Wilson did not approve entirely, but he needed Clarke's support for the shipping bill, and he worked out a compromise with the Arkansan. It was a stipulation, incorporated in the Clarke amendment, permitting the President to delay the grant of independence for the period of one session of Congress if he thought that the time was not ripe. Congress would then have opportunity to amend the bill.[128] "Please say to Senator Clarke, of Ark.," Wilson wrote to Tumulty on January 23, "that the amendment as he has worked it out is satisfactory to me. If the Senate thinks it necessary to take definite action at this time the amendment in this shape is excellently worked out and safeguarded."[129]

The Filipinos were delighted—the Philippine Assembly unanimously approved a resolution endorsing the Clarke amendment on January 25[130]—and Democratic leaders now pressed the Jones bill free of fear that Wilson would veto if it included a definite promise of independence. Gilbert M. Hitchcock of Nebraska, chairman of the Philippines committee of the Senate, presumably spoke for the President after a conference at the White House. He proposed an alternative on February 2 extending the period before independence to between four and six years and permitting the President to postpone independence for an additional year if he thought it wise to do so. But the Senate rejected Hitchcock's proposal by a vote of fifty-eight to twenty-four and then went on to adopt the Clarke amendment by a vote of forty-one to forty-one, with Vice President Marshall breaking the tie.[131] The Senate approved the Jones bill, Clarke amendment and all, by a vote of fifty-two to twenty-four on February 4, with six progressive Republicans joining the Democratic majority.[132]

Everyone assumed that House approval would follow as a matter of course, especially after the insular affairs committee reported the Jones bill favorably on March 1 with the Clarke amendment included verbatim.[133] There was a strong undercurrent of business, conservative,

[128] *ibid.*, January 25, 1916.
[129] W. W. to J. P. Tumulty, January 23, 1916, Wilson Papers.
[130] M. Quezon to W. W., January 25, 1916, *ibid.*
[131] *Congressional Record*, 64th Cong., 1st sess., p. 1998; *New York Times*, February 3, 1916. The Clarke amendment was, actually, adopted in a slightly amended form. Clarke himself had withdrawn the provision for a unilateral American guarantee of Philippine independence for five years if other powers refused to join the United States in making such guarantee. The Senate on February 2 struck out all references to a guarantee of Philippine independence.
[132] *ibid.*, February 5, 1916; *Congressional Record*, 64th Cong., 1st sess., p. 2125.
[133] *New York Times*, March 2, 1916.

and Roman Catholic sentiment against the measure,[134] but this had no impact either on the President or Democratic leaders in Congress. The latter called a caucus of House Democrats on April 26 to obtain a resolution making the Philippine bill a party measure, and Wilson threw in his full weight. "My attention," he wrote in a letter for Representative Jones to read to the caucus, "has been called to a statement in one of the New York papers to the effect that I did not favor passage of the Senate bill known as the Philippine Bill, now pending in the House. I think it important to correct this misapprehension. After giving careful consideration to the bill as it came from the Senate, it has seemed to me highly necessary to the public interest that it should be adopted, and I sincerely hope for its early adoption by the House."[135]

Such words would ordinarily have been tantamount to a command. However, the Roman Catholic hierarchy—fearful that an independent Filipino government would confiscate the Church's extensive property holdings in the islands, with an estimated value of about $44,000,000—apparently requested or instructed Roman Catholic members of the House of Representatives to oppose the Clarke amendment and vote for the original Jones bill as the lesser of two evils. In any event, twenty-eight of them refused to be bound by the resolution calling for approval of the Senate bill with the Clarke amendment, which the caucus adopted after bitter debate on April 27.[136] Thirty Democrats, virtually all of them Roman Catholics of Irish extraction, joined a Republican House membership united solidly for the first time in eight years to reject the Clarke amendment on May 1 by a vote of 193 to 151. Then they approved the original Jones bill and instructed the House members of the conference committee to agree to no provision specifying a date for Philippine independence.[137] As the leader on the

---

[134] e. g., editorial in the *New York Times*, March 3, 1916; H. C. Millar, secretary, Cotton Manufacturers' Association of North Carolina, to C. Kitchin, February 28, 1916, Kitchin Papers; S. C. Mead, secretary, Merchants' Association of New York, to W. W., April 21, 1916, Wilson Papers; J. W. O'Leary, president, Chicago Association of Commerce, to W. W., May 1, 1916, *ibid.*; James Cardinal Gibbons to W. H. Taft, January 12, 1916, Taft Papers, promising to do everything that he could to defeat the Jones bill; W. H. Taft to Cardinal Gibbons, January 16, 1916, *ibid.*, reporting that William Cardinal O'Connell of Boston was strongly opposed to the Jones bill; W. N. Kinkaid, attorney for the Archbishop of Manila, to W. W., February 11, 1916, Wilson Papers.

[135] W. W. to W. A. Jones, April 26, 1916, *ibid.*

[136] *New York Times*, April 27 and 28, 1916; New York *World*, April 29, 1916.

[137] *New York Times*, May 2, 1916; *Congressional Record*, 64th Cong., 1st sess., pp. 7205, 7213-7214.

Republican side explained in a private letter to Taft, Republicans had concluded that their only hope of defeating the Clarke amendment was to meet Democrats half way by accepting the Jones bill.[138]

That was the end of the Clarke amendment. The Senate conferees yielded to the House members when the conference committee, delayed by the crush of other legislation and events, finally met in mid-August 1916. Wilson signed the Jones bill on August 29 with no less pleasure because the Clarke amendment was missing. "The Philippine bill," he said as he signed it, "excites peculiar feelings in me, because there have been times when the people of the Philippine Islands doubted our intentions to be liberally just to them. I hope and believe that this bill is a sufficient earnest to them of our real intentions. It is a very satisfactory advance in our policy of extending to them genuine self-government and control of their own affairs. It is only by such means that any people comes into contentment and into political capacity, and it was high time that we did this act of justice which we have now done."[139] The Filipinos were no less delighted. Some 40,000 persons paraded in Manila to celebrate, and the people of the city presented a silver tablet, inscribed to express their gratitude, to Governor General Harrison to be forwarded to the President.[140]

The first Philippine legislature composed entirely of Filipinos met as stipulated in the Jones Act on October 16, 1916, to mark the beginning of a new epoch in Philippine history and a new chapter in the history of modern colonialism. It was the first virtually autonomous legislative body established by a colonial power in an overseas possession not controlled by emigrants from the mother country. Wilson did not miss some of the significance of the occasion in the following telegram that he sent to Harrison for transmission to the new lawmakers:

> Will you not be kind enough to convey to the members of the legislature of the Philippine Islands, the first legislature to meet under the new Act, my most cordial greetings and best wishes, and will you not express to them the hope that the confidence that has been reposed in them by the people and government of the United States will be abundantly vindicated by their whole course of action and policy? For myself, I look forward with confidence to the growth of self-government in the

[138] Representative C. B. Miller to W. H. Taft, May 2, 1916, Taft Papers.

[139] *New York Times*, August 30, 1916.

[140] F. B. Harrison to W. W., quoted in C. C. Walcott, Jr., acting chief, Bureau of Insular Affairs, to J. P. Tumulty, September 2, 1916, Wilson Papers.

Philippines under this new and happier order of things and am glad to have had a part in taking the great step in advance which has now been taken.[141]

The fight over Brandeis's confirmation came to a crashing climax in May 1916, throwing up the direst challenge of this preconvention period to Wilson's leadership of his party in the movement toward open alignment with advanced progressivism. The first squaring off came during the hearings on the appointment conducted by a subcommittee of the Senate judiciary committee from early February to mid-March. Brandeis had made a host of enemies, including some progressives, during his career as "people's lawyer." They descended on Washington to warn the subcommittee of Brandeis's "infidelity, breach of faith, and unprofessional conduct." Fifty-five eminent Bostonians, including President A. Lawrence Lowell of Harvard and Charles Francis Adams, published a statement on February 11 saying that the nominee did not have "the judicial temperament and capacity" required for service on the nation's highest tribunal. Seven former presidents of the American Bar Association, including Taft, Root, Joseph H. Choate, and Moorfield Storey, affirmed that Brandeis was "not fit" to be a member of the Supreme Court. Brandeis's friends also rushed to Washington to reply and counterattack. The subcommittee members submitted individual reports on April 1. The two Republicans, Albert B. Cummins of Iowa and John D. Works of California, both progressives, were hostile, the three Democrats, William E. Chilton of West Virginia, Duncan U. Fletcher of Florida, and Thomas J. Walsh of Montana, favorable. "The real crime of which this man is guilty," Walsh said, "is that he has exposed the iniquities of men in high places in our financial system. He has not stood in awe of the majesty of wealth. . . . He has been an iconoclast."[142]

---

[141] W. W. to F. B. Harrison, October 14, 1916, *ibid*. A new organic bill for Puerto Rico, which President Wilson had been pressing intermittently since early 1914 and which he had put on the legislative schedule for the first session of the Sixty-fourth Congress, was crowded off the docket by other measures in the spring and summer of 1916. It was finally approved in a much amended form in early 1917 and signed by the President on March 2, 1917. Known also as the Jones Act because sponsored by Representative Jones, it conferred American citizenship on citizens of Puerto Rico, created an elective two-house legislature composed entirely of Puerto Ricans, and gave the legislature virtual autonomy, subject only to the veto of the President of the United States and the review of the American Congress. J. W. Pratt, *America's Colonial Experiment*, pp. 188-190.

[142] A. T. Mason, *Brandeis, A Free Man's Life*, pp. 470-493; the quotation is from p. 493.

Administration leaders were working quietly behind the scenes, counseling and restraining Brandeis's overeager friends. "Atty. Gen.," Brandeis's law partner, E. F. McClennen, wrote from Washington to the nominee at the outset of the hearings, "is very urgent that no effort should be made by anyone which might arouse any suspicion that this appointment sprang from any 'Progressive' source or any other except purely Democratic. The strength is in Democratic party loyalty. This means having [Norman] Hapgood and [George] Rublee figure as little as possible. Also, he believes activity by the Jews is not likely to help with the Bourbon Democrats. They know what this support means in the coming elections, without having it called to their attention."[143] Wilson rather ostentatiously took no part. He made his only comment during these weeks in a private letter to Senator Owen, as follows: "I believe the nomination was the wisest that could possibly have been made, and I feel that few things have arisen more important to the country or to the party than the matter of his confirmation."[144]

It was undoubtedly true, but Democratic leaders on the judiciary committee refused all through April to press for a vote, mainly because at least four Democratic members were wavering, and a solid majority for Brandeis was nowhere in sight. Gregory, actually, was doing all that he could,[145] yet Wilson still carefully avoided giving any impression of interfering, and Brandeis's friends began to wonder whether he really cared. "Feeling here," one of them wrote to Senator James D. Phelan, Democrat of California, "that Brandeis confirmation may fail because of insufficient interest of President. I am convinced that failure of confirmation will lose Wilson many thousand votes in California alone."[146] There were even rumors by early May that the administration would rather see the nomination fail than succeed. "Obviously," Norman Hapgood warned Cary Grayson, "if the Administration cannot hold the party together on this critical matter, the effect on the laboring classes and on liberal opinion generally throughout the country is going to be extremely serious."[147]

Wilson had probably only been waiting for the right moment to intervene. He began to move furtively on May 2, as McClennen reported somewhat cryptically on that day: "There was a conference I am told

[143] E. F. McClennen to L. D. Brandeis, February 3, 1916, Brandeis Papers.

[144] W. W. to R. L. Owen, February 7, 1916, Wilson Papers.

[145] E. F. McClennen to L. D. Brandeis, April 15, 1916, Brandeis Papers.

[146] J. R. Haynes to J. D. Phelan, April 10, 1916, Wilson Papers.

[147] N. Hapgood to C. T. Grayson, May 4, 1916, *ibid.*

with the President today. He is as earnest as ever."[148] He wrote two days later, "The President has been talking to some Senators today and Tumulty says . . . that the President is 'ready to go to the mat' for this appointment."[149] It was all done so quietly that neither reporters nor the head usher at the White House, who kept the official diary, knew what was going on. Wilson, actually, was secretly arranging with Gregory and Senator Charles A. Culberson of Texas, chairman of the judiciary committee, to bring the struggle to a head by a master stroke suggested by George W. Anderson, federal district attorney in Boston. Culberson would write, asking the President to explain his reasons for nominating Brandeis. Wilson would reply, and Culberson would read his letter to the judiciary committee and then give the correspondence to the press. It was done on May 4 and 5. "The President's letter to Senator Culberson is being held in strict confidence, although the fact that it has been sent has been made public," Brandeis's friend reported on May 6. "I knew from the Attorney General that something was going to happen as he was very busy Thursday [May 4] checking up certain facts."[150]

Wilson, using a memorandum prepared by Gregory along lines suggested by Anderson, drafted his letter during the evening of May 4 and on the following day. It follows:

"I am very much obliged to you for giving me an opportunity to make clear to the Judiciary Committee my reasons for nominating Mr. Louis D. Brandeis to fill the vacancy in the Supreme Court of the United States created by the death of Mr. Justice Lamar, for I am profoundly interested in the confirmation of the appointment by the Senate.

"There is probably no more important duty imposed upon the President in connection with the general administration of the Government than that of naming members of the Supreme Court, and I need hardly tell you that I named Mr. Brandeis as a member of that great tribunal only because I know him to be singularly qualified by learning, by gifts, and by character for the position.

"Many charges have been made against Mr. Brandeis. The report of your sub-committee[151] has already made it plain to you and to the country at large how unfounded those charges were. They threw a

[148] E. F. McClennen to L. D. Brandeis, May 2, 1916, Brandeis Papers.

[149] E. F. McClennen to L. D. Brandeis, May 4, 1916, *ibid*.

[150] E. F. McClennen to L. D. Brandeis, May 6, 1916, *ibid*.

[151] Wilson was in error here. There was no single subcommittee report. Each member submitted individual "views."

great deal more light upon the character and motives of those with whom they originated than upon the qualifications of Mr. Brandeis. I myself looked into them three years ago, when I desired to make Mr. Brandeis a member of my Cabinet, and found that they proceeded for the most part from those who hated Mr. Brandeis because he had refused to be serviceable to them in the promotion of their own selfish interests, and from those whom they had prejudiced and misled. The propaganda in this matter has been very extraordinary and very distressing to those who love fairness and value the dignity of the great professions.

"I perceived from the first that the charges were intrinsically incredible by any one who had really known Mr. Brandeis. I have known him, I have tested him by seeking his advice upon some of the most difficult and perplexing public questions about which it was necessary for me to form a judgment. I have dealt with him in matters where nice questions of honor and fair play, as well as large questions of justice and the public benefit, were involved.

"In every matter in which I have made test of his judgment and point of view I have received from him counsel singularly enlightening, singularly clear-sighted and judicial, and, above all, full of moral stimulation. He is a friend of all just men and a lover of the right; and he knows more than how to talk about the right—he knows how to set it forward in the face of its enemies. I knew, from direct personal knowledge of the man, what I was doing when I named him for the highest and most responsible tribunal of the nation."

Wilson went on, commenting on Brandeis's extraordinary achievements as a lawyer and his distinguished public services. He had not, he said, sought or depended on endorsements when he made his choice, although the Attorney General had independently and voluntarily recommended Brandeis for nomination. He then concluded:

"Let me say, by way of summing up, my dear Senator, that I nominated Mr. Brandeis for the Supreme Court because it was and is my deliberate judgment that, of all the men now at the bar whom it has been my privilege to observe, test, and know, he is exceptionally qualified. I cannot speak too highly of his impartial, impersonal, orderly, and constructive mind, his rare analytical powers, his deep human sympathy, his profound acquaintance with the historical roots of our institutions and insight into their spirit, or of the many evidences he has given of being imbued, to the very heart, with our American ideals of justice and equality of opportunity; of his knowledge of

modern economic conditions and of the way they bear upon the masses
of the people, or of his genius in getting persons to unite in common
and harmonious action and look with frank and kindly eyes into each
other's minds, who had before been heated antagonists.

"This friend of justice and of men will ornament the high court of
which we are all so justly proud. I am glad to have had the opportunity
to pay him this tribute of admiration and of confidence; and I beg
that your committee will accept this nomination as coming from me,
quick with a sense of public obligation and responsibility."[152]

Wilson's letter sharpened the horns of the dilemma for wavering
Democrats, as, indeed, he meant it to do. As Brandeis's law partner
in the thick of the fight put it, "The President's letter . . . takes away
the force of the argument that he and the Attorney General would
not object to a rejection. It seems to commit the President to see the
matter through. It makes it very hard for the regulars to waiver [*sic*],
because it would be such an attack on the President's judgment."[153]
That, precisely, was what at least two doubtful Democratic members
of the judiciary committee, John K. Shields of Tennessee and James
A. Reed of Missouri, resented most.[154] How could they and other Democrats vote against Brandeis without confessing that their next presidential candidate was not to be trusted in important matters of state?

McAdoo, Burleson, and Gregory, the three major custodians of the
patronage cornucopia, turned the screws on Democratic senators during the next two weeks.[155] Henry Morgenthau, who had just resigned
as Ambassador to Turkey in order to participate in the presidential
campaign, had a long talk on May 17 with Hoke Smith of Georgia,
upon whom the action of the judiciary committee seemed to hinge.
Smith said that he was now disposed to vote for confirmation, and
that three other Democratic members of the judiciary committee
would follow his lead. He also made it plain that he and other senators resented Wilson's failure to consult them before he nominated
Brandeis. Morgenthau thought that it would be wise for the President
to see Smith after Brandeis had been confirmed "and thereby give

[152] W. W. to C. A. Culberson, May 5, 1916, as published in the *New York Times*,
May 9, 1916.

[153] E. F. McClennen to G. R. Nutter, May 10, 1916, Brandeis Papers.

[154] *New York Times*, May 9, 1916; E. F. McClennen to G. R. Nutter, May 9, 1916,
ibid.

[155] E. F. McClennen to L. D. Brandeis, May 10, 1916, *ibid.*; N. Hapgood to L. D.
Brandeis, May 15 and 16, 1916. *ibid.*

him back his 'self-respect' about which he is much concerned."[156] Wilson replied, "I think the matter goes deep with him and is uncurable, having been born with him, but, of course, I am willing to do anything that I reasonably can to accomplish the great results we have all set our hearts upon."[157]

Wilson said nothing publicly at this time. He did, however, help to swing another wavering Democrat on the judiciary committee, Lee S. Overman of North Carolina, into line by inviting Overman to accompany him on a trip to Charlotte, North Carolina (where Wilson spoke on May 20), and by paying a handsome tribute to Overman in his home town of Salisbury when the presidential train stopped there.[158] Wilson apparently also talked to Senator Shields.[159]

Senator Walsh, one of the Democrats leading the fight for the President, reported on May 20 that there were now enough votes in the upper house for confirmation regardless of what the judiciary committee did.[160] There was a rumor that the committee might make no report at all until after the election in November. That danger, if, indeed, it ever existed, passed on May 22. Hoke Smith came into camp on that day, apparently bringing with him all other undecided Democrats on the committee.[161] It recommended confirmation by a strict party vote, ten to eight, on May 24, and the Senate approved Brandeis's appointment without debate in executive session on June 1 by a vote of forty-seven to twenty-two. Only one Democrat, Francis G. Newlands of Nevada, voted against confirmation.[162] "I am indeed relieved and delighted at the confirmation of Brandeis," the President wrote soon afterward. "I never signed any commission with such satisfaction as I signed his."[163]

No man could miss the significance of the long controversy and its outcome. "The confirmation of Mr. Brandeis is an important milestone in the progress of the republic," Senator Hollis rejoiced. "For the first time within my knowledge the vested interests have gone out to defeat an important nomination, and after using every possible

---

[156] H. Morgenthau to W. W., May 18, 1916, Wilson Papers.
[157] W. W. to H. Morgenthau, May 19, 1916, *ibid.*
[158] J. Daniels, *The Wilson Era—Years of Peace*, pp. 545-547.
[159] N. Hapgood to L. D. Brandeis, May 18, 1916, Brandeis Papers.
[160] T. J. Walsh to R. Cooper, May 20, 1916, Walsh Papers.
[161] E. F. McClennen to L. D. Brandeis, May 22 and 23, 1916, Brandeis Papers.
[162] *New York Times*, May 25 and June 2, 1916.
[163] W. W. to H. Morgenthau, June 5, 1916, Wilson Papers.

source have been soundly beaten."[164] It was a new victory for freedom, the federal district attorney in Boston wrote—"freedom from the trammels of race prejudice; freedom from subservience to the money power; freedom to think and to act and to speak as men ought to think and act and speak in a real democracy."[165]

The Brandeis controversy, as it turned out, was also the opening battle of the presidential campaign, fought even before the party conventions had met. Brandeis's nomination had been the first definite sign of Wilson's intention to stand as the leader of united progressives. His bold leadership and willingness to risk repudiation when the chips were down were, as he undoubtedly meant them to be, pledges of good faith to men who had hitherto had some doubts about his commitment to advanced economic and social reform. There was also reward for doing the right thing. "You may say to the President," a Democrat campaigning in the West later in the summer wrote to Grayson, "that the appointment of Brandeis has had a greater effect upon the Progressives here [in Colorado] than anything else."[166]

Victory in the fight for Brandeis was only one sign that Wilson had survived the crises of the most eventful and danger-laden period of his political career. Indeed, he had done more than survive. He had re-established his domestic leadership in the preparedness and armed ship controversies and set his party upon a new political course. Thus he stood unrivaled and unchallenged among Democrats, the inevitable standard-bearer in the presidential campaign that lay immediately ahead. After grasping the nettle danger in the *Sussex* crisis, he had found new bearings for a rigidly neutral course toward the rival alliances and prepared the way for a dramatic thrust into European affairs. Finally, he would soon recover some measure of control over events that seemed to be hastening the United States and Mexico into war. But of one thing Woodrow Wilson could be certain. Confusions had given way to certitude in domestic and foreign policies, and new crises, if they came, could be met with resolution and courage.

164 H. F. Hollis to E. F. McClennen, June 7, 1916, Brandeis Papers.
165 G. W. Anderson to W. W., June 2, 1916, Wilson Papers.
166 H. Thompson to C. T. Grayson, July 18, 1916, *ibid.*

Bibliography of Sources and Works Cited[1]

The author acknowledges his indebtedness to Constable & Company, Ltd., for permission to quote from *The Letters and Friendships of Sir Cecil Spring Rice*, edited by Stephen Gwynn; and to the Yale University Library, for permission to quote from the letters and diary of Edward M. House.

MANUSCRIPTS

The Papers of the Adjutant General of the United States, War Department Section, National Archives.

The Diary and Papers of Chandler P. Anderson, Library of Congress.

The Papers of Herbert Asquith, Bodleian Library, Oxford.

The Papers of Stockton Axson, William Marsh Rice University Library.

The Papers of Warren Worth Bailey, Princeton University Library.

The Papers of Newton D. Baker, Library of Congress.

The Ray Stannard Baker Collection of Wilsonia, Library of Congress.

"Bernstorff Wireless Despatches—1916," the Papers of Walter H. Page, Harvard University Library.

The Papers of Sir Robert L. Borden, Canadian Public Archives, Ottawa.

The Papers of Louis D. Brandeis, Law Library of the University of Louisville.

The Papers of William Jennings Bryan, Library of Congress.

The Papers of Albert S. Burleson, Library of Congress.

The Papers of Josephus Daniels, Library of Congress.

The Papers of the Department of State, National Archives.

The Papers of Moreton Frewen, Library of Congress.

The Papers of Lindley M. Garrison, Princeton University Library.

The Archives of the German Foreign Office, on microfilm in the National Archives.

The Papers of Carter Glass, University of Virginia Library.

The Papers of Thomas W. Gregory, Library of Congress.

The Diary and Papers of Edward M. House, Yale University Library.

The Papers of Claude Kitchin, University of North Carolina Library.

The Diary, Desk Diary, and Papers of Robert Lansing, Library of Congress.

The Papers of Robert Lansing, Princeton University Library.

The Papers of William G. McAdoo, Library of Congress.

The Papers of Jeff: McLemore, University of Texas Library.

The Papers of Richard Olney, Library of Congress.

The Diary and Papers of Walter H. Page, Harvard University Library.

[1] This bibliography includes *only* works and sources cited in the footnotes in this volume. For a survey of literature and sources dealing with the period 1915-1916, see Arthur S. Link, *Woodrow Wilson and the Progressive Era* (New York: Harper Torchbooks, 1963), pp. 283-314.

The Diary and Papers of Sir Horace Plunkett, Plunkett Foundation, London.
The Diary, Confidential Diary, and Papers of Frank L. Polk, Yale University Library.
The Papers of the Punitive Expedition, War Department Section, National Archives.
The Papers of Theodore Roosevelt, Library of Congress.
The Papers of Hugh L. Scott, Library of Congress.
The Charles L. Swem Collection of Wilsonia, Princeton University Library.
The Papers of William Howard Taft, Library of Congress.
The Papers of Joseph P. Tumulty, Library of Congress.
The Papers of Oswald Garrison Villard, Harvard University Library.
The Papers of Thomas J. Walsh, Library of Congress.
The Papers of Edith Bolling Wilson, Library of Congress.
The Papers of Woodrow Wilson, Library of Congress.
The Woodrow Wilson-Mary Allen Hulbert Correspondence, Princeton University Library.

PUBLIC DOCUMENTS

PUBLICATIONS OF THE UNITED STATES GOVERNMENT

Comptroller of the Currency. *Annual Report of the Comptroller of the Currency, . . . December 6, 1915.* 2 v., Washington, 1916.
Congressional Record, 63rd Cong., 2nd sess. through 64th Cong., 1st sess. Washington, 1914-1916.
Department of State. *Papers Relating to the Foreign Relations of the United States, 1915.* Washington, 1924.
Department of State. *Papers Relating to the Foreign Relations of the United States, 1915, Supplement, The World War.* Washington, 1928.
Department of State. *Papers Relating to the Foreign Relations of the United States, 1916.* Washington, 1925.
Department of State. *Papers Relating to the Foreign Relations of the United States, 1916, Supplement, The World War.* Washington, 1929.
Department of State. *Papers Relating to the Foreign Relations of the United States, The Lansing Papers, 1914-1920.* 2 v., Washington, 1939-1940.

PUBLICATIONS OF FOREIGN GOVERNMENTS

[Germany] Reichstag Commission of Inquiry. *Official German Documents Relating to the World War.* 2 v., New York: Oxford University Press, 1923.
Mexican Foreign Office. *Labor Internacional de la Revolución Constitucionalista de México.* Mexico City: Press of the Secretaria de Governacion, n. d.
Mexican Foreign Office. *Diplomatic Dealings of the Constitutionalist Revolution in Mexico.* Mexico City: Imprenta Nacional, n. d.

CORRESPONDENCE, COLLECTED WORKS, AND DIARIES

Baker, Ray Stannard, and William E. Dodd (eds.). *The Public Papers of Woodrow Wilson, The New Democracy.* 2 v., New York: Harper & Brothers, 1926.

Baker, Ray Stannard. *Woodrow Wilson: Life and Letters.* 8 v., Garden City: Doubleday, Page, and Doubleday, Doran, 1927-1939.

Cambon, Henri (ed.). *Paul Cambon, Correspondance, 1870-1924.* 3 v., Paris: Editions Bernard Grasset, 1940-1946.

Davidson, John Wells (ed.). *A Crossroads of Freedom, the 1912 Campaign Speeches of Woodrow Wilson.* New Haven: Yale University Press, 1956.

Görlitz, Walter (ed.). *Regierte der Kaiser? Kriegstagebücher, Aufzeichnungen und Briefe des Chefs des Marine-Kabinetts Admiral Georg Alexander von Müller, 1914-1918.* Göttingen: Musterschmidt Verlag, 1959.

Gwynn, Stephen (ed.). *The Letters and Friendships of Sir Cecil Spring Rice.* 2 v., London: Constable, 1929.

Hanssen, Hans Peter. *Diary of a Dying Empire,* translated by Oscar O. Winther. Bloomington, Ind.: Indiana University Press, 1955.

Johnson, Walter (ed.). *Turbulent Era, A Diplomatic Record of Forty Years.* 2 v., Boston: Houghton Mifflin, 1952.

Lennox, Lady Algernon G. (ed.). *The Diary of Lord Bertie of Thame, 1914-1918.* 2 v., London: Hodder and Stoughton, 1924.

Seymour, Charles (ed.). *The Intimate Papers of Colonel House.* 4 v., Boston: Houghton Mifflin, 1926-1928.

Tirpitz, Alfred von. *Politische Dokumente von A. von Tirpitz.* 2 v., Stuttgart and Berlin: Cotta, 1924-1926.

MEMOIRS

Bernstorff, Johann H. von. *My Three Years in America.* New York: Scribner's, 1920.

Bethmann Hollweg, Theobald von. *Considérations sur la Guerre Mondiale.* 2 v., Paris: Charles-Lavauzelle & Cie., 1924.

Daniels, Josephus. *The Wilson Era, Years of Peace—1910-1917.* Chapel Hill: University of North Carolina Press, 1944.

Daniels, Josephus. *The Wilson Era, Years of War and After, 1917-1923.* Chapel Hill: University of North Carolina Press, 1946.

George, David Lloyd. *War Memoirs of David Lloyd George.* 2 v., London: Oldhams Press, n. d.

Gerard, James W. *My Four Years in Germany.* New York: George H. Doran Co., 1917.

Grayson, Cary T. *Woodrow Wilson, An Intimate Memoir*. New York: Holt, Rinehart, and Winston, 1960.

Grey, Edward (Viscount Grey of Fallodon). *Twenty-Five Years, 1892-1916*. 2 v., New York: Frederick A. Stokes, 1925.

Harrison, Francis B. *The Corner-Stone of Philippine Independence: A Narrative of Seven Years*. New York: Century Co., 1922.

Helfferich, Karl. *Der Weltkrieg*. 2 v., Berlin: Ullstein and Co., 1919.

Lansing, Robert. *War Memoirs of Robert Lansing*. Indianapolis: Bobbs-Merrill, 1935.

Scott, Hugh L. *Some Memories of a Soldier*. New York: Century Co., 1928.

Tompkins, Frank. *Chasing Villa*. Harrisburg, Pa.: Military Service Publishing Co., 1934.

Tumulty, Joseph P. *Woodrow Wilson As I Know Him*. Garden City: Doubleday, Page, 1921.

Westarp, Kuno, F. V. von. *Konservative Politik im Letzten Jahrzent des Kaiserreiches*. 2 v., Berlin: Deutsche Verlagsgesellschaft, 1935.

Wilson, Edith Bolling. *My Memoir*. Indianapolis: Bobbs-Merrill, 1939.

NEWSPAPERS

American

Armour (S.D.) *Herald*, 1916.
Baltimore *American*, 1916.
Baltimore Catholic Review, 1915.
Baltimore *Sun*, 1916.
Boston *American*, 1915.
Boston Evening Transcript, 1913, 1916.
Boston Herald, 1913, 1916.
Chicago Evening Post, 1916.
Chicago Examiner, 1915.
Chicago Herald, 1916.
Cincinnati *Freie Press*, 1916.
Columbus (Ohio) *Catholic Columbian*, 1915, 1916.
Conrad (Mont.) *Independent*, 1916.
Dallas Morning News, 1916.
Dubuque *Catholic Tribune*, 1916.
Galveston News, 1916.
Hartford Courant, 1916.
Johnstown (Pa.) *Democrat*, 1915-1916.
Kansas City Times, 1915.
Knoxville Journal and Tribune, 1915.
Lincoln *Nebraska Farmer*, 1916.
Los Angeles Examiner, 1916.

Milwaukee Free Press, 1916.
Milwaukee Sentinel, 1916.
New Orleans *Morning Star*, 1915.
New York Evening Post, 1915-1916.
New York Herald, 1916.
New Yorker Herold, 1916.
New York Journal of Commerce, 1915-1916.
New Yorker Staats-Zeitung, 1916.
New York *Sun*, 1915-1916.
New York Times, 1913-1916.
New York *World*, 1915-1916.
Oshkosh (Wis.) *North-Western*, 1916.
Pittsburgh Dispatch, 1916.
Princeton (Minn.) *News*, 1916.
Richmond Times-Dispatch, 1912.
St. Louis *Amerika*, 1916.
Sheridan (Mont.) *Forum*, 1916.
Springfield (Mass.) *Republican*, 1915-1916.
Washington Post, 1916.

FOREIGN

Berlin *Deutsche Tageszeitung*, 1916.
Berlin *Germania*, 1916.
Berlin *Kreuz-zeitung*, 1916.
Berliner Lokal-Anzeiger, 1916.
Berlin *Taegliche Rundschau*, 1916.
Berliner Tageblatt, 1916.
Berlin *Vorwärts*, 1916.
Berlin *Vossische Zeitung*, 1916.
Berlin *Zeitung am Mittag*, 1916.
Frankfurter Zeitung, 1916.
Kölnische Volkszeitung, 1916.
Kölnische Zeitung, 1916.
London *Daily Chronicle*, 1915.
London *Daily Graphic*, 1915.
London *Daily News*, 1915.
London *Pall Mall Gazette*, 1916.
London *Daily Telegraph*, 1915.
London *Times*, 1915.
London *Westminster Gazette*, 1916.
Mexico City *El Democrata*, 1916.
Mexico City *El Pueblo*, 1916.
Paris *Echo de Paris*, 1916.

Paris *L'Homme Libre*, 1916.
Paris *Journal des Débats*, 1916.
Paris *Le Matin*, 1916.
Paris *Petit Journal*, 1916.
Paris *Le Temps*, 1916.
Veracruz *El Dictamen*, 1916.

PERIODICALS

American Federationist, 1916.
Capper's Weekly (Topeka), 1916.
The Christian Advocate (Nashville), 1915-1916.
The Christian Advocate (New York), 1915.
The Churchman, 1915.
Collier's, 1915-1916.
The Commoner, 1915-1916.
The Congregationalist and Christian World, 1915-1916.
Farmer's Open Forum, 1916.
The Independent, 1915-1916.
La Follette's Magazine, 1916.
The Living Church, 1915.
Lutheran Church Work and Observer, 1916.
The Nation (New York), 1915-1916.
The New Republic, 1915-1916.
The Outlook (New York), 1915-1916.
The Presbyterian, 1916.
The Public (Chicago), 1915-1916.
The Spectator (London), 1915.
The Standard, A Baptist Newspaper (Chicago), 1915-1916.
The Survey, 1915-1916.

SIGNED CONTEMPORARY ARTICLES

Brown, L. Ames, "Preparedness for Peace, an Authorized Statement of President Wilson's Plans," *Collier's*, LVIII (September 16, 1916), 12-13.
Bryan, William J., "Distinction Without a Difference," *The Commoner*, XVI (March 1916), 2.
Bryan, W. J., "Do You Want War?" *The Commoner*, XVI (February 1916), 1-2.
Bryan, W. J., "The People VS. the Special Interests," *The Commoner*, XV (October 1915), 1.
Bryan, W. J., "Two Laws Needed," *The Commoner*, XV (December 1915), 5.
Garrison, Lindley M., "Reasonable Preparation," *The Independent*, LXXXIII (August 16, 1915), 226-227.

Harding, Gardner, "Hay Foot! Straw Foot!" *Everybody's Magazine*, xxxv (July 1916), 1-13.

Herrick, Myron T., "Rural Credits," New York *Sun*, April 24, 1916.

Herrick, M. T., "Some Objections to the Federal Farm Loan Act," *North American Review*, cciv (December 1916), 837-849.

La Follette, Robert M., "Brandeis," *La Follette's Magazine*, vii (February 1916), 2.

La Follette, R. M., "Neutrality," *La Follette's Magazine*, vii (September 15, 1915), 1.

La Follette, R. M., "Patriots," *La Follette's Magazine*, vii (November 1915), 1.

Quick, Herbert, "The Rural-Credit Firing Squad," *Saturday Evening Post*, clxxxviii (April 15, 1916), 29-31, 101-102.

Robinson, Leonard G., "Congress Has Bill to Aid Nation's Farmers," *New York Times Magazine*, February 6, 1916, pp. 9-10.

UNSIGNED CONTEMPORARY ARTICLES

"American Law for the Submarine," *Literary Digest*, lii (January 22, 1916), 161-163.

"Another 'Lusitania' Case in the Mediterranean," *Literary Digest*, li (November 20, 1915), 1139-1140.

"Apology for the 'Ancona'; Torpedo for the 'Persia,' " *Literary Digest*, lii (January 15, 1916), 101-103.

"Bringing the War to the United States," *Literary Digest*, li (November 27, 1915), 1207-1209.

"Carranza Mentions the Door," *Literary Digest*, lii (June 10, 1916), 1689-1690.

"Germany's 'Denial' in the Sussex Case," *Literary Digest*, lii (April 22, 1916), 1129-1131.

"How Germany's Reply Is Received," *Literary Digest*, lii (May 13, 1916), 1351-1353.

"Let Us Try to Keep the Peace," *Congregationalist and Christian World*, ci (July 6, 1916), 8.

"The Mexican Murders," *Literary Digest*, lii (January 22, 1916), 157-159.

"The 'Necessity' of War with Mexico," *Literary Digest*, liii (July 8, 1916), 51-53.

"Our Final Word to Germany," *Literary Digest*, lii (April 29, 1916), 1201-1204.

"Our Right to Travel on Armed Merchantmen," *Literary Digest*, lii (March 11, 1916), 625-627.

"A Pacifist Secretary of War," *Literary Digest*, lii (March 18, 1916), 701.

"Preparedness and Politics," *Literary Digest*, li (November 20, 1915), 1143-1145.

"The President Rousing the Nation for Preparedness," *Literary Digest*, LII (February 5, 1916), 269-270.

"A Presidential Peace Message in War-Time," *Literary Digest*, LI (December 18, 1915), 1411-1414.

"Villa's Invasion," *Literary Digest*, LII (March 18, 1916), 700.

SECONDARY WORKS AND ARTICLES

Birnbaum, Karl E. *Peace Moves and U-Boat Warfare*. Stockholm: Almquist & Wiksell, 1958.

Clendenen, Clarence E. *The United States and Pancho Villa*. Ithaca: Cornell University Press, 1961.

Clinard, Outten J. *Japan's Influence on American Naval Power, 1897-1917*. Berkeley: University of California Press, 1947.

Digby, Margaret. *Horace Plunkett, An Anglo-American Irishman*. Oxford: Basil Blackwell, 1949.

Fabela, Isidro. *Historia Diplomática de la Revolución Mexicana*. 2 v., Mexico City: Fondo de Cultura Económica, 1958-1959.

Fischer, Fritz. *Griff nach der Weltmacht: Die Kriegszielpolitik des Kaiserlichen Deutschland, 1914-1918*. Düsseldorf: Droste Verlag, 1961.

Hoelzle, Edwin, "Das Experiment des Friedens im Ersten Weltkrieg, 1914-1917," *Geschichte in Wissenschaft und Unterricht*, 13th Year (August 1962), 465-522.

Kenkel, Joseph F. "The Tariff Commission Movement: The Search for a Nonpartisan Solution of the Tariff Question," unpublished Ph.D. dissertation, University of Maryland, 1962.

Lawrence, David. *The True Story of Woodrow Wilson*. New York: George H. Doran Co., 1924.

Link, Arthur S. *Wilson: The New Freedom*. Princeton: Princeton University Press, 1956.

Link, A. S. *Wilson: The Road to the White House*. Princeton: Princeton University Press, 1947.

Link, A. S. *Wilson: The Struggle for Neutrality, 1914-1915*. Princeton: Princeton University Press, 1960.

Link, A. S. *Woodrow Wilson and the Progressive Era*. New York: Harper, 1954 and 1963.

McDonald, Timothy G. "Southern Democratic Congressmen and the First World War," unpublished Ph.D. dissertation, University of Washington, 1961.

Mason, Alpheus T. *Brandeis, A Free Man's Life*. New York: Viking, 1946.

May, Ernest R. *The World War and American Isolation, 1914-1917*. Cambridge, Mass.: Harvard University Press, 1959.

Pratt, Julius W. *America's Colonial Experiment*. New York: Prentice-Hall, 1950.

Salinas Carranza, Alberto. *La Expedicion Punitiva*. Mexico City: Ediciones Botas, 1936.

Spindler, Arno. *La Guerre Sous-Marine*, translated by René Jouan. 3 v., Paris: Payot, 1933-1935.

Index

Textual material in footnotes is indexed by reference to the page or pages on which the footnote occurs, but without indication that the item appears in a note. Titles, manuscript collections, authors of letters, etc., in footnotes are not indexed when they have merely been cited as references.